DOM CUTHBERT BUTLER

WESTERN MYSTICISM

*The Teaching of Augustine, Gregory and Bernard on
Contemplation and the Contemplative Life*

SECOND EDITION WITH

AFTERTHOUGHTS

HARPER TORCHBOOKS ⟡ The Cathedral Library
HARPER & ROW, PUBLISHERS, NEW YORK

WESTERN MYSTICISM

Printed in the United States of America.

This book was originally published by Constable and Company, Ltd., London, in 1922, and is here printed by arrangement.

First HARPER TORCHBOOK *edition published 1966 by Harper & Row, Publishers, Incorporated, New York, N.Y. 10016.*

Nibil obstat—F. Innocentius APAP, S. Th.M., O.P. Censor Deputatus.

Imprimatur—Edm. Can. Surmont, Vic. Gen. West-monasterii—die 26$_a$ August, 1926

The Library of Religion and Culture
General Editor: Benjamin Nelson

CONTENTS

PART I: SPECULATIVE CONTEMPLATION

1. ST. AUGUSTINE

PREFACE TO SECOND EDITION

ONLY one change of any magnitude has been made in the text; the 'Epilogue' has been shifted to the middle of the book: the reason is given at the commencement of the 'Afterthoughts'. A large amount of fresh matter is added. Nearly eighty pages of 'Afterthoughts' are prefixed, the result of criticisms and questionings made on the book, and of further reading and thought. They are in effect a survey of the active controversies in progress for the past thirty years over the whole field of mystical theology, chiefly among Catholic theologians; they will be found to deal with the most important and vital problems, both practical and speculative, that encompass the domain of contemplation and mysticism. An addition of a dozen pages has been made also to the Appendix, in response to the call for something more definite on the question of natural and non-Christian mysticism.

CUTHBERT BUTLER

Ealing Priory
London, W.5
1st November 1926

PREFACE

A YEAR ago a writer in the *Nation*, under the name 'Curé de Campagne', while reviewing a book on Mysticism, was good enough to say: 'In reading a book on mysticism, we want to know exactly where our guide himself starts from, what are the presuppositions, the governing principles of his investigation. One could read a book on the subject, say, by Abbot Butler of Downside, in complete mental comfort, with one's feet on the fender. One would know where one was, what one started from, what had to be taken for granted.' If the following pages respond in any measure to these expectations, it will be because certain Master-Mystics are allowed to speak for themselves, the author only acting as showman, to introduce the speakers on the scene, call attention to the salient features of what they say, point the moral, and sum up the import of it all. Readers are apt to find long extracts boring, and to skip them with a hurried glance; it would be an entire misconception to take up this book in such frame of mind—because the extracts are the book, and whatever value it may have lies almost wholly in them, the author's personal contribution being little more than a framework in which the extracts are set. I have confidence, however, that anyone who does read these utterances of three of the great religious geniuses of Western Christianity will before long be caught up and carried away by the elevation, the eloquence, and the compelling fascination of the words wherein they lay bare the most intimate and sacred relations of their soul with God.

This book has been twenty years in the making. Among the projects for promoting theological studies that owed their initiation and achievement to the late Dr Swete while Regius Professor of Divinity at Cambridge, was an Association for the Study of Christian Doctrine, the members whereof were each to take up some subject for private study. This was in 1902, and in the original list I am entered for 'Western Mysticism'. The first collection of material from SS Gregory, Bernard, and John of the Cross, was made in 1904. It was an afterthought to include St Augustine; this extension of the field, while adding greatly to the difficulty of the work, without doubt has added equally to its value as a contribution to the history of religion: the sections on St Augustine are certainly the most valuable portions of the book.

There are enough, probably more than enough, books 'about'

mysticism, expounding the writers' ideas thereon: these books contain miscellaneous citations of words of mystics, selected with the object of illustrating and enforcing the theories that the author is propounding. What is needed is a more objective presentation of what the mystics themselves thought about their mysticism, to be determined by a systematic study and formulation of the ideas of a number of the principal mystics, such as is here attempted in the case of three of them. This seems to be the necessary basis for any scientific treatment of the subject.

The title 'Western Mysticism' is explained and justified in the Summary of Part I. It means something different from 'Mysticism in the West', which would be a much wider subject. It means the native mysticism of the West that prevailed in Western Europe during the six centuries from St Benedict to St Bernard, and has characteristics of its own, marking it off from later kinds, and still rendering it peculiarly appropriate for Westerns. Special attention is directed to the section on St Gregory in Part II, being his teaching on the contemplative and active lives. It contains a body of doctrine at once elevated, sane, and practical, that must, it is believed, prove most helpful to the pastoral clergy and to all priests for the regulating of their lives.

CUTHBERT BUTLER

Downside Abbey
1st September 1922

AFTERTHOUGHTS

THE first edition of *Western Mysticism* has had the advantage of careful criticism on the part of competent and thoughtful writers, some of whom, by stressing a certain confusion of mind which they experienced in reading it, have brought home to me the fact that there was a serious structural flaw. The book really divides into two quite distinct parts, dealing with different, though related, problems: Part I, *Speculative*, the nature of Contemplation and the Mystical Experience in itself; Part II, *Practical*, the Contemplative Life and its fusion with the Active in a Mixed Life, properly so called, i.e. one according to St Thomas, and, as I believe, according to St Gregory, and St Augustine before him. Now the 'Epilogue', which stood as the concluding section of the whole book, ought really to have been the conclusion of Part I, and its misplacement was, so I believe, the cause of the sense of confusion felt by many readers. In this new edition the 'Epilogue' has been moved to its rightful place at the end of Part I. Though placed at the beginning, these 'Afterthoughts' are Afterthoughts, suggested by criticisms and questionings made on the book, and by further reading and thought.

§ 1. *Current Controversies on Mystical Theology*

There has been running in France for the past quarter of a century, and with increased intensity during the last half-dozen years, an active controversy among the theologians over the entire ground traversed in these pages. And I found that by the sentence on p. 216, distinguishing between, on the one hand, 'acquired, active, ordinary contemplation', and, on the other, 'infused, passive, extraordinary', I had unwittingly plunged into the thick of the fray. To the best of my knowledge, no account has been given in English of the course of these discussions; yet is the subject-matter of much interest and importance, both theoretical and practical, for the ordering of the spiritual life. Therefore it seems that the most illuminating manner of dealing with the questions that have arisen out of this book, will be to treat them as parts of the general controversy.

The movement of the past quarter of a century may be characterized as a great return to the ideas of antiquity and of the Middle Ages concerning contemplation and its place in the spiritual life.

During the eighteenth and nineteenth centuries the idea had come to be accepted as well established, that, apart from special and unusual calls, the normal mental prayer for all was systematic discursive meditation according to fixed method: this was taken to be the lifelong exercise of mental prayer for those embarked on a spiritual life—priests, religious, nuns, devout layfolk. Contemplation was looked on as something extraordinary, almost identified with visions, revelations, raptures, even stigmatization and levitation, and other such psycho-physical phenomena. Thus contemplation and mystical theology had come to be regarded as wonderful, even miraculous; to be admired from a safe distance, and left alone as dangerous and full of pitfalls. Such was the common view, such the common practice, almost taken for granted at the end of the nineteenth century.

The first to rise up against the prevalent view, and to reassert vigorously, as the old and genuine Christian tradition, the principle that contemplation should be the normal issue of a spiritual life seriously led, and therefore is a thing open to all devout souls, was the Abbé Auguste Saudreau. He in 1896 published *Les Degrés de la Vie spirituelle* (5th ed., 1920), and in 1901 followed up the subject in *La Vie d'Union à Dieu et les moyens d'y arriver* (3rd ed., 1921).[1] The latter book is made up of a catena of extracts from Fathers, theologians, and spiritual writers through the centuries, in proof that the author's position is grounded on the firm Christian tradition of the first sixteen centuries. This book is of first importance. Also in 1901 appeared the great volume of Père Augustin Poulain, S.J., *Les Grâces d'Oraison* (700 pp.); it has had a great vogue, the tenth edition, twenty-first thousand, being issued in 1922.[2] It is a practical treatise on mystical theology; its value is greatly enhanced by the collection of citations of texts that follow each chapter. These books of Saudreau and Poulain have been the principal means of popularizing among Catholics the whole subject of mysticism and contemplation during the past quarter of a century, and of making familiar to devout souls the relatively easy possibilities of the spiritual life.

Unfortunately, perhaps, though in substantial accord on the practical issue of bringing back contemplative prayer into the actual programme of life of devout souls of what degree soever, Saudreau and Poulain differ on a number of points, of theory indeed, but still affecting practice; so that an acute controversy has

---

[1] Both books are translated into English.
[2] It has been translated into English *The Graces of Interior Prayer*, and into German, Italian, and Spanish.

sprung up around their presentations of the fundamental positions of mystical theology. The chief points in dispute will appear sufficiently in what follows; but here the leading combatants must be introduced. And first Mgr Farges, a personage of great consideration as former Director of Saint-Sulpice and of the Institut Catholique of Paris, and as author of a great course of scholastic philosophy in several volumes. He appears as a whole-hearted supporter of Poulain and uncompromising opponent of Saudreau. It is right to mention him prominently, both because of his personal position and authority, and because his treatise on mystical theology has just been published in English.[1] No one can afford to neglect it, as probably the most effective fighting presentation of the side opposed to Saudreau and to what may be called the Dominican school.

For, as might be expected, the Dominicans have intervened, seeking to bring in St Thomas as arbiter on the questions in debate. The foremost among them is Père Garrigou-Lagrange, professor of theology in the Angelico College, Rome; he has made up a series of articles from the Dominican organ of popularization, *La Vie spirituelle*, into a book, *Perfection Chrétienne et Contemplation selon S. Thomas d'Aquin et S. Jean de la Croix* (2 vols., 900 pp., 1923, now in the sixth thousand). Another Dominican theologian, Père Joret, also has made up a volume out of articles in the same periodical, *La Contemplation Mystique d'après S. Thomas d'Aquin* (1923). I have read these two works carefully—even twice through—and with great enlightenment and profit. Their purpose is to show that though St Thomas wrote no treatise on mystical theology, he has laid down in many places of various works principles that cover the subject and can be built up into an intellectual fabric in which the descriptive statements of their experiences by St John of the Cross and St Teresa find their place and can function easily.

It will cause no surprise that over against this Dominican school of mystical theology stands a Jesuit school. Père Bainvel, S.J., Dean of the theological faculty at the Catholic University of Paris, has prefixed to the tenth edition of Poulain a long introduction of a hundred pages, summing up very clearly the state of the question as it stood in 1922, and setting out the points still in controversy between the two schools in the domain of mystical theology.

---

[1] *Mystical Phenomena*, 668 pp. (Burns, Oates and Washbourne, 1926). Part II, on 'accidental or marvellous mystical phenomena', is much less satisfying than Part I in subject-matter and manner of treatment. The Appendices contain important matter.

§ 2. *Prayer of Faith*

Of all the writers called forth by the controversy, he with whom I find myself most fully in accord is neither Dominican nor Jesuit, but Franciscan. In 1903 Père Ludovic de Besse, a Capuchin, intervened in the controversy between Saudreau and Poulain, publishing a small book, *La Science de la Prière*: it has recently been produced in English.[1] Over the practical side of the teaching of my book, the range of questions considered on pp. 308–25, I am pleased at finding that de Besse had forestalled, twenty years beforehand, the substantive positions I was independently led to occupy. Therefore the briefest statement will be given of the heads of his teaching, and thus the points now in controversy will be the most easily understood. He claims, I think rightly, that his book is an exposition, in simple popular form, of the elementary portion of the teaching of St John of the Cross on contemplation. It is a noteworthy feature of the current discussions, how St John is coming more and more to be accepted by all schools as the great exponent of the realms of prayer, contemplation, and mystical theology. Fr de Besse has been well advised in printing as an appendix the more salient parts of the section of the *Living Flame of Love*, on the beginnings of contemplation, from which an extract has been given, text, p. 214.[2] I venture to direct attention to this altogether admirable piece.

Let Fr de Besse speak:
(Chap. ix.) Meditation carefully practised leads on to affective prayer. This in its turn leads just as surely to the 'prayer of faith'. The grace of prayer generally terminates here, for it has reached the degree of ordinary perfection. Beyond that point prayer becomes extraordinary. When a soul is drawn to the prayer of faith, the Holy Spirit inspires no special idea in the intellect, and excites no emotion in the senses. He goes directly to the will and attracts it, revealing His presence to the soul by the light of faith directed towards the highest point of the intelligence, without stirring up the imagination or the lower faculties. Feeling itself thus near to God, the will keenly perceives the need of loving Him, and of entire self-abandonment into His hands. Three things take place at the moment of this prayer. *First*: the mind is roughly stricken, as it were, with a kind of paralysis; it is powerless to devote itself to things divine, or to have any experience of them; before the moment of prayer there was plenty of intellectual vigour; but now when the soul desires to pray there is not one thought forthcoming. *Secondly*: the same phenomenon appears in the senses; the heart is absolutely dry; far from experiencing sweet delightful emotions which direct it towards

---

[1] *The Science of Prayer*, 189 pp. (Burns, Oates and Washbourne, 1925).
[2] In references 'text' means the body of this book.

God, it more often feels only aversion (from prayer) and disgust. But, *thirdly*: the will, on the other hand, is strongly attracted towards God; it feels the need of Him; it has no peace except in adhering to Him. This paralysis of mind and heart is only in regard to God; the soul is absolutely unable to frame any good thought or sentiment to help the will to pray. But the heart and mind are by no means powerless with regard to creatures; on the contrary, the imagination often runs at random, and the senses feel attracted to earthly things: the will alone is drawn towards God.

When these three signs are found together, it is impossible to have any doubt. The Holy Spirit is present, and bestowing the grace of prayer, but not in the same way as before. If the soul wishes to return at whatever cost to one of the previous methods, it resists the Holy Spirit; it neglects the grace offered, and spends its energies in waste, seeking to frame some good thought in the mind, or stir up some pious feeling in the heart. God asks simply for our will, unadorned with good thoughts and sensible devotion: let us then give up our will to Him. Be united with Him by obscure faith in His presence, by one glance full of love, submission, and utter abandonment. Remain peacefully in this state. It is a prayer and a most excellent one.[1]

This, in my judgement, is a faithful presentation of St John's mind.[2] In chapter x. de Besse discusses the various names given to the 'prayer of faith'. This is his name; and, though I do not find it used by St John, it very well expresses his meaning. For faith is the means by which the intellect attains to union with God, obscure faith. Thus he says:

The intellect, if rightly disposed for the divine union, must be pure and empty of all sensible objects, disengaged from all clear intellectual perceptions, interiorly tranquil and at rest, reposing on faith. Such a one must walk by faith, with his understanding in darkness and in the obscurity of faith only: for in this darkness God unites Himself to the intellect.[3]

Similarly Fr Baker describes contemplation:

The soul endeavours to contemplate God in the darkness and obscurity of a blind and naked faith, void of all distinct and express

---

[1] The concluding pages of chapter ix. are one of the few passages on which I have to differ from de Besse. I am unable to follow him in understanding of the prayer of faith, or beginning of contemplation, St John's 'divine touches' or 'substantial contacts' of God and the soul. See the passages cited, text, pp. 12 and 148-149. I agree with Saudreau that they are the very highest manifestation of the mystic union; St John says so: 'The highest condition attainable in this life.'

[2] See passage cited, text, p. 311 (full context in de Besse's appendix); also *Ascent of Mount Carmel*, Bk. II. cc. xii.–xv.

[3] *Ascent of Mount Carmel*, Bk. II. c. ix.

images. Again: A soul without discoursings and curious speculations, without any perceptible use of the internal senses or sensible
images, by a pure, simple, and reposeful operation of the mind, in
the obscurity of faith, simply regards God as infinite and incomprehensible verity, and with the whole bent of the will rests in Him
as her infinite, universal, and incomprehensible good.[1]

Faith being understood in this sense of obscure faith, I think
St John would accept the term 'prayer of faith' for what he means
by the first step in contemplation. But his own term is, 'prayer of
loving attention': so in the oft-cited passage, text, p. 214, and elsewhere: 'learn to abide with attention in loving waiting upon God
in the state of quiet'; 'an attention, or general loving knowledge of
God'; 'a simple, general, and loving attention'.[2]

This same kind of prayer is found described in many places, and
under a variety of names, by St Francis of Sales, in his own writings,
and in the reflection of his teaching found in those of St Jane Frances
of Chantal: such are, 'prayer of simple committal (remise) to God';
'simple dwelling in the presence of God'; 'simple unity and unique
simplicity and repose in the presence of God'; 'holding the spirit
very simply in God, adhering to His operation by a complete
surrender, without making any acts, unless God moves to them,
awaiting what He may be pleased to give me' (St Francis).[3] St Jane
Frances describes such prayer:

There is a prayer of a calm attention of the soul to God, which
tends to moderate the too great activity of the faculties, and which
places it in interior silence and in a repose of its powers. There is
a state of prayer wherein the soul is in this tranquillity; and without
making any act, she is in a real disposition to will all that God
may will to do with her.[4]

---

[1] Sancta Sophia, pp. 400, 503.
[2] Ascent of Mount Carmel, Bk. II. cc. xii., xiv., xxxii.
[3] See citations after Poulain's chapter ii.
[4] Petit Traité sur l'Oraison; English translation, Catholic Truth Society, 1d. Her
writings abound in advice on this kind of prayer and make an excellent commentary on St John of the Cross: (Œuvres de Sainte Chantal, iii. 276–96, 456–64,
532–43.

The resemblance of such prayer to that spoken of by Fr Baker in the chapter of
Sancta Sophia, 'The Prayer of Interior Silence', is evident. In the judgement of
some, including the editor of 1876, this chapter falls under suspicion of 'Quietism';
but Bishop Hedley declares it to be free from any such taint, and sound and safe
in its teaching (Contemplation and Prayer, pp. 82–6). Fr Baker bases this chapter on
a book by de Rojas, a Spanish mystic, condemned, along with a number of
'quietistic' books, in 1689. Bishop Hedley does not see anything unsound in
Fr Baker's citations; he had never seen de Rojas' book; but Poulain says, 'le
quiétisme de cette auteur est assez mitigé' (op. cit. p. 655). It may be said with
confidence that Fr Baker's 'prayer of interior silence' is substantially the same as
the 'prayer of faith', or 'of loving attention'.

This grade of prayer has been greatly popularized in our day by Poulain, under the name 'Prayer of Simplicity'.[1] He says he took this name from a tract of Bossuet's, entitled 'Short and easy way of making the prayer of faith and of the simple presence of God'.[2]

Bossuet says:

We should accustom ourselves to nourish our soul by a simple and loving look on God and on Jesus Christ; and for this we must disengage it gently from reasoning, discourse, and the multitude of affections, in order to keep it in simplicity, regard, and attention, and so bring it nearer and nearer to God. The soul should not stay in meditation, for by its fidelity in mortification and recollection, it ordinarily receives a purer and more intimate prayer, which may be called 'prayer of simplicity', consisting in a simple looking or loving attention to a divine object, be it God Himself or one of His perfections, or Jesus Christ or one of His mysteries. The soul quitting reasoning, uses a sweet contemplation, which keeps it peaceful, attentive, and receptive of any divine impressions the Holy Spirit may communicate.

Of all these names the most expressive, the one which best connotes the nature of this prayer, is St John's 'Prayer of Loving Attention'; and this is the name that will be used in these pages. It can hardly be necessary to note that 'St John' will be St John of the Cross.

St John quite explicitly calls this prayer of loving attention, 'contemplation', and in this there is general agreement with him. But there is much debate as to whether it should be characterized as 'acquired' or 'infused' contemplation, 'active' or 'passive', 'ordinary' or 'extraordinary', 'mystical' or not.

The questions may seem to be merely points of nomenclature and terminology; but there are behind them theological issues, theoretical, but also very practical for those cultivating the interior life.

§ 3. *Acquired Contemplation*

Père Poulain is the protagonist of one school. He lays down his position with great clearness: there is a fundamental distinction between two categories of prayer, ordinary, and extraordinary or mystical. The latter term he thus defines: 'Supernatural acts or states are called mystical, which our own efforts and industry are

[1] It is the subject of chapter ii. of his book. This chapter has been printed separately as a Catholic Truth Society Tract, *The Prayer of Simplicity*.

[2] This tract is printed at the end of Père Grou's *Manuel des Âmes intérieures*, in the French and English editions. It is greatly to be commended.

unable to produce, even feebly, even for a moment.'[1] Thus he refuses the title mystical to any prayer that we can, with the assistance of ordinary co-operating grace, attain to by the practice of self-discipline and mortification, the exercise of virtue, and the cultivation of the habit of prayer. Mystical prayer is for him, no doubt the reward and the crowning of previous endeavours; but still itself is a thing in no way 'achieved', but wholly 'given'. Consequently he ranges the prayer of simplicity, of faith, in the category of ordinary and non-mystical prayer, and calls it 'acquired contemplation', one that can be acquired in some measure by our own industry and exercisings—of course assisted always by divine grace. This setting up of two different kinds of contemplation, one acquired and non-mystical, the other infused and mystical, is vehemently opposed by the other school, by Saudreau and the Dominicans. It is recognized by all that the term 'acquired contemplation' first came into use at the beginning of the seventeenth century, 'contemplation' pure and simple, without qualification, being used by the earlier writers, as SS. Augustine, Gregory and Bernard. On this matter Mgr Farges ranges himself determinedly with Poulain. He contends that though the word 'acquired contemplation' was not employed, the distinction between the two kinds of contemplation was known to various early writers: in particular are cited Richard of St Victor, Walter Hilton, Denis the Carthusian.[2] Farges is insistent that the two kinds of contemplation having been distinguished, and the term 'acquired' having been introduced and having passed into the established vocabulary of mystical theology during the past three centuries, we should no more revert to the old vaguer manner of speaking by discarding the term, than we should discard such terms as 'consubstantial' or 'transubstantiation'. He is able to invoke with much effect, in support of the contention that the distinction of the two kinds of contemplation has become part of the current theology of the Church, the summary of mystical theology given by Benedict XIV in the work on the Canonization of the Saints;[3] also the summary by St Alphonsus Liguori in the Appendix to the *Homo Apostolicus*.

§ 4. *St Teresa and St John of the Cross*

Poulain claims that his rigid definition of 'mystical', cited above, has the authority of St Teresa, and Farges agrees with him; I think

[1] Op. cit. c. i.

[2] The statement, text, p. 216, made on the authority of Pourrat, that the term 'acquired' was used by Denis the Carthusian, is incorrect.

[3] Op. cit. pp. 236–44. He is, of course, careful to point out that such a treatise could only carry the authority of the Pope as private theologian: and it was in fact published before he became Pope.

they are right. The term St Teresa commonly employs is 'supernatural prayer'; this term she uses in a sense of her own, not merely of prayer made under the inspiration of the Holy Ghost and with the assistance of ordinary grace; for in this, the usual theological sense of the term, all real prayer is supernatural: but again and again throughout her writings she makes it plain that by supernatural prayer she means 'that which we cannot acquire or procure for ourselves, no matter what care or what diligence we give to it', it being entirely God's work in the soul; all we can do is to dispose ourselves for it (*passim*). The term 'perfect contemplation', or 'true contemplation' she reserves for the 'prayer of union', that belongs to the 'Fifth Mansion' of the *Interior Castle*, or the 'Third Water' of the *Life* (cc. xvi., xvii.). This appears to be the 'mystical experience' in the full sense, and to be pretty well equivalent to Fr Baker's 'passive unions purely intellectual' (*Sancta Sophia*, p. 531).

The prayer preceding 'union' she calls the 'prayer of quiet'; it belongs to the 'Fourth Mansion' of the *Castle*, or the 'Second Water' of the *Life* (cc. xiv., xv.). She speaks of it as 'touching on supernatural prayer', and 'the beginning of pure contemplation' (*Way of Perfection*, c. xxx. 6).[1] The prayer of quiet is by some writers identified with the prayer of loving attention or of faith; not rightly, I think. The most succinct account of it is in the *Way of Perfection* (c. xxxi. 1):

This prayer of quiet is a supernatural state to which no effort of our own can raise us. All the faculties are calmed, and the spirit realizes that it is close to its God, and that if it drew but a little nearer to Him, it would become one with Him by union. So reverential is the awe felt by such a soul that it dares ask nothing of God. This state resembles a swoon, both exterior and interior, so that the exterior man does not wish to move, but rests; the body feels enjoyment while the spirit is supremely satisfied. The faculties are reluctant to stir; all action seems to impede them from loving God—yet they are not entirely lost, for they can and do realize, by peaceful contemplation, in whose Presence they are. While the prayer of quiet lasts, the soul is so intoxicated with delight and joy that there no longer seems anything left to long for.

This is something different from, something, so to say, on a higher mystical grade than what we have had in the various accounts of the prayer of loving attention. St Teresa calls it 'the beginning of pure contemplation'; and I believe I am right in

---

[1] The references to St Teresa's works are all to the Stanbrook editions, except the *Life*, not edited there; for it Fr Zimmerman's revision of Lewis's translation is used, fourth edition, 1911.

saying that she never uses the word 'contemplation' of anything that falls short of this. Yet I think she recognizes the prayer of loving attention under the name 'interior recollection'. Here a word of explanation is necessary, for she is not quite consistent in her use of the term 'recollection'. In *Way* (c. xx.) she so calls a sort of vocal-mental prayer, a talking with God or Jesus Christ, like the colloquies of Blosius; but this falls in the category of affective prayer, such as may be exercised by those in the 'Third Mansion' of the *Castle*, to be identified with St Francis of Sales's 'devout life'.[1] On the other hand, in the *Life* (cc. xi-xii.) she speaks of 'recollection' and 'quiet' as practically the same thing; but in the *Castle*, her last word on the things of mystical theology, she definitely distinguishes them under the 'Fourth Mansion', so that in it are included two quite different kinds or states of prayer, the prayer of quiet, and that of 'interior recollection', which precedes it. This recollection is most clearly described in the saint's second Relation to Fr Rodrigo Alvarez, S.J.[2]

It is a certain interior recollection of which the soul is sensible; the soul seems to have other senses within itself, then, which bear some likeness to the exterior senses; and thus the soul, withdrawing into itself, seeks to go away from the tumult of its outward senses;[3] for it closes the eyes on purpose that it may neither see, nor hear, nor understand anything but that whereon the soul is then intent, which is to be able to converse with God alone. In this prayer there is no suspension of the faculties and powers of the soul; it retains the full use of them; but the use of them is retained that they may be occupied with God.

In this Fourth Mansion 'the natural is combined with the supernatural': 'it is the one most souls enter'; but 'a person must have dwelt for a long time in the earlier mansions (the Third being the 'devout life') before entering this'.[4] If this more interior form of recollection be not the prayer of loving attention, then it seems that St Teresa does not treat of this prayer at all.

I cannot but think that the trouble among the theologians in great measure arises from the fact that St John applies to the prayer

---

[1] Of the Third Mansion she writes: 'Thanks to His mercy I believe there are many such people in the world: they are very desirous not to offend His Majesty even by venial sins, they love penance and spend hours in meditation, they employ their time well, exercise themselves in works of charity to their neighbours, are well-ordered in their conversation and dress, and those who have a household govern it well' ('Third Mansion', i. 8). This is the 'devout life'.

[2] The Relations are appended to the *Life*, and this one is No. VIII. p. 478, in the 4th English edition, 1911.

[3] Cf. St Gregory on 'recollection', text, p. 69.

[4] See *Castle*, 'Fourth Mansion', iii. 13 and i. 3.

of loving attention, or of faith, the term 'contemplation', and even 'infused contemplation';[1] while St Teresa will not give it the name 'contemplation' at all. I think any one who reads St Teresa will agree with Farges that the action of God on the soul which she regards as the sign of (her) supernatural prayer or contemplation, is not merely a silent working of grace, but an act, of which the soul is sensibly and consciously aware.[2] That this is the fact in higher kinds of prayer, 'union', and even 'quiet', will not be questioned; but in regard to the initial stages of infused contemplation, St John's teaching is that they are imperceptible to the soul, which hardly, or not at all, is aware of what is going on in it: 'The commencement of contemplation is in general secret, and unknown to him who is admitted to it.'[3] Again, St Teresa constantly insists that we should not try in prayer to empty the mind of images or silence the faculties as a preparation for contemplation, but let intellect and will go on working in discursive and affective prayer until God stops them and creates the needed silence. But this, again, is entirely counter to St John's attitude: let the first chapter of Book III of the *Ascent of Mount Carmel* be read, and the difference springs to the eye; indeed the active emptying of the mind and the silencing of the faculties is the burden of the whole treatise.

In these points of difference from St Teresa, St John is, I venture to maintain, in conformity with the older ideas, abundantly evidenced by the great Masters whose teaching makes the stuff of this book. For Augustine, for Gregory, for Bernard, the beginnings of contemplation, the getting under way, is a striving and a struggle of mind and soul to transcend earthly things and fix its gaze on heavenly;[4] and the first step is the stripping the mind of all images and the 'hushing' of the faculties.[5]

It is recognized by Poulain and Farges that with St Teresa came in a new idea of the supernatural character of contemplation, and they maintain that her definition is to be accepted, as not so much an innovation, as an advance in precision of conception and expression concerning the nature of contemplation. And, in fact, her definition of contemplation has come to be commonly accepted. This I believe it was that led to the introduction of the term

[1] Instances will be found in de Besse's Appendix; many more might be cited, see note, p. xxvi.

[2] Op. cit. p. 45.

[3] *Dark Night*, Bk. I. c. ix. Many similar pieces might be cited, as *Ascent*, Bk. II. c. xiv.

[4] Compare St Gregory: 'There is in contemplation a great effort of the mind, when it raises itself up to heavenly things, when it tries to pass over all that is outwardly seen, when it narrows itself that it may be enlarged' (text, p. 66).

[5] See text, pp. 31–34, 69–71; see also the pieces from Dionysius, p. 6.

'acquired contemplation', to denote grades of contemplation not consciously 'supernatural' in St Teresa's sense, but which may, by the help of co-operating grace, be brought about in great measure by the efforts and exercisings of the soul in self-discipline, recollection and prayer: i.e. contemplation that falls short of St Teresa's prayer of quiet, such as the prayer of loving attention, or of simplicity. Kinds of prayer are spoken of simply as 'contemplation' by the older writers, which would not satisfy St Teresa's test; and this fact should not be lost sight of when the recall to the tradition of the earlier centuries is made.

No one can question that St Teresa's own experiences in contemplation and mystical union were of the highest; or that her accounts of her states of prayer probably surpass all others in precision and in graphic delineation of things most difficult to express. But it cannot be denied that there was something in her physical and psychological make-up which rendered her temperamentally peculiarly responsive to onrushes of spiritual influence, and liable to ecstasy, rapture, flights of the spirit.[1] To this, it may be thought, may be attributed her emphasizing, perhaps over-emphasizing, this element as the essential mark of contemplation. It was a pleasure to find in a remarkable tractate, to be spoken of later on, by Père Gardeil, one of the most distinguished of living Dominican theologians, the name 'supernatural contemplation' deliberately given to the prayer of loving attention, or of simplicity, with the note added: 'we take this term (supernatural contemplation) in its obvious sense, and not in the restricted sense that St Teresa gives it.'[2]

Père Joret thinks that the divergence of views among the theologians is in large measure due to the fact that many later writers have been inclined to standardize St Teresa's accounts of her own experiences, as the one universal way of progress in prayer. The charismatic or quasi-charismatic gifts she received have been generalized into absolute tests of the various degrees of prayer. Thus, she speaks as if certain intellectual visions of the Sacred Humanity and of the Holy Trinity which she enjoyed were a constant factor of entry on the Spiritual Marriage; whereas St John and other older mystics record nothing of the kind. Moreover, sanctifying grace in her case led to exterior consequences, the result in large measure of her temperament, physical and psychic. Therefore it is a mistake to look for the same phenomena in all mystics.[3]

---

[1] It is to be remembered that St John of the Cross declares such things to be results of a certain weakness of body or spirit (*Dark Night*, II. i); and that St Teresa herself, when she got to her Seventh Mansion, found that they ceased.

[2] *Structure de la Connaissance Mystique*, p. 25.

[3] *Contemplation*, p. 294.

Poulain and Farges very nearly take St Teresa as practically the final authority, who has spoken the last word, and almost the first word, on the degrees of prayer; and this though she often protests that she relates only what happened to herself, that different souls are led by God in different ways, so that what she exposes is only *a* way, not *the* way, and is not to be made into a general law. The Dominican writers are disposed to take St Thomas, St John of the Cross, and St Teresa, as their authorities; but even this, I venture to think, affords too narrow a basis on which to erect the structure of mystical theology. The testimony of a large number of the representative mystics throughout the ages ought to be systematically studied and formulated, after the manner in which SS. Augustine, Gregory, and Bernard are studied in this book. Only by a comparative method, by the analysis and synthesis of the accounts given by a wide circle of mystics, and viewed from the standpoints alike of theology and of modern psychology, can a broad enough foundation be laid for such a superstructure of mystical theology as will satisfy all desires.

Though there has been a progress in the formulation of mystical theology as a science, the mystical experience itself has not progressed; though the older writers do not use the later terminology of 'union' and 'transformation', they knew these things as experiences. St Augustine's descriptions of intellectual ecstasy—and, indeed, St Gregory's of contemplation—though couched in less developed terminology than that of St Teresa and St John, refer to experiences no whit inferior to theirs, nor to those of Ruysbroeck and later mystics.

Before entering on the discussion of details, the reader will, we believe, be glad to have a broad statement of the whole subject, which, though made by a highly competent authority, has hitherto been overlooked in current discussions.

§ 5. *Bishop Hedley on Contemplation*

It so happens that fifty years ago these questions of theory in regard to contemplation and mystical prayer were treated of by the late Bishop Hedley of Newport, who made on them a pronouncement remarkable for its clear and profound exposition of theological principles, and remarkable as forestalling, twenty years before the tide of reversion to tradition had begun to flow, the great lines of doctrine commonly accepted now. He was a Benedictine, a good theologian, a Thomist with first-hand knowledge of his St Thomas, and he was familiar with the standard spiritual and mystical writers: moreover, he was a spiritual man, a man of prayer. Appearing in a quarterly periodical, his study has been lost to sight, and has not found place in recent discussions; but it deserves to be brought forward, for it is learned, sane, and sober, and perhaps may offer a basis of conciliation on some of the points in dispute. Therefore no apology is needed for directing attention to its most vital passages.[1]

Contemplation is the queen and sovereign act among all the acts of the heart of man. For the perfect flower of the heart is the act of charity; and contemplation is charity or love when it is actual, constant, pure, and flowing under the pressure of the Holy Spirit. Contemplation is not ordinary prayer. Yet it is not one of those extraordinary gifts which humble souls may not aspire to. It is the very aim of the teaching of Fr Baker and his school that 'extraordinary' prayer should be an ordinary state for Christian souls; for priests, for religious, for devout lay folk, and for the poor and unlearned who love God with all their heart. It is true that few arrive at true 'interior' prayer until after many years of patient exercise. But still, in the sense that, with due perseverance and by the help of God, it will come at last, we may say that it is 'ordinary'. It is thus that it differs from ecstasy, rapture, visions and other miraculous supernatural favours. These no one has a right to aspire to or expect.

The whole progress of the 'art' of prayer is supernatural, and depends on the ever-present help of God. Yet because this help, or grace, is always ready, and (up to a certain, not easily determined, point) a matter upon which man may calculate with certainty, we may proceed in our speculation concerning prayer almost as if it were a natural art, depending for its perfection upon the energy of the human will in asceticism and concentration. Not that any one advances in prayer unless, amongst other things, he is fully impressed that God alone can give him the gift of prayer. But the laws of God's gifts and of His grace have become, as a fact, not as a right, the laws of the human soul, when the soul is regenerate.

The end and object of the man of prayer is to attain to contemplation. Yet here we must make careful reservations. We may desire and sigh for contemplation; yet we must be well aware that, in ourselves, we have no power or means to attain to it; and we must not conceal from ourselves that even the virtues and gifts of a sanctified soul do not give us directly the key which will admit us to contemplation. Neither mortification, nor purity of heart, nor humility, nor meditation of point after point, nor the most strenuous exercise of affective aspiration, nor all of these together, can ever produce a state near enough to contemplation to pass into that perfect state by its own force and weight.

[1] It was an article in the *Dublin Review*, 1876, on the re-edition of Fr Baker's *Sancta Sophia* or *Holy Wisdom*. It was reprinted in 1916 as a Catholic Truth Society tract, under the title *Prayer and Contemplation*.

Contemplation is the state in which ordinary prayer becomes perfect. It is not a miraculous state. It is merely the perfection of ordinary supernatural prayer; ordinary, in this sense, that God ordinarily gives it to those who remove obstacles and take the requisite means.

Contemplation is a great and a 'perfect' state of prayer. To arrive at it, sanctifying or habitual grace is not enough; faith, hope, and charity are not enough; there is also required that touch of the finger of God's right hand, and that quick response of the soul thereto, which imply the active operation of the seven great gifts of the Holy Ghost. And among the gifts which confer the privilege of contemplation—gifts which every one not in mortal sin possesses, but which so few stir up within them—the chief are, the gift of knowledge, the gift of understanding, and the gift of wisdom. It is the Gifts of the Holy Spirit which pour on the soul that exquisite and subtle light, that rapture of attention, that spiritual sensibility, as if new senses had been given us, which combine to elevate ordinary meditation and affection into contemplation.

Bishop Hedley gives an account of the act of contemplation. After citing half a dozen descriptions, he makes the following synthesis:

There is a state of mental prayer, ordinarily preceded by less perfect states, which has the following characteristics:

1. It dispenses, to a very great extent, with the use of sensible images or pictures in the mind. Instead of 'pictures', the soul seems overshadowed by a spreading, silent sense as of something near at hand, vague in outline, colourless and dim; such a sense as might fall upon one who watches intently some dark curtain which hides an awful presence.

2. It dispenses with reasoning, or what is called 'discourse'. In the state of prayer which is called contemplation, the mind remains steadfast and fixed in one simple gaze.

3. This intuition is accompanied by ardent love. An intuition by which we gaze upon our last end and only good, not in any abstract way, but as, here and now, our complete joy and perfect bliss, means an intuition of love.

4. Whilst contemplation lasts, the soul does not perceive what she is doing. She is so engaged with God that she does not turn in reflection upon herself. She does not need to invent motives—she has attained, for a time, the object and end of all motive. Hence the dictum of the desert, that 'he who was conscious he was praying, was not yet arrived at perfect prayer'.

Contemplation is 'perfect' prayer, comparatively with the states that precede it; but in itself it is merely the first resting-place of a mountain region in which height reaches beyond height until human thought refuses to follow.

§ 6. *Intellect and Will in Contemplation*

Bishop Hedley here shows himself the Thomist he was, in that he makes contemplation to be primarily an act of the intellect—'the soul fully intent on God, gazing and loving', he describes it, the loving consequent on the seeing. For St Thomas it is in its essence a simple intuition of truth, terminating in an affection of the will.[1] But for another school or tradition, represented by St Bonaventure, contemplation and mystic union lies primarily in the affective order, and is a matter of love, an act of the will, the operations of the intellect being superseded and transcended. For St Thomas, too, the highest and truest knowledge we can have of God in this life is that He utterly transcends any knowledge or idea we can have concerning Him.[2] This is what the author of the old English mystical book the *Cloud* means by the 'Cloud of Unknowing'. His idea is that the soul in contemplation is set between two clouds, one above it, the other below it. The cloud above it, between it and God, impenetrable, is the 'Cloud of Unknowing', against which the soul in contemplation ever beats with 'secret blind stirrings of love' in the will, inarticulate actuations, or else single words, 'God' or 'Love', poured out in swift repetition, like sparks from a burning brand. The cloud below the soul, between it and all creatures, is the 'Cloud of Forgetting', into which it seeks to thrust down all images, thoughts, ideas of creatures, and all words, thus emptying the mind of everything that could disturb it in 'the work' it is about. This 'treading down of the thought of all creatures and holding them under the cloud of forgetting' is man's travail, with the help of grace. But 'the devout stirring of love that is wrought in the will' 'is the work of only God'. 'Therefore do thy work, and surely I promise thee He will not fail in His' (c. xxvi.). Though the 'stirrings' are the movements of grace, still it is the constant burden of the *Cloud* and of its companion *Epistle of Privy Counsel* that they are a 'work' in which the will, or the soul, is industriously at work: 'a naked intent stretching unto God', 'a longing desire evermore working'.[3]

---

[1] Contemplatio pertinet ad ipsum simplicem intuitum veritatis, ... et in affectu terminatur (*Summa*, 2–2ae, q. 180, a. 3).

[2] Hoc est ultimum ad quod pertingere possumus circa cognitionem divinam in hac vita, quod Deus est supra omne id quod a nobis cogitari potest (*De Div. Nom.*, i. lect. 3: cited by Joret).

[3] *Epistle of Privy Counsel*, i. This *Epistle* is printed for the first time in Dom Justin McCann's edition of *The Cloud* (Orchard Books, No. 4, 1924, Burns, Oates and Washbourne). In the same volume is printed, also for the first time, the substantive portions of Fr Augustine Baker's *Secretum sive Mysticum*, an exposition of *The Cloud*.

In his *Exposition of the Cloud* Fr Baker describes the 'stirrings of love' as

certain forced but very facile elevations of the will, that bluntly or blindly heaves itself up towards God, apprehended only according to the general notion of faith, and applies and unites itself unto Him, with a conformity of the will to the Will of God in all things, applying the will unto Him and holding it fast unto Him so long as corporeal frailty will permit. These exercises of love the soul herself (howsoever helped or moved by God) worketh and is the agent.[1]

And so he classes them as 'active' exercises, albeit 'they do not lie in man's power to exercise at his pleasure, but depend upon the power of God, who moves and enables the soul to them' (p. 319): that is, the will does produce them, though in virtue of a special enablement. Fr Baker calls these stirrings 'aspirations':[2]

Aspirations are an exercise by which we immediately aspire to a perfect union with God. In them there is much good love and a kind of union, but not perfect love or perfect union. Aspirations are a certain greedy longing or thirsting after God out of love; but when the soul is come to be united to Him, then do they cease: she being come to enjoy and possess that Good which by her aspirations she aspired and tended unto. But such union ceasing—for it doth not always last—she reneweth her aspirations, by them aspiring to a new union. The which perfect union consisteth in the coupling of the powers of the soul by love and affection to the Spirit of God, all images of creatures being for the time driven and held without. ... The said union I intend to be an active union. For as to the passive union, our author professeth that he will not treat of it, as being a matter too high for him to undertake the expressment of it.[3]

These pieces from the *Cloud* and Fr Baker's *Exposition* have been cited as of interest in themselves, and as showing that both writers are in the line of those who make contemplation lie rather in the will than in the intellect. Fr Baker says:[4]

God only can move the will to this exercise of love, and He doth it immediately, without help of the imagination or understanding. No creature can do it; they can only work in a man's will by causing or using some image in the imagination, the which appearing in the understanding they seek to move the will thereby. The

[1] *Exposition* (see preceding note), pp. 296–301.
[2] Ibid. pp. 314–17: see the full teaching on this subject in *Sancta Sophia*, p. 509 ff.
[3] See piece cited from *Cloud*, c. xxvi, text, p. 8. On passive unions see *Sancta Sophia*, pp. 520 and 531 ff.
[4] *Exposition*, p. 381; cf. *Sancta Sophia*, p. 507.

will being moved by God, will immediately apply itself to God and suffer no thought to go between her and God, or to hinder her union with Him.

An interesting question presents itself: What is the relation between Fr Baker's aspirations and St John's loving attention? Do they speak of different kinds of contemplation, or is the difference one of *nuance*, of emphasis? At first sight they seem to have in mind different states of prayer. Fr Baker lays down clearly that in aspirations the soul, moved by God, itself actuates, until, if so be, there is question of passive union, a rare and extraordinary action of God on the soul. St John on his side urges that 'the soul must be lovingly intent upon God, without distinctly eliciting other acts beyond those to which He inclines it; making no efforts of its own, purely, simply, and lovingly intent upon God' (text, p. 214); and in the piece to be cited just now (p. xxvii.), he says that in loving attention the faculties labour no more, but are all in repose: and similar words occur with great frequency. Yet does he take for granted that there is a certain working of the soul: persons in this state must at least direct their attention lovingly and calmly towards God (text, p. 215), and the attention must be kept fixed (pp. 215-216); by custom the loving attention can come to be secured more or less at will (below, p. xxxii.).

St John's solicitude concerns the protest he makes against the manner of direction prevalent in his time, whereby souls were kept tied down to discursive meditation and explicit acts. That which he is insistent on excluding from the prayer of souls being led by God into the practice of loving attention, is all discourse of the understanding, all meditation and reflection, all images, pictures, forms, all seeking for sensible devotion and fervour, and all acts couched in set forms of words. Whether he would class as acts to be excluded those hardly articulate stirrings of love, those blind upheavings of the soul to God, that are the staple of Fr Baker's aspirations, is at the least very doubtful. After going through again, with this particular point in mind, the section in the *Living Flame* and the *Dark Night of Sense*, the conclusion borne in upon me by many indications is that such aspirations fall within the idea of St John's prayer of loving attention, which, be it noted, he habitually declares to be infused contemplation.[1] Thus, almost in the same words as Fr Baker, he speaks of the soul's 'earnest longing after God' and its 'thirst for God' (*Night of Sense*, xi, 1, 2). Towards the end of the section in the *Living Flame*, while speaking of the

---

[1] *Dark Night*, I. x. 7; xii. I; xiv. I.

mind's emptiness of all distinct perceptions in memory, imagination, understanding, and emotion during the loving attention, he turns to the will: he addresses those directors whom he is objurgating,

You will say, perhaps, that the will, if the understanding have no distinct perceptions, will be idle and without love, because we can love nothing that we do not know. That is true as to the natural actions of the soul. But in the matter of infused contemplation it is not at all necessary for the soul to have distinct knowledge, because God is then communicating to it loving knowledge, which is at the same time heat and light indistinctly, and then according to the state of the understanding love also is in the will. As the knowledge is general and dim, so the will also loves generally and indistinctly. There is no reason, therefore, to be afraid of the will's idleness in this state, for if it ceases to elicit acts directed by particular knowledge, so far as they depend on itself, God inebriates it with infused love through the knowledge which contemplation ministers. These acts of the will which are consequent upon infused contemplation are so much the nobler, the more meritorious, and the sweeter, the nobler the source, God, who infuses this love and kindles it in the soul. Though the soul have no particular comfort in God, distinctly apprehended, though it does not make distinct acts of love, it does find more comfort in Him in that general secret and dim infusion, than if it were under the influence of distinct acts of knowledge.

Speaking of a far higher grade of contemplation, St John says that 'the will burns with the fire of love, longs for God, praises Him and gives Him thanks, worships and honours Him, and prays to Him in the sweetness of love' (text, pp. 149-150). I think, therefore, it may be said that St John, in regard to the earlier stages of infused contemplation, does not differ in substance from the author of the *Cloud* and Fr Baker, though he lays more stress than they on the aspect of tranquil repose in contemplation. And it seems that for him, too, contemplation lies rather in the will than in the intellect.

On this question of intellect or will Père Joret makes a welcome concession, or distinction: 'For St Thomas, contemplation consists in an intellectual act; love is there; but what constitutes the essence of contemplation is the simple gaze on divine truth: without this intuition one may well enjoy a certain mystic union, but one does not properly "contemplate".'[1] This is helpful. St John distinguishes contemplation and union: the former is the characteristic of the state of proficients, the latter of the state of the perfect: 'Souls begin to enter the Dark Night when God is drawing them out of the state of beginners, which is that of those who meditate on the spiritual

---

[1] *Contemplation*, p. 165.

road, and is leading them into that of proficients, the state of contemplatives, that having passed through it, they may arrive at the
state of the perfect, which is that of the divine union with God.'[1]

I have to confess to an abiding uneasy sense when reading the
Dominican writers as to whether St Thomas has in mind really the
same thing as St John and the mystics pure and simple. It would
be a great contribution to the study of mysticism if some Dominican
theologian were to draw out in set form a bare statement of what
St Thomas says on the act of contemplation itself and on union,
without bringing it into relation with St Teresa or St John or any
other mystic, and without theological considerations derived from
the theology of the Gifts. Such misgivings as I feel are engendered
by the sense that the Dominicans seem to consider that there is
some intimate connexion between the study of speculative theology
and contemplation. This comes to the surface often in P. Joret's
book (which on the whole I like better than that of P. Garrigou-
Lagrange); as where he says that the combination of asceticism,
liturgy, and theological study, makes a greater Dominican house
'the ideal abode of contemplation' (p. 174): an idea surely very
different from that of the Egyptian hermits in Cassian (see text,
p. 204).

§ 7. *Points of Mystical Theology*

PASSIVITY.   Of the various points at issue around contemplation,
the question of 'passivity' is probably the one that lies nearest to
the root of the matter. Passivity has commonly come nowadays to
be taken as the test of real contemplation. By passivity is meant that
contemplation itself is wholly the act of God, the soul lying passive
in the hands of God, receiving the gift and not resisting the divine
action; yet accepting and responding by a vital act. The following
words, taken from a review of Mgr Farge's book, well express the
currently received idea:

Mystical or supernatural contemplation is a divine gift, the
result of God's action upon the soul, which is *passive*. There is that
lower kind of contemplation which is called acquired, and which
differs specifically from mystical contemplation, and may be described as active. The essential difference between asceticism and
mysticism, and between mystical contemplation and every other
form of prayer, however perfect, is the element of passivity which
constitutes the former state, and that of activity which constitutes
the latter.

[1] *Dark Night*, I. i.

There is common agreement that such passivity is the mark of the mystical experience in its strictest and fullest acceptation, so that it receives the name, among others, of 'passive union'; but the hard-and-fast limiting of the term 'mystical' to such highest states of prayer as are in the strict sense passive, seems, as has been seen, to be due to the influence of St Teresa. I do not think it will be found that any such rigid line of demarcation emerges from the passages on contemplation brought together in this book from the writings of the three great contemplative Doctors of the West: there appears to be in them a clear sense of the working of the soul, of will and of intellect, in contemplation.[1] It would be of interest to institute a study, from this point of view, of the medieval mystics, the Victorines, SS Thomas and Bonaventure, and the German mystics of the fourteenth century. We have seen that the *Cloud*, and Fr Baker after it, speak of ordinary contemplation as a working of the soul wherein the will is agent.

I can hardly think that anyone, after reading Fr Baker's *Exposition of the Cloud*, or the chapters in *Sancta Sophia* on 'Contemplation' and 'Aspirations', will class 'aspirations' as 'acquired contemplation'; yet does he speak of them as an active exercise, as 'active mystical contemplation', and as leading up to a 'perfect active mystical union', which in turn is likely to obtain from God the extraordinary grace of a passive union.

Whether and how much Fr Baker's road differs from St John's we cannot say: St John has spoken as no one else has of the initial stages of contemplation, infused contemplation; and he has spoken as few others have of the highest heights of the spiritual life; but he has hardly spoken of the intermediate stages Fr Baker's road is different from St Teresa's, yet does it reach the same goal. It is a gradual ascent, without break of continuity, from discursive meditation, through affective prayer and forced acts of the will, to aspirations and contemplation, and to active union. It is the road he travelled along himself, and we know that it brought him to the 'passive union purely intellectual', which is the Fifth and Sixth of St Teresa's Mansions; and into the 'great desolation', which is St John's 'night of the spirit';[2] and we may surely believe that it led him through that into the 'state of perfection' portrayed in the last chapter of *Sancta Sophia*, which is nothing less than St Teresa's Seventh Mansion, the state which she and St John call the 'spiritual marriage' or 'transforming love'. These three concluding chapters of *Sancta Sophia* treat of the same heights of the spiritual life, of

---

[1] See, for instance, pp. 34, 65, 70-71, and *passim*.
[2] Fr Baker's *Confessions*, pp. 59-81.

prayer and contemplation and union, as are spoken of in the most advanced pages of St Teresa, St John of the Cross, or B. John Ruysbroeck. And in so far as Fr Baker's road of approach may differ somewhat from theirs, it only shows that more than one path leads to the summit of God's mountain, and that it is a misconception to map it out as if there were only a single track.

On the matter of passivity, it is worth noting that Père Joret declines to follow the extreme ideas of some recent writers: he points out that not until St Teresa's Sixth Mansion does prayer become completely passive; in the Fourth and Fifth, 'quiet' and 'union', some effort is needed; yet is such prayer 'mystical contemplation'.[1]

MYSTICAL. So much on passivity. Another term much controverted is the word 'mystical'. One school of mystical theologians limits its use strictly to contemplation that is fully passive—this is the position of Poulain and Farges; another school, to which belong de Besse and Saudreau, extend it so as to include the prayer of loving attention or of simplicity. On this question excellent words have been written in a recent book, *Darkness or Light*, by Fr Henry Browne, S.J., to which we shall revert more than once. He sets up a psychological rather than a theological test for 'mystical'. The natural, normal, mode of operation of the mind during its present state of union with the body, is by sense impressions, images, concepts, 'intelligible species', reasoning; when it operates in another mode, without these means it is acting mystically. Fr Browne says: 'In theory it is necessary, unless we want to be lost in hopeless confusion, to state firmly that, as soon as one ceases to use discourse of the faculties, so soon one's prayer begins to be passive and one is really entering on the mystic road' (op. cit. p. 138). This seems to afford a true and easily applicable discriminant delimiting the frontier between mystical and non-mystical prayer. According to it, the prayer of loving attention, or of simplicity, is rudimentary mystical prayer.

The unduly rigid idea of 'mystical' is responsible for Poulain's difficulties over St John's 'Night of Sense': the description of the 'loving attention' quite tallies, as he sees, with the prayer of simplicity; yet St John calls it 'infused contemplation'. As Poulain's position is that the prayer of simplicity is 'acquired', not 'infused', and therefore not mystical, he has to postulate in the Night of Sense 'a latent quietude' that distinguishes it from the prayer of simplicity, and makes it a rudimentary mystical state, in the restricted

---

[1] *Contemplation*, p. 105. The four 'Waterings' of the *Life* correspond to the Third Fourth, Fifth, and Sixth 'Mansions' of the *Castle*.

sense of 'mystical' (op. cit., c. xv.). But we have seen that this is a misconception.

ORDINARY AND EXTRAORDINARY. These terms again give rise to much controversy. We have heard Bishop Hedley make a synthesis, almost a paradox: contemplation is extraordinary prayer, but it ought to be an ordinary state for Christian souls. Some writers use 'ordinary' as meaning usual; among them de Besse: his chapter xiii. is entitled 'The prayer of faith [loving attention] a common grace.' He says:

The grace of contemplation is granted with truly divine generosity to souls who devote themselves generously to prayer. It is not a miraculous gift; it is not an indication of a perfect life; it is a means of raising the soul to sanctity. 'Nearly all generous souls who remain faithful to prayer receive, sooner or later, the grace of obscure contemplation [i.e. prayer of faith]. As soon as these souls have acquired the power of discerning and corresponding with this grace they can practise at will the prayer of faith, which is an ordinary mystic prayer.'[1]

Poulain and de Besse, while differing as to whether prayer of faith, or of simplicity, should be classed as mystical and infused, are agreed that it is the term of ordinary prayer, and that higher kinds, as St Teresa's prayers of quiet or of union, are extraordinary, or even miraculous. Fr Baker extends upwards the range of ordinary contemplation—he does not, I think, ever use the term 'acquired':

Mystic contemplation or union is of two sorts: (1) Active and ordinary, being indeed an habitual state of perfect souls by which they are enabled, whensoever fit occasion shall be, to unite themselves actively and actually to God by efficacious, fervent, amorous, and constant, yet withal silent and quiet, elevations of the spirit. (2) Passive and extraordinary; the which is not a state but an actual grace and favour from God, by which He is pleased at certain times, according to His free good pleasure, to communicate a glimpse of His majesty to the spirits of His servants, after a secret and wonderful manner.[2]

The most recent writers of the Dominican school carry the thing still further. They say that the epithet 'extraordinary' belongs only to such phenomena as visions, auditions, revelations, raptures, ecstasies, and the other psycho-physical phenomena, which, though

[1] Op. cit. p. 181.   [2] Sancta Sophia, p. 505.

frequent concomitants of contemplation and mystical states, still are not of its essence, but only accidental adjuncts. These, being of the nature of *gratiae gratis datae*, like the charismata of the Corinthians, are properly 'extraordinary' gifts, and are never legitimate objects of desire or prayer. But contemplation in itself, and apart from such manifestations, is in the normal course of God's providence and of the workings of the Holy Spirit, by sanctifying grace and by the sevenfold gifts, in the hearts and souls of the regenerate. Even the highest degrees of contemplation and mystical union, such as we hear the great mystics describe in the pages of this book, are held to be but the prolongation and culmination of the supernatural life of the soul coming to its fullest fructification in this life, an advanced glimpse or taste of the union of heaven. Thus, though extraordinary *in fact*, in that few reach the higher states of mystic union, such union is not extraordinary *in itself* or *in its nature*, but the growth of ordinary sanctifying grace working, so to say, intensively in congenial and well-prepared soil. And so these higher mystic experiences, apart from rapture and ecstasy, etc., are not to be called 'extraordinary', but 'eminent': that they are so rare is to be attributed to the same sorts of reasons that make perfection and heroic sanctity so rare. This is the theory propounded by the Dominicans as being that of St Thomas, or at least the outcome of his teaching. It finds its most vigorous exponent in Père Garrigou-Lagrange. It is in fact part of a larger theory to which we shall revert presently.

§ 8. *Mixed Contemplation*

It may seem that these 'afterthoughts' have been labouring interminably abstract questions of theory; nay, even only of definition and terminology: yet it is not so: they are intimately bound up with those issues of practical personal devotion and religion that were a principal motive of the writing of this book (pp. 131-132, 222-223). And so I call attention to a letter, really a tractate, by a Carmelite theologian, printed by P. Garrigou-Lagrange in *Perfection Chrétienne et Contemplation* (pp. 745-769). We have seen that, whether the idea goes further back or not, the name 'acquired' contemplation was devised by Carmelite theologians at the beginning of the seventeenth century in view of St Teresa's very rigid conception of 'supernatural' contemplation. The letter is an explanation of the teaching of these Carmelites on acquired contemplation. It shows that by it they mean hardly more than affective prayer or the simpler kind of recollection spoken of by St Teresa in c. xxviii. of the *Way* (see above, pp. xvii-xviii.). But between mere acquired contemplation and that which is fully passive—St Teresa's 'supernatural'—they recognize a 'mixed contemplation', which is in a measure acquired, and yet is really infused, the initiative of the soul joining itself to the divine motion, and the acts of acquired contemplation alternating with those of infused. This is the initial kind of contemplation; and to it this Carmelite theologian explicitly says belong St John's prayer of loving attention (of faith or of simplicity) in the *Night of Sense* and the oft cited section of the *Living Flame*, and also St Teresa's 'interior recollection' of the Fourth Mansion (above, pp. xviii-xix.).[1]

This may be illustrated by a useful passage from St John himself, *Ascent of Mount Carmel*, Bk. II. c. xv:

It may be asked, whether proficients, those whom God has begun to lead into the supernatural knowledge of contemplation—[i.e. the prayer of loving attention (see c. xiv.)]—are, in virtue of this commencement, never again to return to the way of meditation, reflections, and natural forms [phantasmata, concepts, etc.]? To this I answer, that it is not to be supposed that those who have begun to have this pure and loving knowledge are never to meditate again or attempt it. For in the beginning of their advancement the habit of this is not so perfect as that they should be able at pleasure to perform the acts of it.[2] Neither are they so far advanced beyond the state of meditation as to be unable to meditate and make their reflections as before and to find therein something new. Yea, rather, at first, when we see that our soul is not occupied in this quiet or knowledge, it will be necessary to have recourse to reflections, until we attain to the habit of it in some degree of perfection. Such will be the case when, as often as we apply ourselves to meditation, the soul reposes in this peaceful knowledge, without the power or the inclination to meditate; because, until we arrive at this, sometimes one, sometimes the other, occurs in this time of proficiency in such a way that often the soul finds itself in this loving or peaceful attendance upon God, with all its faculties in repose; and very often also will find it necessary, for that end, to have recourse to meditation, calmly and with moderation. But when this state is attained to, meditation ceases, and the faculties labour no more; for then we may rather say that intelligence and sweetness are wrought in the soul, and that it itself abstains from every effort, except only that it attends lovingly upon God, without any desire to feel or see anything further than to be in the hands of God, who now communicates Himself to the soul thus passive, as the light of the sun to him whose eyes are open. Only, we must take care that no other lights of knowledge, or forms, or figures of meditation, of a more palpable kind intervene.

---

[1] Op. cit. p. 763, note.
[2] This seems of first importance: it implies that when the state of loving attention grows more perfect and more habitual, the acts of it may be performed at will.

This passage seems to speak the language of practical experience and of good sense. On similar lines Mgr Farges, while maintaining the propriety and reality of the distinction between acquired and infused or mystical contemplation, taking the latter in St Teresa's full sense of 'supernatural', still is prepared to grant that there is an intermediate prayer between infused or mystical contemplation and ordinary or ascetic prayer, such that the highest degree of the prayer of simplicity would border on the lowest degree of the prayer of quiet, such a contemplation being partly infused and partly acquired; and to the rest in God which would result from it, has been given the name of quasi-quiet, for it would not entail any real suspension of the working of the powers of the soul. It is a mistake to recognize only a single form of contemplation, or only two, while in fact there are several.[1]

After so much abstract discussion a concrete example will perhaps help to clear ideas. The following is a description of a kind or state of prayer that is fairly common among devout souls whose profession it is to cultivate the interior life and prayer as a set exercise:

One sets oneself to pray, say for the regulation half-hour;

empties the mind of all images, ideas, concepts—this is commonly done without much difficulty;

fixes the soul in loving attention on God, without express or distinct idea of Him, beyond the vague incomprehensible idea of His Godhead;

makes no particular acts, but a general actuation of love, without sensible devotion or emotional feeling: a sort of blind and dumb act of the will or of the soul itself.

This lasts a few minutes, then fades away, and either a blank or distractions supervene: when recognized, the will again fixes the mind in 'loving attention' for a time. The period of prayer is thus passed in such alternations, a few minutes each, the bouts of loving attention being, in favourable conditions, more prolonged than the bouts of distraction.

Such prayer, on the one hand, seems to fall within the limits of Bishop Hedley's 'contemplation', 'gazing and loving'; and certainly to be St John's 'loving attention', and therefore initial 'infused contemplation'; on the other hand, it is 'acquired' by the act of the will, in again and again directing and fixing the mind in loving attention on God.

In view of the foregoing discussions I do not feel any need of

[1] *Mystical Phenomena*, pp. 81–3.

changing what is written on pp. 216-217; only I would now avoid the sharp contrast between acquired and infused contemplation, because they often overlap; and I would wish the last paragraph on p. 217 to be understood of 'mixed' contemplation. With St Teresa's prayer of quiet, and still more with the prayer of union, a change comes in, a new element—the element which she designates 'supernatural', in her peculiar sense of the word. This change Père Joret explains theologically by saying that up to this point the prayer is made in virtue of co-operating grace, but afterwards by operating grace.[1] Above this line lie the various manifestations of the mystical experience spoken of by the mystics—passive union, experimental perception of God, substantial divine touches, intellectual vision, transforming love, spiritual marriage. Whether such experiences are to be termed extraordinary or ordinary (in whatever sense), I range myself with those who hold that there is a difference in kind between them and those lowlier contemplations that have so far mostly been occupying our attention.

§ 9. Practical Agreements

Meantime, while the controversy on questions of theory is working itself out, we may be thankful that fairly general agreement has been arrived at concerning certain points affecting the practice, alike of devout souls embarked on a spiritual course of self-discipline and prayer, and of those that direct them. These points of agreement may be summed up under three heads.

1. It seems to be a practically acquired result that discoursive meditation is no longer looked on as the normal lifelong mental prayer of devout souls. It has become recognized that if things be allowed to run their natural course, meditation will in due time (probably no very long time) pass into affective prayer, and this again into prayer of loving attention or of simplicity, i.e. contemplation; and that souls, as soon as they show the signs of ripeness for the change, should be instructed and encouraged to respond to the leading of the Holy Ghost. This, of course, is the burden of the teaching of St John of the Cross in the outburst on 'direction', printed as appendix by de Besse.[2] It was also the universal traditional teaching of the first sixteen centuries. How the change came about towards the close of the sixteenth century is set forth by Saudreau in an interesting section of the book La Vie d'Union à Dieu,

[1] Contemplation Mystique, p. 102.
[2] It is taken from The Living Flame of Divine Love, stanza iii., ed. 1864, pp. 265–88; ed. 1891, pp. 463–89; ed. 1912, pp. 75–106: de Besse gives only summary of some portions; but the piece is well worth studying in its entirety.

entitled 'Déviation de la doctrine traditionnelle.' The older Orders
have always, on the whole, naturally clung to the old ideas, and
gladly welcome the return to the old ways. And it seems that in the
Society of Jesus Père Poulain's book has brought it about, that the
line of mystic teachers, beginning with St Ignatius himself, which
has at all times existed alongside of another current, is now in fair
way to become predominant. This conclusion seems to be justified
in regard to the French Jesuits by the whole tenor of Père Bainvel's
Introduction to the latest edition of Poulain; and in regard to those
of English-speaking countries, by the closing words of the altogether
admirable final chapter of Fr Henry Browne's book, *Darkness or
Light*:

> If we look at our own time, we shall find that Jesuit writers have
> been and are in the forefront of those who are working for the
> revival of mysticism and for the abandonment of that mechanical
> spirit of meditation, which, however it may have been called for
> by special circumstances in the past, can hardly be thought suited
> to the exigencies of our generation.[1]

2. It follows that not only the prayer of loving attention, but the
higher, and even highest, grades of contemplation and mystical
prayer, are, in the same way as perfection or heroic sanctity, a
lawful object of desire, aspiration, and humble prayer on the part
of all. This means, of course, contemplation and mystical prayer in
itself, as distinguished from elements properly extraordinary, as

---

[1] The whole thoughtful chapter will well repay reading, as will the whole book.
Quite recently Fr Robert Steuart, S.J., has published a small *Map of Prayer*
(Burns, Oates and Washbourne, 6*d*.), which gives a clear and excellent summary
of the steps in prayer, up to and including the prayer of loving attention. He is in
full agreement with Fr Browne as to the propriety and desirability of encouraging
all souls that show the signs of such invitation, to pass out of meditation and on
to such contemplation. He points out that the term 'contemplation' as used by
St Ignatius in the *Exercises*, has a meaning quite different from the ordinary
traditional one.

The fact that St Ignatius in the *Exercises* is silent concerning contemplation and
contemplative prayer has been, probably, the principal reason why so many of
the spiritual writers of the Society have looked on meditation as the normal lifelong mental prayer of devout souls. But if Père Poulain's account of the *Exercises*
be correct, this difficulty vanishes. He says: 'This book is intended for a thirty days'
retreat, and presupposes a man with a certain desire to be generous towards God,
but kept back either by ignorance with regard to the means to be taken, or by
his weakness. The *Exercises* are skilfully combined for his gradual development in
generosity, and, if he is capable of it, his being led on to heroism' (op. cit. c. ii.
§ 51; *Prayer of Simplicity*, p. 70). But a month is, ordinarily speaking, all too short
a time to pass in meditation for the mind to be attuned to contemplation; and
so St Ignatius, naturally, does not speak of it in his great retreat. But Poulain
seems to make quite clear what the Saint's mind was, that after the retreat his
disciples should pursue the traditional courses of prayer, as he did very eminently
himself (op. cit. c. ii., §§ 68, 73).

visions, revelations, prophecy, rapture, and so forth; these by universal consent never are lawful objects of prayer or desire. Poulain, who, by force of his definition, makes all mystical prayer 'extraordinary', 'supernatural' in St Teresa's sense, yet agrees with the others that the mystic union is a lawful and good object of desire and prayer, and shows that this is the traditional teaching (op. cit. c. xviii-xix.).

3. The third point on which there has come about general agreement is the sharp distinction between contemplation or even mystic union in itself, and the accidental accessories that often accompany it—visions, locutions, raptures, trances, and so forth. This is important, for in recent times the tendency has been to throw more and more emphasis on this the non-essential and, it may be added, undesirable side of mysticism, and indeed in great measure to identify mysticism with it. I have been at pains to show that this was not the mind of SS. Augustine, Gregory, Bernard; and it was not the mind of St John of the Cross, who relentlessly rules out all such things. The depreciation of such manifestations reaches its highest pitch in the Dominican writers. Père Garrigou-Lagrange lays down the position that the simplest prayer made by the force of sanctifying grace, is of a higher supernatural grade than such miraculous gifts as prophesying future events, giving sight to the blind, or raising the dead to life: the reason being that the first is supernatural by its very nature, the others supernatural only in their mode—sight and life being natural things (pp. 9-10, 42). In this he has St Paul with him, who says that charity is more excellent than the gifts of prophecy or healing or miracles. All such charismata, as visions, locutions, revelations, are intrinsically of less worth than sanctifying grace and the Gifts of the Holy Ghost, the highest work of which in the soul is mystic prayer and union.

§ 10. *General Call to Mystic Union*

Up to this point it is possible to rejoice wholeheartedly in the movement that is carrying practical teaching on spiritual prayer back to the old ways of Christian tradition. We can agree with Père de Besse that the prayer of faith, contemplation, 'is a much more common grace than is supposed. If every soul to whom it is offered corresponded faithfully, contemplatives—[that is, those frequently and easily exercising acts of contemplation]—would be innumerable, both in convents and even in the world' (p. 55):—I would add, and especially in the ranks of the clergy, pastoral and other, according to the teaching of St Gregory. But the Dominican theologians carry the matter of theory much further, and the well-known Jesuit, Père de la Taille, goes at any rate a long way with them, though more guardedly.[1] The theory is enunciated in the following statement, printed on the title-page as the motto of Père Garrigou-Lagrange's book: 'The normal prelude of the vision of heaven, infused contemplation, like heaven, is by docility to the Holy Spirit, by prayer and the Cross, accessible to all.' This idea was put forward, in its clearest expression, by a Spanish Dominican, Padre Arintero, in a book whereof the sub-title was 'The heights (las alturas) of contemplation accessible to all.'[2] He thus sums up the position:[3]

Perfection lies in the full development of baptismal grace. All baptized receive the seven Gifts of the Holy Ghost, with which we can, by being faithful and docile, arrive at fulness of life and intelligence, therefore at the fruitive or mystic union. And short of that we shall ever be children, never reaching the age of discretion or of the perfect man: indeed we shall be the slothful servants of the Gospel, for not having cultivated the gifts received at baptism.

Garrigou-Lagrange formulates the theory thus:[4]

There are not two ways of perfection, the ordinary (intended for all), and an extraordinary (by way of contemplation and mystical life), a special vocation, to which not all fervent souls may aspire. There is only one unitive way, which by docility to the Holy Spirit, growing ever more and more perfect, leads to a mystic union, more and more intimate. This is not of itself or by its nature extra-ordinary, but the perfect order, the full development of charity, realized actually in souls truly generous, at least towards the end of life, if they live long enough. It may well be that owing to lack of proper guidance, or of favourable surroundings, or as the result of a nature strongly carried to exterior activities, some generous souls may not arrive at the mystic life until after a time longer than the usual span of life. But this is accidental and does not touch the essential law of the full development of the life of grace. This summit is not reached without infused contemplation.

Garrigou-Lagrange gives some two hundred pages of explanations of this thesis (pp. 419-627). He seems to fluctuate between

---

[1] His study, L'Oraison contemplative, a review article, was reprinted as a little tract of 40 pp. (Paris, Beauchesne, 1921; in English, Burns, Oates and Washbourne, 1926, 1s.). It is of highest quality and should be read by all interested in these matters. P. Bainvel in the Introduction to Poulain makes an analysis with some criticisms and hesitations, and prints two letters of de la Taille in response (lv., lxxxi.).

[2] The sub-title was withdrawn in the latest edition of Cuestiones misticas (Farges, p. 638).

[3] Cited by Bainvel, 'Introduction,' p. l., from letter of Arintero to Farges.

[4] Perfection et Contemplation, pp. 191-2.

substantial mitigations and reassertions of the extreme features of
the theory. Thus he explains 'all' as 'all the just,' 'all in the state
of grace,' even 'all living interior lives.' That it can be said of these
last, that infused contemplation is accessible to them, by infused
contemplation meaning the initial stages, St John's prayer of loving
attention, is a proposition that might easily be accepted as substantially true; and on p. 409 he does recognize 'simple amorous
attention to God' as being the mystic state. It is also laid down that
there may be an active form as well as the contemplative form of
the mystic life (pp. 381, 417). Such explanations, were they firmly
offered, would go a long way towards rendering the theory accept-
able. But the premises are such that, when directly faced, they press
on inexorably to the most extreme positions of Arintero. Thus we
meet such propositions as these: 'The *full* perfection of charity in
this life cannot exist without mystic contemplation' (p. 209); 'Without having passed through the twofold purifications of the Night
of Sense and the Night of the Spirit (treated of by St John in the
Dark Night of the Soul),[1] one cannot attain to (on ne saurait atteindre)
the full perfection of Christian life' (p. 428); 'All the just are called,
at any rate in a general and remote way, to the transforming union
of St Teresa's Seventh and highest Mansion—that is, to the Spiritual
Marriage of St John of the Cross, and such mystic experiences as
he speaks of in the extracts in text, pp. 149-154;—and if they be
faithful to this remote call they will have another call, individual
and more immediate and pressing' (pp. 321, 457).

This last pronouncement means that there has been some infidelity in the case of every baptized person, of everyone who has
been in the state of justification, who does not attain to the very
highest kinds of mystical experience; this is substantially the same
as Arintero's classing all such as among the 'slothful servants'. Such
doctrine gives rise to many questionings. It has been combated by
Farges and by Bainvel, and in a long letter to *La Vie Spirituelle*,
printed by Garrigou-Lagrange, pp. [58]-[79]. Any set discussion
would require a long article; but certain thoughts may find utterance here. And first, Is this the teaching of Our Lord? There is no
trace of anything of the kind in the synoptic gospels, surely, nor
even in St John.[2] I do not perceive it in the teachings of SS.

[1] The 'Night of the Spirit' is the 'Great Desolation' of Fr Baker's *Sancta Sophia*.
[2] St Teresa interprets the petition of the Lord's Prayer, 'Thy Kingdom come',
and also the 'living water' of John vii. 37, 38, and elsewhere, as meaning mystical
contemplation. Such interpretations or applications of texts have their place in
sermons and discourses and spiritual books; but no exegete of Holy Scripture
would say that that is the real meaning of the texts, what our Lord had in mind;
no more than he would accept St Augustine's interpretation of the hundred and
fifty-three great fishes of John xxi. 11 as having any exegetical value.

Augustine, Gregory, or Bernard—St Gregory seems even counter to it (text, pp. 173-174, 188); nor do I perceive it explicitly, or even implicitly, in the many pieces cited from St Thomas by Garrigou-Lagrange and Joret.

The case of St Gregory comes naturally to mind. His laments are well known, that by becoming Pope he had lost the gift of contemplation which he had enjoyed in the monastery, because of the troubles, anxieties, responsibilities, and constant flood of distractive business inherent in the Papacy.[1] Yet was he without doubt fulfilling God's will; nor can it be supposed that the change implied any lessening in perfection of charity, any falling away in sanctity. Surely it must be thought that the devoted performance of the trying duties of his state of life effected in his soul a purification as thorough as if he passed through the mystical Night of the Spirit.

This example of St Gregory brings out the obvious fact that there are states of life, some of them even the holiest, the conditions of which render practically impossible, even for a saint, the higher grades of contemplation and mystical experience: and yet surely is such a one doing God's will in being in these conditions. It is agreed that personal perfection, sanctity, lies in the perfection of charity, in the perfection with which the commandment, 'Thou shalt love the Lord thy God,' is carried out. It is agreed that it is possible and open to man to love God perfectly, and so attain to the highest perfection and sanctity, in any path or condition of life. Also, the manner of exercising this perfect love of God will be different in different conditions: the perfection of the pastoral priest is different in mode from the perfection of the Carthusian; the perfection of a married person in some calling in the world is different from the perfection of a bishop: there are endless modes of perfection, forms in which sanctity may be attained. In any state of life there is no limit to the degree of personal perfection that may be reached, even unto heroic sanctity—and not in spite of, but by means of, the duties of that state of life. This is God's will in regard to each one, and by the faithful and religious performance of the duties of our state of life we are doing God's will and obeying His commandment, which, so the Best Authority has assured us, is the supreme test of love of God; and he who does this perfectly has, so far forth, attained to perfect love of God and to perfection. This is possible, is open, in any condition of life, even the busiest and most distractive.

But the mystical state and the higher grades of contemplation ordinarily are the issue and the culmination of a prolonged system-

---

[1] Preface to *Dialogues*, and *Ep*. i. 5, ad Theoctistam, cited text, p. 182.

atic course of prayer, demanding an amount of time and a concentration that is hardly compatible with the duties of a busy life in the world;—hardly compatible with the life of a pastoral priest in a large modern town parish. Far be it from me to say that such may not receive, as the reward of devoted zeal in the ministry, real mystical consolations; and surely all such may exercise the contemplation of the prayer of loving attention: still the faithful performance of the duties of the pastoral office in such conditions must, as St Gregory experienced in the Papacy, make practically impossible that tranquillity of mind and those long hours of prayer that are the normal conditions of the higher mystical experiences. Yet, without any doubt at all, may such a faithful pastor be a saint, and in the fullest sense of the word. And so I find it difficult to accept the theory that perfection of charity, or even heroic sanctity, are, in the individual, necessarily connected with the higher mystical experiences. P. Garrigou-Lagrange admits that in the active life, without the gifts of contemplation, there may be a great generosity that may merit the name of perfection, but is not the *full* perfection of the Christian life.[1] He has here in view a piece of academic theological theory; for he admits, too, that many of these souls, whose perfection is of the inferior grade, may be more advanced in virtue and in true charity than others who have received the highest kinds of infused contemplation. Words of St Alphonsus Liguori bear on the points under discussion:[2]

After the earlier stages of prayer [up to and including St Teresa's prayer of quiet], God makes the soul pass on to union, and union with God should now be the one object of the soul. But that the soul should attain to perfection, passive union is not necessary, it is enough for it to arrive at active union. Active union is perfect uniformity with the Will of God, wherein certainly consists the whole perfection of divine love. This union is necessary, but not a passive union [i.e. the mystical union of St Teresa's Fifth Mansion, which he refers to]. In heaven we shall see very many who without this sort of supernatural graces will be more glorious than those who have received such graces.

The above passage is somewhat abridged, but in the full text, and throughout the tractate, St Alphonsus claims to be giving St Teresa's teaching. And therefore it will be very much to our purpose to cite a piece from St Teresa wherein this same doctrine is very unmistakably set forth. It comes in the *Castle*, chapter iii. of

---

[1] Op. cit. p. [77].
[2] Instruction on the 'Direction of Spiritual Souls', appendix to *Homo Apostolicus*, § 16.

the Fifth Mansion. In the first two chapters has been described the prayer of Union. This is for St Teresa true and perfect contemplation, a fully supernatural state, the psychological side of which is a suspension or absorption in God of all the faculties and powers of the soul, yet so far without physical rapture: it seems to be the same as Fr Baker's 'passive union purely intellectual.' Then in chapter iii. she goes on:

The advantage of entering this fifth mansion is so great that it is well that none should despair of doing so because God does not give them the supernatural gifts described above. With the help of divine grace true union can always be attained, by forcing ourselves to renounce our own will and by following the will of God in all things. If this be our case I can only declare that we have already obtained this grace from God. There is, then, no need to wish for that other delightful union described above, for its chief value lies in the resignation of our will to that of God, without which it could not be reached. Oh how desirable is this union [i.e. of will] ...

Is it necessary, in order to attain to this kind of divine union, for the powers of the soul to be suspended? [for St Teresa the characteristic feature of the mystical prayer of union.] No; God has many ways of enriching the soul and bringing it to these mansions besides what might be called 'a short cut'. I own that the work will be much harder; but then it will be of higher value, so that your reward will be greater if you come forth victorious; yet there is no doubt it is possible for you to attain this true union with the will of God. This is the union I have longed for all my life, and that I beg Our Lord to grant me; it is the most certain and the safest. But alas, how few of us ever obtain it!

The whole chapter is well worth reading; it is very striking, working round to love of others as the practical test of the 'true union of our will with the will of God.' St Teresa, as she often insists, was no theologian, and she may be mistaken in the above passage; but she had a great gift of thinking and writing clearly—of saying what she meant, and meaning what she said; and the plain meaning of this passage, when read as a whole, has been truly grasped by St Alphonsus in the distinction he draws between the 'active union' of the will with God's Will, and the 'passive union' of the mystical states; and the French Carmelites in their translation rightly interpret it as meaning that St Teresa recognizes two ways of arriving at union, a mystic way and a non-mystic. This, of course, is quite counter to the theory of Saudreau and the Dominican writers, and Garrigou-Lagrange more than once tries to come to grips with St Teresa's words[1]—unsuccessfully, it seems to me. He

[1] Op. cit. pp. 307, 308, 313, 586.

cites only small fragments that give no proper idea of the force of the chapter as a whole; and by treating the prayer of union described by St Teresa in the Fifth Mansion as ecstatic, he makes it fall in the category of 'extraordinary' states, according to his own definition, and therefore outside of the 'normal' development of the spiritual life, and a thing not to be desired or prayed for. To say that the suspension of the powers of the mind is not for St Teresa an essential feature of the prayer of union of her Fifth Mansion, is counter to her language and to her thought. But Garrigou-Lagrange does not seem to reflect how this ruling out of the prayer of union, of the passive union of St Alphonsus or of Fr Baker (text, pp. 11-12), and of the mystical experience properly so called, shakes his general theory, and indeed makes it rock.

I will only add that St Benedict seems to be of the same mind as St Teresa; for he gives the assurance that any one who mounts his Twelve Degrees of Humility, in which there is nothing of mystic contemplation, but much of the renunciation of one's own will, will come straightway to the perfect love of God.

Great discussion goes on whether there be two 'unitive ways' or only one. There is much to be said for the view that they are not one nor two, but many, just as there are many mansions in our Father's House.

§ 11. *The Mystic Experience and Theology*

These 'afterthoughts' have so far been concerned mainly with the practical side of the theme of this book, that dealt with in Part II, and it has been possible to welcome a great general movement going on in ever-increasing volume for the past third of a century, in the direction of the ideas that motived the writing of this book—a broadening out of the conception of mental prayer and contemplation, till contemplation should become once again what it was in olden times, the recognized goal of the spiritual life, the normal full growth of grace in the regenerate soul. We must now turn, more briefly, to the problem envisaged in Part I, the nature of the mystical experience itself in its highest and most complete manifestation, and the validity of the claim of the great mystics in regard to their most characteristic experience. What that claim is, is set forth unmistakably in the Prologue, in the words of certain mystics voicing their own experiences; while in the Epilogue the evidence of the great Christian mystics, pre-eminently St John of the Cross, is accepted as proof of validity. The claim was formulated as the experimental perception of the Being and Presence of God in the soul; or the entering of the soul into conscious direct contact with God.

This I had ventured to put forward as the outstanding problem of mysticism, the issue on which mysticism, properly so called, as an element in the philosophy of religion, must ultimately stand or fall. And so it was a disappointment to find that P. Garrigou-Lagrange seems to pass this question by completely. It is matter for regret that P. Poulain pressed much too far this direct perception of God, making it the essential element of states truly mystical, so that he would not accord the name to any kind of prayer or any religious experience from which the perception of God's Being is absent. But there are many experiences certainly mystical without such direct sense of God.

I cannot but think that Poulain's really most valuable book is marred by the defects of his temperament; he was by profession a mathematician, and he proceeds in mystical theology by a mathematical method of clear-cut definitions, propositions, and proofs, of which the subject-matter is not patient. A great deal of the obscurity and divergences reigning in the sphere of mystical theology are due to a too rigid and mechanical pressing of theories to their extreme conclusions. Thus, in reacting against this exaggeration of Poulain's, Saudreau goes too far in the opposite direction, maintaining that the experimental perception of God is not an element of the mystical experience at all; he holds that the expressions of the mystics that seem to assert some such thing are to be taken as figures of speech, metaphors, and signify that the Presence of God is not directly perceived, but only inferred from the effects of love, devotion, surrender felt in the soul.[1] He seems to make an exception for St John of the Cross's substantial touches, placing them apart as a practically unique experience.[2] It was disconcerting to find Garrigou-Lagrange endorsing this position of Saudreau in more than once place,[3] and citing, with an evident sense of relief, words of Cardinal Billot, that the immediate perception of God by the mystics was an invention of P. Poulain.[4] This, of course, is not the

---

[1] One of the principal pieces cited in support of this interpretation is St Bernard's account of his mystic experience (text, pp. 101–102). But other passages of St Bernard (pp. 104–106) are in line with the statements of the great mystics.

Saudreau deals with the matter with great fulness in an appendix of fifty pages to the second edition of *L'État Mystique* (1921). Farges stoutly defends, against Saudreau, the position that the language of the mystics cannot be explained away as metaphorical, and that their claim of an experimental perception of God, a certain immediate apprehension, is philosophically and theologically sound (*Mystical Phenomena*, pp. 58 ff., 266 ff., 611 ff.).

[2] *The Mystical State*, p. 95.

[3] Op. cit. pp. 301, 331, 576 ('perfectly conformable to St Thomas's principles').

[4] Ibid. p. [86].

case; in the pieces cited from Fr Baker (text, pp. 11-12) the very words 'real experimental perception of God's presence' occur. Though Poulain is mistaken in making such experience the characteristic feature of all grades of infused contemplation and of all mystical states, the claim of the great mystics is, in one way or another, that in the heights of the mystic experience they have got into immediate conscious contact with the Being of God—be it expressed as experimental perception of His Presence in the soul, or as substantial touch, or as passive union, or as intellectual intuition: all this, be it noted, is something quite different from the vision of God's Essence as supposed to have been granted to Moses and St Paul (text, pp. 55-62). In order to have clearly before his mind the nature of the claim of the mystics, let the reader go over the set of citations in the Prologue and the series of pieces from St John of the Cross in the Epilogue: he will see that it really is what is set forth above, and that the language cannot reasonably be explained away as figurative or metaphorical. The claim may be unfounded, an illusion; but that is what it is.

And so, when I found P. Garrigou-Lagrange denying it, and P. Joret passing it over in his book on 'Contemplation according to St Thomas,' and other Dominicans ruling it out, I began wondering if there was any place for this claim of the mystics within the limits of Thomist theology and psychology. And therefore I experienced a sense of relief and of joy when a friend put in my hands the tractate of Père Gardeil, *La Structure de la Connaissance Mystique*.[1] Gardeil is a veteran theologian of the Dominicans, and his tractate impresses me greatly as a masterly and convincing exposition, marked by singular modesty withal, showing how St Thomas's theological doctrine and the witness of the great mystics can really be worked together into a single structure without any watering down of what the mystics have to tell of their experiences. The following formulation of the great question of mysticism leaves nothing to be desired:

Can we touch God in this life by an immediate contact, and have of Him an experience truly direct and substantial? The saints affirm it, and their descriptions of the prayer of union, of ecstasy, of the spiritual marriage, are all full of this sort of quasi-experimental perception of God within us (p. 47).

To this vital question of mysticism, thus posed with the utmost clarity, Gardeil gives an affirmative answer, and he holds that the

---

[1] It is a reprint, 95 pp., of four articles in the *Revue Thomiste*, 1924.

mystics' claim lies within the lines of St Thomas's theology. But it takes him nearly a hundred pages to work up to this conclusion—pages, be it said, of quite extraordinary interest. The foundations are laid in the fullest and most literal assertion of the principle of philosophy no less than theology, of the presence of the Creator, the First Cause, in all creatures, and especially in rational creatures; and of the in-dwelling of the Holy Ghost, and of the Blessed Trinity, in the soul that is in the state of grace. This presence of God is stressed to its fullest meaning, as not merely by His Immensity or Power, but as being the substantial presence of God by His Essence in the 'fund', or centre, or essence of the soul. He shows that of two kinds of knowledge or consciousness, and of these two only, St Thomas uses the term 'perception', 'percipere'; viz. of the soul's consciousness of itself—a matter of everyday psychology—and of the mystic's consciousness of God as present in his soul. Gardeil's theory is based on the analogy of these two kinds of perception, or awareness, to which the term 'cognition' is not applicable. For 'cognition' in our present state of union of soul and body, 'knowledge', is dependent on sense-impressions, phantasmata, intelligible species, concepts, abstract and general ideas derived from material things; whereas the soul's perception of itself is direct, without such intermediate forms; and so is it with the soul's perception in the mystic experience of God present in it—the perception is direct, quasi-experimental, as the mystics say. This perception of God is, according to the principles of St Thomas's theology, to be ascribed to the 'supra-conceptual'—'supra-intentional' is Gardeil's technical scholastic term[1]—working of the Gift of Wisdom, which is for Thomists the operating force in the higher grades of contemplation. And Gardeil consequently rejects two theories that have been in these controversies put forward to meet the difficulty inherent in the idea of the mind working without concepts or species; for non-conceptual activities of the mind are as great a bugbear to modern psychologists, as non-intentional activities without intelligible species are to scholastic psychologists.

The first of the theories rejected turns on a point of highly technical scholastic psychology; still, as it looms large in the *Mystical Phenomena* of Mgr Farges, lately translated into English and likely to be widely read, it is worth while to take note of Gardeil's utter rejection. Farges maintains, as the teaching of St Thomas, that in contemplation the place of the ordinary means of knowledge, viz., phantasmata, concepts, ideas, species, is taken by 'impressed

[1] 'Intentional knowledge' means that the object known is presented to the mind not directly, but by the means of a representative idea (p. 5).

species' infused in the mind by God. Garrigou-Lagrange contests this at length, and Gardeil pronounces it alien to the tradition of the mystics and to sane philosophy and theology, especially that of St Thomas (p. 74). Readers of *Sancta Sophia* will remember that Fr Baker has recourse to a similar theory (pp. 505-7, 520, 532 [1]); but it will be noted that he does so only in compliance with what he conceived to be the dicta of the schools, that the soul cannot in this life operate without the means of 'species'. Had he realized that the best Thomist teaching declares the highest mystical states to be independent of such need, he would surely have felt relieved at being freed from the necessity of postulating such a theory, in no way demanded by the personal experience of mystics.

And on the other hand, Gardeil argues at great length against the view which we have just seen to be maintained by Saudreau and endorsed by Garrigou-Lagrange, that God's presence is not directly perceived in the mystic experience, but only inferred from its effects on the soul. This Gardeil rejects as an inadequate account of the phenomenon, and he strongly asserts, as St Thomas's real and most profound teaching on the subject, the immediacy of the soul's perception of God in the state of full union, that of St Teresa's Fifth Mansion, and Sixth and Seventh. These last twenty-five pages of his tractate are, for me, beyond all compare the most illuminating and most satisfying treatment of the mystical problem from the side of pure theology.

§ 12. *The Mystic Experience and Psychology*

This matter of the immediate perception of God in the mystic experience is so vital that I feel emboldened to try to sketch another line of approach laid down by another Dominican theologian, Père Noël, the translator and editor of the works of John Tauler, the great Dominican German preacher and mystic of the fourteenth century. Buried away in the middle of the fourth volume, 1911, is a striking 'Exposé doctrinal (pp. 316-57) of the teaching of Tauler and the other masters of the Rhenish mystical school concerning the 'fund' or 'apex' of the soul, its very essence. The subject has been touched on in the text, pp. 139-140, and a passage from Blosius is there given, which sufficiently explains the idea underlying the doctrine. Noël's thesis is that this teaching of the 'fund' of the spirit is a proper development of St Thomas's conception, taken over from St Augustine, of the 'mens', as being the essence of the soul, the root

---

[1] Also in the *Exposition of the Cloud*.

of its powers or faculties.[1] The feature of the study that is especially to our purpose may be set forth thus:

While the soul is united to the body, the man, the composite being, is dependent for his knowledge as human being on the bodily senses, St Thomas's axiom standing firm, that nothing is in the intellect that was not first in sense, the intellectual concepts being derived from phantasmata by processes of abstraction, ratiocination, and so forth. But the soul, 'mens', is 'an incorporeal principle, subsisting of itself,' having as a spirit its own proper operation, that is, a process of intelligence. This power of intellection, independently of bodily senses and phantasmata, the soul will exercise between death and the resurrection—as a separated spirit it will see God intuitively, directly without intermediary. This power of intuition the soul possesses radically even when united to the body, and exercises, but in a rudimentary way. It has an intuitive perception of itself, indeterminately, and also it can have an indeterminate perception of God present within it. 'There is thus a sort of doubling of the "ego". On the one side is the "man", with an exterior knowledge, which he can form for himself by abstraction, clear, precise, evident; and on the other an incorporeal subsistent principle, which also knows, but imperfectly and confusedly, without abstracting, in an intuitive way: and these two modes work alongside of each other, simultaneously, no confusion being possible' (op. cit. p. 335).

But the 'mens', the fund or essence of the soul, is capable of greater things than this: it is the seat of the image of God and of the Holy Trinity; and, according to P. Noël, it is the region in which works the supernatural virtue of faith. It is also capable of special illuminations from God, and it is the field of the higher mystic experiences. Noël sums up the constant burden of Tauler's teaching on this subject, which he declares to be wholly conformable to St Thomas's mind:

Do you wish to live truly of the divine life, to submit yourself fully to the illuminations of the Primary Truth, to experience the direct irradiations of the Divinity? Leave matter and the senses, go forth from this visible world, quit creatures, pass over the matter that encloses you, the sensations that hold you in, the imaginations that keep you captive, the thoughts and sublime concepts which you take for the Primary Truth, but which are only a magnificent though fragile scaffolding of your reason. Raise yourself above your reason, above your human intelligence which nourishes itself on phantasms, images, sensible species; descend into the fund and the

---

[1] See article by Gardeil, 'Le "Mens" d'après S. Augustin et S. Thomas d'Aquin', *Revue des Sciences philosophiques et théologiques*, 1924.

inmost recess of your soul:—there you will find the pure and subsistent spirit; there you will find the dwelling-place of God; there
you will find God. This spirit by nature resembles God, God has
made it for Himself. There God descends by grace and love, and
only there can He descend. We are accessible to the visit of God
only by those summits of our soul that, like Himself, are wholly
spiritual (p. 351). There the divine Essence places itself, without
intermediary of any kind, in face of the intelligence (p. 340).

Noël seems to be aware that he is sailing over very deep water,
and that some may deem his position in parts dangerous; but he is
firm that he is exposing the mind not only of Tauler but of St
Thomas. And his study bears the fullest Dominican authorization,
P. Gardeil being one of the censors. It is in its entirety worthy of the
best consideration of those interested in mystical problems.[1]

I need not say what a pleasure it is to find how near the little
sketch offered (text, pp. 199-205) of the theological and psychological bases of mysticism comes to the principles so solidly established by such eminent Dominican theologians as PP. Gardeil
and Noël.

The Dominican approach to the consideration of mysticism is
primarily from the side of theology; but Père Joseph Maréchal,
S.J., approaches it from the side of phenomenal psychology. He is
professor of psychology at Louvain and is well versed in the methods
and the literature of modern experimental psychology, and he
brings all this knowledge to bear on the subject of contemplation
and mystical experience. His contributions have been articles in
various philosophical periodicals, and of these he has republished
three very substantial studies in a recent volume, *Études sur la
Psychologie des Mystiques* (pp. 267; 1924). He is conversant with the
most recent treatment of the phenomena of mysticism at the
hands of modern psychologists, as William James and H. Delacroix.
He declares that on the phenomenal side all the experiences of the
mystics lie within the range of psychological science, except the
very highest, that of full union, as described in St Teresa's Fifth
Mansion, and in the similar narrations of other mystics. The idea
of non-conceptual workings of the mind is abhorrent to psychologists,
and so their disposition is to reduce the state of mystical union
to a mental blank, a mere unconsciousness. But while admitting
that this may be true of certain kinds of quasi-mystical absorption,
especially oriental, often deliberately induced by methods akin
to hypnotism, Maréchal has no difficulty in showing that as an

---

[1] Some illuminating notes of Noël, as on pp. 50 and 60, on the 'mens', and the
'fund' or 'apex' of the spirit, deserve to be read.

account of the ecstatic unions of the great mystics, such an idea
is wholly inadequate and untrue, their ecstasies being highly
wrought states of religious consciousness and of spiritual activity.
As he says, if the merely psychological explanations be accepted,
then must the whole body of testimony of the mystics be rejected.
He holds that the true scientific attitude is to accept that testimony,
even though it be something transcending the data of psychology.

He sums up in the language of psychology the affirmations of the
mystics under two heads, negative and positive (op. cit. p. 245):

1. The affirmation of negative characteristics which separate
radically the ecstatic state from psychological states, normal or
abnormal, of ordinary life: the effacement of the empiric self, the
abandonment of imagery and spatiality, the absence of all multiplicity,—that is, in a word, the cessation of conceptual thought.
The ecstasy is negative.

2. On the other hand, the affirmation that this suspension of
conceptual thought is not complete unconsciousness, but rather an
enlargement, an intensification, or even a higher form, of intellectual
activity.
The ecstasy is positive.

But these two affirmations are contradictory on every imaginable
hypothesis, save one: viz., that the human intelligence can arrive,
in certain conditions, to an intuition proper to it; in other words,
that the intelligence, in place of constructing analogically and
approximatively its object in materials derived from the senses, can
sometimes attain this object in an immediate assimilation.

The general run of psychologists will, he says, recoil from this
consequence, and prefer to expurgate the documents of mysticism
of one or other of these affirmations—Maréchal thinks unscientific-
ally, and that considerations derived from ontology and theology
must be brought in to supplement those of experimental psychology.

§ 13. *The Vision of God*

The accounts offered by the different authorities as to *what* takes
place in the highest mystic states are very perplexing, because they
all differ so greatly in the theories put forward, and also because all
claim to be following St Thomas, and all cite him extensively in
support of their views. Maréchal holds that the characteristic
feature of the higher mystic states, and the one that separates them
from 'ordinary contemplation'—such as the Dionysian 'darkness'—
is that there takes place in them an active, and not merely sym-

bolical, presentation of God to the soul, with its psychological correlative of an immediate intuition of God by the soul (p. 253). Here, he says, we have a definition, clear and sufficient, of supernatural mysticism. And in an article, 'L'Intuition de Dieu dans la Mystique Chrétienne' (*Recherches de Science Religieuse*, 1914), to be reproduced in Vol. II of the *Études*, he interprets this intuition of God as the vision of the Divine Essence, spoken of by St Augustine and St Thomas (text, pp. 55-62).

Such a position, it will at once be seen, is quite different from that of the Dominican theologians. They seem to fight shy of this item of St Thomas's teaching, so as to place it outside the pale of discussion on the theory of mysticism: Gardeil, I think, makes no reference to it at all; Garrigou-Lagrange considers St Paul's vision to be a grace so extraordinary as to transcend anything spoken of by St Teresa or St John of the Cross;[1] Joret says that St Thomas restricts it to the two cases of Moses and St Paul[2]—a statement which, I think, cannot be sustained. Mgr Farges correctly interprets St Thomas's mind: the vision of God's Essence is possible in this life, but in a state of rapture, and not only to Moses and St Paul; but it is an exceedingly rare grace, and it is miraculous—'miraculose' St Thomas uses of it more than once.[3]

And hence arises an objection to Maréchal's definition of supernatural mysticism: it would place the essence of mysticism, the real thing, within the borders of the definitely miraculous. He makes this definition apply only to the 'higher mystical states'; he does not make it clear where he draws the line between 'ordinary Dionysian contemplation' and the 'higher states,'—whether the prayer of union of St Teresa's Fifth Mansion falls below or above the line: certainly I can see in it nothing to suggest a vision of the divine Essence. St Thomas and St Augustine hold that the condition of such vision is an entire alienation of the senses in a vehement ecstasy, a rapture so profound as to be a deathlike trance.[4]

It was a surprise to find Maréchal claiming that the whole tradition of the mystics until the sixteenth century was that the mystic experience is the vision or intuition of God's Essence. The statement is counter to what we see to be the teaching of St Gregory and St Bernard (text, pp. 87-88, 119-120); it is counter to the explicit judgement of St John of the Cross (text, pp. 61-62), who certainly thought that his own elevations in contemplation never had been

---

[1] *Perfection et Contemplation*, p. 333.

[2] *Contemplation Mystique*, pp. 23-4, 243, 304.

[3] The only discussion in English of this curious point of theology is that of Farges, op. cit. pp. 58-80.

[4] See St Augustine, text, pp. 51, 57.

such; I do not recollect this claim to be made by St Teresa; it is not found in the series given in the Prologue, of the accounts of their mystical experiences recorded by the mystics. For it must be insisted on definitely that the direct intuition or vision of the divine Essence would be something greatly more than the experimental perception of God's Being and Presence in the soul, or the substantial touches, or the unions, by which the mystics do describe their experience; it is also quite different from visions, even intellectual, such as those which St Ignatius and St Teresa had of the Holy Trinity.

There seem to be four or five definite personal claims on the part of accredited Christian mystics to have had such vision of the divine Essence (see Poulain, c. xviii., Nos. 60, 75, 76, 77, 78; and Farges, p. 63). The most arresting is that of B. Angela of Foligno, who declared it to have been made known to her that the unutterable manifestation of God, which she had over and over again, is really the good possessed by the blessed in heaven—that, and nothing else—though in less measure, the least in heaven possessing it more fully than any one ever could on earth ('Vision' VIII).

When dealing with this question of the Vision of God's Essence I was careful to say that I was not concerned with the truth or the possibility of the idea put forward by St Augustine and taken up by St Thomas, but only with the ascertaining what their idea was (text, p. 55). In view, however, of the prominence given to that idea in recent discussions, especially those of P. Maréchal, it seems to be desirable to go into the subject itself. So far as the view is current, that even in this life, in certain conditions, the divine Essence can be, and has been, seen by man, it rests mainly on St Thomas; but I believe it is true to say that in all his treatment of it, direct or incidental, he simply follows St Augustine, reproducing his arguments and applying his method of treatment: it is a simple adoption and endorsement of St Augustine's idea, without any contribution of St Thomas's own. Consequently this whole piece of theological thought and theory has its intellectual basis in the motives that caused St Augustine to adopt it. These motives are given in full in the passages cited from St Augustine, text, pp. 53-59. It will therein be seen that the two cases relied on by St Augustine for his affirmative answer, the two cases in which he holds that the essential vision of God has certainly been given, are Moses and St Paul. St Paul figures much more largely with St Thomas; but it will be seen that for St Augustine the real strength of the case lies in Moses.

St Paul, describing his mystical experience (2 Cor. xii.), speaks of visions and revelations, and says he was caught up (rapt) to the 'third heaven', to 'Paradise'. What these expressions mean is very uncertain; St Thomas offers various interpretations (2-2, q. clxxv. a. 3). But St Paul does not claim to have *seen* anything, but to have heard 'unspeakable words'. There is nothing whatsoever to suggest that he had any vision of God's Essence. St Augustine seizes on the words 'whether in the body or out of the body I know not,' as offering an escape from the force of God's word to Moses, 'Thou canst not see My Face, for man shall not see Me and live' (Exod. xxxiii. 20): St Paul was thrown into a rapture or trance so profound that his soul had for the time being left his body, and he was not 'alive' in the full sense of the word (see St Augustine's argumentation). Thus St Paul's case comes in only secondarily, as affording a means of surmounting a difficulty; and St Thomas in one place (*de Veritate*, q. xiii. a. 2) recognizes that the strength of the case lies in Moses, for he argues that as Moses, the minister of the Old Testament, had this privilege, it would be improbable that St Paul, the minister of the New, should not have had the like.

And so we are thrown back on the case of Moses, and on St Augustine's line of argument whereby he arrives at the conclusion that, in spite of God's apparent refusal of the request as impossible (Exod. xxxiii.), the wording of Num. xii. 8 shows that it afterwards was granted, and Moses did see God 'in that substance whereby He is God,' in His divine Essence. The argument is Scriptural, based on the texts Num. xii. 8 and Exod. xxxiii. 13, 18, 20. Augustine used an Old Latin version, a literal translation of the Septuagint Greek in these verses. A comparison of these texts with the Vulgate or the Authorised, or better still, the Revised Version, will show that in the points critical for Augustine's argument, the Hebrew text differs from the Greek and OldLatin (for Num. xii. 8, see text, pp. 55-56). It will be seen that the crucial point for Augustine's argument is the term 'in specie' (Gk. ἐν εἴδει), in Num. xii. 8, to which he gives its full philosophical force of 'essence': but there is no equivalent in the Hebrew; the Vulgate 'palam', and R.V. 'manifestly', correctly render the text. As for the last clause of the text 'claritatem Domini vidit,' 'claritas' is δόξα in the Gk., but 'similitude' in A.V. and 'form' in R.V. A very competent Hebraist tells me the word probably signifies 'some sort of real manifestation, God allowing Himself to be seen under this or that visible form, a theophany.' To take either 'species' or 'claritas' as meaning the divine Essence is to depart altogether from the sense of the Hebrew words.

Thus it would seem that the whole conception of Moses, or of

St Paul, having had the vision of God's Essence, is built upon St Augustine's misinterpretation of a mistranslation of a biblical text.

The biblical texts adverse to any such idea are very cogent. Besides that of Exodus just cited, 'Man shall not see Me and live,' St Paul declares that God 'dwelleth in light unapproachable, whom no man hath seen, nor can see' (i Tim. vi. 16); and St John: 'No man hath seen God at any time' (i. 18, 1 Ep. iv. 12). What men have seen has always been some figure or form, as in the theophanies, never the divine Essence Itself. In face of this biblical evidence, and of the grave philosophical difficulties involved, it may well be thought that but for St Augustine's ill-founded speculation, accepted and endorsed by St Thomas, the idea of the vision of God's Essence by any man would not have found a place in theological tradition.

§ 14. *Summary of Results*

In concluding this survey of debates in progress among the theologians, it may be of use to gather up into definite propositions the impressions and conclusions that seem, at any rate to the present writer, to emerge.

1. It cannot be held that the mystic experience claimed by the mystics is ordinarily the vision of the divine Essence, such as, according to SS. Augustine and Thomas, was granted to Moses and St Paul. Such vision, if it ever has been granted to man in this life, is the rarest of all mystical favours, and is definitely miraculous (St Thomas).

2. Quite different from such vision of God's Essence is the 'perception' of His Being and Presence, experimental, direct, which, in one way or another, the mystics do claim as the culmination of their experiences in the higher kinds of contemplation. Such 'supraconceptual', 'supra-intentional', perception is within the lines of Thomistic psychology and theology (so P. Gardeil), and is to be accepted as a religious fact on the consistent evidence of the great Christian mystics. To this perception, and to nothing short of it, should be given the name 'Mystical Experience'.

3. Père Poulain goes too far in making this experience the essential feature of mystical states and of infused contemplation, ruling out of the domain of mysticism, and of contemplation proper, all states, all prayer, not marked by such perception of God. There are in fact frequent phases of prayer and contemplation, really infused and mystical, from which such experience is absent.

4. In reacting against Poulain, Abbé Saudreau has gone too far in the opposite direction, maintaining that such perception of God is no part of the mystical experience; that God's Presence is not directly perceived, but only inferred from the fervour, sweetness, devotion experienced in mystical states of prayer; and that any direct perception of God is found only in a very small number of cases, almost unique, for which he creates the special category of 'angelic contemplation' ('super-eminent', Garrigou-Lagrange).

So much on the speculative question, What takes place in the higher mystical experiences? To turn now to the practical side:

5. The 'contemplative life,' objectively taken as an external manner of life ordered with the one object of facilitating contemplation, from which is excluded to the utmost possible all works and activities that could distract or impede the soul in advancing to that goal—such a life as that of Carthusians, Carmelite nuns, Poor Clares—is a very special vocation, the call of but few, and requiring quite peculiar gifts of character and temperament.

6. But 'contemplation,' even the high kinds of it, if easier in such a life, is by no means restricted to it. In theory it lies open to all, and may be found and exercised in any state of life whatsoever. This is most definitely the teaching of SS. Augustine, Gregory, Bernard, and of St Thomas according to the Dominican theologians.

7. That contemplation lies open to all, all at any rate who are trying to lead seriously a good Christian life, is literally and unreservedly true of the initial grades of contemplation, spoken of under the names prayer of loving attention, of faith, of simplicity, of simple regard. Such prayer is, according to St John of the Cross, infused contemplation; and it ought to be, and is, ordinarily within the reach of men of good will laying themselves out to lead a spiritual life—priests, religious, good lay folk living 'the devout life' as laid down by St Francis of Sales. All these are to be instructed and encouraged so as to be able and ready to respond to any enablement of grace for exercising such prayer, according to the conditions of their state of life.

8. Speaking in the abstract, it cannot be said that any one is debarred from the higher, and even highest, grades of contemplation. And for one who has entered on the course of the spiritual life, and especially for any one who is exercising the prayer of loving attention, the higher kinds of contemplation and mystical experience are legitimate and proper objects of aspiration, desire and humble prayer, in the same kind of way that heroic sanctity is a good object of prayer.

9. But that every one, or every baptized person, is intended

according to the normal way of God's Providence, to reach these higher mystical states, in such sense that the fact of not doing so always spells some initial infidelity to grace, or is to be attributed to spiritual sloth, or implies some kind of failure, is, I believe, a teaching to be rejected, though it seems to be held by some of the Dominican theologians (Arintero and Garrigou-Lagrange). The life of the vast majority of devout servants of God is cast, by virtue of the vocation in which they are called by God's Providence and Will, in conditions of this workaday world wherein the very performance of God's Will in the duties of their state renders impossible those opportunities for such prayer and recollection as are the ordinary means of attaining to grades of contemplation above that of the prayer of loving attention.

10. Yet who will question that such as these may, by living their lives in the perfect performance of God's Will in all the duties of their state of life, attain to the perfection of charity, even in an heroic degree; and that, without being raised to the higher mystical states? We have had it on the authority of St Teresa and St Alphonsus, and of St Benedict before them, that perfect love of God, and perfect union with Him, may be attained by entire renunciation of our own will, and perfect conformity to God's Will, and this without the mystic union. And the same seems to be Our Lord's lesson in the Gospels.

11. Consequently the teaching seems to be very questionable that stresses the idea that the normal thing, the thing according to God's intention, is that every one should pass through the Night of the Spirit, and attain to the highest mystical state of the Spiritual Marriage, as described by St Teresa in the Seventh Mansion, or by St John of the Cross in the *Canticle* and the *Living Flame*, on the ground that this is the ordinarily appointed means of attaining to the perfection of charity. It may be difficult to lay hold on the flaw in the chain of reasoning as presented by P. Garrigou-Lagrange; but the religious sense recoils from the conclusions and implications.

12. I hope it may not be deemed over venturesome for one not pledged by profession to any particular Catholic theological school to wonder if the rigid methods of speculative theology that are being applied, really are helpful towards explaining the nature and the facts of mystical theology and of contemplation. We all believe that the Holy Ghost is really and by His Substance dwelling in the souls of the just, of all who are in God's grace and friendship. We know that He sheds abroad in the hearts of such the love of God (Rom. v. 5), and with love the other infused virtues and the Gifts and Fruits of the Spirit. And we know that all prayer, and all

contemplation, is due to His working in us. We know, too, that the mystic experience and union is the culmination of the working of the Holy Spirit in souls conspicuously generous in self-denial and in devotion, and pliable in responding to His inspirations and guidance. We know that all true mystical graces are the working of the Holy Ghost.

Many would be best satisfied to leave it there, without seeking to specify the functions of the individual Gifts—of Intelligence, Knowledge and Wisdom—in bringing about the result. There are no doubt minds to whom such schematizations and the diagrams provided by P. Garrigou-Lagrange may appeal; but there are others to whom they do not. I confess myself one of the latter; and I have a feeling that many of the difficulties that have arisen in the discussions under survey are occasioned by an undue pressing of theological theories.

P. Joret in his chapter 'Les Dons du Saint-Esprit,' wherein he gives a lucid exposition of St Thomas's doctrine on the Gifts, is careful to point out that what is of Faith is no more than such Scriptural ideas as have just been set forth; all else is matter only of theological speculation (op. cit. p. 40). Not that there is any difficulty about the general idea that contemplation is due principally to the Gift of Wisdom. But that the 'mystical life' is distinguished from the 'ascetical' in that the latter is marked by the 'human', the former by the 'supra-human' mode of the operation of the Gifts, does seem a piece of very speculative theology.

So far on questions of principle; there remain a few questions of definition and terminology.

13. It seems that the term 'acquired contemplation', as contrasted with infused, had better be abandoned. St John of the Cross knows of no prayer intermediate between discursive meditation (including affective prayer and acts) and infused contemplation, the prayer of loving attention. But it should be recognized that in this prayer, although infused by God, there is an element of effort on the part of the will, in placing the mind in the state of recollection and attention, and in keeping the attention fixed on God by recalling it when it wanders, or reviving it when it fades away.

14. The words 'ordinary' and 'extraordinary' are applied to prayer and contemplation in such different ways by accredited writers, that it seems impossible to conciliate them; it is a matter of definition.

15. 'Mystical' also is used in very different ways. P. Poulain's use is much too restricted and rigid. On the other side, some uses are unduly loose; bouts of sensible devotion should not be spoken

of as mystical contemplation. Of all the definitions proposed, Fr Henry Browne's (above, pp. xxix-xxx.) seems the most distinctive: Prayer is mystical which is made without discourse of the faculties, without phantasmata or images, almost without words; the will, as Fr Baker puts it, 'heaving itself up, blindly and bluntly, to God' (above, p. xxv.), and the mind working in a way outside the ordinary laws of phenomenal psychology.

16. An agreed terminology in mystical theology is greatly to be desired. If the above psychological test of mystical prayer be accepted, the prayer of loving attention, of faith, is not only infused but mystical: but nothing less than it is mystical. The term 'mystical experience' could be usefully restricted to that experimental perception of God, however expressed, that is the real claim of the mystics in their higher states of contemplation and union,—the assertion, on the validity of which depends the religious and philosophical importance of mysticism properly so called.

Above all, it is greatly to be desired that the use of the words 'mysticism', 'mystical', be strictly confined to this religious and philosophical meaning, all current vague, misleading, improper uses, which bring the whole subject into confusion and disrepute, being rigorously eschewed. Essential mysticism should not be identified with occasional accidental concomitants, as visions, revelations, raptures, or other psycho-physical phenomena. In particular, Catholic writers should refrain from giving the title mystical to curious experiences and manifestations bordering on those of Spiritism; to intimations, second sight, telepathy; or to religious 'queer stories'. For all such phenomena there is an accepted scientific term: they are 'psychic', not 'mystic'. This word should be jealously reserved for its proper traditional religious sense, given it in the beginning by 'Dionysius'—the secret knowledge or perception of God in contemplation.

PART I: SPECULATIVE

CONTEMPLATION

PROLOGUE

WHAT MYSTICISM IS

THE writings of the mystics may be studied from three distinct points of view:

(1) They may be read for the sake of their religious philosophy and their theology.

(2) Or they may be taken as affording material for the study of that branch of modern psychology called Psycho-physiology, the borderland between mind and body, which investigates such phenomena as auto-suggestion, auto-hypnotism, ecstasy and trance, and such-like frequent psycho-physical concomitants of higher states of prayer.

(3) And lastly, they may be studied for the sake of their mysticism itself, as a religious experience.

Each one of these aspects of the writings of the great mystics has its own interest and its own value, recognizedly of a high order; but in the following pages the last-named of these objects of study is the one predominantly pursued. The purpose of this book is to set forth, in their own words, as a co-ordinated body of doctrine, what three great teachers of mystical theology in the Western Church have left on record concerning their own religious experience, and the theories they based on it.

It is incumbent on anyone writing a book on Mysticism to make plain at the outset the meaning to be attached to the word. There is probably no more misused word in these our days than 'mysticism'. It has come to be applied to many things of many kinds: to theosophy and Christian science; to spiritualism and clairvoyance; to demonology and witchcraft; to occultism and magic; to weird psychical experiences, if only they have some religious colour; to revelations and visions; to other-worldliness, or even mere dreaminess and impracticability in the affairs of life; to poetry and painting and music of which the motif is unobvious and vague. It has been identified with the attitude of the religious mind that cares not for dogma or doctrine, for church or sacraments; it has been identified also with a certain outlook on the world—a seeing God in nature, and recognizing that the material creation in various ways symbolizes spiritual realities: a beautiful and true conception, and one that was dear to St Francis of Assisi, but which is not mysticism according to its historical meaning. And, on the other side, the meaning of the term has been watered down: it has been said that the love of God is mysticism;[1] or that mysticism is only the Christian life lived on a high level; [2] or that it is Roman Catholic piety in extreme form. [3]

Against all this stands the perfectly clear traditional historical meaning, handed down in the Christian Church throughout the centuries, not subject to confusion of thought until recent times.

Here it is necessary to explain that in the Latin Church the word used was not 'mysticism', but 'contemplation'. The word 'mystic' was originally used in connexion with the Greek mysteries, as the Eleusinian. The Christian use of the word is due to the writer now known as pseudo-Dionysius, probably of the fifth century, who gave the title 'Mystical Theology' to the little treatise that was the first formulation of a doctrine on the subject. Though this treatise was at an early date translated into Latin and became well known in the West the old word 'contemplation' held its ground, so that 'mystical' did not become current until the later Middle Ages, and 'mysticism' is a quite modern word. Consequently, 'contemplation' is the word that will be met with in St Augustine, St Gregory, and St Bernard, to designate what is now commonly called 'the mystical experience.'

The claim consistently and unequivocally made by the whole line of great mystics found, perhaps, its simplest and most arresting expression in these words of St Augustine: 'My mind in the flash of a trembling glance came to Absolute Being—That Which Is.'[4] This claim, as uttered by Augustine, has been recognized as the claim of the mystics, and has been formulated by recent writers of various schools of thought in such ways as these:

A (conscious) direct contact of the soul with Transcendental Reality.

A direct and objective intellectual intuition of Transcendental Reality.

The establishing conscious relation with the Absolute.

The soul's possible union in this life with Absolute Reality.[5]

These definitions or descriptions are couched in the terminology

[1] Joly, *Psychologie des Saints.*
[2] Dom Salvinian Louismet, of Buckfast Abbey, in a recently published series of booklets.
[3] Harnack, cited by Inge, *Christian Mysticism,* App. A.
[4] '(Mens mea) pervenit ad Id quod est in ictu trepidantis aspectus' (*Confessions,* vii. 23; the entire passage is cited below, pp. 31-32).
[5] The first two of these formulations are from Fr A. B. Sharpe's *Mysticism,* pp. 74, 96; the third from Evelyn Underhill's *Mysticism,* p. 97; the fourth from an article in Hastings's *Encyclopaedia of Religion and Ethics* (ix. 83) by Mr Rufus

of metaphysics; for the Christian and the Theist, 'The Absolute', 'Absolute Being', 'Absolute Reality', 'Transcendental Reality', are God. And so the mystic's claim is expressed by Christian mystics as 'the experimental perception of God's Presence and Being,' and especially 'union with God'—a union, that is, not merely psychological, in conforming the will to God's Will, but, it may be said, ontological of the soul with God, spirit with Spirit. And they declare that the experience is a momentary foretaste of the bliss of heaven.

This claim of the mystics will be illustrated by a selection of passages from representative Catholic mystics. The passages are chosen not as depicting the effects of the experience on the soul, but as stating the mystics' belief as to what took place; they are chosen for the sake of the objective, not the subjective, information they purport to give, and they all may be taken as autobiographical, describing the personal experience of the writer.

It is well to warn the reader that much of the language used will appear hardly intelligible, and may even give rise to doubts as to the mental balance of some of the writers. It has to be asserted strongly that the great mystics were not religiously mad; nor were they pious dreamers: far from it—they were, most of them, peculiarly sane and strong men and women, who have left their mark, many of them, for good in history. The obscurity and apparent extravagance of their language is due to their courage in struggling with the barriers and limitations of human thought and language in order to describe in some fashion what they experienced in the height of the mystic state. The same explanation is to be given of any seeming pantheistic tendency in their language when attempting to describe their union with God; no matter what the terms may be in which they speak of the transformation of the soul or its absorption in God, the Catholic mystics are insistent in asserting that the soul retains its own individuality and full personality in the unions either of this life or of eternity.

It is to be understood that there are phases and stages of mysticism that fall short of the supreme experiences laid claim to in the following extracts. But for the sake of a clear understanding of the nature of mysticism, and of the problems that encircle it, it is essential that its claim be made to stand out distinctly in all the naked daring of

---

Jones, a nonconformist and author of an important book on the subject. In App. A. to his *Christian Mysticism* Dean Inge brings together and criticizes a miscellaneous but interesting collection of definitions of mysticism. That of Professor Pringle Pattison (Seth) may be quoted: It is 'the endeavour of the human mind to grasp the Divine Essence or the ultimate reality of things, and to enjoy the blessedness of actual communion with the Highest. It maintains the possibility of direct intercourse with this Being of beings.'

its most extreme expression. Only so shall we know what we are really talking about. In this way, too, we shall know, not other people's ideas about mysticism, but what the mystics themselves thought it to be.

PSEUDO-DIONYSIUS (*Cent. V.*)

Do thou, in the intent practice of mystic contemplation, leave behind the senses and the operations of the intellect, and all things that the senses or the intellect can perceive, and all things which are not and things which are, and strain upwards in unknowing, as far as may be, towards the union with Him Who is above all being and knowledge. For by unceasing and absolute withdrawal from thyself and all things in purity, abandoning all and set free from all, thou wilt be borne up to the ray of the divine Darkness that surpasseth all being (*Mystical Theology*, i.).

Unto this Darkness which is beyond Light we pray that we may come, and through loss of sight and knowledge may see and know That Which transcends sight and knowledge, by the very fact of not seeing and knowing; for this is real sight and knowledge (ibid. ii.).

(The mind) enters into the really mystic Darkness of Unknowing wherein it renounces all the perceptions of the understanding, and abides in That Which is wholly intangible and invisible, belonging wholly to Him that is beyond all, through being by inactivity of all cognition united in its highest part to Him Who is wholly unknowable, and by knowing nothing knows in a manner that is above understanding (ibid. i. *fin.*).

The divine Darkness is the unapproachable light in which God is said to dwell; ... in this everyone enters who is found worthy to know and to see God by not knowing or seeing Him, really being in Him Who is above sight and knowledge (*Letter* v.).

Besides the knowledge of God obtained by processes of philosophical and theological speculation, 'there is that most divine knowledge of God which takes place through ignorance, in the union which is above intelligence, when the intellect, quitting all things that are, and then leaving itself also, is united to the superlucent rays, being illuminated thence and therein by the unsearchable depth of wisdom' (*de div. Nom.* vii. 3).

'Dionysius,' as the Father of scientific Mystical Theology, is rightly given the first place. Augustine, Gregory, Bernard might come next, but their witness is to be found abundantly in what follows, and need not be anticipated in this place. The two latter speak for the early Middle Ages, the 'Benedictine Centuries'; so we pass on to the later period, beginning with a younger contemporary of St. Bernard.

RICHARD OF ST VICTOR, *Canon Regular of St Augustine,*
died 1173

The third grade of love is when the mind of man is rapt into the abyss of the divine light, so that, utterly oblivious of all exterior things (exterior*um*?), it knows not itself and passes wholly into its God. And so in this state is held in check and lulled to deep sleep the crowd of carnal desires. In this state, while the mind is alienated from itself, while it is rapt unto the secret closet of the divine privacy, while it is on all sides encircled by the conflagration of divine love, and is intimately penetrated and set on fire through and through, it strips off self and puts on a certain divine condition, and being configured to the beauty gazed upon, it passes into a new kind of glory (*de IV Gradibus Violentae Caritatis*, Migne, Patr. Lat. cxvi. 1220).

ST THOMAS AQUINAS, Dominican, died 1274
(*This section I owe to Dom. John Chapman*)

St Thomas in *de Veritate*, quaest. xviii. 1, distinguishes three ways of knowing God: (1) In the state after the Fall we need a kind of mirror in which to see a likeness of God, for we know Him only through His creatures. (2) But in the state of innocence this means was not needed, but only a means which was a kind of *species* of the thing seen, because God was seen by a spiritual light, flowing upon man's mind from the divinity, which was an express likeness of the uncreated Light. (3) But in heaven not even this means is necessary, but God's own Essence is the means by which It is seen. But St Thomas adds that the second kind of knowledge is still given to man: in contemplation, God is seen by a means which is the Light of Wisdom, which uplifts the soul to perceive the Divine, but not so that the divine Essence be immediately seen (as in heaven); and in this fashion by grace It is seen by the contemplative after the state of sin, though this took place in the state of innocence with greater perfection (ibid. ad 4).

This 'Light of Wisdom' is the first of the seven gifts of the Holy Ghost (*Comm. in Sent.* III. dist. xxxv. qu. ii. art. 1, sol. 1): 'the gift of Wisdom goes forward to a (so to speak) *deiform* and (as it were) *explicit* contemplation of the articles which Faith holds after a human manner (as it were) under a veil.' And so also the second gift: 'If the mind be so far uplifted by a supernatural Light that it is introduced to the perception of spiritual things themselves, this is above human measure; and it is caused by the gift of Understanding' (ibid. art. 2, sol. 1).

NOTE.—St Thomas teaches that these are not the ordinary effects of the gifts of the Holy Ghost, which are all infused at Baptism, and are necessarily present in all Christians who are not in mortal sin; but they represent a higher stage, and belong to the *gratiae gratis datae* spoken of by St Paul in 1 Cor. xii (*Summa Theol.* 22ae, qu. xlv. art. 5). But the gift of Understanding is always a 'supernatural light' (*Summa Theol.* 22ae, qu. viii. art. 1); it is compatible with Faith, for it is at best an imperfect 'understanding' in this life.

'THE CLOUD OF UNKNOWING'. (An anonymous English treatise of 14th century)

For at the first time when thou dost [this work], thou findest but a darkness, and as it were a cloud of unkowing, thou knowest not what, saving that thou feelest in thy will a naked intent unto God. This darkness and this cloud is, howsoever thou dost, betwixt thee and thy God, and telleth thee that thou mayest neither see Him clearly by light of understanding in thy reason, nor feel Him in sweetness of love in thine affection. And therefore shape thee to bide in this darkness as long as thou mayest, evermore crying after Him that thou lovest. For if ever thou shalt feel Him or see Him, as it may be here, it behoveth always to be in this cloud in this darkness. And if thou wilt busily travail as I bid thee, I trust in His mercy that thou shalt come thereto.

Then will He sometimes peradventure send out a beam of ghostly light, piercing this cloud of unknowing that is betwixt thee and Him; and shew thee some of His privity, the which man may not, nor cannot speak. Then shalt thou feel thine affection inflamed with the fire of His love, far more than I can tell thee, or may or will at this time. For of that work, that falleth only to God, dare I not take upon me to speak with my blabbering fleshly tongue: and shortly to say, although I durst I would do not (cc. 3 and 26).

BLESSED JOHN RUYSBROECK, Canon Regular of St Augustine, died 1381

In this storm of love two spirits strive together: the Spirit of God and our own spirit. God, through the Holy Ghost, inclines Himself towards us; and thereby we are touched in love. And our spirit, by God's working and by the power of love, presses and inclines itself into God; and thereby God is touched. From these two contacts there arises the strife of love, at the very deeps of this meeting; and in that most inward and ardent encounter each spirit is deeply wounded by love. These two spirits, that is, our own spirit and the Spirit of God, sparkle and shine one into the other, and each shows to the other its face. This makes each of the spirits yearn for the other in love. Each demands of the other all that it is; and each offers to the other all that it is, and invites it to all that it is. This makes the lovers melt into each other. God's touch and His gifts, our loving craving and our giving back: these fulfil love. This flux and reflux causes the fountain of love to brim over: and thus the touch of God and our loving craving become one simple love. ... Thereby the spirit is burned up in the fire of love, and enters so deeply into the touch of God, that it is overcome in all its cravings, and turned to nought in all its works, and empties itself (*Adornment of the Spiritual Marriage*, Bk. II. c. 54).

Elsewhere: The possession of this Superessential Love is a simple and abysmal tasting of all good and of eternal life; and in this tasting we are swallowed up above reason and without reason, in the deep Quiet of the Godhead, which is never moved. That this is true we can only know by our own feeling, and in no other way. For how this is, or where, or what, neither reason nor practice can come to know. For that abysmal Good which we taste and possess, we can neither grasp nor understand; neither can we enter into it by ourselves or by means of our exercises. And so we are poor in ourselves, but rich in God (*The Sparkling Stone*, c. 9: *John of Ruysbroeck*. London, Dent, 1916).

Such passages, and others even more bewildering, abound in all the writings of Ruysbroeck. It is well to say definitely that they have reference to experiences in this life, not in the next (ibid. c. 11). It is not surprising that such language should have occasioned suspicion of pantheistic tendencies; but Ruysbroeck constantly protects himself against this by repeated assertions that the soul never, in this life or in the next, can be so transformed in God as to lose its individuality or its proper essence. The recent confirmation of his cultus as a Beatus, with concession of Mass and Office, by the Holy See in 1908, must be taken as an official recognition of the soundness of his doctrine and its immunity from Pantheism or other taint.

LOUIS OF BLOIS (BLOSIUS), *Benedictine Abbot, died 1566*

It is a great thing, an exceeding great thing, in the time of this exile to be joined to God in the divine light by a mystical and denuded union. This takes place where a pure, humble, and resigned soul, burning with ardent love, is carried above itself by the grace of God, and through the brilliancy of the divine light shining on the mind, it loses all consideration and distinction of things, and lays aside all, even the most excellent images, and all liquified by love, and, as it were, reduced to nothing, it melts away into God. It is then united to God without any medium, and becomes one spirit with Him, and is transformed and changed into Him, as iron placed in the fire is changed into fire, without ceasing to be iron. It becomes one with God, yet not so as to be of the same substance and nature as God. ... In the faculty of intellect it perceives the surpassing illumination of the Sun of Justice, and learns divine truth; and in the faculty of love it feels a certain glow of quiet love, or contact of the Holy Spirit, like a living fountain, flowing with streams of eternal sweetness; and thus it is introduced into sublime union with God. The soul, having entered the vast solitude of the Godhead, happily loses itself; and enlightened by the brightness of

most lucid darkness, becomes through knowledge as if without
knowledge, and dwells in a sort of wise ignorance. And although it
knows not what God is, to Whom it is united by pure charity,
although it sees not God as He is in His glory, it yet learns by
experience that He infinitely transcends all sensible things, and all
that can be apprehended by the human intellect concerning Him.
It knows God by this intimate embrace and contact better than the
eyes of the body know the visible sun. This soul well knows what
true contemplation is (*Spiritual Mirror*, c. 11).

Again: When through love the soul goes beyond all working of
the intellect and all images in the mind, and is rapt above itself,
utterly leaving itself, it flows into God: then is God its peace and
fullness. It loses itself in the infinite solitude and darkness of the
Godhead; but so to lose itself is rather to find itself. The soul is, as
it were, all God-coloured, because its essence is bathed in the
Essence of God—plane tota deicolor est, quia essentia eius essentiâ
Dei perfusa est (*Spiritual Instruction*, c. 12, § 2. This whole chapter
may be read).

ST JOHN OF THE CROSS, *Carmelite, died 1591*

The end I have in view is the divine Embracing, the union of the
soul with the divine Substance. In this loving, obscure knowledge
God unites Himself with the soul eminently and divinely (*Ascent of
Carmel*, ii. c. 24).

This knowledge consists in a certain contact of the soul with the
Divinity, and it is God Himself Who is then felt and tasted, though
not manifestly and distinctly, as it will be in glory. But this touch
of knowledge and of sweetness is so deep and so profound that it
penetrates into the inmost substance of the soul. This knowledge
savours in some measure of the divine Essence and of everlasting life
(ibid. ii. c. 26).

O gentle subtile touch, the Word, the Son of God, Who dost
penetrate subtilely the very substance of my soul, and, touching it
gently, absorbest it wholly in divine ways of sweetness. ... What the
soul tastes now in this touch of God, is, in truth, though not perfectly, a certain foretaste of everlasting life. It is not incredible that
it should be so, when we believe, as we do believe, that this touch
is most substantial, and that the Substance of God touches the substance of the soul.[1] Many saints have experienced it in this life. The
sweetness of delight which this touch occasions baffles all description
(*Living Flame*, stanza ii. §§ 18, 22; old ed. lines iii. iv).

The soul prays to see the Face of God, which is the essential communication of His Divinity to the soul, without any intervening
medium, by a certain knowledge thereof in the Divinity. This is
something beyond sense and divested of accidents; inasmuch as it is

---

[1] Cf. 'the divine touches in the substance of the soul with the loving Substance
of God'—en la sustancia del alma de la amorosa sustancia de Dios (*Dark Night*,
ii. c. 23).

the contact of pure substances—that is, of the soul and the Divinity (*Canticle*, stanza xix. 3).

A most sublime and sweet knowledge of God and of His attributes overflows into the understanding from the contact of the attributes of God with the substance of the soul (ibid. stanza xiv. 16).

The knowledge of substance is given the soul, stripped of accidents and phantasms, because it is given to that [part of the] understanding which philosophers call passive or 'possible', because without any action on its part it receives passively. This is the highest delight of the soul, because it is in the understanding, which is the seat of fruition, as theologians think, and fruition is the vision of God (ibid. 19, literal translation).

With this compare St Thomas, above.

ST FRANCIS OF SALES, *Bishop of Geneva, died 1662*

He speaks habitually of the soul's perception in contemplation of the divine Presence (*Treatise of the Love of God*, Bk. vi. cc. 8, 9); also of the soul's union with God (Bk. vii.). Of it he says:

When the union of the soul with God is most specially strict and close, it is called inhesion or adhesion, because by it the soul is caught up, fastened, glued and affixed to the divine Majesty, so that she cannot easily loose or draw herself back again (ibid. vii. 3).

My heart melted when he spoke (*Canticle* v. 6).

As melted balm that no longer has firmness or solidity, the soul lets herself pass or flow into What she loves: she does not spring out of herself as by a sudden leap, nor does she cling as by a joining or union, but gently glides, as a fluid and liquid thing, into the Divinity Whom she loves. She goes out by that sacred outflowing and holy liquefaction, and quits herself, not only to be united to the well-Beloved, but to be entirely mingled with and steeped in Him. The outflowing of a soul into her God is a true ecstasy, by which the soul quite transcends the limits of her natural way of existence, being wholly mingled with, absorbed and engulfed in, her God (ibid. vi. 12).

FR AUGUSTINE BAKER, *English Benedictine, died 1641*

Mystic writers do teach that the proper end of a contemplative life is the attaining unto an habitual and almost uninterrupted perfect union with God in the supreme point of the spirit; and such a union as gives the soul a fruitive possession of Him, and a real experimental perception of His divine presence in the depth and centre of the spirit, which is fully possessed and filled with Him alone. The effects of this blessed perceptible presence of God in perfect souls are unspeakable and divine. ... They become after an inexpressible manner partakers of the divine nature; yea, one spirit, one will, one love with Him, being in a sort deified, and enjoying as much of heaven here as mortality is capable of (*Sancta Sophia*, p. 42).

Of intellectual passive unions, the supreme and most noble that may be had in this life is that whereby God is contemplated without any perceptible images, by a certain intellectual supernatural light darted into the soul, in which regard it draws much towards an angelical contemplation; for herein, though God be not seen as He is, yet He is clearly seen that He is, and that He is incomprehensible. Mystic authors call this rather a divine passive union than contemplation; a union far more strait and immediate than any of the former (ibid. p. 532).

By the foresaid passive union a soul hath a distinct view of God, her original. ...

By such fiery trials and purifications, as also by so near approaches as are made to the fountain of beauty and light in passive unions, love is exalted to its perfection (ibid. p. 542).

In this 'divine inaction' (*passim*[1]) the soul hath lost the free disposal of her own faculties, acting by a portion of the spirit above all the faculties, and according to the actual touches of the Divine Spirit, and apprehending God with an exclusion of all conceptions and apprehensions ... and is immediately united to God (ibid. p. 545).

BLAISE PASCAL, died 1662

After his death was found stitched into the lining of his doublet what is called his 'memorial', a scrap of parchment with a rough drawing of a flaming cross, and around it a few words whereby he tried to keep alive the memory of a mystic experience. They are even startling in their directness and simplicity:

In the year of grace 1654 Monday, 23 November, the day of St Clement, Pope and Martyr, and others in the Martyrology; the eve of St Chrysogonus, Martyr, and others; from about half-past ten in the evening till about half an hour after midnight.

FIRE

God of Abraham, God of Isaac, God of Jacob,
Not of the philosophers and the learned.
Certitude. Joy. Certitude. Emotion. Sight. Joy.
Forgetfulness of the world and of all outside of God.
The world hath not known Thee, but I have known Thee.
Joy! joy! joy!   Tears of joy.
My God, wilt Thou leave me?
Let me not be separated from Thee for ever.

(Facsimile in Abbé Bremond's *Sentiment Religieux en France*, iv, 368.)

[1] 'Divine inaction' means God's action in the soul.

Of all the attempts to describe such experiences these barely articulate, incoherent exclamations of Pascal—the intellectual, the philosopher, the master of language and style—are, for me, beyond all compare the most eloquent and the most realistic.

MOTHER ISABEL DAURELLE, Carmelite nun, died 1914

During prayer on the evening of the third day I entered the interior of my soul, and seemed to descend into the giddy depths of an abyss where I had the impression of being surrounded by limit-less space. Then I felt the presence of the Blessed Trinity, realizing my own nothingness, which I understood better than ever before, and the knowledge was very sweet. The divine Immensity in which I was plunged and which filled me had the same sweetness.

This grace gradually grew weaker, but lasted for a long while. For many months I never opened a book during prayer; it was enough for me to descend into the abyss. My soul resembled a tiny shell floating peaceful and solitary upon a shoreless ocean. What a joy it was! Now I often say to myself: 'let me descend!' but the scene is changed: I can no longer find the deep abyss nor the infinite space around me—The good God has come to the surface.

The light which has filled my soul has not come from books but from the Holy Ghost, although I have had neither ecstasies nor visions. My prayer time always passed either in dryness and in struggling against distractions, in trying to forget the pains in my stomach, or in keeping my mind at rest in the presence of God, Whom I felt within my heart. I think the latter was a form of prayer of quiet, an obscure contemplation in which the Master instructed me without the sound of words. I felt with delight that He was beautifying my soul.

Without seeing anything with the eyes either of the body or the soul, I realized that God was present, I felt His gaze bent on me full of gentleness and affection, and that He smiled kindly upon me. I seemed plunged in God. My imagination was submissive and did not act. I did not hear any noise that might be going on around me. My soul looked fixedly into the gaze invisibly bent on me, and my heart repeated untiringly: 'My God, I love Thee!' While reiterating it with obscure but deep joy, I longed that the divine gaze, the spiritual Sun, should cause the virtues to flourish in my soul, and was conscious that this longing was granted, and that this profound peace and simple act of love concealed an incomprehens-ible activity. Sometimes I used to plead for souls, but as a rule I did not pause for that, being convinced that to repeat: 'My God, I love Thee!' pleased Him better and included all the rest (*Mother Isabel of the Sacred Heart*, pp. 41-43. London, Kingscote Press, 1916).

A great variety of passages, asserting the same claims made in divers ways by a number of Catholic mystics, may be found among the well-selected body of 'Extracts' that follow each chapter of the book *Les Grâces d'Oraison* (English translation, *The Graces of Interior Prayer*, Kegan Paul, 1910) of Père Poulain, S.J. Some of his psychological and theological speculations and explanations have given rise to criticism and controversy. But his thesis that the criterion of fully mystical states lies in the experimental perception of the presence of God in the soul, is proved in his book by a cloud of witnesses among the mystics.

The foregoing extracts make clear what the consistent claim of the classic mystics has been, asserted with an insistence and a conviction that is most impressive. And the great problem of mysticism, the crucial question, is: Whether this claim be objectively true? Does it express the reality, or is it a delusion of those that believe they have enjoyed such experiences? On the answer to this question depends the place of mysticism as an object of religious study. If it be negative, the writings of the mystics would retain indeed their philosophical and psychological interest, and their value as manuals of instruction on the spiritual life and the exercise of prayer; but mysticism would not be the culminating point of religious experience, the last word in the philosophy of religion. Fr Sharpe is probably right in saying that if 'mysticism' is to lose its recognized traditional meaning, the use of the word should be dropped—it should not be applied to other things quite different from it.

The answer to the essential question ought to be at least largely conditioned by the evidence of the mystics themselves, for it is the only first-hand evidence we have got. Many may think the thing ruled out by its mere statement, so extravagant, so impossible, is the claim. Such, however, is not the answer of the philosophical thought of the day. So modern-minded a thinker as Dean Inge has said: 'That the human mind, while still "in the body pent," may obtain glimpses of the eternal order, and enjoy foretastes of the bliss of heaven, is a belief which I, at least, see no reason to reject. It involves no rash presumption, and is not contrary to what may be readily believed about the state of immortal spirits passing through a mortal life.'[1] And William James leaves the reality of the mystical experience as claimed by the mystics an open question, a matter of evidence, with a clear preparedness of mind to accept it as true, and certainly as a thing that science has no right to deny off-hand.[2]

And so let us, without more ado, turn to our three great mystical Doctors of the Western Church, to see what they have to tell us.

---

[1] *Light, Life, and Love: Selections from the German Mystics of the Middle Ages*, p. xxxvii.
[2] *Varieties of Religious Experience*, p. 427; the words are given in full below, in the Epilogue, pp. 137-138.

The study of their mystical doctrine, or teaching on contemplation, will furnish us with authentic first-hand material for considering, and attempting to answer in the Epilogue of this Part not only this, the most fundamental question, but also many lesser ones, raised by the subject of mysticism.

CONTEMPLATION

1. ST AUGUSTINE

ANALYSIS

ST AUGUSTINE

St Augustine's *Confessions* is a Christian classic so widely read that his personality is among the best known in history. There is therefore no need to give more than the bare dates and facts of his life. He was borne at Thagaste in North Africa, not far from Carthage, in 354. In 374 he became a Manichaean and remained such for some ten years, after which he went to Rome and to Milan as teacher of rhetoric. The story of his conversion is known to all. The beginnings of his return to Catholicism were due to the fact that in 385 some books of the neo-Platonists, without doubt Latin translations of Plotinus, came into his hands and greatly impressed him (*Conf.* vii.), so that from that time onward he accepted the main principles of the neo-Platonic philosophy, and his whole intellectual outlook, his mysticism included, was coloured by it to the end. The conversion took place in 386, and he was baptized by St Ambrose the following year. Shortly afterwards he returned to Africa and formed a religious community. In 391 he was ordained priest, and in 396 he became bishop of Hippo, and so continued until his death in 430.

The greatness of Augustine as thinker, writer, theologian, champion of the Church, saint, is recognized universally with admiration unreserved. He is on all hands acknowledged to be the dominant figure in Western Christianity.[1] Every aspect, it may be said, of his teaching has been made the object of special study, so that an array of treatises, monographs, books of all kinds and sizes has been produced, dealing separately with his philosophy, his psychology, his theology in its several branches, his philosophy of history, his theory of politics, and a number of other subjects. One conspicuous exception there is. Not yet, I believe, has his mystical theology been made the object of special study. Well-known extracts from the *Confessions* are made in books on mysticism; but never yet has there been a systematic presentation of his teaching on contemplation and the kindred topics. Here, then, appears to be a lacuna, which, from the point of view of Augustine and of mysticism alike, it is well worth while trying to fill up.

[1] The best source known to me for careful and detailed general information on every topic concerning St Augustine are the 300 columns of Abbé E. Portalié's three articles in the *Dictionnaire de Théologie Catholique*, edited by Vacant and Mangenot (Paris, 1903).

Augustine is for me the Prince of Mystics, uniting in himself, in a manner I do not find in any other, the two elements of mystical experience, viz. the most penetrating intellectual vision into things divine, and a love of God that was a consuming passion. He shines as a sun in the firmament, shedding forth at once light and heat in the lustre of his intellect and the warmth of his religious emotion.

Augustine is in himself the refutation of a number of popular misconceptions about mysticism and mystics. One of these is the notion often heard that mysticism is a reaction and protest against ecclesiasticism, sacramental system, dogma, church authority, institutional religion. But Augustine was pre-eminently a churchman, nay a militant one, a subtle theologian, an almost fierce dogmatist. Another is the notion that mysticism represents an antagonism between personal religion, the religion of the Spirit it has been called, and a religion of authority. But it is acknowledged on all hands, for it is evident, that in Augustine the three elements of well-balanced religion, the personal, the institutional, the intellectual, are triumphantly conciliated; and we are all of us, in our measure, little Augustines in this regard. Sometimes it is said that a vigorous play of the intellect is an impediment to mystical contemplation. Yet who has been a greater intellectualist than Augustine, with his keen joy in philosophical speculation, and his ever-flowing output of intellectual writing, that to this day has influenced Western theological thought as none other since St Paul? Again, the theory that vacancy from external works and occupations is a condition of contemplation, and that mystics are impracticable dreamers, is shown in Augustine to be untrue. For he was full of business, a bishop devoted to his flock, a popular preacher, a letter-writer ever ready to answer, even at great length, the questions put to him. These and other popular errors, often almost taken for granted by serious writers, are put out of court by the single case of Augustine.

We may now turn to our study of his mystical theology and doctrine on contemplation, which, if I be not mistaken, will prove to be of a religious value quite extraordinary. His teaching has to be picked up from many isolated passages scattered widespread through his writings; but there are certain continuous passages containing a more sustained exposition. The principal are the following:

Confessions, vii. 16, 23; ix. 23-25; x. 65; *Enarratio in Psalmum* xli. (heb. xlii.); *de Quantitate Animae*, 74, 75, 76; *de Genesi ad litteram*, xii.; *Ep.* cxlvii. *de Videndo Deo*; *c. Faustum*, xxii. 52-58; *de Civitate Dei*, xix. 1, 2, 19; *Sermons*, ciii. civ.

In the 'Enarration' on Psalm xli. St Augustine gives a continuous exposition which may fairly claim to be a doctrine of contemplation. We shall open the investigation of his teaching on mysticism with a consideration of this piece as a whole. The text is first given, in condensed form, the Oxford 'Library of the Fathers' being used, and is followed by a short commentary.

Like as the hart desireth the water-brooks, so longeth my soul after Thee, O God.

2. This psalm is sung as 'a Psalm for Understanding' (title). For what understanding is it sung? Come, my brethren, catch my eagerness; share with me in this my longing: let us both love, let us both be influenced with this thirst, let us both hasten to the well of understanding. Let us then long for it as the hart for the brook; let us long for that fountain whereof another Scripture saith, *For with Thee is the fountain of life.* For He is both the Fountain and the Light; for it is *In Thy Light that we shall see light.* If He is both the Fountain and the Light, with good reason is He the Understanding also, because He both filleth the soul that thirsteth for knowledge, and every one who hath 'understanding' is enlightened by a certain light; not a corporeal, not a carnal one, not an outward, but an inward light! There is, then, a certain light within, not possessed by those who understand not. Run to the brooks; long after the water-brooks, *With God is the fountain of Life;* a fountain that shall never be dried up: in His light is a light that shall never be darkened. Long thou for this light: for a certain fountain, a certain light, such as thy bodily eyes know not; a light, to see which the inward eye must be prepared; a fountain, to drink of which the inward thirst is to be kindled. Run to the fountain; long for the fountain; but do it not anyhow, be not satisfied with running like any ordinary animal; run thou like the hart.

3. But perhaps Scripture meant us to consider in the hart another point also. The hart destroys serpents, and after the killing of serpents, it is inflamed with thirst yet more violent. The serpents are thy vices; destroy the serpents of iniquity, then wilt thou long yet more for the Fountain of Truth. Whilst thou art yet indulgent to thy vices, thy covetousness or thy appetite, when am I to find in thee a longing such as this, that might make thee run to the waterbrooks? When art thou to desire the Fountain of Wisdom, whilst thou art yet labouring in the venom of iniquity? Destroy in thyself whatever is contrary to the truth, and when thou hast seen thyself to be comparatively free from irrational passions, be not contented to stay where thou art, as if there was nothing further for thee to long for. For there is yet somewhat to which thou mayest raise thyself, even if thou hast already achieved that triumph within, that there is no longer within thee a foe to hinder and to thwart thee. For perhaps if thou art the hart, thou wilt already say to me: 'God knows that I am no longer covetous, that I no longer set my heart on the property of any man; that I am not inflamed by the passion of unlawful love; that I do not pine away with hatred or ill-will

against any man'; and as to all other things of this description, thou wilt say: 'I am free from them'; and perhaps thou wouldest fain know wherein thou mayest find pleasure. Long for the water-brooks; God hath wherewith to refresh thee, and to satisfy thee when thou comest to Him, athirst, like the swift-footed hart, after the destruction of the serpents.

5. Such a hart then, being yet in a state of 'faith' only, not yet in 'sight' of what he believes, has to bear with adversaries, who mock the man who believes, and cannot show them that in which he believes, saying, *Where is thy God?*

7. Meditating night and day on this taunt, I have myself sought to find my God, that if I could I might not believe only, but might see also somewhat. For I see the things which my God hath made, but my God Himself I do not see.

The effort of mind to attain to the knowledge and sight òf God through creatures is described in a striking passage: he interrogates the earth, the heavenly bodies, his own body, his soul in its highest and most spiritual mental operations. He goes on:

Is God, then, anything of the same nature as the soul? This mind of ours seeks to find something that is God. It seeks to find a Truth not subject to change, a Substance not capable of failing. The mind itself is not of this nature: it is capable of progress and of decay, of knowledge and of ignorance, of remembering or forgetting. That mutability is not incident to God.

8. Having therefore sought to find my God in visible and corporeal things, and found Him not; having sought to find His Substance in myself, and found Him not, I perceive my God to be something higher than my soul. Therefore that I might attain unto Him *I thought on these things, and poured out my soul above myself*. When would my soul attain to that object of its search, which is 'above my soul,' if my soul were not to pour itself out above itself? For were it to rest in itself, it would not see anything else beyond itself; and in seeing itself, would not, for all that, see God. Let then my insulting enemies now say, *Where is thy God?* Aye, let them say it! I, so long as I do not *see*, so long as my happiness is postponed, *Make my tears my bread day and night.* I seek my God in every corporeal nature, terrestrial or celestial, and find Him not: I seek His Substance in my own soul, and I find it not; yet still have I thought on these things, and wishing to see *the invisible things of my God, being understood by the things made*, I have poured forth my soul above myself, and there remains no longer any being for me to attain to (tangam), save my God. For it is *there* is the 'house of my God'. His dwelling-place is above my soul; from thence He beholds me; from thence He governs me and provides for me; from thence He appeals to me, and calls me, and directs me; leads me in the way, and to the end of my way.

9. But He Who has His house very high in secret place, hath also

on earth a tabernacle. His tabernacle on earth is the Church. It is here that He is to be sought, for it is in the tabernacle that is found the way by which we arrive at the house. *For I will go into the place of Thy admirable tabernacle, even unto the house of God.* God's tabernacle on earth is the Faithful. How much is there I admire in this tabernacle:—the self-conquest and the virtues of God's servants. I admire the presence of those virtues in the soul; but still I am walking in *the place of the tabernacle.* I pass beyond these also; and admirable though the tabernacle be, yet when I come to *the house of God*, I am even struck dumb with astonishment. It is there, in the sanctuary of God, in the house of God, is the fountain of understanding. It was going up to the tabernacle the Psalmist arrived at the house of God. It was thus, that whilst admiring the members of the tabernacle, he was led on to the house of God: by following the leadings of a certain delight, an inward mysterious and hidden pleasure, as if from the house of God there sounded sweetly some instrument; and he, whilst walking in the tabernacle, hearing a certain inward sound, led on by its sweetness, and following the guidance of the sound, withdrawing himself from all noise of flesh and blood, made his way on even to the house of God. For he tells us of his progress and of his guidance thither; as if we had been saying, 'You are admiring the tabernacle here on earth; how came you to the sanctuary of the house of God?' and he says, *'In the voice of joy and praise, the sound of keeping holiday.'* In the house of God there is a never-ending festival; the angelic choir makes an eternal holiday, the presence of God's face, joy that never fails. From that everlasting, perpetual festivity there sounds in the ears of the heart a mysterious strain, melodious and sweet, provided only the world do not drown the sounds. As he walks in this tabernacle, and considers God's wonderful works for the redemption of the faithful, the sound of that festivity charms his ears and bears the *hart* away to *the water-brooks.*

10. But seeing that 'the corruptible body presseth down the soul,' even though we have in some way dispersed the clouds by walking as longing leads us on, and for a brief while have come within reach of that sound, so that by an effort we may catch something from that house of God; yet through the burden, so to speak, of our infirmity, we sink back to our usual level and relapse to our ordinary state (consueta). And just as there we found cause for rejoicing, so here there will not be wanting an occasion for sorrow. For that hart that *made tears its bread day and night*, borne along *by longing to the water-brooks* (that is, to the inward sweetness of God), *pouring forth his soul above himself*, that he may attain to what is above his own soul, walking *unto the place of the admirable tabernacle, even unto the house of God*, and led on by the delight of that inward spiritual sound to feel contempt for exterior things and be ravished by things interior, is but a mortal man still; is still groaning here, still bearing about the frailty of the flesh, still in peril in the midst of the offences of this world. He therefore gazes on himself, as if he were coming from that other world; and says to himself, now placed in the midst of these sorrows, comparing these with the things to see which he had

entered in there, and after seeing which he had come forth from thence, '*Why art thou cast down, O my soul, and why dost thou disquiet me?*' Lo, we have just now been gladdened by certain inward delights; with the mind's eye we have been able to behold, though but with a momentary glance, something not susceptible of change: why dost thou still disquiet me, why art thou still cast down? For thou dost not doubt of thy God. For now thou art not without somewhat to say to thyself in answer to those who say, *Where is thy God?* I have now had the perception of something that is unchangeable: 'why dost thou disquiet me still?' And as if his soul was silently replying to him, 'Why do I disquiet thee, but because I am not yet there, where that delight is, to which I was rapt as it were in passing. Am I already drinking from this fountain with nothing to fear? Have I no longer anything to be anxious about, as if all my passions were conquered and thoroughly subdued? Is not my foe, the devil, on the watch against me? Wouldst thou have me not disquiet thee, placed as I am yet in the world, and on pilgrimage from the house of God?' Still *Hope in God* is his answer to the soul that disquiets him, etc.

This, surely, will, I think, be acknowledged by even the most objective exegete to be a noble piece of exegesis—a masterpiece of its kind. For however little it may express the real thought of the Psalmist, still, without doing violence to the text, it makes his words, with rare skill, serve as the basis of a statement of mystical doctrine forestalling the lines laid down by the great mystics of later times. The passage is characteristic alike in the warmth of its devotion, in its intellectual method, and in the eloquence and elevation of its language. It will repay a careful study.

In § 2 Augustine sets in the forefront the vague yet intense longing for something not clearly known, yet strongly desired, which is the motive power impelling one destined to ascend the Mount of Contemplation to embark on the dark and difficult way that lies before him. The mystics are all agreed as to the necessity of this great desire as the condition of success in the pursuit of the Contemplative Life. Here, too, is emphasized that characteristic doctrine of the mystics—the special inward light enlightening with spiritual understanding the minds of those who cultivate the inner life.

In § 3 is set forth, as a preliminary condition of contemplation, the necessity of the destruction of vices in the soul and the elimination of imperfections. Herein lies the feature which marks off true mysticism from the counterfeits which so often, especially in these our days, masquerade in its name. It is the constant teaching of the great mystics that there can be no progress in prayer without mortification; no contemplation without self-denial and self-discipline seriously undertaken; no real mysticism without asceticism, in its full

sense of spiritual training. After all, this is only the teaching of the
Gospel: the clean of heart shall see God. And so Augustine, like all
genuine mystics, warns us that this destruction of vices must first be
secured; only so can anyone press on to the shrine of contemplation.

Though remembering, in § 5, that he is now only in a state of
'faith' and not yet of 'sight', still in § 7 the Psalmist desires to find
God, that he may not only believe, but may also see somewhat.
Here is formulated the fundamental Postulate of Mysticism: that
it is possible in this life to see somewhat of God—to have an experimental perception of Him.

§ 7 continues in an eloquent passage describing the soul's search
for God throughout creation. It is the search for a Truth not subject
to change, a Substance not capable of failing.

§ 8. This the mind cannot find in creatures; not in itself. It must
mount up above itself, to where God dwells.

§ 9. Finally, it is the contemplation of the virtues of God's servants,
and admiration at His gifts in them, that carries the soul up to the
threshold of God's dwelling-place. This idea, that that which gives the
soul its final lift up to the mystic height is the consideration of the
holiness of God's faithful servants, is (to me) a unique, but surely
a striking and a fruitful, conception. We no doubt owe it to the
exegetical necessities of the Psalm. The more normal teaching of the
mystics, that God is found within the soul, is of course taught by
Augustine in various places, as will appear later on.

And so he comes to the mystic experience itself. Then is he struck
dumb with astonishment. It is as if some strains of the music of the
heavenly festival reached the ear of his heart, leading him on by a
mysterious inward delight. And led on by the sweetness of this inward sound, withdrawing himself from all noise of flesh and blood,
charmed by that melodious strain that comes from the court of
Heaven, he is borne along to the 'water-brooks'—'that is, to the
inward sweetness of God' (§ 10).

The imagery of music to express the mystic experience occurs (so
far as I know) only here in Augustine, though it is employed by
other mystics, as Richard Rolle.[1]

In § 10 are more precisely described the phenomena of the actual
mystical experience. The soul, coming for a brief while within reach
of the sound of the music of heaven, is gladdened by inward de-

[1] In the following passage, for instance, Rolle expresses the mystical experience
as 'the inshedding and receiving of this heavenly and ghostly sound, the which
belongs to the songs of everlasting praise and the sweetness of unseen melody.
Whiles I took heed to praying to heaven with my whole desire, suddenly, I wot
not in what manner, I felt in me the noise of song, and received the most liking
heavenly melody which dwelt with me in my mind' (*Fire of Love*, p. 71, ed.
Comper, 1914).

lights and the mind's eye is able to behold, though but with a momentary glance, Something not susceptible of change. The act of contemplation is here characterized as 'the perception of Something Unchangeable,' accompanied by a wondrous inward joy. Its effect on the soul is to make it feel contempt for exterior things, and be ravished by things interior. But after the brief moment of realization, the soul, weighed down by the burden of its infirmity, sinks back to its ordinary level and its normal experience: and this return, as it were, from the other world is an occasion of sorrow, and of longing for a renewal of the experience. Here is emphasized what is the testimony of all the mystics as to the transient nature of the act of contemplation.

The foregoing passage is the most considerable and complete of Augustine's descriptions of the process and nature of the mystic experience. But there are in the *Confessions* definitely autobiographical relations of the way in which he attained to contemplation. These passages will be adduced in the proper place.

The attempt will now be made to present in orderly sequence, under certain main headings, St Augustine's full doctrine on mysticism and contemplation, all the principal passages that I have been able to collect from his writings being duly co-ordinated, and reproduced mostly in his own words, but sometimes in compressed form. The general outlines correspond in main features to those under which the doctrine of St Gregory and that of St Bernard will be presented. In the case of each Doctor the subject matter will be treated under two heads: in Part I, the Nature of Contemplation; and in Part II, the Relations between the Contemplative and the Active Lives.

St Augustine's teaching on the nature of contemplation may be formulated under the following aspects:
He gives in one place a definition or description of contemplation in general: It is the directing a serene and straight look on the object to be looked at.[1]

(1) *The Contemplation of God is the lot of the Blessed in heaven; in it consists their essential eternal happiness.*

The contemplation of God 'face to face' is promised to us as the end of all our actions and the perfection of all our joys (*de Trin.* i. 17).

---

[1] 'Serenum atque rectum aspectum in id, quod videndum est, dirigere' (*de Quant. Anim.* 75).

In the contemplation of God is the end of all good actions, and everlasting rest, and joy that never will be taken from us (ibid. i. 20).

That vision of God whereby we shall contemplate the unchangeable and to human eyes invisible Substance of God, alone is our summum bonum, for the attaining to which we are commanded to do whatever we rightly do (ibid. i. 31).

The contemplation of God will be the highest reward of the saints (ibid. xii. 22).

(2) *Though Contemplation really belongs to the next life, in this life some beginnings of it are possible, some passing glimpses or intuitions of divine things.*

Thus he says: Contemplation is only begun in this life, to be perfected in the next (*Tract. in Ioan.* cxxiv. 5).

Even in this life our soul hungers and thirsts for God, and we can find real satisfaction only in Him. This truth is enunciated in St Augustine's celebrated formulation of what may be called the Great Mystic Postulate: Thou hast created us for Thyself, and our heart is restless till it rest in Thee (*Conf.* i. 1).

A. PRELIMINARY PHASES

(3) *The Remote Preparation for Contemplation lies in the Purification of the Soul.*

For Augustine, as for all true mystics, the indispensable condition of contemplation is such a purification of the soul as will render it fit for the ascent to the contemplation of God: a purification which is the result of a long process of self-denial and self-conquest, of mortification and the practice of virtue—in short, asceticism in the broad and full meaning of the word, viz. 'training'.

This is the teaching, for instance, of Cassian, who divides spiritual knowledge into two branches: *practical*, which consists in the elimination of faults and acquiring of virtues; and *theoretic*, which consists in the contemplation of divine things. There is no arriving at contemplation without a serious pursuit of practical discipline—asceticism—for 'in vain does one strive for the vision of God, who does not shun the stains of sin' (*Coll.* xiv. 1, 2). And so, in such a book as Fr Augustine Baker's *Sancta Sophia*, being 'Directions for the Prayer of Contemplation,' the section of Mortification, conceived identically with Cassian's practical discipline, occupies nearly as much space as that of Prayer. This truth is asserted, too, in the classical division of the spiritual life into the three phases of Purgation, Illumination, and Union, the first being that process of self-discipline and reformation and readjustment of character which is the necessary preparation for entry into the higher degrees of the spiritual life.

And it is remarkable that in the treatise *de Quantitate Animae*, written shortly after his baptism, St Augustine forestalls, in fact though not in nomenclature, this received division of later writers into the purgative, illuminative, and unitive ways. He distinguishes seven grades or degrees (gradus) in the functions or operations of the soul: it is the principle of life, of sensation, of intelligence, of morality; the fifth grade he characterizes as 'tranquillitas', the calming of the passions; the sixth as 'ingressio', the approach to contemplation; the seventh as contemplation. These last three correspond in idea to the familiar stages of purgation, illumination, and union. He uses, indeed, the actual word 'purgation', but of the fourth grade. He summarizes them thus: In the fourth God purges the soul, in the fifth He reforms it, in the sixth He leads it in, in the seventh He feeds it.[1] The last two, 'ingressio' and 'contemplatio', will be spoken of again; but the fourth and fifth represent the process of ethical reconstruction and transformation of the self, the conflict with sin and the establishment of the soul in good, the difference between the two grades lying in this, that what was effected in the fourth is made permanent in the fifth: 'for it is one thing to purify the soul, and another to keep it pure; one thing to restore it when sullied, another not to suffer it to become sullied again.' And more than once is the truth insisted on, that not until this purification of the soul has been effected, not until it has been 'cleansed and healed,' can it proceed to contemplation.[2]

And indeed this same truth is proclaimed throughout the *Confessions*—the portrayal of an emergence alike from intellectual error and from moral disorder. The latter it was that for a long while held back the mind from its flight to God and hindered it from fixing its gaze upon Him. Not till the struggle had issued in full moral victory and regeneration could Augustine attain to that clear vision of heavenly things and that intimate realization that afterwards were his not infrequent experience. And so in certain premonitory experiences and elevations during the pre-Christian neo-Platonist phase described in Book vii. of the *Confessions*, before he had emancipated himself from sinful habits, of the first, viz. vision, he says: 'When first I knew Thee, Thou didst take hold of me, that I might see there was Something to see, but that I was not yet such as to see it' (16); and of the second, viz. realization, wherein he did attain to a momentary glimpse: 'I was fully con-

---

[1] *De Quant. Anim.* 79, 80.   [2] *Op. cit.* 73, 74, 75.

vinced there was One to Whom I might cleave, but that I was not yet such as to cleave to Him' (23). Thus it is Augustine's witness that there was for him neither clear vision of God nor union with Him, until both mind and heart should be effectively purged: Blessed are the clean of heart, for they shall see God.

(4) *The Proximate Preparation for Contemplation lies in the processes called 'Recollection' and 'Introversion.'*

The word 'recollection' is taken, not in its present, secondary, sense of remembering, but in its primary sense of gathering together and concentrating the mind. It consists first in the effort to banish from the mind all images and thoughts of external things, all sense perceptions and thoughts of creatures; then the reasoning processes of the intellect are silenced, and by this exercise of abstraction a solitude is produced wherein the soul may operate in its most spiritual faculties. This shutting off all external things from the mind, and emptying it of distracting thoughts, which is the object of 'recollection', is the prelude to that entering of the mind into itself that is effected by 'introversion', which is a concentration of the mind on its own highest, or deepest, part. In the account of the soul's quest for God through creatures, in *Enar. in Psalm.* xli. (see above, p. 22), the process of introversion is described as the final step before the soul finds God. Thus: 'the mind abstracts itself from all the bodily senses, as interrupting and confounding it with their din, in order to see itself in itself, and know itself as mirrored in itself' (§ 7); and again, it is by 'abstracting its attention from all noise of flesh and blood' that it arrives at God (§ 9).

The philosophical, or rather theological, explanation of the reason and meaning of introversion has been clearly set forth by Bishop Ullathorne:

Let it be plainly understood that we cannot return to God unless we enter first into ourselves. God is everywhere, but not everywhere to us. There is but one point in the Universe where God communicates with us, and that is the centre of our own soul. There He waits for us; there He meets us; there He speaks to us. To seek Him, therefore, we must enter into our own interior (*Groundwork of the Christian Virtues*, p. 74).

The most noteworthy of Augustine's various descriptions of the soul's search for God through the ascending grades of creation, wherein the mind finally turns itself in upon itself, mounting through its progressively more and more spiritual faculties, till it finds God at once in and above itself, is the elaborate and eloquent passage in Book x. of the *Confessions* (12-38), which Mr Montgomery

singles out as an acute and true psychological analysis of the
phenomena of consciousness and sub-consciousness—memory,
Augustine calls it.[1] In it he describes his own seeking to find God
throughout the different regions of consciousness—how, turning inwards on itself, his mind passed successively through those regions
that contain the images of material things, and those that contain
the 'affections' of the mind—not merely emotions, but purely
intellectual phenomena, 'ideas'—till at last he entered 'into the very
seat of the mind.'

Thou remainest unchangeable over all, and yet hast vouchsafed
to dwell in my memory, since I learnt Thee. And why seek I now
in what place thereof Thou dwellest, as if there were places therein?
Sure I am, that in it Thou dwellest, since I have remembered Thee,
ever since I learnt Thee, and there I find Thee, when I call Thee
to remembrance. Where then did I find Thee, that I might learn
Thee? For in my memory Thou wert not, before I learned Thee.
Where then did I find Thee, that I might learn Thee, but in Thee
above me ? (loc. cit. 36, 37). It culminates in the following fine
piece, embodying the normal teaching of the mystics on God's
immanence in the soul: Too late loved I Thee, O Beauty so old,
yet ever new! too late loved I Thee. And behold Thou wert within,
and I abroad, and there I searched for Thee. Thou wert with me,
but I was not with Thee. Thou calledst, and shoutedst, burstedst
my deafness. Thou flashedst, shonedst, and scatteredst my blindness.
Thou breathedst odours, and I drew in breath, and pant for Thee.
I tasted, and hunger and thirst. Thou touchedst me, and I was on
fire for Thy peace (38).

The question raised in the above passage, Whether God is to be
found within the soul or above it, is solved in the following striking
utterance, declared by the latest editor to be one of his memorable
phrases, wherein the simultaneous truth of both ideas, the immanence and the transcendence of God, is affirmed:

Thou wert more inward to me than my most inward part, and
higher than my highest (Conf. iii. 11).

[1] St Augustine, p. 117. The Confessions is the work which, more than any other,
supplies material for the study of St Augustine's mysticism. The edition by
Dr Gibb and Mr Montgomery ('Cambridge Patristic Texts', 1908) will be found
the most serviceable; it supplies a critical text, based on that of the Vienna
'Corpus', and explained in a running commentary of useful notes. Pusey's translation in the Oxford 'Library of the Fathers' has been reprinted in handy form in
'Everyman's Library' (Dent). A somewhat modernized translation was made by
Dr Bigg in the 'Library of Devotion' (Methuen), but it closes with Book ix. [The
early one, by Sir Tobie Matthew, 1620, is printed in 'Orchard Books' (Burns
and Oates).]

There are certain passages in the *Confessions* strongly autobiographical in character, and therefore wholly convincing, describing with great power and rare eloquence Augustine's own elevations to the mystic experience, wherein the processes of recollection and introversion and the subsequent contemplation are very vividly depicted. It would be a pity to break up these passages into fragments in order to illustrate severally the different elements: for their value lies largely in their delineation of the experience as a whole. So they will be here recited in their entirety, as a basis for the coming study.

B. Autobiographical Passages

The thought and the language of the following pieces are strongly coloured by Plotinus, whose philosophy was the vehicle whereby Augustine habitually formulated to himself and others his experiences of mind and soul. The first two of these realizations of the mystic experience are taken from the Seventh Book of the *Confessions*, which depicts the phase that intervened between the abandonment of Manichaeism and the full embracing of Catholic Christianity, while he was captivated by the religious Platonism of Plotinus.

After speaking at some length of what he had found 'in the books of the Platonists,' he says:

And being by them admonished to return into myself, I entered even into my inmost self, Thou being my Guide. I entered and beheld with the eye of my soul, above the same eye of my soul, above my mind, the Light Unchangeable. ...[1] And Thou didst beat back the weakness of my sight, streaming forth Thy beams of light upon me most strongly, and I trembled with love and awe (*Conf.* vii. 16).

More precise in details is the following powerful piece:

Step by step was I led upwards, from bodies to the soul which perceives by means of the bodily senses; and thence to the soul's inward faculty to which the bodily senses report external things, which is the limit of the intelligence of animals; and thence again to the reasoning faculty, to whose judgement is referred the knowledge received by the bodily senses. And when this power also within me found itself changeable, it lifted itself up to its own intelligence, and withdrew its thoughts from experience, abstracting itself from the contradictory throng of sense images, that it might find what that light was wherein it was bathed when it cried out that beyond

---

[1] The passage wherein he explains what this Light is, is given at a later place (pp. 43-44).

all doubt the unchangeable is to be preferred to the changeable; whence also it knew That Unchangeable: and thus with the flash of one trembling glance it arrived at THAT WHICH IS. And then at last I saw Thy 'invisible things understood by the things that are made'; but I could not sustain my gaze, and my weakness being struck back, I was relegated to my ordinary experience, bearing with me but a loving memory and a longing for what I had, as it were, perceived the odour of, but was not yet able to feed upon (*Conf.* vii. 23).

There is a special interest in the circumstance that these experiences, evidently in full sense mystical, were pre-Christian, or at any rate pre-Catholic;[1] and they are couched in great measure in the very language of Plotinus.[2] This is true also in some degree of the description of the fully Catholic experience in the well-known scene at Ostia, just before Monica's death, when mother and son opened to each other their inmost thoughts, and together strove to rise to a realization of the heavenly joys.

We were discoursing together alone, very sweetly, and we were enquiring between ourselves in the presence of the Truth, which Thou art, of what sort the eternal life of the saints was to be. With the lips of our souls we panted for the heavenly streams of Thy fountain, the fountain of life which is with Thee, that, sprinkled with that water to the measure of our capacity, we might attain some poor conception of that glorious theme. And as our converse drew to this conclusion, that the sweetest conceivable delight of sense in the brightest conceivable earthly sunshine was not to be compared, no, nor even named, with the happiness of that life, we soared with ardent longing towards the 'Self-same' [i.e. the unchanging God], we passed from stage to stage through all material things, through heaven itself, whence sun and moon and stars shed their radiance upon earth. And now we began a more inward ascent, by thinking and speaking and marvelling at Thy works. And so we came to our own minds, and we passed beyond them, that we might come unto the region of unfailing plenty, where Thou feedest Israel for ever with the food of truth. There Life is the wisdom by which all things come to be, both those that have been and those that are to be; and the Life itself never comes to be, but is as it was and shall be ever more, because in it is neither past nor future but present only, for it is eternal. And as we talked and yearned after it, we touched it—and hardly touched it—with the full beat (toto ictu) of our heart. And we sighed and left there impawned the firstfruits of the spirit, and we relapsed into articulate speech, where the word has beginning and ending (*Conf.* ix. 23, 24).

---

[1] He did not yet accept the Catholic doctrine of the Incarnation or the divinity of Christ (ibid. 25).

[2] See notes in edition of Gibb and Montgomery (Cambridge 1908).

It is a common teaching of mystic writers that introversion is effected by a successive silencing of the faculties of the mind and of the powers of the soul, till the actuations become blind elevations to God; and in the 'Quiet' thus produced, the very being of the soul—the 'Ground of the Spirit', the later mystics call it—comes into immediate relation with the Ultimate Reality which is God. This silencing of the faculties is systematically pursued in, for instance, the work of St John of the Cross, *The Ascent of Mount Carmel*; and it is described with much eloquence and power by Augustine in the continuation of the foregoing passage:

We said then: If the tumult of the flesh were hushed; hushed the sense impressions (phantasiae) of earth, sea, sky; hushed also the heavens, yea the very soul be hushed to herself, and by not thinking on self transcend self; hushed all dreams and revelations which come by imagery; if every tongue and every symbol, and all things subject to transiency were wholly hushed: since, if any could hear, all these say: 'We made not ourselves, but He made us who abideth for ever.'—If then, having uttered this, they too should be hushed, having roused only our ears to Him who made them; and He alone speak, not by them but by Himself, so that we may hear His word, not through any tongue of flesh nor angel's voice nor sound of thunder, not in any similitude, but His voice whom we love in these His creatures—may hear His Very Self without intermediary at all—as now we reached forth and with one flash of thought touched the Eternal Wisdom that abides over all:—suppose that experience were prolonged, and all other visions of far inferior order were taken away, and this one vision were to ravish the beholder, and absorb him and plunge him in these inward joys, so that eternal life were like that moment of insight for which we sighed—were not this: Enter into the joy of thy Lord![1] (*Conf.* ix. 25).

Those familiar with the later literature of mysticism and with the mystics' records of their own souls' flights to God, are sure to be struck by one feature of the foregoing passages. In all of them, those from the *Confessions* as well as that from the 'Enarration' on Psalm xli., Augustine's accounts of the process whereby the soul mounts up

[1] This passage is reminiscent of Plotinus, *Enn.* v. i. 1–3, translated by Dean Inge, *Plotinus*, i. 205, and by Taylor, *Select Works of Plotinus*, edited by Mead ('Bohn's Philosophical Library'), p. 162. The following are the most striking resemblances: The soul ought first to examine its own nature to know whether it has the faculty of contemplating spiritual things, and if it ought to embark on the quest. ... The soul makes itself worthy to contemplate by ridding itself, through quiet recollection, of deceit and of all that bewitches vulgar souls. For it let all be quiet; not only the body which encompasses it, and the tumult of the senses; but let all its environment be at peace. Let the earth be quiet, and the sea and air, and the heaven itself calm (Inge).

to contemplation are for the most part intellectual in idea and in language, sometimes being frankly Plotinian. Western mystics commonly represent contemplation as attained to by and in absorption in prayer; but for Augustine it seems to have been primarily an intellectual process—informed, indeed, by intense religious warmth, but still primarily intellectual. It is the search for Something not subject to change, that leads the soul up to God, and it is represented as a great effort of intellect and will. This is very interesting and valuable; especially as it will be shown in the sequel that the religious experience described by Augustine as the culmination of these efforts, was, without any doubt, identical in kind with those described by the later mystics.

C. THE ACT OF CONTEMPLATION

Some of the principal descriptions of the Act of Contemplation have already been cited, but there are many others throughout the writings of Augustine. His characterizations are of quite unusual interest and value, from the vivid autobiographical, and therefore convincing, character of so many of them; from the intellectual and philosophical acumen of him who experienced them; and from the lofty eloquence with which they are related. Their many-sidedness, too, is a most noteworthy feature: he uses every sort of conception, intellectual and symbolic, as the vehicle for expressing the intimate relations into which his soul came with God. It seems that these efforts of him who was undoubtedly, on the whole, the greatest religious genius in Western Christianity, to express his highest religious experiences, must be worthy of careful study. A detailed analysis of all these passages, so far as I have been able to collect them, will therefore be made, and in the most important cases the actual Latin words will be given in the footnotes. The statements will be grouped according to the idea under which the Object contemplated is conceived.

Sometimes the Object contemplated is expressed in the terms of pure metaphysics. Such are:

Ultimate Reality

Augustine so describes the culmination of his own earliest experience: 'In the flash of a trembling glance my mind came to Ultimate Reality, Absolute Being—That Which Is.'[1]

Elsewhere: 'God has given to His spiritual saints not only to believe, but to understand divine things,' and contemplation, 'wis-

---

[1] 'Mens mea pervenit ad id quod est in ictu trepidantis aspectus' (*Conf.* vii. 23).

dom,' 'lies in cognition and love of That Which always is and unchangeably abides, namely God.'[1]

Contemplation is 'the striving to understand those things that really and supremely are'; when attained to it is 'the full enjoyment of the highest and truest Good'; by it we attain to 'that highest Cause, or highest Author, or highest Principle of all things.'[2]

The Unchangeable

The intellectual or philosophical conception by which Augustine predominantly thinks of God is as the Being that is not subject to change: 'He truly Is, because He is unchangeable' (de Nat. Boni, 19). It was mainly the intellectual necessity he felt for Something Unchangeable as the basis and background of things changeable, that led him, more than anything else, out of Manichaeism into Christianity, and in his search for God he usually represents his mind as passing ever upwards through the grades of things subject to change, till it arrives at that Being 'in Whom there is no variation.'

And so his mystical experiences are often expressed in terms of this idea: e.g. as a perception of something unchangeable;[3] a beholding with the mind's eye something unchangeable;[4] a learning something divine and unchangeable.[5] The same fundamental idea runs through the following descriptions of the act of contemplation, as the perception of unchangeable Good;[6] as some vision of unchangeable Truth;[7] as the search for some unchangeable Truth.[8] Or again, the Light unchangeable; as where he says he 'saw with the eye of his soul, above his mind, the Light unchangeable';[9] or 'arrived by some kind of spiritual contact at the Light unchangeable.'[10]

These partly neo-Platonic, partly Joannine conceptions of Truth and Light are favourite ideas with Augustine when speaking of contemplation and mystic experience.

---

[1] 'Cognito et dilectio eius quod semper est et incommutabiliter manet, quod Deus est' (Enar. in Psalm. cxxxv. 8).

[2] 'Appetitio intelligendi ea quae vere summeque sunt ... perfructio summi et veri boni ... perventuri ad summam illam Causam, vel summum Auctorem, vel summum Principium rerum omnium' (de Quant. Animae, 75, 76).

[3] 'Aliquid incommutabile persensi' (Enar. in Psalm. xli. 10).

[4] 'Acie mentis aliquid incommutabile, etsi perstrictim et raptim, perspicere potuimus' (ibid.).

[5] 'Divinum et incommutabile aliquid discitur' (c. Faust. xxii. 54).

[6] 'Cernere incommutabile bonum' (ibid. xxii. 53).

[7] 'Aliqua visio incommutabilis veritatis' (de Cons. Evang. i. 8).

[8] 'Aliquam quaerit incommutabilem veritatem' (Enar. in Psalm. xli. 7).

[9] 'Vidi oculo animae meae supra mentem meam lucem incommutabilem' (Conf. vii. 16).

[10] 'Pervenire spiritali quodam contactu ad illam incommutabilem lucem' (Serm. lii. 16).

But in order to make sure that we understand him aright, it is necessary to institute a brief study of his psychological theory of perception and cognition, or, as it is called, his Ideology, a matter wherein the interpretation of his mind has given rise to keen controversy between rival schools of philosophy. We shall confine ourselves to setting forth in order what he says.

Excursus on St Augustine's Ideology

His Ideology is to be studied mainly in the Twelfth, last, Book of the work *de Genesi ad litteram*. It is primarily concerned with St Paul's vision when rapt to the Third Heaven; but as a basis of the discussion of visions, principles are laid down governing also ordinary perception and cognition.[1]

Augustine distinguishes three kinds of perception, following the three kinds of objects perceived:[2]

Corporal, whereby are seen physical things.

Spiritual, whereby are seen images of physical things not present, be it in memory or in imagination. Augustine apologizes for this unusual use of the word 'spiritual', based (surely improperly) on 1 Cor. xiv. 15; it has in fact often led to misunderstandings of his meaning, of which 'imaginary' is the best equivalent.

Intellectual, whereby are seen things in no way physical, incapable of being represented by images, being the objects of the pure intellect: this perception he would call 'mental', 'were there such a word' (*de Gen. ad. litt.* xii. **6-9**, 15-20).

He neatly illustrates his theory by the case of one reading the Commandment, 'Thou shalt love thy neighbour as thyself'; the actual letters are seen by corporal perception, the absent neighbour's image by spiritual (imaginary) perception, and the abstract idea 'love' by intellectual (ibid. **6**, 15; **11**, 22).

In most places he couples together the first two kinds of perception, corporal and spiritual (imaginary), as both being the perception of things changeable, and therefore the objects of science (scientia), as distinguished from wisdom (sapientia), whereby are

---

[1] In the older editions *de Genesi ad litteram*, like most of Augustine's longer works, has a twofold numbering; the paragraphs are numbered right through with Arabic figures, and there is also a division into greater sections, or chapters, with Roman figures. In the latest edition—that of the Vienna Corpus—only the latter numbering is given, but in Arabic figures. Consequently, for convenience of reference, both systems of numbering are given here for the passages of *de Genesi ad litteram*, the greater sections being marked with Arabic numbers in clarendon type.

[2] 'Vision' is the word he uses: it is taken most frequently in its objective sense, meaning the thing seen; but sometimes in its subjective or psychological sense, meaning the act of seeing.

perceived things not subject to change, eternal. Elsewhere he distinguishes wisdom and science: 'to wisdom pertains the intellectual cognition of things eternal; to science the rational cognition of things temporal' (de Trin. xii. 25).

In corporal and spiritual (imaginary) perception the soul is liable to error; but in things intellectually seen it is not liable to error—if there be any error, it is because the soul does not really intellectually see; for what it intellectually sees is true (de Gen. ad. litt. xii. 25, 52). Similarly elsewhere. 'Intellectual perception is not liable to error; for either: he who thinks something else than what is, does not intellectually see; or: if he does intellectually see, it follows it is true' (ibid. 14, 29).[1]

Augustine terms the objects of intellectual vision 'intellectualia' and 'intelligibilia' indiscriminately, saying that the attempt to make a distinction would be over-subtle (10, 21).

As objects of pure intellectual perception he enumerates the mind itself; every good disposition (affectio, πάθος) of the soul, or virtue, as charity, joy, peace, longanimity, and the rest, by which it draws near to God; lastly, God Himself (24, 50).

Also in the treatise de Trinitate, at the end of Book xii., he discourses of 'intelligibilia'. To wisdom pertain those things that neither have been nor are to be, but are; and because of that eternity in which they are, they are said to have been, to be, and to be about to be, without any changeableness of time: they always have had the selfsame being, and they always will have it. They abide, not fixed in local spaces like bodies; but in an incorporeal nature 'intelligibilia' are so present to the gaze of the mind, as visible and tangible things in places are present to the bodily senses. The 'rationes' of sensible things existing in place, abide intelligible and incorporeal not in local spaces: the squareness of a square figure abides as an incorporeal and unchangeable 'ratio' (de Trin. xii. 23).

Here we are in the presence of Plato's doctrine of Ideas, and it will be of interest to give St Augustine's Christianized formulation of that doctrine:

Ideas are certain primary or principal forms (principales formae), or 'ratios' of things, abiding and unchangeable, which themselves have not been formed, and by this fact are eternal and always remaining the same, which are contained in the divine Intelligence. And whereas themselves neither come into being nor perish, everything is said to be formed according to them, that can come into

---

[1] 'Intellectualis visio non fallitur. Aut enim non intelligit, qui aliud opinatur quam est; aut si intelligit, continuo verum est' (29). Cf. 'In intellectualibus visis (anima) non fallitur: aut enim intelligit, et verum est; aut si verum non est, non intelligit' (52).

being and perish, and everything that comes into being and perishes.

Each thing is created according to its own proper 'ratio'; but these 'ratios', where are they to be supposed to be except in the Mind itself of the Creator?

But if these 'ratios' of things to be created, or that have been created, are contained in the divine Mind, and there is nothing in the divine Mind but what is eternal and unchangeable, it follows that not only are they ideas, but they are true, because they are eternal, and remain the same and unchangeable; and by participation in them it comes about that everything is whatever it is.

And these 'ratios' may be called 'ideas', or 'forms', or 'species', or 'ratios' (*Lib. de div. Quaest.* lxxxiii. 46).

In each kind of perception the objects perceived are seen in a light that is of a higher order than themselves. In corporal vision physical things are seen in the light of the heavenly bodies (or of some fire, *de Pecc. Mer.* i. 38); in spiritual or imaginary vision the images of physical things are seen in 'a certain incorporeal light proper to itself' (*de Gen. ad. litt.* xii. 30, 58). This evidently is a mere makeshift, and I do not know any other place where Augustine attempts to define the light wherein are seen the objects of spiritual or imaginary vision.

In regard to intellectual vision, sometimes he speaks in the same vague way of the light wherein 'intellectualia' or 'intelligibilia', the Platonic Ideas, are seen: 'It is to be believed that the nature of the intellectual mind has been so made, that being brought into contact (subjuncta) with 'intelligibilia' in the natural order, by the disposition of the Creator, it sees them in a certain incorporeal light *sui generis*, as the eye of the flesh sees the things around in this corporeal light' (*de Trin.* xii. 24).

But in *de Genesi ad litteram*, xii. it is laid down that in intellectual vision the light wherein the soul sees all truly intellectual objects (omnia veraciter intellecta), is God Himself. 'Different [from the things intellectually seen] is that light itself whereby the soul is so enlightened that it beholds all things truly the object of the intellect. For that light is God Himself' (31, 59).[1] It is to be noted that this passage was written in 415, when Augustine had been twenty years a bishop, and it was his constant teaching. Thus in the (authentic) *Soliloquies*, of 387: 'God is the intellectual (intelligible) Light, in Whom and from Whom and by Whom shine intellectually all things that do intellectually shine'—i.e. as objects of pure intellect (i. 3).[2]

---

[1] For the Latin see below, pp. 53-54.

[2] 'Deus intelligibilis lux, in quo et a quo et per quem intelligibiliter lucent quae intelligibiliter lucent omnia.'

The central portions of *de Civitate Dei* were written about 415-20. In them we find the following: He praises the Platonists for having said that 'the light of our minds for learning all things is the same God Himself by Whom all things were made' (viii. 7). And: 'The incorporeal soul is in such wise illumined by the incorporeal light of the simple Wisdom of God, as the body of the air is illumined by corporeal light' (xi. 10). In the elevation described in *Confessions*, vii. 16, he says he 'found by the eye of his soul, above his mind, the Light unchangeable', which he goes on to recognize as God (the passage is given below, p. 44). And in c. 23, when seeking by what light his mind was bedewed (aspergitur) when it recognized that the unchangeable is greater than the changeable, 'he found the unchangeable and true eternity of Truth above his changeable mind'.

It is hardly necessary to say that Truth for Augustine means not subjective or logical truth—the conformity of thought to reality— but objective or ontological truth, that first and sovereign Truth which, in common with all Christian thinkers, he ultimately identifies with the Divine Being. Thus: 'Where I found Truth, there found I my God, the Truth Itself' (*Conf.* x. 35); and 'Thou art the Truth' (ibid. 66). The passage in the *Soliloquies* already referred to brings out Augustine's identification of this and the kindred great Abstracts with God: 'I invoke Thee, O God, the Truth, in Whom and from Whom and by Whom are true all things that are true' (i. 3). And he continues in parallel sentences of Wisdom, Life, Beatitude, Goodness, Beauty, Light, identifying each of them with God, 'in Whom and from Whom and by Whom' they are participated in by creatures.

Similar to the piece just cited from *Confessions*, vii. 23, are the following:

The human mind when judging of things visible is able to know that itself is better than all visible things. But when, by reason of its failings and advances in wisdom, it confesses itself to be changeable, it finds that above itself is the Truth unchangeable (*Lib. de div. Quaest.* lxxxiii. 45).

The human mind recognizes truth only in the Truth and Light of God: A man hears either man, or even angel, speaking; but, that he may feel and know that what is said is true, his mind is bedewed (aspergitur) inwardly with that light that abides eternal (*de Pecc. Mer.* i. 37).

The Truth unchangeable shines like a sun in the soul, and the soul becomes partaker of the very Truth (*de Gen. c. Manich.* i. 43).

There is the Truth unchangeable, containing all things that are unchangeably true, which belongs not to any particular man, but to all those who perceive things unchangeable and true; as it were in wondrous ways a secret and public light, it is present and offers itself in common (*de lib. Arb*. ii. 33).

Finally all truths are perceived in the unchangeable Truth itself: If you and I both see that what you say is true, and both see that what I say is true: where do we see this? Not I in you, nor you in me; but both of us in the unchangeable Truth itself, which is above our minds (*Conf*. xii. 35).

The passages cited, which cannot be explained away as metaphors, show that, according to Augustine, the human mind perceives 'ideas', 'intelligibilia', in some way in the Light of God, and grasps all truth in the Truth unchangeable, which is God. Hence his Ideology, or theory as to how the mind comes to the knowledge of 'intelligibilia', is the theory of the divine illumination. This theory, under the influence of St Augustine's authority, held sway in the early Middle Ages, until it was generally supplanted by St Thomas Aquinas's Aristotelian teaching on the subject. But it was perpetuated in the Franciscan school of St Bonaventure;[1] and St Thomas, while rejecting it, allowed it to be tenable and quite probable.[2]

Any critique of the theory would be out of place here. It can only be said that it is a piece of St Augustine's Platonism; it is in no way Pantheism; nor is it the theory of Innate Ideas; nor is it Ontologism—all which systems have laid claim to it. It could not be said to mean that God Himself is seen when 'intelligibilia' are seen in His Light or in His Truth, any more than that the sun necessarily is seen when objects are seen in its light.

D. MYSTICISM OR PLATONISM?

What has been set forth in the foregoing excursus puts us in a position to estimate the import of a number of expressions habitually used by St Augustine, and liable to be understood of mystical experiences. Such are: 'searching after and contemplating truth';[3] 'seeking after, and finding, and knowing, and perceiving, and

---

[1] See tractate of St Bonaventure, 'Utrum quidquid certitudinaliter cognoscitur a nobis cognoscatur in ipsis rationibus aeternis?' first published, along with tractates on the same subject by other Franciscan doctors, at Quaracchi in 1883.

[2] He is discoursing of the 'intellectus possibilis' and the 'intellectus agens'. After explaining that the latter is that which in the perception of 'intelligibilia' plays the same part as light in the perception of colour, he says that some Catholic doctors with much probability have made God Himself the 'intellectus agens'. His words are: 'Intellectus agens dicitur qui facit intelligibilia in potentia esse in actu, sicut lumen quod facit colores in potentia visibiles, esse actu visibiles'; and then: 'Quidam Catholici doctores satis probabiliter posuerunt ipsum Deum esse intellectum agentem' (*In Lib. ii. Sentent*. dist. 17, quaest. 2. art. 1).

[3] *c. Faust*. xxii. 56.

intuing truth';[1] contemplation is 'delight in the light of con-spicuous truth';[2] and in one place it is asked: 'What is happier than he who has the enjoyment of unshaken and unchangeable and most excellent truth?'[3] In the mouth of a later mystic such expressions would rightly be understood of fully religious contemplation and mystical experience; but with Augustine they need mean hardly more than the operations of the speculative intellect, the intellectual apprehension of philosophic or theological truth. It has to be re-membered that, for Augustine, every 'intelligible' perceived by the mind, every abstract or universal, 'the squareness of a square figure', is an unchangeable and eternal truth, perceived by the mind in some way in the Unchangeable Truth itself, and seen in the divine Light of God. So he calls such perception 'the intellectual cognition of things eternal', or 'the cognition of intelligible and supreme things that are everlasting' (de Trin. xii. 25).

There is a tendency, I think, to exaggerate greatly the neo-Platonism of the early treatises, particularly those composed between conversion and baptism, and to minimize the element of very real Christian and religious feeling that pervades them; still they are an ordered attempt to provide a philosophy of Christian belief in the ideas and terms of the most generally accepted and most spiritual philosophic system of the time, the neo-Platonism which Augustine loved as the means, humanly speaking, that had led him back to his Catholic faith. At a later date he corrected the exaggerated in-tellectualism of these early treatises;[4] but to the end he continued a convinced and devoted Platonist. His early position was that 'the Platonists with the change of very few words and opinions would become Christians'.[5]

This renders it necessary to examine with care and make quite sure that words currently taken as spoken of mystical experiences and conveying mystical doctrine, really do so. And indeed, when we consider the expressions he uses—'a glance at That Which Is', 'the perception of something Unchangeable', 'spiritual contact with the Light Unchangeable'—we may well wonder whether, under such cold intellectual and philosophical terms, he really describes the same religious experiences as do the mediaeval and later mystics in so many a passage all aglow with exuberant religious emotion, as they speak of their unions with God. Are they not, rather, the

---

[1] de Civ. Dei, xix. 19.　　　[2] Conf. xiii. 23.
[3] de lib. Arb. ii. 35.　　　[4] Retractationum, lib. i.
[5] De Vera Relig. 7. There is in the 'Introduction' to Gibb and Montgomery's edition of the Confessions (Cambridge), a sane and sensible conciliation of the Confessions and the Dialogues in regard to Augustine's intellectual and religious position just after the conversion. Also Montgomery, St Augustine, c. ii.

language of an exalted Platonism describing only the higher operations of the intellect? In other words, the question has to be faced:
Is it Mysticism, or is it Platonism?

The answer to this question is not really in doubt. The longer
pieces cited in the course of this study are not susceptible of the
suggested interpretation, and manifestly speak of religious experiences the same in kind as those described by the other great mystics·
In support of this position the following piece is of especial interest:
commencing in what seems to be mere Platonism, it develops quite
naturally into a mysticism of the highest type:

> If one be lifted up into the region of 'intellectualia' and 'intelligi-
> bilia,' where without any likeness of bodies the perspicuous truth is
> seen ... there the one and whole virtue is to love what you see, and
> the supreme happiness to possess what you love. For there the blessed
> life is drunk in from its fountain, whence are sprinkled some drops
> on this human life ... There is seen the brightness of the Lord, not
> by any vision corporeal or spiritual, but by sight (per speciem) so
> far as the human mind is capable of it, by God's grace, that He may
> speak mouth to mouth to him whom He has made worthy of such
> colloquy—the mouth, that is, not of the body but of the mind
> (de Gen. ad. litt. xii. 26, 54).

The piece is quoted in its entirety at a later place, the Latin text
being given (p. 53): it is there dealt with more fully; here it will
suffice to say that the whole of it just cited refers to experiences
during the present life.[1]

Conversely, in the striking passage in the 'Enarration' on Psalm
xli., the experience there described culminates in the cold metaphysical formula, 'We were able by a momentary glance of our
mind to gaze on Something Unchangeable'; and yet the whole context is aglow with the fire and warmth of the highest and purest
Christian mysticism (see pp. 20-24, especially §§ 9, 10).

Similarly, the piece cited in a later place (p. 51) from *Sermon* lii. 16,
describes in the very language of the mystics the supreme mystic
experience; and yet here, too, the culmination is clothed in a metaphysical garb: 'spiritual contact with the Light unchangeable.'

The remarkable passage at the end of the treatise *de Quantitate
Animae*, written just after baptism, has already been referred to.
Here Augustine speaks of the highest grades in the operations or
functions of the soul:

> The soul realizes how great it is in every way; and when it realizes

---

[1] This is true even of the expression 'drinking the blessed life in its fountain'.
In the early treatise *de Beata Vita* the term 'blessed life' is used of the knowledge
of truth and enjoyment of God that is had in this life.

this, then with a great and unbelievable confidence it makes its way unto God, that is, unto the very contemplation of Truth, and that most high and secret reward, for which such labour has been undergone.[1] And the highest spiritual state of the soul in this life consists in the vision and contemplation of Truth, wherein are joys, and the full enjoyment of the highest and truest Good, and a breath of serenity and eternity, such as certain great and incomparable souls have described in some measure, who, we believe, have seen and see such things. And I dare aver that if we with constancy follow the course that God commands, we shall by the Power of God and His Wisdom arrive at the First Cause of all things, and intellectually see It.[2]

This passage unquestionably describes the act of religious contemplation and the mystic experience. The reference to the experience of 'certain great and incomparable souls' is without doubt to the ecstasies of Plotinus and Porphyry, to be cited in Appendix. His admiration for the neo-Platonists was great, especially in the early days of conversion and baptism, when he spoke of them as 'magni homines et pene divini' (de Ordine, ii. 28).

The following shorter passage seems to speak unmistakably of the 'experience of the mystics':

To some it has been granted by a certain holy inebriation of mind, alienated from fleeting temporal things below, to gaze on the eternal light of Wisdom.[3]

Compare: If the glorious cup of the Lord intoxicate you, it shall be seen indeed in a certain alienation of your mind, but an alienation from the things of earth to those of heaven (Enar. in Psalm. ciii. 3, 13).

And it will be felt that only he could have spoken, as follows, who had enjoyed to the full the religious experience of the mystics: What do I love, when I love Thee? It is a certain light that I love, and melody and fragrance and embrace that I love when I love my God—a light, melody, fragrance, food, embrace of the inner man; where for my soul that shines which space does not contain, that

[1] 'Ingenti quadam et incredibili fiducia pergit in Deum, id est, in ipsam contemplationem veritatis, et illud, propter quod tantum laboratum est, altissimum et secretissimum praemium' (de Quant. Anim. 74).

[2] 'In ipsa visione et contemplatione veritatis, qui ultimus animae gradus est, quae sint gaudia, quae perfructio summi et veri boni, cuius serentitatis atque aeternitatis afflatus, quid ego dicam? Dixerunt haec quantum dicenda esse iudicaverunt, magnae quaedam et incomparabiles animae, quas etiam vidisse ac videre ista credimus. Illud plane ego nunc audeo tibi dicere nos si cursum quem nobis Deus imperat, et quem tenendum suscepimus, constantissime tenuerimus, perventuros per virtutem Dei atque sapientiam ad summam illam Causam, vel summum Auctorem, vel summum Principium rerum omnium: quo intellecto,' &c. (ibid. 76). 'Quo intellecto' means that it will be seen as an object of intellectual vision.

[3] 'Quibus donatum est, sancta quadem ebrietate alienatae mentis ab infra labentibus temporalibus, aeternam lucem Sapientiae contueri' (c. Faust. xii. 42).

sounds which time does not sweep away, that is fragrant which the breeze does not dispel, and that tastes sweet which fed upon is not diminished, and that clings close which no satiety disparts. This it is I love when I love my God (*Conf.* x. 8).

God the Object of Contemplation

In a number of places the Object contemplated, and described after the manner of the Platonists under the great Abstract Ideas, is definitely identified with the Christian God.

To begin with, the phrase 'Id Quod Est,' That Which Is, in the mystical elevation described in *Confessions*, vii. 23, is a refrain of the words of God to Moses in Exodus iii. 14: 'Dixit Deus ad Moysen: Ego Sum Qui Sum. Ait: Sic dices filiis Israel: Qui Est, misit me ad vos.' 'God said to Moses: I Am Who Am. He said: So shall you say to the children of Israel: He Who Is, hath sent me to you.' And so Absolute Being, of which Augustine obtained a glance, is God.

In the elevation of *Confessions*, vii. 16 (cited above, p. 31), after saying that he beheld above his soul, above his mind, the Light Unchangeable, he goes on to define the nature of that Light:

Not this ordinary light which all flesh may look upon, nor as it were a greater of the same kind, as though the brightness of this should be manifold brighter, and with its greatness take up all space. Not such was this Light, but other, yea, far other from all these. Nor was It above my soul, as oil is above water, nor yet as heaven above earth: but higher than my soul, because It made me; and I below It, because I was made by It. He that knows the Truth, knows what that Light is; and he that knows It, knows Eternity. Love knoweth It. O eternal Truth, and true Love, and lovable Eternity! Thou art my God, to Thee do I sigh day and night (*Conf.* vii. 16).

In the following pieces, too, God is the object of contemplation:

Wisdom, that is contemplation (as he explains), consists in the knowledge and love of That Which always is and unchangeably abides, namely God (*Enar. in Psalm.* cxxxv. 8).

I sought my God, that if possible I might not only believe, but even see somewhat (*Enar. in Psalm* xli. 7).

Similarly he speaks explicitly of 'contemplating the beauty of God' (*de Moribus Eccl. Cath.* 66), and simply of 'contemplating God' (*de Civ. Dei*, xix. 19).

The Mystic Union

Later mystics commonly designate their experience as Union with God. St Augustine does not employ this term; yet there are passages

in which he equivalently expresses the same idea. That in which
he most nearly approaches an utterance of the idea of union is the
one wherein he speaks of arriving in this life at 'some kind of
spiritual contact with the Light unchangeable.'[1]

Others are the following:

We strained ourselves [in the effort to realize eternal life], and
with one flash of thought touched on that Eternal Wisdom, which
abideth above all.[2]

What is that which gleams through me and strikes my heart
without hurting it; and I shudder and I kindle? I shudder inasmuch
as I am unlike it; I kindle inasmuch as I am like it. It is Wisdom,
Wisdom's self, which gleameth through me.[3]

The context shows that the Wisdom is the substantial Wisdom
of God, the Second Person of the Holy Trinity.

So in 'the holy inebriation' of ecstasy 'the eternal light of Wisdom
is beheld';[4] but 'the gaze of the mind is not able to be attuned to
the light of the Wisdom of God'.[5]

In a passage referring to contemplation exercised in this life, it is
said that corporeal images are stirred up, even when somewhat of
the spiritual and unchangeable substance of divinity is being heard.[6]

Similarly, in contemplation, 'something divine and unchangeable
is learned.'[7]

Such passages as these plainly describe the experience that the
later mystics speak of under the term union. And Augustine's
accounts of the characteristic phenomena of such experiences tally
perfectly with those of the other mystics—he may be compared
especially with Gregory and Bernard in the sequel.

Rapturous Joy

According to all the mystics who speak from first-hand experience,
rapturous joy, ecstatic delight, is a constant accompaniment of one
of the closer spiritual unions of the soul with God. To this joy

[1] 'Pervenire spirituali quodam contactu ad illam incommutabilem lucem'
(*Serm.* lii. 16).
[2] 'Extendimus nos et rapida cogitatione attingimus aeternam Sapientiam super
omnia manentem' (*Conf.* ix. 25).
[3] 'Quid est illud, quod interlucet mihi et percutit cor meum sine laesione? et
inhorresco et inardesco: inhorresco, in quantum dissimilis ei sum; inardesco, in
quantum similis ei sum. Sapientia, Sapientia ipsa est, quae interlucet mihi'
(ibid. xi. 11).
[4] 'Aeternam lucem Sapientiae contueri' (*c. Faust.* xii. 42).
[5] 'Acies mentis mei non potuit contemperari luci Sapientiae Dei' (*Serm.* lii. 16).
[6] 'De vetere vita carnalibus sensibus dedita corporeae concitantur imagines,
etiam cum aliquid de spirituali et incommutabili substantia divinitatis auditur'
(*c. Faust.* xxii. 54).
[7] 'Divinum et incommutabile aliquid discitur' (ibid.).

Augustine refers again and again in passages convincing by their eloquence and by their unmistakable personal character.

For instance, of the experience described in *Confessions*, vii 16, wherein he attained to a sight of the Light Unchangeable, he says: 'Thou didst stream forth Thy beams of light upon me most strongly, and I thrilled with love and awe.'

The idea of interior sweetness and joy is the dominant note in the long mystical passage in the 'Enarration' on the forty-first Psalm:

> a mysterious and hidden interior pleasure;
> something melodious and sweet to the ears of the heart;
> ravished by desire to the inward sweetness of God;
> rejoiced by a certain inward sweetness.[1]

He speaks of 'a holy inebriation' (*c. Faust.* xii. 42); of being 'fixed with sweet delight in the contemplation of Truth' (ibid. xxii. 56); of the delight of the human heart in the light of Truth (*Serm.* clxxix. 6); of 'arriving at a shrine of quiet' (*Ep.* cxx. 4); of 'a breath of serenity and eternity' (*de Quant. Anim.* 76).

This last piece deserves to be quoted more fully:

> The soul in contemplation will arrive at that most high and secret reward for sake of which it has so laboured; and in which are such joys, such a full enjoyment of the highest and truest Good, such a breath of serenity and eternity, as are indescribable.[2]

In more than one place he definitely gives utterance to the idea that the joy felt in the mystical experience is a foretaste of the joy of Heaven, which is but as a perpetual prolongation of those momentarily experienced during the heights of contemplation.

Thus, when 'in a flash of thought he touched the Eternal Wisdom,' he declares:

> Were this prolonged, and the vision ravish and absorb and wrap up its beholder in inward joys, so that life might be for ever like that one moment of understanding; were not this the entry into the joy of Heaven? (*Conf.* ix. 25).

Similarly:

Sometimes Thou dost admit me to an interior experience most unwonted, to a wondrous sweetness, which, if it be brought to pass

---

[1] 'Interiorem nescio quam et occultam voluptatem: nescio quid canorum et dulce auribus cordis: raptus desiderio ad interiorem dulcedinem Dei: iam quadam interiore dulcedine laetati' (*Enar. in Psalm.* xli. 9, 10).
[2] *De Quant. Anim.* 74, 76 (Latin cited above, p. 43).

in me, there will be something which will not be this life [i.e. I shall have a foretaste of eternal life.][1]

Transiency of the Experience

Here again St Augustine's descriptions of his experiences tally perfectly with those given by the great mystics. They speak of contemplation as a sustained effort of the soul, by recollection and introversion, to mount to God; when successful, the soul enjoys a brief period—often but momentary—of supreme exaltation in the contemplation of God and union with Him; this is followed by a recoil whereby the soul falls back from its height into its normal work-a-day state, wherein it recuperates its forces for another flight.

This whole process is exactly and eloquently described by Augustine in various passages. The struggle upward of the soul to raise itself above earthly things and ascend to the contemplation of God is vividly depicted in the passages from the Seventh and (especially) the Ninth Books of the *Confessions*, cited under §B, above.

In these same passages the transient and momentary character of the experience itself is brought out by such expressions as these:

In the pre-Christian experience, described in language largely Plotinian, when his mind reached to Absolute Being, it was 'in the flash of a trembling glance';[2] and in that other later experience, when mother and son together soared aloft to some realization of the heavenly life, they 'barely touched it with the whole beat of the heart,'[3] and 'in swift thought they touched the Eternal Wisdom';[4] so that the experience was but 'a moment of comprehension.'[5] Elsewhere it is said that the experience is enjoyed 'briefly and hastily, and as it were in passing,'[6] nor 'can it be endured for long.'[7]

Such momentary supreme elevations are followed by a recoil of the soul, beaten back to its normal conditions. This falling away from the height with such difficulty attained is described by all the mystics, and by Augustine in many places.

After experiencing at times a wondrous inward delight, I fall back again, weighed down by my miseries, and am absorbed again in my normal state (solita) (*Conf*. x. 65).

---

[1] 'Aliquando intromittis me in affectum multum inusitatum introrsus ad nescio quam dulcedinem, quae si perficiatur in me, nescio quid erit, quod vita ista non erit' (*Conf.* x. 65).
[2] 'In ictu trepidantis aspectus' (*Conf.* vii. 23).
[3] 'Attingimus eam modice toto ictu cordis' (ibid. ix. 24).
[4] 'Rapida cogitatione attingimus' (ibid. 25).
[5] 'Momentum intelligentiae' (ibid.).
[6] 'Perstrictim et raptim—quasi per transitum' (*Enar. in Psalm.* xli. 10).
[7] 'Vidi nescio quid quod diu ferre non potui' (Serm. lii. 16).

Speaking of an ecstasy:

He had seen somewhat wonderful, which he could not long endure, and he was recalled from God to his normal human condition (*Serm.* lii. 16).

The following piece gives utterance to the sorrow felt by the mystics at the loss of the supreme experience and the longing whereby they are consumed for its renewal:

After he had attained to the Vision of Absolute Reality, he says: Thy invisible things, understood by those that are made, I saw, but I was not able to fix my gaze thereon; but my infirmity being struck back, I was thrown again on my normal experience (*solita*), carrying with me only a memory that loved and desired what I had, as it were, perceived the odour of, but was not yet able to feed upon (*Conf.* vii. 23).

We may refer back also to *Enarratio in Psalmum* xli. § 10, already cited (pp. 23-24).

It is noteworthy that in one place the reversion to normal experience is said to be a return to articulate speech. After telling how he and Monica, in the endeavour to realize the joy of the life of the saints in heaven, 'touched it slightly with the whole force of the heart,' he goes on:

We sighed, and left there impawned the first-fruits of the spirit, and we lapsed to vocal expressions of our mouth, where the word spoken has beginning and end.[1]

Such failure of the power of articulate speech, even when there is no suggestion of ecstasy or trance, is a characteristic feature of such mystic experiences and of higher states of prayer, frequently mentioned by the mystics, from Cassian onwards.[2]

Effects of the Experience

Mention has already been made of the important passage in the treatise *de Quantitate Animae*, §§ 73-76, in certain aspects the most important for our purposes of all Augustine's utterances, being the nearest approach to a formulation of a theory of Mystical Theology. Herein, as has been observed (above, p. 27), the later division of the course of the spiritual life into the Purgative, Illuminative, and Unitive Ways, is clearly foreshadowed in the later of the 'grades',

---

[1] 'Remeavimus ad strepitum oris nostri, ubi verbum et incipitur et finitur' (*Conf.* ix. 24).
[2] An analysis and summary of Cassian's teaching on contemplation and prayer may be found in my book, *Benedictine Monachism*, pp. 63-7, 78-82.

or functions of the soul there distinguished. The seventh and highest grade, 'or rather mansion, to which the steps (gradus) lead up,' consists in the vision and contemplation of Truth. After speaking of this contemplation in itself as the full enjoyment of the 'summum bonum', and declaring that it brings the soul to the Great First Cause and Principle of all things,[1] the passage enlarges upon the intellectual effects on the mind of such a contemplation:

When it has been achieved, we shall truly see the vanity of all things under the sun, and we shall discern how far distant are mundane things from those that really are. Then shall we know how true are the Articles of Faith (credenda) that have been enjoined, and how well and wholesomely we have been nourished by Mother Church. We shall see into the nature of our bodies so as to consider the Resurrection of the Flesh to be as certain as the rising of the sun. We shall have such understanding of the Mystery of the Incarnation and the Virgin Birth, as to brush aside impatiently all cavilling. And such pleasure is there in the contemplation of Truth, such purity, such sincerity, such undoubting faith, that one now feels one had never really known what previously we had seemed to know; and death is no longer feared, but desired as the greatest gain, that the soul may be free to cleave wholly to the whole Truth (de Quant. Anim. 76: compressed and in some measure paraphrased).

In a letter written about the same time he speaks in like strain:

When, after calling upon God for aid, I begin to rise to Him, and to those things which are real in the highest sense, I enjoy at times such a vivid realization of things that abide, that I am surprised that I should require any process of ratiocination in order to persuade myself of the reality of things as truly present to me as I am to myself (Ep. iv. 2).

Here again St Augustine is in harmony with the great mystics, many of whom declare that an effect of their contemplations and unions was a clearer perception of the truths of the Catholic Faith and a deeper insight into the secret things of God—the Divine Being and Attributes, the Mysteries of the Trinity and Incarnation, the nature of the soul itself, and the workings of the cosmic laws of God's governance of the Universe. Such claims are made by Ruysbroeck, St John of the Cross, St Teresa, St Ignatius, and are formulated by Fr Augustine Baker in the following passage, which, like his other descriptions of the high mystic states, is certainly autobiographical:

In regard of the understanding, there is a divine light communicated, not revealing or discovering any new verities, but affording a

[1] Passages cited pp. 42–43.

most firm clear assurance and experimental perception of those verities of Catholic religion which are the objects of our faith, which assurance the soul perceives to be divinely communicated to her. O happy evidence of our Catholic belief. No thanks to them that believe after such sight, which is more evident than anything we see with our corporal eyes (*Sancta Sophia*, p. 533).

To sum up; in answer to the question: Is it Mysticism or Platonism? the evidence adduced shows, beyond all possibility of doubt, that St Augustine's contemplations were the same in kind, were as fully religious experiences, as the highest and most spiritual contemplations and unions of the great Christian mystics.

It remains, in order to complete the exposition of his teachings on the nature of contemplation, to investigate two special points: psycho-physical phenomena and ecstasy; and the vision of God attainable in this life.

E. Psycho-physical Phenomena: Ecstasy

In the autobiographical passages wherein St Augustine relates his own mystical experiences, there is no suggestion of any of the psycho-physical phenomena, such as ecstasy and trance, that figure so largely in the history of mysticism, as frequent accompaniments of absorption in contemplation: there is, I say, no suggestion that St Augustine's elevations of the spirit and contemplations produced any effects, quasi-hypnotic or other, in his body. Yet the phenomena of ecstasy, with its alienation of the senses, were familiar to him. The place wherein he deals ex professo with the problems involved in these phenomena, is the last Book of *de Genesi ad litteram*, a psychological discussion arising out of St Paul's description of his great mystical experience (2 Cor. xii. 2-4); but he deals with these same problems also incidentally in many passages of his works.

The physical side of ecstasy is thus described:

When the attention of the mind is wholly turned away and withdrawn (penitus avertitur atque abripitur) from the bodily senses, it is called an ecstasy. Then whatever bodies may be present are not seen with the open eyes, nor any voices heard at all (*de Gen. ad litt.* xii. **12**, 25). It is a state midway between sleep and death: The soul is rapt (rapitur) in such wise as to be withdrawn (avertatur) from the bodily senses more than in sleep, but less than in death (ibid. **26**, 53).

Its causes are thus stated: Ecstasy is a departure (excessus) of the mind, which sometimes happens by fright, but sometimes by some revelation, through an alienation of the mind from the senses of the body, in order that to the spirit may be shown what is to be shown (*Enar. in Psalm.* lxvii. 36); cf. *Enar.* ii. *in Psalm.* xxx. serm. i. 2, where it is similarly said that ecstasy is caused by fright or by rapt attention (intentio) to things above, so that in some way things below drop out of memory (consciousness).

In a fully religious ecstasy the subject 'is withdrawn from the bodily senses and is carried away unto God and afterwards is restored to his mortal members'[1] (*Serm.* lii. 16).

The following speculations on St. Paul's words, 'Whether in the body or out of the body, I know not,' throw light on St Augustine's ideas of the psychology of ecstasy:

He did not know whether, when rapt to the third heaven, he was in the body, as the soul is in the body when the body is said to live, be it of one awake or of one asleep, or when in ecstasy the soul is alienated from the bodily senses; or whether his soul had altogether gone forth from his body, so that the body lay dead, until, when the revelation was over, his soul was restored to the dead members: so that he did not awake as one asleep, nor, as one alienated in ecstasy, return to his senses; but as one dead, came to life again. But because, when his soul was alienated from his body, it was uncertain whether it left his body quite dead, or after some manner of a living body the soul was there, but his mind carried away to see or hear the unspeakable things of that vision—for this reason, perhaps, he said: Whether in the body or out of the body, I know not; God knoweth (*de Gen. ad litt.* xii. 5, 14).

See also comment on same text in the *Liber de videndo Deo* (*Ep.* cxlvii.), cited below (p. 58).

In this passage a distinction is drawn between the soul (anima) which during an ecstasy remains in the body, and the mind (mens) which is withdrawn from the bodily senses. In most of the places that deal with the phenomena of ecstasy it is the mind (mens or animus) that is said to be alienated from the body; but in some it is the soul (anima) or even the person. The passage just cited, being that wherein he strives with most precision to attain to scientific accuracy, may be taken as the truest expression of his thought; and it is also the one most in harmony with the data of psychology. According to it Augustine's idea of what takes place in ecstasy is an alienation of the mind from the bodily senses, but not of the soul from the body.

So much on the psycho-physical side of ecstasy.

The more spiritual or religious side—that which takes place in

---

[1] 'Abreptus a sensibus corporis et subreptus in Deum: redditus mortalibus membris.'

the soul when in this condition—is delineated in the following piece, which, like the rest, bears unmistakable characteristics of being the record of actual personal experience:

'*I said in my ecstasy: I am cast forth from the sight of Thy eyes*' (Ps. xxx. 23). It seems to me that he who said this had lifted up to God his soul, and had poured out above himself his soul (Ps. xli. 5, O.L.), and had attained by some spiritual contact to the Light unchangeable, and had been unable, through weakness of sight, to endure it; but had fallen back into his feebleness and languor, and had compared himself with that Light, and had felt that he could not yet attune the glance of his mind to the light of the wisdom of God. This he had done in an ecstasy withdrawn from the senses of the body, and carried away unto God; and when he was recalled from God to his normal human condition he said: I said in my ecstasy. For he saw somewhat wonderful in the ecstasy which he could not long endure; and being restored to his bodily frame and to the many thoughts of mortal things, he said: I am cast forth from the sight of Thy eyes (*Serm.* lii. 16).

In certain places, above all in Book xii. of *de Genesi ad litteram*, in passages wherein thought and language vie with each other in the effort to rise to the supreme heights of human experience, Augustine describes the nature of the experiences of the soul—and manifestly of his soul—in its most spiritual contemplations, while in the state of ecstasy.

It is necessary here to refer back to what was set forth in the 'Excursus on Augustine's Ideology', on the distinction of the three kinds of perception or vision: corporeal, spiritual or imaginary, and intellectual. His doctrine on the content of ecstasy, on what takes place in mind and soul during it, is based on this division.

Frequently in ecstasy it is a case of the second kind of vision, the 'spiritual' (imaginary), as in St Peter's ecstasy, when he saw the sheet let down from heaven, with four-footed beasts and creeping things; but sometimes it is a case of the third, or 'intellectual', the soul being raised to the realm of things purely intellectual (intellegibilia).[1]

---

[1] The twofold kind of vision in ecstasy is brought out also in the following: Ecstasy is an alienation of the mind from the senses of the body, that the spirit of a man taken up by the divine Spirit may be free to attend to the receiving and beholding images: as to Peter was shown the sheet let down from heaven. ... (Or) the mind may be so affected that it comprehends not images of things, but beholds the things themselves, as wisdom and justice are intellectually seen, and every unchangeable and divine species (i.e. 'idea' in the divine mind, p. 52)—'ita mens afficitur ut non rerum imagines coniecturali examinatione intelligat, sed res ipsas intueatur, sicut intelligitur sapientia et iustitia omnisque incommutabilis et divina species' (*De diversis Quaest. ad Simplicianum,* i. Quaest. i. 1).

If, as one is rapt from the senses of the body, so as to be among those images of bodies which are seen by the spirit (imagination); in the same way may one be rapt from them also, so as to be lifted up into that region of intellectual or intelligible things, where without any image of body the perspicuous truth is perceived and is obscured by no mists of false opinions; there the virtues of the soul have no scope for their operations or labours: for neither is there lust to be restrained by temperance, nor adversities to be borne by fortitude, nor iniquity to be punished by justice, nor evils to be avoided by prudence. There the sole and all-embracing virtue is to love what you see, and the supreme happiness to possess what you love. For there the blessed life is drunk at the fountain head, whence there drop some sprinklings on this human life, that amid the trials of this world one may live with temperance, fortitude, justice, and prudence. Since it is for the sake of attaining unto that where will be an untroubled quiet, and an ineffable vision of truth, that the labour is undertaken of restraining oneself from pleasure, and enduring adversities, and helping the needy, and resisting deceivers. There is seen the brightness of the Lord, not by any symbolic vision, whether corporal or spiritual (imaginary); but by 'species', not by enigmas (aenigmata), in so far as the human mind can grasp it, according to the grace of God who takes hold of it, that God may speak mouth to mouth to him whom He hath made worthy of such colloquy: not the mouth of the body, but of the mind.[1]

The term 'species' will frequently occur in what follows. The contrast between 'fides' and 'species' is based on St Paul, 2 Cor. v. 6, 7: 'scientes quoniam dum sumus in corpore, peregrinamur a domino: per fidem enim ambulamus et non per speciem.' Gr. διὰ πίστεως οὐ διὰ εἴδους. The English versions all translate: 'We walk by faith, not by sight'; but R.V. adds in margin: Gr. 'appearance'. In other N.T. passages εἶδος, species, is translated ' form', e.g. in the one most akin, John v. 37: 'Ye have neither heard God's Voice at any time, nor seen His Form.'

The familiar 'walking by faith, not by sight,' certainly fails to render the meaning of εἶδος and 'species'; nay, even suggests one altogether inadequate, at any rate according to Augustine's mind. The Lexicon says that in philosophical writings εἶδος is used as equivalent to 'essence'; I do not find this meaning of 'species' in the

---

[1] 'Porro autem, si quemadmodum raptus est a sensibus corporis, ut esset in istis similitudinibus corporum, quae spiritu videntur, ita et ab ipsis rapiatur, ut in illam quasi regionem intellectualium vel intellegibilium subvehatur, ubi sine ulla corporis similitudine perspicua veritas cernitur, nullis opinionum falsarum nebulis offuscatur, ibi virtutes animae non sunt operosae ac laboriosae. ... Una ibi et tota virtus est amare quod videas et summa felicitas habere quod amas. Ibi enim beata vita in fonte suo bibitur, unde aspergitur aliquid huic humanae vitae... Ibi videtur claritas domini non per visionem significantem sive corporalem sive spiritalem, sed per speciem non per aenigmata, quantum eam capere humana mens potest, secundum adsumentis Dei gratiam, ut os ad os loquatur Deus ei quem dignum tali conloquio fecerit, non os corporis, sed mentis, sicut intelligendum arbitror, quod de Moyse scriptum est (de Gen. ad litt. xii. 26, 54; ed. Zycha, 'Corpus Viennense').

Dictionaries, but it appears to be Augustine's, as 'per speciem qua Deus est quidquid est,' cited below from *de Gen. ad litt.* xii. **28**, 56 (p. 56).[1] Accordingly the word 'species' is used untranslated wherever it occurs. Augustine is not forcing St Paul by taking 'per speciem' as meaning 'by essence'. Similarly St Paul's 'in aenigmate' (1 Cor. xiii. 12) is left untranslated, as neither 'darkly', nor 'in a riddle', represents its full meaning.[2]

In the foregoing passage the 'untroubled, quiet, and ineffable vision of truth' seems principally to refer to the joys of the future life; but the remainder—all that is reproduced in the Latin text— describes experiences enjoyed by some souls while still in this life, and does not refer to the vision of God in the life everlasting: this is clear from the passage itself, and from the context, the entire book being concerned with the phenomena of the different kinds of vision, or perception, in this life.

St Augustine's distinction as to the objects perceived in the two kinds of ecstasy, corresponds to that drawn by later mystics between contemplations and unions that are sensible, and those that are purely intellectual (St Teresa, St John of the Cross, and especially Fr Baker, *Sancta Sophia*, pp. 520 and 531).

We now come to perhaps the most difficult piece with which we shall have to deal, that wherein Augustine seeks to determine the object perceived in ecstasy of the highest and most purely intellectual kind. I translate quite literally and give the Latin.

Among the intellectual objects of vision, some are seen in the soul itself, as the virtues: ... these are intellectually seen. Distinct, however [from things intellectually seen], is that Light Itself, whereby the soul is so enlightened that it beholds, whether in itself or in that Light, all things truly the object of the intellect. For that Light is God Himself; but the soul, although rational and intellect- ual, is a creature made after His image, which when it endeavours to fix its gaze on that Light, quivers through weakness and is not able. Yet still thence [i.e. from the Light] is whatever it intellectu- ally perceives as it is able. When it is borne away thither, and with- drawn from the bodily senses [i.e. in ecstasy] is more expressly presented to that vision, not in local space but in some way of its

---

[1] Compare: 'Species in re mutabili qua est quidquid illud est' (*de Civ. Dei*, viii. 6). In the passage on the Platonic Ideas cited in the Excursus (p. 52), 'species' is given along with 'forma' and 'ratio', as the equivalent of 'idea'.

[2] Augustine gives the following explanation of 'aenigma' in reference to St Paul: Velamen omni modo intercludit aspectum; aenigma vero, tamquam per speculum, nec evidentissimam detegit speciem, nec prorsus obtegit veritatem (*de div. Quaest. ad. Simp.* ii. *init.*).

own, even above itself it sees That by help of which it sees whatever
it intellectually sees even in itself.[1]

The words 'illi expressius visioni praesentatur' are just translated
literally, because I am not sure of their meaning. Pusey, who cites
the passage in illustration of *Confessions* vii. 23, takes 'visioni' objectively and translates: 'The soul is placed more expressly in the
presence of That Vision,' i.e. the divine Light.

This is, to me, a difficult passage, and its meaning in various
points obscure. But it seems to show that, in St Augustine's conception, in an ecstasy of the intellectual order, the soul not only
sees 'in' the divine Light, but in some way sees that divine Light
which is God Himself. This gives rise to the main question discussed
in this place by St Augustine: Whether in this life any man has
ever seen the divine Essence.

F. THE VISION OF GOD

In this same Book xii. of *de Genesi ad litteram*, and in *Ep.* cxlvii.,
called also *Liber de videndo Deo*, St Augustine discusses whether and
how God can be seen in His Essence in this life, as in the next. In
what follows no attempt is made to consider the philosophical and
theological bearings of St Augustine's positions, or to determine
whether they be true; the treatment is a purely historical attempt
to ascertain what his teaching was, and to indicate briefly its effect
on subsequent thought.

The classic cases on which the discussion turns are those of Moses
and St Paul.

In regard to Moses, Augustine bases the discussion on the text in
Num. xii. 8, which he cites thus: 'Os ad os loquar ad illum in specie
et non per aenigmata, et claritatem Domini vidit.' This Old Latin
is an exact rendering of the Septuagint; and the Hebrew, as represented in the Revised Version, is practically the same: 'My servant
Moses is not so: with him will I speak mouth to mouth, even
manifestly, and not in dark speeches; and the form of the Lord shall
he behold.' The Vulgate differs somewhat: 'I speak to him mouth

---

[1] 'Sic etiam in illo genere intellectualium visorum alia sunt quae in ipsa anima
videntur, velut virtutes ... ipsae intellectualiter videntur ... Aliud autem est ipsum
lumen, quo inlustratur anima, ut omnia vel in se vel in illo veraciter intellecta
conspiciat. Nam illud iam ipse Deus est, haec autem creatura, quamvis rationalis
et intellectualis ad eius imaginem facta, quae cum conatur lumen illud intueri
palpitat infirmitate et minus valet. Inde est tamen quidquid intellegit sicut valet.
Cum ergo illuc rapitur et a carnalibus subtracta sensibus illi expressius visioni
praesentatur, non spatiis localibus, sed modo quodam suo, etiam supra se videt,
quo adiuta videt quidquid etiam in se intellegendo videt' (*de Gen. ad litt.* xii. 31,
59, ed. Zycha).

to mouth; and plainly and not by riddles and figures doth he see the Lord.' Augustine takes 'species' in his text as signifying 'essence' (see above, pp. 53-54), and comments as follows:

Moses longed to see God in that substance whereby He is God [i.e. in His divine Essence], not by any similitude of a bodily creature, but by His 'species', as far as a rational and intellectual creature can grasp it, withdrawn from all bodily sense and from all significative image (enigma) of the spirit [that is, from the two lower kinds of vision].[1]

This is St Augustine's account of what Moses asked God to manifest to him, as narrated in Exod. xxxiii.; and though it is not said there that the request was granted—nay, though it is rather implied that it was not: Man shall not see My Face and live—still he looks on the text in Num. xii. 8 as proving that the request was granted, and that Moses did see the divine Essence—'he saw', vidit. His explanation of how this could be is the following:

In that 'species' whereby He is God He speaks beyond all words more secretly and immediately by an ineffable speech, where whoso

[1] 'Concupiverat videre Deum, non utique sicut viderat in monte nec sicut videbat in tabernaculo, sed in ea substantia, qua Deus est, nulla adsumta corporali creatura, quae mortalis carnis sensibus praesentetur, neque in spiritu figuratis similitudinibus corporum, sed per speciem suam, quantum eam capere creatura rationalis et intellectualis potest sevocata ab omni corporis sensu, ab omni significativo aenigmate spiritus.'

Then Moses's petition in Exod. xxxiii. is described: 'Ostende mihi Temet ipsum manifeste ut videam Te'; and again: 'Ostende mihi claritatem tuam'; and the answer: 'Non videbit homo faciem meam et vivet.' Augustine continues: 'Nisi tamen concupitam et desideratam Dei claritatem Moyses videre meruisset, non in libro Numerorum diceret Deus: Os ad os loquar ad illum in specie et non per aenigmata, et claritatem Domini vidit. Neque enim hoc secundum substantiam corporis, quae carnis sensibus praesentatur, intellegendum est; nam utique sic loquebatur ad Moysen facie ad faciem, contra in contra, quando tamen dixit ei: Ostende mihi Temet ipsum. Illo ergo modo in illa specie, qua Deus est, longe ineffabiliter secretius et praesentius loquitur locutione ineffabili, ubi Eum nemo vivens videt vita ista, qua mortaliter vivitur in istis sensibus corporis, sed nisi ab hac vita quisque quodammodo moriatur sive omnino exiens de corpore sive ita aversus et alienatus a carnalibus sensibus, ut merito nesciat, sicut Apostolus ait, utrum in corpore an extra corpus sit, cum in illam rapitur et subvehitur visionem.

'Quapropter si hoc tertium visionis genus, quod superius est non solum omni corporali, quo per corporis sensus corpora sentiuntur, verum etiam omni illo spiritali, quo similitudines corporum spiritu, non mente cernuntur, tertium caelum appellavit Apostolus, in hoc videtur claritas Dei, cui videndae corda mundantur. Unde dictum est: Beati mundicordes, quia ipsi Deum videbunt, non per aliquam corporaliter vel spiritaliter figuratam significationem tamquam per speculum in aenigmate, sed facie ad faciem, quod de Moyse dictum est "os ad os," per speciem scilicet, qua Deus est quidquid est, quantulumcumque Eum mens, quae non est quod Ipse, etiam ab omni terrena tale mundata, ab omni corpore et similitudine corporis alienata et abrepta capere potest. ... Cur autem non credamus, quod tanto Apostolo, rapto usque ad istam excellentissimam visionem, voluerit Deus demonstrare vitam, in qua post hanc vitam vivendum est in aeternum?' (de Gen. ad. litt. xii. 55, 56 (27, 28).

sees Him will not live with that life with which we mortals live in the bodily senses; but unless he be in some sort dead to this life, whether as having wholly departed from the body, or as being so withdrawn and alienated from the carnal senses that he knows not whether he be in the body or out of the body, he is not rapt and uplifted to that vision (de Gen. ad litt. xii. 27, 55).

In this kind of vision is seen the brightness (claritas) of God, not by some corporal or spiritually figured signification, as through a glass in an enigma, but face to face, or, as Moses, mouth to mouth; that is, by the 'species' by which God is what He is, how little soever the mind, even when cleansed from all earthly stain, and alienated and carried out of all body and image of body, is able to grasp Him (ibid. 28, 56).

St Paul also 'was rapt unto this transcendent vision, wherein we may believe that God vouchsafed to show him that life wherein, after this life, we are to live for ever' (ibid.).

The Third Heaven whereunto St Paul was rapt is that which is seen by a mind so separated and removed and wholly withdrawn from the carnal senses and cleansed, that those things which are in that Heaven, and the very Substance of God, and God the Word, in the charity of the Holy Ghost, it is able ineffably to see and to hear (ibid. 34, 67).[1]

It is difficult to decide which was written first, Book xii. of de Genesi ad litteram or the Liber de videndo Deo (Ep. cxlvii.); both seem to have been composed about 415. The problem envisaged in the second work is the vision of God by the just in heaven; but the question of the possibility of God being seen in His Essence by one still in this life, is handled on lines parallel to those just recited. The relevant passages are cited in the footnotes (next page).

The desire of the truly pious, by which they long and eagerly are inflamed to see God, is to see Him not under any appearance, but in the Substance in which He is That He is. This was Moses's desire, to see God in His own Nature, as He will be seen by the saints in heaven, as He is. He was not satisfied that God should speak to him 'face to face' under a figure or appearance, but asked: Show me Thyself openly, that I may see Thee.

The possibility is discussed as follows:

The question may be raised, How the Very Substance of God

---

[1] 'Si caelum tertium recte accipimus ... quod mente conspicitur ita secreta et remota et omnino abrepta a sensibus carnis atque mundata, ut ea quae in illo caelo sunt, et ipsam Dei substantiam Verbumque Deum, per quod facta sunt omnia, per caritatem Spiritus Sancti ineffabiliter valeat videre et audire: non incongruenter arbitramur et illuc esse Apostolum raptum et ibi fortassis esse Paradisum omnibus meliorem et, si dici oportet, paradisum paradisorum' (de Gen. ad litt. 67 (34).

could have been seen by some while still in this life,—unless it be that the human mind may be divinely rapt from this life to the angelic life, before it be separated from the flesh by ordinary death. So was he rapt, who heard unspeakable words that man may not utter, where to such a degree occurred a withdrawal of the attention from the senses of this life, that he declared he knew not whether he was in the body or out of the body: that is, whether, as is wont to happen in a more vehement ecstasy, his mind was alienated from this life to that, the bond with the body remaining; or whether there was a complete severance, as happens in real death. Thus it comes about that that is true which was said: No one can see My face and live,—because the mind must be withdrawn from this life when it is carried away to the ineffableness of that vision; and also, that it is not incredible that even this transcendent revelation has been granted to certain holy men not yet dead in the full sense that they continued to be corpses for burial (op. cit. 31).

St Augustine goes on to declare his belief that Moses's petition was granted, and that he saw God 'as He is', with the contemplation of the saints in heaven.[1]

Whatever may be thought of it, St Augustine's meaning in the above passages is not in doubt—they speak for themselves with

[1] (N.B.—In these passages 'species' has meaning 'appearance' or 'form'.) 'Desiderium veraciter piorum, quo videre Deum cupiunt et inhianter ardescunt, non, opinor, in eam speciem [='appearance'] contuendam flagrat, qua ut vult apparet, quod Ipse non est; sed in eam substantiam, qua Ipse est quod est. Huius enim desiderii sui flammam sanctus Moyses ostendit. (God while speaking to Moses 'face to face') erat in ea specie qua apparere voluerat, non autem Ipse apparebat in natura propria, quam Moyses videre cupiebat' (§ 20).

'Nunc quaeritur quo modo videatur Deus non ea specie, qua et in isto saeculo quibusdam voluit apparere, sed quo modo videatur in illo regno, ubi Eum filii eius videbunt, sicuti est. Tunc quippe satiabitur in bonis desiderium eorum, quo desiderio flagrabat Moyses, cui loqui ad Deum facie ad faciem non sufficiebat et dicebat: Ostende mihi Temet ipsum manifeste, ut videam Te' (§ 26).

'Deinde potest movere, quo modo iam ipsa Dei substantia videri potuerit a quibusdam in hac vita positis, propter illud quod dictum est ad Moysen: Nemo potest faciem meam videre et vivere, nisi quia potest humana mens divinitus rapi ex hac vita ad angelicam vitam, antequam per istam communem mortem carne solvatur. Sic enim raptus est, qui audivit illic ineffabilia verba quae non licet homini loqui, ubi usque ad ea facta est ab huius vitae sensibus quaedam intentionis aversio, ut sive in corpore sive extra corpus fuerit, id est utrum, sicut solet in vehementiore exstasi, mens ab hac vita in illam vitam fuerit alienata manente corporis vinculo, an omnino resolutio facta fuerit, qualis in plena morte contingit, nescire se diceret. Ita fit ut et illud verum sit quod dictum est: Nemo potest faciem meam videre et vivere, quia necesse est abstrahi ab hac vita mentem quando in illius ineffabilitatem visionis adsumitur, et non sit incredibile quibusdam sanctis nondum ita defunctis, ut sepelienda cadavera remanerent, etiam istam excellentiam revelationis fuisse concessam' (§ 31).

'Quod dicere institueram, desiderio eius (Moysis) etiam illud, quod petierat, fuisse concessum, in libro Numerorum postea demonstratum est, ubi Dominus dicit se apparere Moysi per speciem, non per aenigmata, ubi etiam addidit dicens: Et gloriam Domini vidit: ... ut quem ad modum concupiverat, videret Deum sicuti est, quae contemplatio cunctis filiis in fine promittitur' (§ 32). (Ed. Goldbacher, 'Corpus Viennense'.)

unmistakable clearness.[1] St Thomas so understood them, and accepted their teaching quite definitely.[2] Probably on this range of subjects there is no better commentator on St Thomas than the seventeenth-century Spanish Dominican, Vallgornera, and his summing up is: 'Ergo in doctrina Divi Thomae Moyses et Paulus in via viderunt divinam essentiam per modum transitus.'[3] But though St Thomas takes these two as palmary instances, it is not the case that he would limit to Moses and St Paul the Vision of God's Essence, but implies that to others also may have been, and has been, granted the same vision: this appears clearly from the passages referred to in the de Veritate.[4]

We have to consider St Augustine's position on this point. I think that, like St Thomas, he does not limit this supreme vision to Moses and St Paul, but holds that it is enjoyed by others. The passage cited from the Liber de videndo Deo speaks of its being granted to 'certain holy men'—though, expressed thus generally, it is open to the contention that the reference is solely to the two cases explicitly spoken of. But the concluding words of § 54 of de Genesi ad litteram, xii. (cited above, § E, p. 53) seem to show that the case of Moses is

[1] The Augustinian theologian Berti, while recognizing their meaning, puts forward the view that St Augustine changed his mind at a later date. He relies chiefly on de Trin. ii. 27; but the question there discussed is whether Moses saw the divine Essence with his bodily eyes (Berti, Opus de theol. Disciplinis, Lib. iii. c. vi.). Moreover, the dates assigned for writing of de Trin. are 400–16, of de Genesi ad litteram 401–15; consequently de Trin. ii. was prior to de Genesi ad litteram xii. Other authorities, too, say that he changed his mind; I can see no evidence of it in the passages cited in support of this view. Certainly in the 'Retractations', written in 426, in neither chapter, on de Genesi ad litteram or de videndo Deo, does he retract or make any reference to what he has taught on this point. St Augustine's paramount authority has secured for his theory a certain amount of hesitating acceptance from later theologians. St Thomas's acceptance is due, it may safely be said, to his reverence for St Augustine. But it is counter to the general trend of theological thought, even among the mystics, and has been a source of embarrassment to St Thomas's commentators.

[2] 'Summa, secunda secundae', quaest. clxxv. 'de Raptu', arts. 3 and 4; clxxx. 'de Vita Contemplativa', art. 5: more fully De Veritate, quaest. x. art 11, xiii. arts. 2, 3 and 4. We may cite his words in Comment on 2 Cor. xii. 2–4: 'Paulus dicitur raptus ad tertium caelum, quia sic fuit alienatus a sensibus et sublimatus ab omnibus corporalibus, ut videret intelligibilia nuda et pura eo modo quo vident angeli et anima separata; et quod plus est, etiam ipsum Deum per essentiam, ut Augustinus expresse dicit. ... De Moyse autem, quod viderit Deum per essentiam, patet'—and he reproduces St Augustine's argument (In Ep. ii. ad Cor. xii. Lectio i).
[3] Mystica Theologia D. Thomae, 1662; ed. 1911, i. 485.
[4] According to Haeften, Bañez, the great Dominican commentator on St Thomas, does definitely limit this privilege to Moses and St Paul (Haeften, Monasticae Disquisitiones, Comm. in Vitam S.P.B., p. 169). Besides the places in St Thomas referred to in text, cf. 'Summa' Pars Prima, quaest. xii. art 11, ad. 2: 'supernaturaliter et praeter communem ordinem mentes aliquorum in hac carne viventium, sed non sensibus carnis utentium, usque ad visionem suae essentiae elevavit (Deus), ut dicit Augustinus de Moyse et de Paulo.' Here it seems that these two are only examples of the 'some', 'aliqui', who have been raised to the vision.

introduced in illustration of the account there given of what is experienced by anyone raised to the highest kind of intellectual vision, evidently not looked upon as a thing practically unattainable.

This seems to be borne out by another passage, the meaning of which, however, I confess is not clear to me:

The unchangeable Creator and also Moderator of changeable things so regulates all till the beauty of the entire world breaks forth like the great song of some ineffable musician; and thence pass to the eternal contemplation of 'species' those that rightly serve God, even while it is the time of faith.[1]

Whatever it may mean, this passage, based on St Paul's contrast, 'We walk by faith and not by "species",' seems to assert the possibility of contemplation by 'species' even in this life, 'the time of faith'.

It may be of interest here to refer to the passage wherein he likens St John to the Eagle, in that 'he contemplated with steady gaze the interior and eternal Light,' which for Augustine is God Himself.[2]

An interesting question arises: Did St Augustine believe that he himself had had such a vision of the divine Essence? There is nothing in the strictly autobiographical accounts (cited in § B) of his own elevations of spirit that need imply this. It is true he speaks of them as if he believed they were momentary foretastes and participations of the heavenly life; but this seems to refer only to the rapturous joy felt in these experiences, according to the testimony of all the mystics. It would, I think, be unduly pressing his words to argue that as the Beatific Vision is the essential happiness of Heaven, he therefore virtually claims to have had momentary views of it: I believe he means no more than that the joy was so great that he could imagine none greater.

It is true also that he speaks of his mind touching the eternal Wisdom, seeing the Light unchangeable, gazing on perspicuous Truth. But such expressions must not be unduly pressed in the case of so thorough a Platonist as was St Augustine. After his full conversion to Catholic Christianity his Platonism continued ineradicable, and he used the thoughts and language of Plato's philosophy, as interpreted by the neo-Platonic school, as the vehicle for the

---

[1] ' ... donec universi saeculi pulchritudo, velut magnum carmen cuiusdem ineffabilis modulatoris excurrat, atque inde transeant in aeternam contemplationem speciei qui Deum rite colunt, etiam cum tempus est fidei' (*Ep.* cxxxviii. 5). The language suggests the possibility that this passage may refer to some sort of (what is called) 'cosmic rapture', rather than a vision of God.

[2] 'Aquila ipse est Joannes, sublimium praedicator et lucis internae atque aeternae fixis oculis contemplator' (*Tract. in Ioan.* xxxvi. 5).

formulation and expression of Christian truth and theology, just as naturally and whole-heartedly as did St Thomas use those of Aristotle. Thus to argue from one of St Augustine's expressions, that as the divine Truth is to be identified with the divine Being, therefore to 'see the unchangeable Truth' is to see the divine Essence, would be, perhaps, in the case of St Thomas a valid argument, but I venture to think in the case of St Augustine it is not. It has to be remembered that he held that every truth perceived by the human mind is seen in the unchangeable Truth above the mind, which is the very Truth of God;[1] also that every idea that is the object of the pure intellect is seen in the unchangeable Light above the mind, which is God himself.[2] This does not, of course, mean that in all intellectual cognition this divine Light is itself seen, just as physical objects may be seen in the light of the sun without the sun itself being seen. But the conclusion of the passage in § 59 of *de Genesi ad litteram*, xii. does imply that the divine Light can be, and sometimes is, Itself directly seen. Moreover, it is impossible to read the account of the highest intellectual vision, cited above,[3] without the conviction that it describes a personal experience, wherein Augustine believed had been seen the Brightness of the Lord by 'species', not by enigma, in the same manner as Moses had seen it.

It is not asserted here that St Augustine had ever in fact been accorded such a vision of God's Essence, but only that it seems probable he believed he had. As was said at the outset of this inquiry, the philosophical or theological correctness or possibility of Augustine's idea is no concern of ours here; we are concerned only with ascertaining what his idea was.

Meantime it would be extravagant to suppose that Augustine believed that this supreme vision is always seen in intellectual contemplation, or is attained to in all ecstasies, even intellectual, or is a constant factor of the mystic experience. The following passages show this, speaking the language that is usual among theologians:

There is another life which is immortal, in which there are no ills. There we shall see face to face what here is seen through a mirror in enigma, even when great progress has been made in contemplating truth (*Tract. in Ioan.* cxxiv. 5).

In this life contemplation is rather in faith, and with a very few through a mirror in enigma, and in part, in some vision of unchangeable Truth (*de Cons. Evang.* i. 5).

With this compare St John of the Cross: 'It is believed that God showed his own Essence to Moses. These essential visions, such as

---

[1] *Conf.* xii. 35. [2] *De Gen. ad litteram,* xii. 59 (p. 77).
[3] Ibid. xii. 54 (p. 75).

those of St Paul, Moses, and our Father Elias, are transient and of
most rare occurrence, and scarcely ever granted, and to very few;
for God shows them only to those who, like these, are the mighty
ones of His Church and Law' (*Ascent of Carmel*, ii. 24).

The idea that a transient visitation of the *lumen gloriae* is imparted
by the fact of the mystical union, so that the difference between the
beatific vision of heaven and the mystical vision of persons still living
on earth is merely that the one is habitual and permanent, and the
other transient and exceptional (Sharpe, *Mysticism*, pp. 94, 95),
seems, as an account of normal mystical experience, to be little
conformable to the teaching of the best-accredited mystics, or (I
believe) of the theologians.

CONTEMPLATION

2. ST GREGORY THE GREAT

ANALYSIS

ST GREGORY THE GREAT

St Gregory was a Roman, born in Rome of a senatorial family about the year 540. After following the course of liberal studies of the day, he entered public life, and sometime before 573 became Prefect of the City and Governor of Rome. In 574 he determined to forsake his career in the world and become a monk; and having turned his ancestral palace on the Caelian Hill into a monastery, he entered as a monk there, and in all probability in due time became the abbot. He was sent in 579 to Constantinople as the Pope's Apocrisiarius or Nuncio, and passed six years there. While there he composed the famous book of *Morals on Job*, that will figure so largely in these pages, and addressed it in a series of familiar conferences to the little community of his monks he had brought with him from Rome. After his return to Rome he was in 590 elected Pope. He died in 604.

The story of his life and his works has been well told by Mr F. H. Dudden.[1] Here it will suffice to say that he is recognized on all hands as one of the very greatest, if not the greatest, of the Popes. His activities and his influence in every other sphere have been made the object of appreciative study, but as a mystic and teacher of mystical theology he has been strangely overlooked by recent writers on mysticism.[2] Yet he was the recognized master thereon throughout Western Europe during the five centuries of the early Middle Ages, and, along with St Augustine and pseudo-Dionysius, he was St Thomas's principal authority over the range of subjects comprised under contemplation and contemplative life.

Collections of extracts on contemplation from St Gregory's writings are made by Blosius in *Psychagogia*, Book iv., and by Abbé Saudreau in *Vie d'Union avec Dieu*; but quite half these passages are from the doubtful or certainly spurious Commentaries on Kings, on the Canticle and on the Penitential Psalms. In the following pages only the certainly authentic works will be used, and they will be found to furnish ample material. St Gregory wrote no set treatise on mystical theology; his teaching is to be found embedded in his

---

[1] *Gregory the Great: his Place in History and Thought*, 2 vols., 1905; a shorter account in Abbot Snow's *St Gregory the Great: his Work and his Spirit*, 1892.

[2] The most surprising omission of St Gregory is in the recent good, and in most cases adequate, work of Abbé Pourrat, *La Spiritualité Chrétienne*. His treatment of SS Augustine and Bernard is quite satisfactory, but St Gregory's spiritual teaching is despatched in a page, and without a word on contemplation.

principal writings, and is manifestly the record of his personal experiences. The chief continuous passages wherein he sets forth his teaching are the following:

Morals on Job: v. 52-66; vi. 55-61; viii. 49, 50; x, 31; xviii. 88-90; xxiii. 37-43; xxiv. 11, 12; xxxi. 99-102.

Homilies on Ezechiel: i. iii. 9-14; v. 12, 13: ii. i. 16-18; ii. 7-15; v. 8-20.

Pastoral Rule: i. 5, 6, 7; ii. 5, 7.

It will be found that in his teaching on contemplation St Gregory stands where we should expect the Roman to stand, midway between St Augustine and St Bernard—less intellectual than St Augustine, less emotional than St Bernard. But if he falls short of the elevation of the former and of the unction of the latter, he has a value all his own for his Roman actuality and practicality; nor will he be found devoid either of eloquence or of devotion.

One of the *Homilies on Ezechiel* (Bk. ii. Hom. ii.) is a complete sermon on the contemplative and active lives, and the nature of contemplation. So far as I know, the only modern writer who has used it is Bishop Ullathorne in the chapter on 'Prayer' in the book *Christian Patience*. The second portion of it (§§ 12-14) is given in *Benedictine Monachism* (p. 83) as a summary of St Gregory's teaching on contemplation. It is here reproduced in order to provide a preliminary general idea as to St Gregory's mind on the subject.

12. There is in contemplation a great effort of the mind, when it raises itself up to heavenly things, when it fixes its attention on spiritual things, when it tries to pass over all that is outwardly seen, when it narrows itself that it may be enlarged. And sometimes indeed it prevails and soars above the resisting darkness of its blindness, so that it attains to somewhat of the unencompassed Light by stealth and scantily; but for all that, to itself straightway beaten back it returns, and out of that light into which panting it had passed, into the darkness of its blindness sighing it returns. In the wrestling of Jacob with the Angel, the Angel symbolizes the Lord, and Jacob, who contends with the Angel, represents the soul of each perfect man who exercises contemplation. Such a soul, when it strives to contemplate God, as if placed in a wrestle, now comes uppermost, because by understanding and feeling it tastes somewhat of the unemcompassed Light; and now falls underneath, because in the very tasting it faints away. Therefore, so to say, the Angel is worsted when by the innermost intellect God is apprehended.

13. Almighty God, when He is now known through desire and intellect, dries up in us every fleshly pleasure; and whereas aforetime we seemed to be both seeking God and cleaving to the world, after the perception of the sweetness of God, the love of the world grows feeble in us, and the love of God alone waxes strong; and

while there increases in us the strength of inmost love, without doubt the strength of the flesh is weakened.

The sweetness of contemplation is worthy of love exceedingly, for it carries away the soul above itself, it opens out things heavenly, and shows that things earthly are to be despised; it reveals things spiritual to the eyes of the mind, and hides things bodily.

14. But we must know that so long as we live in this mortal flesh no one so advances in power of contemplation as to fix the mind's eyes as yet on the unencompassed ray itself of Light. For the Almighty God is not yet seen in this brightness, but the soul beholds something beneath it, by the which refreshed it may progress, and hereafter attain to the glory of the sight of Him. When the mind has made progress in contemplation it does not yet contemplate that which God is, but that which is under Him. But in that contemplation already the taste of interior quiet is experienced. And as it is, so to say, partial and cannot now be perfect, rightly is it written in the Apocalypse: 'There was silence in heaven about half an hour.' For heaven is the soul of the righteous. When therefore the quiet of contemplation takes place in the mind, there is silence in heaven; because the noise of earthly doings dies away from our thoughts, that the mind may fix its ear on the inward secret. But because this quiet of the mind cannot be perfect in this life, it is not said that there was silence in heaven a whole hour, but about half an hour: because as soon as the mind begins to raise itself, and to be inundated with the light of interior quiet, the turmoil of thoughts soon comes back, and it is thrown into disorder from itself, and, being disordered, it is blinded.

St Gregory's conception of contemplation gathered from this and other passages, I summarized as follows in *Benedictine Monachism* (p. 59):

It is a struggle wherein the mind disengages itself from the things of this world and fixes its attention wholly on spiritual things, and thereby raises itself above itself, and by dint of a great effort mounts up to a momentary perception of the 'unencompassed Light', as through a chink; and then, exhausted by the effort and blinded by the vision of the Light, it sinks back wearied to its normal state, to recuperate its spiritual strength by exercising the works of the active life, till in due time it can again brace itself for the effort of another act of contemplation.

This is in full accord with the general teaching of mystics; but there is a strongly marked and most convincing personal tone running through all St Gregory's descriptions of the various phases in the process of contemplation. It will be well to distinguish the phases, and to bring out his teaching on each of them.

A. Preliminary Phases
Remote Preparation: Purgation

It was shown at some length that according to St Augustine's mind the remote preparation for contemplation, and its indispensable condition, is a prolonged and serious exercise in self-discipline, self-control, self-denial, and the cultivation and practice of the virtues:—that is, Christian asceticism, when rightly understood as a course of training in the spiritual life. There is no need to labour the point that St Gregory's view is the same. Most of his teaching on contemplation is contained in the *Morals on Job*, and thus is set in a solid background of Christian ethical practice, recognized on all hands as being of a high religious order.

One of the principal passages on contemplation is *Morals*, Book vi. 56-61. Here we find such warnings as these: The mind is first to be cleansed from the affection for temporal glory and from all taking pleasure in carnal concupiscence, and then to be raised up to the ken of contemplation (58). Again: It is needful that every perfect man first discipline his mind in virtuous habits, and afterwards lay it up in the granary of rest, i.e. contemplation (60). And this fundamental truth breathes through the entire work.[1]

St Gregory insists in particular that for contemplation a special measure of love is requisite:

It is necessary that whoever eagerly prosecutes the exercises of contemplation, first question himself with particularity, how much he loves. For the force of love is an engine of the soul, which, while it draws it out of the world, lifts it on high (*Mor.* vi. 58).
The greatness of contemplation can be given to none but them that love (*Hom. in Ezech.* II. v. 17).

Thus for St Gregory, as for all true mystics, purification, purgation, is the first stage in the spiritual life. In the following piece the order is: (1) mortification; (2) active good works; (3) contemplation.

Whoever has already subdued the insolencies of the flesh, has this task left him, to discipline his mind by the exercises of holy working; and whosoever opens his mind in holy works, has over and above to extend it to the secret pursuits of inward contemplation (*Mor.* vi. 56).

Proximate Preparation: Recollection, Introversion

St Gregory describes very precisely the manner in which the mind sets itself to get under way in raising itself to contemplation. His

---

[1] Cf. also *Mor.* v. 54, 55.

formal teaching on this point is contained in another of the *Homilies on Ezechiel* (II. v.).

The preliminary condition for contemplation is that the mind has been through a process of spiritual training, whereby it is able to empty itself of images and sense perceptions: 'it must first have learned to shut out from its eyes all the phantasmata of earthly and heavenly images, and to spurn and tread underfoot whatever presents itself to its thought from sight, from hearing, from smell, from bodily touch or taste, so that it may seek itself interiorly as it is without these sensations' (9).

Only when this power has by practice been acquired is the soul able to take the first step in contemplation, viz. 'Recollection': 'the first step is that the mind recollect itself—gather itself to itself' (se ad se colligit). The second step is 'Introversion': 'that it should see itself as it is when recollected' (9); should turn its eyes inwards upon itself, and consider itself thus stript of sense perceptions and free from bodily images. In this way the soul 'makes of itself a ladder for itself' (sibi de seipsa gradus ascensionis facit, 8), and mounts to the third stage, 'Contemplation': 'that it rise above itself, and make the effort to yield itself up to the contemplation of the invisible Creator.'[1]

This passage, extending over §§ 8-20 of the *Homilies on Ezechiel*, II. v., is the one piece in St Gregory's writings that may claim to be in any way a scientific or psychological exposition of the process of contemplation. Striking passages of the kind have been adduced from St Augustine, wherein is described under the act of introversion the soul's search to find God within itself, a search which for St Augustine appears to have been a process predominantly intellectual, but culminating in a fully religious experience. St Gregory's passage on introversion, though of greatly inferior power, is of much interest, as being the only account he gives, known to me, of the intellectual side of contemplation. It is difficult in places to understand, and very difficult to translate, the doctrine of contemplation being couched in terms of an allegorical interpretation of the doors and windows of Ezechiel's Temple. An attempt will be made to reproduce the teaching positively, detached as far as may be from the references to the Temple, and in a contracted form. He starts from the words of Ezechiel xl. 13, 'A door against a door,' that is, an inner door opposite to an outer one. He proceeds:

8. In the cognition of the Almighty God our first door is faith, and

---

[1] 'Primus gradus est ut se ad se colligat; secundus ut videat qualis est collecta; tertius ut super semetipsam surgat, ac se contemplationi Auctoris invisibilis intendendo subiciat' (*loc. cit.* 9).

our second is sight (species) to which, walking by faith, we arrive. For in this life we enter the door of faith, that afterwards we may be led to the other. And the door is opposite the door, because by the entrance of faith is opened the entrance of the vision of God. But if any one wishes to understand both these doors as of this life, this by no means runs counter to a sound meaning. For often we desire to contemplate (considerare) the invisible nature of Almighty God, but we are by no means able; the soul, wearied by these difficulties, returns to itself and uses itself as a ladder by which it may mount up, that first it may consider itself, if it is able, and then may explore, as far as it can, that Nature which is above it. But if our mind be distracted (sparsa) by earthly images, it can in no way consider either itself or the nature of the soul, because by how many thoughts it is led about, by so many obstacles is it blinded.

9. And so the first step is that it collect itself within itself (recollection); the second, that it consider what its nature is so collected (introversion); the third, that it rise above itself and yield itself to the intent contemplation of its invisible Maker (contemplation). But the mind cannot recollect itself unless it has first learned to repress all phantasmata of earthly and heavenly images, and to reject and spurn whatever sense impressions present themselves to its thoughts, in order that it may seek itself within as it is without these sensations. So they are all to be driven away from the mind's eye, in order that the soul may see itself as it was made, beneath God and above the body, that receiving life from What is above, it may impart life to that which it governs beneath. ...

When the soul, stript of bodily images, is the object of its own thought, it has passed through the first door. But the way leads from this door to the other, that somewhat of the nature of the Almighty God may be contemplated. And so, the soul in the body is the life of the flesh; but God, who gives life to all, is the life of souls. And if life that is communicated (vita vivificata) is of such greatness that it cannot be comprehended, who will be able to comprehend by his intellect of how great majesty is the Life that gives life (vita vivificans)? But to consider and to grasp this fact is already in some measure to enter the second door; because the soul from its estimate of itself gathers what it should think concerning the unencompassed Spirit, who incomprehensibly governs what He has incomprehensibly created.

11. When the soul raised up to itself understands its own measure, and recognizes that it transcends all bodily things, and from the knowledge of itself passes to the knowledge of its Maker, what is this, except to see the door opposite the door? However much it strive, the soul is not able fully to fathom itself; how much less the greatness of Him who was able to make the soul. But when, striving and straining, we desire to see somewhat of the invisible Nature, we are fatigued and beaten back and driven off: and if we are not able to penetrate to what is within, yet already from the outer door we see the inner one. For the very effort of the looking is the door, because

it shows somewhat of that which is inside, although there be not yet the power of entering.

So much for recollection and introversion: what is said in §§ 17-20 of *Hom. in Ezech.* II. v. on contemplation will be reproduced under the next heading, B.

The foregoing account of the process of contemplation may be illustrated by the following shorter pieces:

When with marvellous efforts it strives to rise up from corporeal things and images, it is a great thing indeed if the soul, thrusting aside the bodily form, be brought to the knowledge of itself, so as to think of itself without bodily figure, and by thus thinking of itself, to prepare a pathway to contemplate the substance of eternity. In this way it exhibits itself to itself as a kind of ladder, whereby in ascending from outward things it may pass into itself, and from itself may tend unto its Maker (*Mor.* v. 61, 62).

The three stages—recollection, introversion, contemplation—are found in the short passage:

The appearance (species) of corporeal figures the soul has drawn to itself within through the infirmity of the body. But to its utmost power it is on its guard that, when it is seeking Truth, the imagination of circumscribed vision shall not delude it, and it spurns all images that present themselves to it. For since it has fallen by them beneath itself, it endeavours without them to rise above itself; and after it has been in unseemly manner scattered over the Many, it strives to gather itself together to the One (in unum se colligere nititur), that, if it can prevail by the great force of love, it may contemplate the Being that is one and incorporeal (*Mor.* xxiii. 42).

With these may be contrasted a less intellectual account of contemplation:

When the word of God is read in secret, and the mind, conscious of its faults, strikes itself with the spear of sorrow or pierces itself with the sword of compunction, and can do nothing but weep and by its tears wash away its stains; then also at times is it caught up to the contemplation of things on high, and in the desire of them is tortured with a sweet weeping. ... And because it cannot yet cleave to heavenly things, in its fervour it finds rest in tears, being wearied out (*Hom. in Ezech.* 11. ii. 1).

B. AUTOBIOGRAPHICAL PASSAGES

Under this heading were given in the section on St Augustine certain wonderfully vivid and convincing descriptions of his personal experiences in contemplation. In St Gregory's writings I know of only one such definitely personal piece, and in it he hardly more than makes the claim to have frequently enjoyed contemplation. But there are a number of passages which, though not explicitly autobiographical, certainly are really such, being undoubtedly his endeavours to express what he had experienced.

The autobiographical piece occurs in the well-known lament at the beginning of the *Dialogues*, wherein the Saint deplores the loss of the spiritual light he had enjoyed in his monastery, before the cares of the Papacy weighed upon him:

My sad mind, labouring under the soreness of its engagements, remembers how it went with me formerly in the monastery, how all perishable things were beneath it, how it rose above all that was transitory, and, though still in the body, went out in contemplation beyond the bars of the flesh (*Dial.* i. Pref.).

Speaking elsewhere of his manner of life in the monastery, he says he was able to keep his mind almost continually on the stretch in prayer.[1] This shows that it was in prayer he found contemplation.

Of St Gregory's descriptions of contemplation, that which follows those of recollection and introversion just cited from *Hom. in Ezech.* II. v. will first be given, in order to keep more or less together that which is the most scientific and formal exposition of his doctrine on mysticism. The Latin of this and the subsequent pieces is given in the footnotes.

He starts from the text 'Slanting windows in the chambers' (Ezech. xl. 16):

17. In slanting, or splayed, windows that part by which the light enters is narrow, but the inner part which receives the light is wide; because the minds of those that contemplate, although they have but a slight glimpse of the true light, yet are they enlarged within themselves with a great amplitude. For even the little they see, they are scarcely able to hold. It is very little indeed that those who contemplate see of eternity; but from that little the fold of their minds is extended unto an increase of fervour and love.

18. He who keeps his heart within, he it is who receives the light of contemplation. For they that still think immoderately of external things, know not what are the chinks of contemplation from the eternal light. For that infusion of incorporeal light is not received along with the images of corporeal things; because while only visible things are thought of, the invisible light is not admitted to the mind.[2]

---

[1] 'In monasterio positus valebam in intentione orationis pene continue mentem tenere' (*Hom. in Ezech.* I. xi. 6).

[2] '*Et fenestras obliquas in thalamis*'.

'In fenestris obliquis pars illa per quam lumen intrat angusta est, sed pars interior quae lumen suscipit lata, quia mentes contemplantium quamvis aliquid

One of the descriptions of the act of contemplation occurs in the continuous explanation of St Gregory's theory in *Homilies on Ezechiel*, II. ii. which has been cited (p. 66) as the basis of this exposition of his mystic doctrine (§ 12); it should be read again—the Latin is given in the footnote.[1]

Other descriptions occur in the *Morals on Job*; such are the following (Oxford Library of Fathers):

The mind of the elect already bears down all earthly desires beneath itself, already mounts above all the objects that it sees are of a nature to pass away, is already lifted up from the enjoyment of things external, and closely searches what are the invisible good things, and in doing the same is frequently carried away into the sweetness of heavenly contemplation; already it sees something of the inmost realities as it were through the mist, and with burning desire strives to be admitted to the spiritual ministries of the angels; it feeds on the taste of the unencompassed Light, and being carried beyond self, disdains to sink back again into self. But forasmuch as the corruptible body still weighs down the soul, it is not able to cleave for long to the Light which it sees in a momentary glimpse. For the mere infirmity of the flesh drags down the soul, as it mounts above itself, and brings it down sighing to think of lowly cares and wants[2] (*Mor.* viii. 50).

Sometimes the soul is admitted to some unwonted sweetness of interior relish, and is suddenly in some way refreshed when breathed

---

[1] tenuiter de vero lumine videant, in semetipsis tamen magna amplitudine dilatantur. Quae videlicet et ipsa quae conspiciunt capere pauca vix possunt. Exiguum quippe valde est quod de aeternitate contemplantes vident, sed ex ipso exiguo laxatur sinus mentium in augmentum fervoris et amoris; et inde apud se amplae fiunt, unde ad se veritatis lumen quasi per angustias admittunt. Quae magnitudo contemplationis concedi nonnisi amantibus potest.

'Qui cor intus habet ipse quoque lumen contemplationis suscipit. Nam qui adhuc exteriora immoderatius cogitant, quae sint de aeterno lumine rimae contemplationis ignorant. Neque enim cum corporearum rerum imaginibus illa infusio incorporeae lucis capitur, quia dum sola visibilia cogitantur, lumen invisibile ad mentem non admittitur' (*Hom. in Ezech.* II. v. 17, 18).

[1] 'Est autem in contemplativa vita magna mentis contentio, cum sese ad caelestia erigit, cum in rebus spiritualibus animum tendit, cum transgredi nititur omne quod corporaliter videtur, cum sese angustat ut dilatetur. Et aliquando quidem vincit, et reluctantes tenebras suae caecitatis exsuperat, ut de incircumscripto lumine quiddam furtim et tenuiter attingat; sed tamen ad semetipsam protinus reverberata revertitur, atque ab ea luce ad quam respirando transiit, ad suae caecitatis tenebras suspirando rediit' (*Home in Ezech.* II. ii. 12).

[2] 'Ecce enim electorum mens iam terrena desideria subicit, iam cuncta quae considerat praeterire transcendit, iam ab exteriorum delectatione suspenditur, et quae sint bona invisibilia rimatur, atque haec agens plerumque in dulcedinem supernae contemplationis rapitur, iamque de intimis aliquid quasi per caliginem conspicit, et ardenti desiderio interesse spiritalibus angelorum ministeriis conatur; gustu incircumscripti luminis pascitur, et ultra se evecta ad semetipsam relabi dedignatur; sed quia adhuc corpus quod corrumpitur aggravat animam, inhaerere diu luci non valet, quam raptim videt. Ipsa quippe carnis infirmitas transcendentem se animam retrahit, atque ad cogitanda ima ac necessaria suspirantem reducit' (*Mor.* viii. 50).

on by the glowing spirit; and is the more eager the more it gains a taste of something to love. And it desires that within itself which it feels to taste sweet within, because it has in truth, from the love of its sweetness, become vile in its own sight; and after having been able in whatever way to enjoy it, it discovers what it has hitherto been without it. It endeavours to cling closely to it, but is kept back from its strength by its own remaining weakness; and because it is unable to contemplate its purity, it counts it sweet to weep, and sinking back to itself, to strew the tears of its own weakness. For it cannot fix its mind's eye on that which it has with hasty glance seen within itself, because it is compelled by its own old habits to sink downwards. It meanwhile pants and struggles and endeavours to go above itself, but sinks back, overpowered with weariness, into its own familiar darkness. A soul thus affected has to endure itself as the cause of a stubborn contest against itself, and all this controversy about ourselves causes no small amount of pain, when we are engaged in it, whatever pleasure may be blended therewith[1] (ibid. xxiii. 43).

The intervening mist of evils is first washed away from the eye of the mind by burning sorrow; and then it is illumined by the bright coruscations of the unencompassed Light flashing upon it. When this is in any way seen, the mind is absorbed in a sort of rapturous security; and carried beyond itself, as though the present life had ceased to be, it is in a way remade in a certain newness [it is re-freshed in a manner by a kind of new being: Oxf. Lib.]. There the mind is besprinkled with the infusion of heavenly dew from an inexhaustible fountain; there it discerns that it is not sufficient for that to which it has been carried, and from feeling the Truth, it sees that it does not see how great Truth itself is[2] (*Mor.* xxiv. 11).

It will be of interest to consider how far, if at all, these passages may be beholden to St Augustine. St Gregory was well versed in

[1] 'Aliquando (anima) ad quamdam inusitatam dulcedinem interni saporis admittitur, ac raptim aliquo modo ardenti spiritu afflata renovatur; tantoque magis inhiat, quanto magis quod amet degustat. Atque hoc intra se appetit quod sibi dulce sapere intrinsecus sentit, quia videlicet eius amore dulcedinis sibi coram se viluit; et postquam hanc utcunque percipere potuit, quid sine illa dudum fuisset invenit. Cui inhaerere conatur, sed ab eius fortitudine sua adhuc infirmitate repellitur; et quia eius munditiam contemplari non valet, flere dulce habet, sibique ad se cadenti infirmitatis suae lacrimas sternere. Neque enim mentis oculum potest in id quod intra se raptim conspexerit figere, quia ipso vetustatis suae usu deorsum ire compellitur. Inter haec anhelat, aestuat, super se ire conatur, sed ad familiares tenebras suas victa fatigatione relabitur. Anima sic affecta contra semetipsam grave certamen tolerat semetipsam, et omnis haec de nobis contro-versia, cum nos afficit, quamvis delectatione permixta, non modicum dolorem parit' (*Mor.* xxiii. 43).

[2] 'Prius a mentis acie exurente tristitia interposita malorum caligo detergitur, et tunc resplendente raptim coruscatione incircumscripti luminis illustratur. Quo utcunque conspecto, in gaudio cuiusdam securitatis absorbetur, et quasi post defectum vitae praesentis ultra se rapta, in quadam novitate aliquo modo recreatur. Ibi mens ex immenso fonte infusione superni roris aspergitur; ibi non se sufficere ad id quod rapta est contemplatur, et veritatem sentiendo videt quia quanta est ipsa veritas non videt' (*Mor.* xxiv. 11).

St Augustine's writings, and, as Mr Dudden shows,[1] his theology is little more than a popularization of that of Augustine, which he presented in the form that remained current throughout the early Middle Ages, so that the staple theology of those ages was in the main that of St Augustine as diluted by St Gregory.

For all that, in the passages describing his mystical experiences, traces of any dependence on Augustine seem to be few and slight. Only a single expression occurs in those just cited recalling verbally St Augustine's language:—The soul 'aliquando ad quamdam inusitatam dulcedinem interni saporis admittitur' (*Mor.* xxiii. 43); cf. Augustine: 'Aliquando intromittis me in affectum multum inusitatum introrsus ad nescio quam dulcedinem' (*Conf.* x. 65).

The pieces portraying the height of contemplation, *Morals*, xxiv. 11, and *de Genesi ad litt.*, xii. 54 (p. 53), may be compared, especially the sentences: 'ibi mens ex immenso fonte infusione superni roris aspergitur' (Greg.), and 'ibi beata vita in fonte suo bibitur, unde aspergitur aliquid huic humanae vitae' (Aug.); but there is no real resemblance of thought.

Perhaps more striking are: 'primitias sui spiritus in caelestis patriae amore ligant' (Greg. *Hom. in Ezech.* i. v. 13), and 'reliquimus ibi religatas primitias spiritus' (Aug. *Conf.* ix. 24).

In bringing out the momentary character of the act of contemplation Augustine uses the expressions: 'Perstrictim et raptim, quasi per transitum' (*Enar. in Psalm.* xli. 10); and in Gregory we find in the same connexion 'per transitum' (*Hom. in Ezech.* i. v. 12), and 'raptim' frequently. There may here be borrowing.

Again, in describing the recoil or revulsion which follows the act of contemplation, they both use the text, Wisd. ix. 15: 'the corruptible body weigheth down the soul' (Aug. *Enar. in Psalm.* xli. 10, *Serm.* lii. 16, *c. Faust.* xxii. 53; Greg. *Mor.* v. 58, viii. 50, xvii. 39, xxx. 53); and there is a general resemblance in the descriptions. But it is a resemblance not of language, but of the mental state described, which is a common experience of those who have attained to contemplation.

In short, it is likely that St Gregory was familiar with the mystical passages of St Augustine's writings, and it is possible he borrowed the expressions 'inusitata dulcedo' and 'per transitum'; but there is no reason for thinking that his passages are based on St Augustine's, or are anything else than the first-hand expression of genuine personal experience.

---

[1] *Gregory the Great*, ii. 293, 468.

(C, D). The Act of Contemplation

When dealing with St Augustine's descriptions of contemplation we found it necessary to examine his idea of the nature of the act of contemplation under two headings, a supplementary section, D, being introduced in order to find the answer to the question: Is what he speaks of merely Platonism, or is it real religious mysticism? In the case of St Gregory there is no room for any question of the kind, for he was neither Platonist nor adherent of any philosophical school.[1] Though highly intelligent, he was not pre-eminently intellectual, and what he tells of contemplation is nothing else than the endeavour to utter, as well as he can, experiences which he looked on as purely religious, in language uncoloured by any system of philosophy.

It is true he uses the same sort of expressions as Augustine, and speaks of contemplation as 'the search for Truth', and 'the contemplation of Truth'; as 'a sight of the true Light' or of 'the eternal Light.'[2] But in his mouth the words Truth and Light lack the deep content they have in Augustine's: they are not the great, vital, ontological Realities that the Platonic Ideas were to Augustine. They are but the commonplaces of theological language taken over from St John.

I do not find that St Gregory anywhere explicitly identifies this Truth with God; but there can be no doubt that by the 'Boundless Truth' (incircumscripta Veritas, *Mor.* v. 66) he means God Himself. And he does identify with God the 'Eternal Light' and the 'True Light'.[3] But there is no suggestion of Augustine's conceptions that all truth is perceived in the unchangeable Truth above the mind, and that the Light in which purely intellectual truths are seen is God Himself.

Truth and Light

For all that, it will be instructive, as in the case of Augustine, to group under headings Gregory's ways of speaking of contemplation. In the first place, then, we saw that there was a series of passages wherein Augustine spoke of the Object contemplated in the language of pure metaphysics. Of this I find in Gregory only a

[1] The only passage known to me that in any way may re-echo neo-Platonic ideas is that cited from *Mor.* xxiii. 42, above (p. 71), which speaks of the Many and the One; but this is probably due to Augustine (see p. 159; but cf. *St Luke* x. 41, 42).

[2] *Mor.* xxiii. 42, v. 66; *Hom. in Ezech.* II. v. 17, 18.

[3] 'Lux aeterna, quae Deus est' (*Mor.* xxv. 11); 'Lumen verum, Creator videlicet noster' (ibid. xxv. 9).

single instance, where he says that in contemplation 'the One and Incorporeal Being, "Esse", is contemplated.'[1]

We saw how Augustine depicts his elevations to contemplation as the result of the effort to attain to the Being that it is not subject to change. In Gregory no such intellectual hunger for the Unchangeable manifests itself. In one place, describing contemplation, he speaks of 'transcending all things changeable and inhering in the Unchangeable' (*Mor.* xxii. 35).

Augustine's predominant idea of the object of contemplation is 'Truth', the ontological Truth that is God Himself. With Gregory also the effort to attain to contemplation is to search for the Truth,[2] and its achievement is to contemplate or to feel the Truth.[3] More fully: Contemplation is 'a subtle tasting of the savour of boundless, or unencompassed, Truth,'[4] and 'the receiving the food of love from the pasture of contemplated Truth.'[5]

But St Gregory's favourite symbol, to which he returns again and again in describing contemplation, is Light. He conceives of God as the boundless or unencompassed Light—'Lumen incircumscriptum'—and contemplation is the endeavour 'to fix the eye of the heart on the very ray of the unencompassed Light.'[6] With this may be compared his description of the Beatific Vision enjoyed by the Saints in Heaven: 'To behold God's face and see the unencompassed Light.'[7] But in this life 'no one is able to fix the mind's eye on the unencompassed ray itself of Light'[8]: all it can do is 'to attain to somewhat of the unencompassed Light by stealth and scantily.'[9] To this we shall return in § F.

The 'unencompassed Light' constantly recurs as the object of contemplation: the effort to attain to contemplation is the desire to see the unencompassed Light, the striving to gaze on its radiance, the gaping at it; the achievement of contemplation is to attain to somewhat of it, by understanding and feeling to taste somewhat of it, to be fed on its taste, to be illumined by its flash or coruscation.[10]

He uses the same epithets as Augustine: thus he speaks of the

---

[1] 'Ut unum atque incorporeum Esse contempletur' (ibid. xxiii. 42).

[2] Ibid. xxiii. 42.

[3] Ibid. v. 66, xxiv. 11.

[4] 'Saporem incircumscriptae veritatis contemplatione subita subtiliter degustare' (ibid. v. 66).

[5] 'Amoris pastum de pabulo contemplatae veritatis accipere' (*Hom. in Ezech.* I. v. 12).

[6] 'Cordis oculum figere in ipso radio incircumscriptae lucis intendit' (*Mor.* xxiii. 42).

[7] 'Gloriae Conditoris assitere, praesentem Dei vultum cernere, incircumscriptum lumen videre' (*Hom. in Evang.* xxxvii. 1).

[8] *Hom. in Ezech.* II. ii. 14.

[9] Ibid. 12.

[10] *Mor.* vi. 59, x. 13 *bis*; *Hom. in Ezech.* II. ii. 12 *bis*; *Mor.* viii. 50, xxiv. 11.

Light eternal of contemplation, the Light invisible, the Light incorporeal, an infusion whereof is received in contemplation;[1] of the true Light, somewhat whereof may scantily be seen;[2] of the inward Light, a sight whereof flashes in the soul with a ray of brightness by the grace of contemplation,[3] but which man, placed in darkness, knows not as it really is;[4] of the unchangeable Light which does not in contemplation burst forth as it is on the mind's eye;[5] of the incorruptible Light;[6] of the supernal Light which our contemplation discloses to us, agape for it, and anon hides from us, failing through weakness.[7]

For St Gregory, contemplation is to pass into the Light;[8] to inhere in it, to see it hastily and taste it scantily;[9] it is to gaze on the very Fountain of Light.[10] This Light is the Light of Truth which, though not yet perceived as it is, still is let into the mind as it were through a narrow slit.[11]

'The chink of contemplation' is a favourite symbol with St Gregory: in contemplation the eternal or unencompassed Light is seen as is a sunbeam coming through a chink.[12] This is a suggestive idea, and perhaps brings out more simply than any other description his conception of the nature of contemplation. The infinite divine Light is the figure under which he conceives God's Essence: man cannot look directly on It, but may see Its ray, subdued and indistinct, as a sunbeam passing through a chink into a darkened room.

God the Object

But whatever be the figures and symbols employed, God is the Object contemplated. One in contemplation is on fire to see the face of the Creator; it is an effort to contemplate God; in contemplation God is apprehended by the innermost intellect, and with the inmost sweetness.[13] Similarly, those in contemplation endeavour to behold with their mind the brightness of the Creator,[14] and a knowledge of the divine Presence is contemplated and felt.[15] The mind is caught up to unwonted ground when it explores the Essence of the Divinity.[16]

Whoever is so rapt by contemplation, as, being raised up by divine grace, already to engage his thought on the choirs of angels,

[1] *Hom. in Ezech.* II. v. 18.   [2] Ibid. 17.
[3] *Mor.* xxiii. 41.   [4] Ibid. xxvii. 67.
[5] Ibid. v. 53.   [6] Ibid. xxxi. 101.
[7] Ibid. v. 58.   [8] *Hom. in Ezech.* II. ii. 12.
[9] *Mor.* viii. 50.   [10] Ibid. xxx. 8.
[11] *Hom. in Ezech.* II. v. 16, 17.
[12] *Mor.* v. 52; *Hom. in Ezech.* II. v. 16, 18.
[13] *Hom. in Ezech.* II. ii. 8, 12, 13: 'apprehenditur Deus.'
[14] *Mor.* xxx. 8.   [15] Ibid. xxiv. 12.   [16] Ibid. v. 62.

and fixed on things on high to hold himself aloof from all action below, is not contented with beholding the glory of angelic brightness, unless he is able to behold Him also Who is above angels. For the vision of Him is alone the true refreshment of our mind. Hence, from these choirs of angels he directs the eye of his mind to contemplate the glory of the Majesty on high: and not seeing it, he is still hungry: and at length [in the next life] seeing it he is satisfied. But while weighed down by the interposition of the corruptible flesh, we cannot see God as He is (*Mor.* xxxi. 99, 100).

In contemplation it is the divine Wisdom that is contemplated, and even touched: When in contemplation we are brought to the contemplation of Wisdom, the mere immensity thereof, which by itself lifts man to itself, denies the human mind full knowledge, so that it should by touching (tangendo) love this Wisdom, and yet never by passing through penetrate it (*Mor.* xxii. 50).

In one place is the suggestion that in contemplation God's Voice speaks in the soul:

By the grace of contemplation the Voice of the Supernal Intelligence occurs in the mind. ... The words of God are perceived in the ear of the heart ... and by supernal grace we are led to understand higher things (*Hom. in Ezech.* II. i. 17, 18).

Fervour and Joy

After this brief analysis of the more intellectual side of St Gregory's conception of contemplation, it will be well to cite a few passages of a more general character, giving a fuller account, and bringing out those elements of fervour, love, and rapturous joy which are the constant characteristics of the descriptions of their contemplations left by the great mystics.

The first passage is of interest in that it associates contemplation with prayer; this we did not find explicitly in Augustine, though it is certainly implied in many places.

When the mind, employed in prayer, pants after the form (species) of its Maker, burning with divine longings, it is united to that which is above, it is disjoined from that below; it opens itself in the affection of its fervent passion, that it may take in, and while taking in kindles itself; and whilst, with longing desire, the soul is agape after heavenly objects, in a marvellous way it tastes the very thing it longs to get (*Mor.* xv. 53).

Holy men, with the feeling of delight, are caught away unto interior things from the strife of temporal desires, so that whilst their mind is stretched wholly to the love of God, it is not rent and torn by any useless anxieties, and it hides itself in the bosom of inward love from all the disquietudes of external things (ibid. v. 9).

Falling back upon herself [from a contemplation] the soul is drawn to Him with closer bonds of love, Whose marvellous sweetness, being unable to bear, she has but just tasted of under an indistinct vision (*Mor.* v. 53).

When the mind tastes that inward sweetness, it is on fire with love (ibid. v. 58).

Many passages give utterance to the sweetness and joy which Gregory, like Augustine and Bernard and all the mystics, experienced in his contemplations and unions:

The soul is admitted to a certain unwonted sweetness of inward savour (*Mor.* xxiii. 43); it seeks after, and attains to, the sweetness of inward knowledge (ibid. xxx. 39); it is caught away to the sweetness of supernal contemplation (ibid. viii. 50); it tastes a wondrous sweetness (ibid. v. 53); it touches by a foretaste the sweetness of inmost delight, and knows the sweetness of eternal delight (*Hom. in Ezech.* i. v. 12). Thus it is absorbed in the joy of a certain security (*Mor.* xxiv. 11); it is brought into the secret joys of quiet (*Hom. in Ezech.* ii. v. 16); it is overflowed by the light of inmost quiet (ibid. ii. ii. 14); and it already tastes with inward savour the rest that is to come (ibid. i. iii. 9).

Some of these passages show that St Gregory shared the thought explicitly uttered by St Augustine (above, p. 46), that the height of contemplation is a momentary experience, a transient glimpse and foretaste, of the heavenly joys. So elsewhere: It is very little that those raised to contemplation see of eternity (*Hom. in Ezech.* ii. v. 17); still they do attain to a subtle knowledge of eternity (*Mor.* v. 66). Elsewhere contemplation is spoken of as an irradiation of the light of the heavenly country (ibid. x. 17). Often the mind is so hung aloft in divine contemplation, that it already rejoices that it perceives by a certain image somewhat of that eternal liberty which eye hath not seen nor ear heard (*Hom. in Ezech.* ii. i. 17).

Such experiences in contemplation often surpass the power of utterance and even of comprehension:

Their minds are inflamed with the love of that interior brightness, which they are able neither to see as it is, nor to utter as they see it (ibid. i. v. 13).

Often the mind of him that loves is filled with so great a gift of contemplation, that it has power to see what it has not the power to utter. The inundation of the Holy Spirit in exuberant outpouring is gathered in the soul of one in contemplation, when his mind is full beyond what he is able to comprehend (*Mor.* xv. 20).

Transiency

The transiency and momentariness of the act of contemplation is insisted on habitually by St Gregory in such expressions as these:

The contemplation is enjoyed by stealth and scantily, by stealth and in passing, delicately, suddenly, not fixedly but by snatch[1]— 'raptim', which word constantly occurs in the descriptions of contemplation.[2]

It was St Gregory's experience, as we have seen it to have been St Augustine's, that the soul can maintain itself in the act of contemplation only for a brief moment, and then, exhausted by the effort, it falls back to its normal state. This recoil is graphically and eloquently described in various passages, some of which have already been cited (*Hom. in Ezech.* II. ii. 12; *Mor.* viii. 50, xxiii. 43), (pp. 66, 73-74).

Others follow:

When the mind is suspended in contemplation; when, exceeding the narrow limits of the flesh, with all the power of her ken she strains to find something of the freedom of interior security, she cannot for long rest standing above herself, because though the spirit carries her on high, yet the flesh sinks her down below by the yet remaining weight of her corruption (*Mor.* v. 57).

Not even in the sweetness of inward contemplation does the mind remain fixed for long, in that, being made to recoil by the very immensity of the light, it is called back to itself. And when it tastes that inward sweetness, it is on fire with love, it longs to mount above itself; yet it falls back in broken state to the darkness of its frailty (ibid. v. 58).

After the contemplation described in *Morals*, xxiv. 11 (cited above p. 74):

The effort of the mind is driven back when directed towards the contemplation of Truth, by the bright encircling of its boundless nature. ... It accordingly falls back speedily to itself, and having seen as it were some traces of Truth before it, is recalled to a sense of its own lowliness (loc. cit. 12).

Like other mystics, Gregory tells of the ineffaceable memory of the experience once enjoyed, and the longing for its renewal:

Such an one, returning to good works, feeds on the memory of God's sweetness, and is nourished by pious acts without and holy

---

[1] 'Furtim et tenuiter' (*Hom. in Ezech.* II. ii. 12, II. v. 17); 'furtim et per transitum' (ibid. I. v. 12); 'subtiliter, subita contemplatio' (*Mor.* v. 66); 'non solide sed raptim' (ibid. v. 58).
[2] 'Raptim' (*Mor.* v. 58, viii. 49, 50, xxiii. 43, xxiv. 11).

desires within; and they strive always to utter the memory of it by recollecting it and speaking of it (*Hom. in Ezech.* I. v. 12).

Effects of Contemplation on the Soul

The principal effects, as expressed by St Gregory, may be grouped under the following heads:

(*a*) *Self-knowledge.*—The higher the elevation whereat the mind of man contemplates the things that are eternal, so much the more, terror-struck at her temporal deeds, she shrinks with dread, in that she thoroughly discovers herself guilty in proportion as she sees herself to have been out of harmony with that light which shines in the midst of darkness above her; and then it happens that the mind, being enlightened, entertains the greater fear, as it more clearly sees by how much it is at variance with the rule of truth (*Mor.* v. 53). (Compare *Mor.* xxiii. 43).

(*b*) *Humility* (cf. *Hom. in Ezech.* I. viii. 17).—The more that holy men advance in contemplation, the more they despise what they are, and know themselves to be nothing, or next to nothing (*Mor.* xxxv. 3).

This is like Fr Baker's teaching, that only by a Passive Union can one attain to an experimental realization of one's fundamental nothingness, and thereby to essential humility (*Sancta Sophia*, 316 ff., 534).

(*c*) *Fervour and love.*—It is very little that those who contemplate can see of eternity, but by that little the folds of their minds are extended unto an increase of fervour and love (*Hom. in Ezech.* II. v. 17).

Other passages have already been cited to the same effect (*Mor.* v. 53, 58).

(*d*) *Lessens concupiscence.*—It dries up in us every fleshly pleasure, and weakens the strength of the flesh (*Hom. in Ezech.* II. ii. 13; see the whole piece, p. 66).

(*e*) *Temptations.*—Commonly he who is most carried away in contemplation is most harried by temptation: and so, often it is wont to happen to some who make good progress, that while contemplation carries their mind above itself, temptation also immediately follows, that it be not puffed up by those things to which it is carried; so that the temptation may weigh it down lest the contemplation should puff it up, and the contemplation raise it up lest the temptation should sink it. For if contemplation so raised the mind that temptation was altogether wanting, it would fall into pride; and if temptation so weighed it down that contemplation did not lift it up, it would surely fall into sin (*Hom. in Ezech.* II. ii. 3).

It often befalls that the Spirit raises up the mind to things aloft, and, for all that, the flesh assails it with importunate temptations; and when the mind is drawn to contemplate heavenly things, it is beaten back by the images presented to it of illicit actions. For the sting of the flesh suddenly wounds him whom holy contemplation was carrying off outside the flesh, and at once the flight of contemplation illumines and the importunity of temptation obscures one and the same mind (*Mor.* x. 17).

E. PSYCHO-PHYSICAL PHENOMENA: ECSTASY

The examination of St Augustine's teaching on this subject led to the highest elevations of religious experience. It is not so with St Gregory. Still, the matter of the physical side of contemplation and ecstasy, emphasized as it has been in more modern times, must always be of importance; and the ideas thereon of any great practical mystic, as Gregory pre-eminently was, must needs repay study and prove a valuable contribution to the psychology of religious experience.

In the passages already cited, and in many others, St Gregory habitually speaks of the soul being 'rapt' in contemplation (rapere, rapi); of its being borne out of itself, or above itself, or above the world, or being carried beyond the confines of the flesh. We have to inquire whether such terminology implies those psycho-physical phenomena—rapture, trance, ecstasy, alienation of the mind or of the senses—that are the frequent concomitants of certain phases of the mystic life, certain states of prayer. The most satisfactory answer will be given by supplying the material for forming a first-hand judgement.

By contemplation we are lifted up above ourselves (*Hom. in Ezech.* i. iii. 1).

Our mind becomes above itself (*Dial.* ii. 35).

The mind, passing beyond the barriers of flesh, endeavours to go above itself (*Mor.* x. 31).

We are lifted up outside the confines of the flesh (ibid. x. 13).

I strove daily to become outside the world, outside the flesh (*Ep.* i. 5).

The mind becomes above the world—outside the world (*Dial.* ii. 35).

The mind cannot stand for long above itself (in contemplation) (*Mor.* v. 57).[1]

---

[1] 'Per contemplationem super nosmetipsos tollimur.'
'Anima fit super semetipsam.'
'Carnis claustra transgrediens super semetipsam ire conatur.'
'Extra carnis angustias sublevati.'
'Extra mundum, extra carnem fieri.'
'Mens superior existat mundo ... extra mundum fuit' (p. 87).
'Mens stare diu super semetipsam non potest.'

The following are instances of the word 'rapere', 'rapi':

Contemplation ravishes (rapit) the soul above itself (*Hom. in Ezech.* II. ii. 13).

The mind is caught up above itself (*Dial.* ii. 35), beyond itself (*Mor.* xxiv. 11), outside itself (ibid. x. 17).

Caught up inwardly above themselves, they fix their mind on high (*Mor.* vii. 53).

Caught up in God (*Dial.* ii. 35).

These are only specimens of expressions constantly occurring; the following passages will supply the proper interpretation.

On the fact that the same words, 'He returned to himself,' are used of the Prodigal Son and of St Peter, Gregory comments:

In two ways we are led out of ourselves: either by sinful thoughts we fall below ourselves, or by the grace of contemplation we are raised above ourselves. The Prodigal fell below himself; but Peter, whose mind was rapt in ecstasy, was out of himself indeed, but above himself. Each 'returned to himself'—the former when, conscience smitten, he forsook his evil ways; the latter when from the height of contemplation he returned to the normal state of intellect as before. When the ardour of contemplation bears one aloft, he leaves himself beneath himself (*Dial.* ii. 3).

Desiring nothing, fearing nothing in this world, I seemed to myself to stand as it were on the summit of things; for he is lifted up 'upon the high places of the earth' who in his mind despises and tramples down even the things which in the present world seem high and glorious (*Ep.* i. 5, ad Theoctistam).

Merely to love things above is already to mount on high (*Mor.* xv. 53).

Speaking of his own contemplation in his monastery, he says:

My mind, while still enclosed in the body, did yet by contemplation pass beyond the barriers of the flesh[1] (*Dial.* Pref.).

Similarly:

The mind by the force of its contemplation is carried out of the flesh, while by the weight of its corruption it is still held in the flesh[2] (*Mor.* x. 13).

While in the world it is out of the world[3] (ibid. xxii. 35).

---

[1] 'Retentus corpore ipsa iam carnis claustra contemplatione transibat.'
[2] 'Contemplationis suae vi extra carnem tollitur, quae corruptionis suae pondere adhuc in carne retinetur.'
[3] 'In mundo extra mundum est.'

These passages show that St Gregory's ordinary language, as adduced above, is figurative and has no reference to psycho-physical phenomena. The only passages known to me that can suggest any such interpretation are the two following:

Often the mind of the righteous is so suspended in contemplating things on high, that outwardly their face seems to have been struck with stupefaction (obstupuisse) (*Mor.* xii. 35).

After the struggles of labour [in contemplation], after the waves of temptations, the mind is often hung aloft in a transport (in excessu suspenditur), in order that it may contemplate a knowledge of the divine Presence (ibid. xxiv. 12).

These two passages do seem to suggest something of the nature of physical concomitants of contemplation; but they are on the most ordinary, the least abnormal and questionable, grade of such phenomena, and hardly find a place among those bodily effects of prayer and contemplation discoursed of so largely by modern writers on mysticism and by mental physiologists. They suggest little more than a profound absorption of mind. It is certain that St Gregory's frequent expressions that in contemplation the mind is carried out of the body or out of the world, do not mean any such phenomenon as that called by St Teresa 'the flight of the spirit', and described in *Interior Castle*, 'Sixth Mansion', c. v.

He does speak of alienation of mind:

Because fright when it strikes the mind makes it alien from itself, the Latin interpreters sometimes translate ecstasy by fright, as in the Psalm: 'I said in my fright (pavor) I am cast away from the face of thy eyes,' where not 'fright' but 'ecstasy' (departure, 'excessus') might have been said; but 'fright' was used in place of 'ecstasy', because the mind is alienated in fright just as in ecstasy (*Mor.* xxvii. 31).

This may remind us of the passage cited from St Augustine (*Enar. in Psalm.* lxvii. 36, above, p. 51), where it is said that fright may cause an ecstasy or alienation of mind from the senses.

A perusal of the foregoing pieces shows that there is little to be learned from St Gregory on any psycho-physical concomitants of contemplation, as raptures, alienations, and so forth. All this side of mysticism seems to have been outside of his horizon. And yet it must be felt that the experiences he describes in such a passage as that cited in § B from *Morals*, xxiv. 11 (p. 74), though falling far short in power of expression, still does describe a religious mystical experience the same in kind and degree as even the highest and most intellectual of St Augustine's elevations of spirit, as told in the passage from *de Genesi ad litteram*, xii. 54, cited above (p. 52).

It is necessary to examine with especial attention the passage wherein St Gregory describes St Benedict's great mystical experience (*Dial.* ii. 35); because the language employed suggests elevations of spirit beyond what is suggested in the passages portraying Gregory's own experiences; because it has given rise to the question whether St Benedict is to be joined to the group of supreme mystics who have enjoyed in this life the vision of God; and also because St Gregory here formulates a theory in explanation of such experiences.

Let St Gregory first describe the vision:

While Benedict was standing at the window of the tower, beseeching Almighty God, suddenly, at dead of night, looking out he saw that a light shed from above had dissipated all the darkness of the night, and was shining with such splendour that the light that had shone forth amid the darkness surpassed the day. And a very wonderful thing followed in that spectacle: for, as afterwards he himself narrated, the whole world, gathered as it were under one ray of the sun, was brought before his eyes. And while he fixed the steady gaze of his eyes in this splendour of the shining light, he saw the soul of Germanus, bishop of Capua, carried to heaven by the angels in a fiery ball.

On the interlocutor Peter expressing wonder how the whole world could be seen by one man, St Gregory expounds his own theory as to the vision:

To the soul that sees the Creator every created thing is narrow. For however little it be of the light of the Creator that it beholds, all that is created becomes to it small: because by the very light of the inmost vision the bosom of the mind is enlarged, and it is so expanded in God that it is above the world. But the seer's soul itself becomes also above itself, and when in the light of God it is rapt above itself, it is broadened out interiorly; and while raised aloft it looks downwards, it understands how small is that which in its lowly estate it could not understand. Therefore the man of God, who, looking on the fiery globe, saw also angels returning to heaven, assuredly could see these things only in God's light. And so, what wonder is it if he saw the world gathered together before him, who, being raised up in the light of his mind, was out of the world? And that the world is said to have been gathered before his eyes, it is not that the heaven and earth were contracted, but the seer's mind was enlarged, who, being rapt in God, could see without difficulty all that is beneath God. In that light, therefore, which shone on his outward eyes, there was a light in his inward mind, which, by ravishing the seer's mind to things above, showed him how small were all things below.[1]

It will be noticed that the various expressions suggesting rapture, alienation, departure from the world occur here in their most acute form. And yet St Gregory says that at the height of the vision St Benedict thrice called out with a loud voice to the deacon Servandus, who was in the room beneath, to come up and see the wonder, and related to him what had occurred. Thus it is seen that, even in an experience that seems to have transcended any of his own, St Gregory represents St Benedict as retaining full possession of his mind and external senses, and as in no wise carried away by ecstasy, rapture, or trance. This is strong and decisive confirmation of the view already expressed, that all such psycho-physical phenomena were outside of St Gregory's horizon.

F. THE VISION OF GOD

St Gregory's doctrine on the Vision of God possible in this life is in marked contrast to what we have seen was St Augustine's; his practical Roman mind could not easily attune itself to the elevations of such a thorough-going Platonist as Augustine, and his customary teaching, embodying his own settled view, is that God cannot be seen or known as He is by mortal man in this life. A number of quite clear passages show this.

One such occurs in the long continuous exposition found in *Homilies on Ezechiel*, II. ii (p. 66). Others occur in other of these Homilies:

On Ezechiel ii. 1: *Visio similitudinis gloriae Domini*. He does not say:

[1] 'Animae videnti Creatorem angusta est omnis creatura. Quamlibet etenim parum de luce Creatoris aspexerit, breve ei fit omne quod creatum est; quia ipsa luce visionis intimae mentis laxatur sinus, tantumque expanditur in Deo ut superior existat mundo. Fit vero ipsa videntis anima etiam super semetipsam; cumque in Dei lumine rapitur super se, in interioribus ampliatur; et dum sub se conspicit exaltata, comprehendit quam breve sit quod comprehendere humiliata non poterat. Vir ergo Dei, qui intuens globum igneum, angelos quoque ad caelum redeuntes videbat, haec proculdubio cernere nonnisi in Dei lumine poterat. Quid itaque mirum si mundum ante se collectum vidit, qui sublevatus in mentis lumine extra mundum fuit? Quod autem collectus mundus ante eius oculos dicitur, non caelum et terra contracta est, sed videntis animus est dilatatus, qui in Deo raptus videre sine difficultate potuit omne quod infra Deum est. In illa ergo luce quae exterioribus oculis fulsit, lux in interiore mente fuit, quae videntis animum quia ad superiora rapuit, ei quam angusta essent omnia inferiora monstravit' (*Dial.* ii. 35; ed. Mittermüller, 1880).

Compare terminology: 'Quanto se foras per desideria dilatant, tanto ad receptionem illius sinum cordis angustant' (*Mor.* v. 50).
'Laxatur sinus mentium' (*Hom. in Ezech.* II. v. 17).
'Laxato mentis sinu' (*Mor.* iv. 62).
'Ad eadem desideria laxato mentis sinu dilatentur' (ibid. v. 6).
'Sinum cordis extendere' (ibid. vi. 55).
'Dilatet ... angustet' (ibid. vi. 57, xxiv. 12; *Ezech.* II. ii. 12).

The vision of the glory, but of the likeness of the glory; that it may be shown that with whatever effort the human mind strains, even if it have repressed the phantasies of bodily images from its thoughts, and have removed from the eyes of its heart all finite spirits, still while placed in mortal flesh it is not able to see the glory of God as it is. But whatever of it that is which shines in the mind, is a likeness, and not itself (*Hom. in Ezech.* i. viii. 30).

The following are from the *Morals*:

With whatever force the eye of our mind in the exile of this life strains after the light of eternity, it is not able to penetrate it; and when we raise the gaze of our mind to the ray of the supernal Light, we are clouded over by the obscurity of our weakness. While man is yet weighed down by the corruptible flesh, he is by no means able to see the eternal Light as it is. The mind often is so inflamed that, though it be placed in the flesh, it is caught up (rapitur) to God, every carnal thought being subdued; but, for all that, it does not see God as He is (*Mor.* iv. 45).

So long as we are beset by the corruptions of the flesh, we in no wise behold the brightness of the divine Power as it abides unchangeable in itself, in that the eye of our weakness cannot endure that which shines above us with intolerable lustre from the ray of His Eternity (ibid. v. 52).

The Divinity never imparts Himself as He is to those that contemplate Him while still in this life, but shows forth His Brightness scantily to the blinking eyes of our mind (ibid. v. 66).[1]

Whatever progress any one may have made when placed in this life, he does not as yet see God in His real appearance (per speciem), but in enigma and through a glass. Holy men raise themselves up to lofty contemplation, and yet they cannot see God as He is. They resolutely direct the keenness of their intention, but they cannot yet behold Him nigh, the greatness of Whose brightness they are not at all able to penetrate. For the mist of our corruption darkens us from the incorruptible Light; and when the light can both be seen in a measure, and yet cannot be seen as it is, it shows how distant it is. And if the mind already saw it perfectly it would not see it as it were through fog [or darkness—'per caliginem'] (*Mor.* xxxi. 101).

Here we meet an idea that became classical in the literature of mysticism in the West—with that of the East I am not conversant— that contemplation in this life is as seeing the sun through a fog or cloud. It is based on the verse of the psalm: 'Caligo sub pedibus eius'—'Darkness is under his feet' (Ps. xvii. 10), thus commented on by St Gregory: 'By those beneath He is not seen in that brightness wherewith He exercises dominion among those above' (*Mor.* xvii. 39).

This is the ground idea of the remarkable English fourteenth-

[1] Cf. *Mor.* xxiii. 39, xxxi. 100.

century mystical treatise, *The Cloud of Unknowing*, and it is a symbol much used by the later mystic writers. I am not in a position to affirm that the conception, so far as Western mystical thought is concerned, originated with St Gregory; but I do not recollect having met it in the West before him: not in St Augustine, with whose mode of thought it would not be consonant, for he speaks of St John as having 'contemplated the interior and eternal Light with steady gaze'—'fixis oculis' (*Tract in Ioan.* xxxvi. 5).

In the passage cited at length in § B, from *Morals*, viii. 50 this idea of seeing through a fog occurs: When the mind is caught up in contemplation 'it beholds something of the inmost realities as through a fog.'[1]

It occurs also in the following piece:

Whatever the progress in virtue, the mind does not yet compass any clear insight into eternity, but still looks on it under the fog of some sort of imagining (sub cuiusdam caligine imaginationis). And so it is called a vision of the night. And therefore, as contemplating the ray of the interior Sun, the cloud of our corruption interposes itself, nor does the unchangeable Light burst forth such as It is to the weak eyes of our mind, we as it were still see God in a vision of the night, since we must surely go darkling (caligamus) under an uncertain contemplation (*Mor.* v. 53).

This teaching of the indistinctness of the vision and knowledge of God revealed in contemplation runs through the whole section, *Morals*, v. 52-66; it is summed up in these sentences:

When the mind is hung aloft in the height of contemplation, whatever it has power to see perfectly is not God. ... Then only is there truth in what we know concerning God, when we are made sensible we cannot fully know anything concerning Him (*Mor.* v. 66).

The following passage from this section is of interest, as the only one of St Gregory (known to me) of a theologico-philosophical character:

Every man that apprehends something of the Eternal Being by contemplation, beholds the same through His co-eternal Image. When then His Eternity is perceived as far as the capability of our frail nature admits, His Image is set before the eyes of the mind, in that when we really strain towards the Father, as far as we receive Him we see Him by His Image, i.e. by His Son. And by that Image which was born of Himself without beginning, we strive in some sort to obtain a glimpse of Him who hath neither beginning nor ending (*Mor.* v. 63, 64).

[1] 'De intimis aliquid quasi per caliginem conspicit.'

Thus the settled teaching of St Gregory, discordant from that of St Augustine, but concordant with ordinary theology in the West, is that even in the highest contemplation in this life God is never seen as He is. Yet in a single passage St Augustine makes his influence felt, and St Gregory reproduces his idea:

As long as we live this mortal life, God may be seen by certain semblances, but by the actual appearance (species) of His Nature He cannot, so that the soul, being breathed on by the grace of the Spirit, should by certain figures behold God, but not attain to the actual power of His Essence[1] (ipsa vis eius essentiae). ... [Moses' request—'Show me Thyself'—is thus interpreted:] He was athirst to perceive, through the Brightness of His uncircumscribed Nature, Him Whom he had begun to see by certain semblances, that so the supernal Essence might be present to the eyes of his mind, in order that for the vision of Eternity there might not be interposed to him any created semblance with the circumstances of time. ... By persons living in this mortal flesh, Wisdom, which is God, was able to be seen by certain circumscribed images, but not able to be seen by the uncircumscribed Light of Eternity. But if by certain ones still living in this corruptible flesh, yet growing in incalculable power by a certain piercingness of contemplation, the Eternal Brightness of God is able to be seen,[2] this is not at variance with the words of Job: 'Wisdom is hidden from the eyes of all the living'; because he that sees Wisdom, which is God, wholly dies to this life, that henceforth he should not be held by the love thereof. He who sees God dies by the mere circumstance alone, that either by the bent of the interior, or by the carrying out of practice, he is separated with all his mind from the gratifications of this life. Hence yet further it is said to Moses: 'No man shall see me and live': as though it were plainly expressed, 'No man ever at any time sees God spiritually and lives to the world carnally' (Mor. xviii. 88, 89).

Here it is admitted that the 'eternal Brightness of God' may be—has been—seen by some still in this life, by a piercing contemplation. And in the following paragraph it is laid down that God's Brightness and His Nature are identical.[3]

Thus, 'to see the eternal Brightness of God' is to see the divine

[1] 'Quamdiu hic mortaliter vivitur, videri per quasdam imagines Deus potest, sed per ipsam naturae suae speciem non potest, ut anima, gratia spiritus afflata, per figuras quasdam Deum videat, sed ad ipsam vim eius essentiae non pertingat. ...'

[2] 'Sapientia, quae Deus est, in hac mortali carne consistentibus et videri potuit per quasdam circumscriptas imagines, et videri non potuit per incircumscriptum lumen aeternitatis. Sin vero a quibusdam potest in hac adhuc corruptibili carne viventibus, sed tamen inaestimabili virtute crescentibus, quodam contemplationis acumine aeterna Dei claritas videri,' &c.

[3] 'Neque illi simplici et incommutabili essentiae aliud est claritas et aliud natura, sed ipsa ei natura sua claritas, ipsa claritas natura est' (loc. cit. 90).

Nature. In his careful and valuable summary of St Gregory's theology, Mr. Dudden makes him draw a distinction between the knowledge of God's Nature and the knowledge of His Essence: 'God's
Nature is the object of the knowledge of angels and blessed spirits,
and sometimes of mortal men, raised in contemplation; but God's
Essence can be known only by Himself, and cannot be the object of
the knowledge of any created intelligence.'[1] I am not prepared to
accept this distinction between God's Nature and His Essence as
being really St Gregory's; for it is not in itself theologically sound,
and it is not to be found in the places referred to in the note as
justifying it. The principal of these is as follows:

Then Almighty God is found out by clear thought, when, the
corruption of our mortality being once for all trodden underfoot, He
is seen by us, taken up (into heaven) in the Brightness of His
Divinity. ... In the height of the rewarding [i.e. in heaven] the
Almighty may be found in the appearance (per speciem) afforded
to contemplation, but not in perfection. For though sooner or later
we see Him in His Brightness, yet do we not fully behold His
Essence. For the mind, whether of angels or men, while it gazes
toward the unencompassed Light, shrinks into little by the mere fact
that it is a creature (*Mor.* x. 13).

All that is said here is that even in the Beatific Vision of heaven
no created intelligence can see **fully** God's Essence or ever know
Him as He knows Himself (cf. *Mor.* xviii. 92, 93). In the passage,
Morals xviii. 88, it seems hardly possible to draw any distinction
between God's Nature and Essence in the expressions: God cannot
be seen by the very 'species' of His Nature; and: the soul does not
reach to the very power of His Essence (see Latin in note, p. 90).
And so it is not doubtful that when, in the next paragraph (89),
he says that it may be possible that by some in this life 'the eternal
Brightness of God has been seen', he allows, in contradiction to his
own constant teaching everywhere else, but in agreement with
St Augustine, that the divine Nature or Essence may have been seen
(partially) in contemplation by some in this life. But when we compare St Gregory's passage with those wherein St Augustine gives
utterance to his speculations, its lower level of thought is all too
painfully apparent, and especially in the sense attached to that
'dying to the world' which both take to be the condition of such a
contemplation. For Augustine it is an ecstasy the highest and most
spiritual that can fall to the lot of man, as St Paul's, wherein he knew
not 'whether he was in the body or out of the body'; for Gregory it
is no more than the spiritual commonplace of dying to the love and

[1] *Gregory the Great*, ii. 313.

the pleasures of the world. This watering down of Augustine's sublime conceptions would open wide the gate to the Vision of God to almost all comers in the spiritual life, as the condition admits of many degrees, and so is relatively easy of fulfilment. So that it is a satisfaction to reflect that the whole idea is not St Gregory's own, and is foreign to his true range of thought.

It remains to consider whether St Gregory intended to assert that in the vision described in *Dialogues* ii. 35 (cited above, p. 86), St Benedict saw the divine Essence. He unquestionably asserts that St Benedict saw God—'animae videnti Creatorem'—and that he beheld somewhat, albeit little, of the light of God; that he was caught up in the light of God, and what he saw, he saw in the light of God.

St Thomas in *Quodlibetales* i. 1 (cf. *Summa* 2 2^{ae} quaest. clxxx. art. 5, ad 3) formally discusses the question and concludes negatively, basing himself on St Augustine's teaching that only in an ecstasy involving entire alienation of the mind from the bodily senses can God's Essence be seen; whereas St Gregory's narrative shows that St Benedict was not in such ecstasy, for he called out to his disciple to come up and see the vision. If St Augustine's view be accepted, it is clear that St Benedict did not enjoy this supreme vision. But our question is: Did St Gregory believe St Benedict to have had the vision of God's Essence? rather than: Did St Benedict really have it? And it has been seen that St Gregory did not demand the condition postulated by St Augustine, but only one of spiritual death to the world that certainly was amply fulfilled in St Benedict. Haeften shows that the question has been discussed among the later scholastics, some of whom do not regard St Thomas's solution as final.[1] St Bernard held that St Gregory's words mean that St Benedict was momentarily raised to the manner of knowledge of the angels, who see God face to face, contemplate His wisdom clearly in itself, and know creatures in God.[2]

When we remember that in one place St Gregory, against his customary teaching, does hold the vision of God's Essence to be attainable in this life, it is difficult to understand the extraordinary language he uses of St Benedict otherwise than does St Bernard; but as in the case of St Augustine, the question what St Gregory meant, is quite distinct from the question whether his meaning is in conformity with the reality.

[1] *Monasticae Disquisitiones*, Comm. in Vitam S.P.B., p, 168.
[2] *Serm. de Diversis*, ix. 1. (see below, p. 120).

CONTEMPLATION

3. ST BERNARD

ANALYSIS

ST BERNARD

ST BERNARD was born in 1090 in Burgundy. He was of noble parentage, and at the age of twenty-two he entered the newly-founded monastery of Citeaux, the cradle of the Cistercian Order. Three years later he was sent to make the foundation at Clairvaux, of which house he was abbot until his death in 1153. The Cistercians being a strictly reformed branch of the Benedictines, their life at the beginning was one of prayer, of manual labour, of austerity, of silence, and of strict seclusion. Judged by this standard, never was there a life less Cistercian than Bernard's. He travelled all over Western Europe on missions for popes and potentates; he preached a Crusade; he controlled bishops, popes, and councils; he was mixed up in all the controversies of the day, whether of theology or ecclesiastical politics; he was the dominant ecclesiastical and religious force of the time.[1] It was a life of prodigious and ceaseless activities; and the wonder of it is that to the end he continued not only the saint, but also the great contemplative that he was. This result must be attributed partly to his intellectual temperament, but mainly to his immense and overmastering love of God and of Our Lord Jesus Christ.

Intellectually he was the 'Last of the Fathers', the child of the patristic age that was passing away. He combated the beginnings of the scholastic movement, and in what he says on contemplation and mysticism there is no trace of the new methods of scholasticism which his great contemporaries, Hugh and Richard of St Victor, were already applying to a systematic presentation of a doctrine of mystical theology. Like St Gregory, he wrote no formal treatise on the subject; his doctrine has to be extracted from numerous stray passages, wherein he discourses on what is patently his own personal experience.

In the excellent study, *La Spiritualité Chrétienne*, vol. ii., 'Le Moyen Age', Abbé P. Pourrat devotes nearly one hundred pages to St Bernard. The greater part is concerned with the spiritual life in general, the section on 'Mystical Theology' covering only sixteen pages. In the former part is brought out with admirable clearness St Bernard's teaching on mortification, humility, perfection, meditation, prayer; and, above all, on devotion to the mysteries of Our

---

[1] The best modern life of St. Bernard is that of Abbé E. Vacandard, 2 vols. 1895. From another point of view, Cotter Morison's *St Bernard* is very remarkable, as showing the sympathy and admiration entertained for St Bernard by a Positivist.

Lord's Life—the Infancy, the episodes of the Passion, the Cruci-
fixion: also devotion to the Blessed Virgin and to the angels. It is
Pourrat's judgement that in the sphere of personal devotional life
it was St Bernard who principally shaped the Catholic piety of the
later Middle Ages and also of modern times. This is especially true
of his expression of tender devotional love for the Humanity of Our
Lord, and for His Mother. With this view Dean Inge is in substantial accord:

> His great achievement was to recall devout and loving con-
> templation to the image of the crucified Christ, and to found that
> worship of Our Saviour as the 'Bridegroom of the Soul', which in
> the next centuries inspired so much fervid devotion and lyrical
> sacred poetry (*Christian Mysticism*, 140).

My treatment of St Bernard's mystical theology was completed
before Pourrat's second volume had come into my hands.

The principal source of St Bernard's mystical theology is the
series of eighty-six sermons on the Canticle of Solomon—the 'Song
of Songs'; like St Gregory's *Morals* preached as conferences to his
monks. There is little on the subject to be found in his other writings
which is not to be found also, and more fully, in these sermons. The
Sermons on the Canticle have been translated into English by the late
S. J. Eales (1896). This translation is in great measure a paraphrase,
though a good one for its purpose. It has been taken as the basis of
the citations that follow; but it has been controlled throughout and
made more exact, especially in places where it seemed necessary to
secure literal accuracy.

In laying down the lines of a spiritual course, St Bernard, starting
from the opening words of the Canticle—'Let him kiss me with the
kisses of his mouth,'—describes the three stages of the spiritual life,
purgative, illuminative, unitive, under the imagery of the threefold
kiss of Christ's Feet, of His Hand, and of His Mouth. This idea is
worked out at length in *Canticle* iii. and iv.: We must first kiss the
Feet of Christ, falling prostrate in sorrow and repentence for our
sins; next we must kiss His Hand, which will lift us up by bestowing
upon us the grace of continence, the fruits worthy of penance, and
works of piety, and so make us stand upright; and then:

> When we have with many prayers and tears obtained these two
> former graces, at length we perhaps venture to lift our eyes to that
> Countenance full of glory, for the purpose not only to gaze upon it,
> but (I say it with fear and trembling) to kiss; because the spirit
> before us is Christ the Lord, to Whom, being united in a holy Kiss,
> we are by His condescension made to be one spirit with Him
> (*Cant.* iii. 5).

(In the kiss of the Feet) are dedicated the first-fruits of conversion; (the kiss of the Hand) shall be accorded to those who are making progress; but (the kiss of the Mouth) is rarely experienced, and by those only who are perfect. ... There are then three states of progress of souls, sufficiently well known at least to those who have experienced them, when, as far as is possible in these weak bodies of ours, they are enabled to take knowledge either of the pardon which they have received for their evil actions, or the grace which has enabled them to do good ones; or, lastly, of the very presence of Him Who is their patron and benefactor (ibid. iv. 1).

It is well at the outset to say a word on the imagery of the *Sermons on the Canticle*. Being based on the Canticle itself, the exposition is couched in the language of human love. St Bernard did not invent this method of interpretation: it had been in vogue for centuries and was the Christian tradition (see Eales, op. cit., 'Introductory Essay', and Inge, *Christian Mysticism*, App. D). It is often looked on with misgiving, as by Dean Inge, on the score of danger of erotic or sensuous elements. The matter will have to be gone into more fully at a later place. Here it will suffice to call attention to the fact that a twofold allegorical interpretation of the Bridegroom and Bride of the Canticle runs through the *Sermons*: (i) the Bridegroom is Jesus Christ and the Bride is the Church—this is in accordance with St Paul and the Apocalypse; but (ii) when the bride is the soul of the devout individual man, the Bridegroom is not Jesus Christ in His Humanity, but the Divine Word, the Logos, the Second Person of the Holy Trinity—in more than one place He is called 'the Bridegroom-Word', 'Verbum Sponsus' (*Cant.* lxxiv. 3). In a small number of cases this rule is broken and Jesus Christ is spoken of as the Bridegroom of the individual soul; but they are so few as to be negligible. In the following passage St Bernard makes clear what is his customary practice:

Take heed that you bring chaste ears to this discourse of love; and when you think of these two lovers, remember always that not a man and a woman are to be thought of, but the Word of God and a soul. And if I shall speak of Christ and the Church, the sense is the same, except that under the name of the Church is specified not one soul only, but the united souls of many, or rather their unanimity (*Cant.* lxi. 2).

Still, for Bernard it is the Church that primarily is the Bride:

Though none of us would presume so far as to venture to say that his soul was the Spouse of the Lord; yet, since we are members of the Church, which justly glories in that name, and in the fact which that name signifies, we may claim not unjustly a participation in that glory (ibid. xii. 11).

The spirituality of St Bernard's conception of the 'Mystic Kiss' of Christ is seen in the following piece:

(The Kiss of His Mouth) signifies nothing else than to receive the inpouring of the Holy Spirit. ... The Bride has the boldness to ask trustingly that the inpouring of the Holy Spirit may be granted to her under the name of a Kiss. When the Bride is praying that the Kiss may be given her, her entreaty is for the inpouring of the grace of this threefold knowledge [i.e. of Father, Son and Holy Ghost], as far as it can be experienced in this mortal body. ... This gift conveys both the light of knowledge and the unction of piety (*Cant.* viii. 2-6).

In presenting St Bernard's teaching on mystical theology the attempt will be made to follow, as far as possible, the general lines of the scheme whereby was unfolded the teaching of St Augustine and that of St Gregory; but it has to be said that St Bernard's more discursive and emotional style does not lend itself easily to such cut-and-dried treatment as was possible in the case of St Gregory, and even of St Augustine.

A. PRELIMINARY PHASES

Remote Preparation: Purgation

Like SS Augustine and Gregory, St Bernard is insistent that the necessary preparation and indispensable condition for progress in contemplation is the serious exercise of asceticism, of self-discipline, mortification, and the practice of the virtues. This appears in such passages as the following:

Perhaps you desire the repose of contemplation, and in this you do well. ... But it would be a reversing of the proper order to ask for the reward before having earned it, and to grasp at the mid-day meal before performing the labour. The taste for contemplation is not due except to obedience to God's commandments. ... 'What then would you have me to do?' In the first place I would have you cleanse your conscience from every defilement of anger and murmuring and envy and dispute; and that you should hasten to banish from your heart all that evidently conflicts with the peace which ought to reign among brethren, and the obedience due to your elders. In the next place I would wish you to adorn yourself with the flowers of good works and laudable studies of every kind, and seek the sweet perfumes of virtues ... and endeavour to employ yourselves in them ... that your conscience may everywhere be fragrant with the perfumes of piety, of peace, of gentleness, of justice, of obedience, of cheerfulness, of humility (*Cant.* xlvi. 5, 7).

The course of the spiritual life is sketched as follows:

The Physician draws near to the wounded man. ... What is it that it is needful he should first do? ... The ulcer of inveterate evil custom must be cut away with the sharp blade of a sincere repentance. But this cannot be done without severe pain; let that, then, be alleviated with the healing ointment of devotion, which is, in fact, the comfort caused by the hope of forgiveness. Of that hope is born the mastery which is acquired over our passions, and the victory over sin. Then are applied the remedy of penance, the poultice of fasts, of vigils, of prayers, and of other exercises of the repentant. Let him be nourished in labour with the food of good works, that he fail not. That good works are nourishment to the soul may be learned from the words: 'My meat is to do the will of Him that sent me.' Therefore let works of piety accompany the labours of penitence which strengthen the soul. ... Now food arouses thirst and drink is needed. To the nourishment of good works let there be added therefore the draught of prayer. ... Prayer is as wine which maketh glad the heart of man ... it moistens the dry soil of the conscience, it brings about the perfect absorption of the food of good actions, and distributes them into all the members of the soul; strengthening faith, giving vigour to hope, rendering charity active and yet well ordered, and shedding an unction over the whole character.

When a sick man shall have partaken of food and of drink, what remains for him to do but to repose, and in the quiet of contemplation to recover himself after the toils of busy life? (*Cant.* xviii. 5, 6).

Proximate Preparation: Recollection, Introversion, Devotion

Though what St Bernard says explicitly on this point is little in comparison with what we have heard from SS Augustine and Gregory, still it is enough to show that he is in agreement with them, and with all contemplatives, that the first stage in rising to contemplation is 'recollection', the act whereby the soul 'recollects itself, gathering itself to itself (se in se colligens; cf. St Gregory, above, p. 69), and detaches itself from human affairs, in order to contemplate God' (*de Consid.* v. 4). It spurns the use of things and of the senses, so far as human frailty permits, in order to soar up to contemplation (ibid. 3).

Words cited below (pp. 115-116) show that for Bernard, as for Augustine and Gregory, a condition for contemplation is the banishment from the mind of all phantasmata of corporeal images and of all sense perceptions.

The process of 'introversion' is indicated as follows:

Let us seek the understanding of the invisible things of God by

those things that are made; but if the soul sees them to be understood in other creatures, she must needs see them far more fully and
understand them much more delicately in the creature made in the
image of God, that is in herself (*Serm. de div.* ix. 2).

We have seen that for Augustine the effort to attain to contemplation was an intellectual search, wherein the mind mounted up
through the successive grades of things subject to change, until it
reached Unchangeable Being; and that for St Gregory, too, it was
a psychological process. For Bernard the method of rising to contemplation was simply piety, devotion, and prayer, as appears in
many places.

Often we approach the altar and begin to pray with a heart lukewarm and dry. But if we steadily persist, grace comes suddenly in
a flood upon us, our breast grows full of increase, a wave of piety
fills our inward heart; and if we press on, the milk of sweetness conceived in us will spread over us in fruitful flood. The Bridegroom
then speaks thus: 'Thou hast, O my Spouse, that which thou prayest
for [i.e. the mystic kiss]' (*Cant.* ix. 7).

You if you shall enter into the house of prayer in solitude and
collectedness of spirit, if your mind be thoughtful and free of care,
if standing in the presence of God before some altar, you touch, as
it were, the portal of heaven with the hand of holy aspiration and
longing; if, having been brought among the choirs of the saints by
the fervour of your devotion, you deplore before them your troubles
and miseries, you plead your necessities with frequent sighs and
groans too deep for utterance, and entreat their compassion; if, I
say, you act thus, I have full confidence in Him Who said: 'Ask, and
ye shall receive', and I believe that if you persevere in knocking, you
shall not go away empty (ibid. xlix. 3).

The grace of contemplation is granted only in response to a longing and importunate desire: Nevertheless He will not present Himself, even in passing, to every soul; but to that soul only which is
shown, by great devotion, vehement desire, and tender affection, to
be His Bride, and to be worthy that the Word in all His beauty
should visit her as a Bridegroom (ibid. xxxii. 3).

B. AUTOBIOGRAPHICAL PASSAGE

At this point in the presentation of the teaching of SS Augustine
and Gregory, before passing on to the detailed examination of their
accounts of the Act of Contemplation itself, were intercalated autobiographical passages, wherein they describe their own highest
personal experiences in contemplation. St Bernard similarly provides us with a long passage of singular eloquence and beauty, in
which he sets himself to describe his own experience. It is one of the
most remarkable attempts to picture the mystical experience in the

whole literature of mysticism. It dates from the closing years of
his life.

But now bear with my foolishness for a little. I wish to tell you, as
I have promised, how such events have taken place in me. It is
indeed a matter of no importance. But I put myself forward only
that I may be of service to you, and if you derive any benefit, I am
consoled for my egotism; if not, I shall have displayed my foolishness. I confess, then, though I say it in my foolishness, that the Word
has visited me, and even very often. But although He has frequently
entered into my soul, I have never at any time been sensible of the
precise moment of His coming. I have felt that He was present; I
remember that He has been with me; I have sometimes been able
even to have a presentiment that He would come; but never to feel
His coming or His departure. For whence He came to enter my
soul, or whither He went on quitting it, by what means He has
made entrance or departure, I confess that I know not even to this
day. ... It is not by the eyes that He enters, for He is without colour;
nor by the ears, for His coming is without sound; nor by the nostrils,
for it is not with the air but with the mind that He is blended; nor
again does He enter by the mouth, not being of a nature to be eaten
or drunk; nor lastly is He capable of being traced by the touch, for
He is intangible.

You will ask, then, how, since the ways of His access are thus incapable of being traced, I could know that He was present? But He
is living and full of energy, and as soon as He has entered into me
He has quickened my sleeping soul, has aroused and softened and
goaded my heart, which was in a state of torpor and hard as a stone.
He has begun to pluck up and destroy, to plant and to build, to
water the dry places, to illuminate the gloomy spots, to throw open
those which were shut close, to inflame with warmth those which
were cold, as also to straighten its crooked paths and make its rough
places smooth, so that my soul might bless the Lord and all that is
within me praise His Holy Name. Thus, then, the Bridegroom-
Word, though He has several times entered into me, has never made
His coming apparent to my sight, hearing, or touch. It was not by
His motions that He was recognized by me, nor could I tell by any
of my senses that He had penetrated to the depths of my being. It
was, as I have already said, only by the movement of my heart that
I was enabled to recognize His presence, and to know the might of
His power by the sudden departure of vices and the strong restraint
put upon all carnal affections. From the discovery and conviction of
my secret faults I have had good reason to admire the depths of His
wisdom; His goodness and kindness have become known in the
amendment, whatever it may amount to, of my life; while in the
reformation and renewal of the spirit of my mind, that is, of my
inward man, I have perceived in some degree the loveliness of His
beauty, and have been filled with amazement at the multitude of
His greatness, as I meditated upon all these things.

But when the Word withdrew Himself, all these spiritual powers and faculties began to droop and languish, as if the fire had been withdrawn from a bubbling pot; and this is to me the sign of His departure. Then my soul is necessarily sad and depressed until He shall return and my heart grow warm within me, as it is wont, which indeed is the indication to me that He has come back again.

After having, then, such an experience of the Word, what wonder that I should adopt for my own the language of the Bride, who recalls Him when He has departed, since I am influenced by a desire, not indeed as powerful, but at least similar to hers. As long as I live that utterance shall be in my mind, and I will employ, for the recalling of the Word, that word of recall which I find here in the word 'Return'. And as often as He shall leave me, so often shall He be called back by my voice; nor will I cease to send my cries, as it were, after Him as He departs, expressing the ardent desire of my heart that He should return, that He should restore to me the joy of His salvation, restore to me Himself. I confess to you, my sons, that I take pleasure in nothing else in the meantime, until He is present Who is alone pleasing to me (*Cant.* lxxiv. 5, 6, 7, compressed).

C. The Act of Contemplation

In one place St Bernard gives a definition of contemplation in general, as contrasted with consideration or meditation:

Contemplation is concerned with the certainty of things, consideration with their investigation. Accordingly contemplation may be defined as the soul's true and certain intuition of a thing, or as the unhesitating apprehension of truth. Consideration is thought earnestly directed to investigation, or the application of the mind searching for the truth [the modern 'meditation'] (*de Consid.* ii. 5, trans. G. Lewis).

St Bernard recognizes very clearly the place and the use of meditation in the spiritual life (*de Consid. passim*, cf. Pourrat, op. cit. 52-7).

He distinguishes two kinds of contemplation—of intellect and of heart:

There are two kinds of transport (excessus) in holy contemplation: the one in the intellect, the other in the heart (affectus); the one in light, the other in fervour; the one in discernment, the other in devotion (*Cant.* xlix. 4).

The Contemplation of the Heart

St Bernard dwells chiefly on the 'contemplation of the heart', and it is in this that he principally places the mystic experience, or, as it is otherwise called, the state of passive union. A description of this contemplation has been given in the autobiographical passage already cited; another is given in the following:

(In the times of the Patriarchs) the manifestation of God was made from without, by appearances visible to the senses, or words heard by the ears. But there is still another manner in which God is discerned, differing from those, inasmuch as it is inward: when God deigns of His own accord to make Himself known to a soul that seeks for Him and lavishes on that seeking the entire love and ardour of its affections. And this is the sign of His coming thus to a soul, as we are taught by one who had experienced it: 'A fire will go before Him and burn up His enemies round about.'

For it is needful that in every soul in which He is about to appear such an ardour of sanctified longing should go before His Face as to consume every impurity of evil thoughts and works, and so to prepare a place for the Lord. And then the soul knows that the Lord is at hand, when it feels itself consumed in that fire, and it says with the Prophet: 'From above hath He sent fire into my bones'; and again: 'My heart was hot within me, and while I was musing the fire burned forth.'

After a soul has been thus pressed by frequent aspirations towards God, or rather by continual prayer, and is afflicted by its longings, it is sometimes the case that He who is so earnestly desired and longed for, has pity on that soul and makes Himself manifest to it; and I think that, led by its own experience, it will be able to say with the prophet: 'The Lord is good to them that wait for Him, to the soul that seeketh Him.'

But be most careful not to allow yourself to think that we perceive anything corporeal or by way of images in this union (mingling, 'commixtio') of the Word with the soul. I am saying only that which the Apostle says, that 'he that is joined to God is one spirit'. I go on to express, in what words I am able, the transport (excessus) of a pure soul unto God, or the loving descent of God into the soul, comparing spiritual things with spiritual. That union (conjunctio), then, is made in the spirit, because God is a spirit, and is moved with love for the beauty of that soul which He may have seen to be walking according to the Spirit, and to have no desire to fulfil the lusts of the flesh, especially as He knows that it is filled with ardent love for Himself. A soul in this condition, with such feelings and so beloved, will be far from content that the Bridegroom should manifest Himself to her in the manner which is common to all, that is by the things which are made; or even in the manner peculiar to a few, namely, by dreams and visions; such a soul desires that by a special privilege He should descend from on high into her, and pervade her wholly in the deepest affections, and to the very ground of the heart. She desires that He whom she loves should not show Himself to her in an outward shape, but should be, as it were, inpoured into her; that He should not merely appear to her, but should enter into and possess her; nor is it doubtful that her happiness is so much the greater, as He is within rather than without (*Cant.* xxxi. 4-6).

Throughout the *Sermons on the Canticle* such expressions abound as the following, describing the experiences of the soul in the mystic union; it is an inpouring of the Spirit (viii. 2); an inpouring of the sweetness of holy love (xxxii. 2); an inpoured savour of heavenly sweetness (xxxi. 7); a virtue which changes the heart, and a love which fires it (lvii. 7); a wave of piety (ix. 7); a taste of the Presence of God (xxxi. 7); the soul is inwardly embraced (xxxii. 2); drawn into the secret of the Divinity (xlix. 4); set aglow with the love of God (lvii. 7); sweetly refreshed with delicious love (l. 4); experiences joy ineffable (lvii. 11). Indeed there is hardly a page but supplies some such expression.

Like Augustine, Bernard speaks of the mystic union as a momentary foretaste of heaven. In the tractate *de Gratia et libero Arbitrio*, after laying down that in this life, freedom of enjoyment (libertas complaciti), that is, freedom from misery, is not attainable, he says:

But it is to be recognized that those who by transport (excessus) of contemplation are at times rapt in spirit, are able to taste some little fragment of the sweetness of supernal felicity, and as often are free from misery as they thus are carried away. These indeed, even in this flesh, though rarely and momentarily, experience the freedom of enjoyment (15).

And after describing the union he exclaims: 'So, so is it in heaven, I do not doubt' (*Cant.* lii. 2).

The Contemplation of the Intellect

Though St Bernard's emphasis is on the 'contemplation of the heart', his 'contemplation of the intellect' is of greater interest for the psychology and theology of mysticism. This is 'a sweet and familiar contemplation of things heavenly, intellectual (intelligibilia) and divine, in which are drunk with pleasure deep draughts of the hidden and sacred meanings of truth and wisdom' (*Cant.* xxxv. 2).

The following longer piece describes such contemplation:

When the Lord comes as a consuming fire and His Presence is understood in the power by which the soul is changed and in the love by which it is inflamed; when all stain of sin and rust of vices have been consumed in that fire, and the conscience has been purified and calmed, there ensues a certain sudden and unwonted enlargement of mind and an inpouring of light illuminating the intellect, either for knowledge of Scripture or comprehension of mysteries. But not through open doors, but through narrow apertures does that ray of so great brightness penetrate, so long as this sorry wall of the body subsists (*Cant.* lvii. 7, 8).

The closing words remind us of St Gregory's chinks through which the ray of divine Light passes (above, p. 78).

The following passage Dom John Chapman comments on in the article 'Mysticism, Roman Catholic', in Hastings's *Dictionary of Religion and Ethics*, as being 'perhaps the earliest account of the distinction between *pure contemplation*, in which reason as well as imagination remains in darkness, and nothing is understood by it, and *revelation* in which the pure intellectual conceptions are made comprehensible by means of the imagery or words which the mind habitually employs.' I adopt his translation:

'Pendants of gold and studs of silver'. This means, I think, nothing else than to weave certain spiritual likenesses, and to bring the most pure meanings of divine wisdom into the sight of the mind which is contemplating, in order that it may perceive, at least by a mirror and in an enigma, what it cannot at all as yet look upon face to face. What I speak of are things divine, and wholly unknown but to those who have experienced them, how, that is, in this mortal body, while yet the state of faith endures and the substance of the clear Light is not yet made manifest, the contemplation of pure truth can yet anticipate its action in us, at least in part; so that some, even among us, to whom this has been granted from above, can employ the Apostle's words, 'Now I know in part', and again, 'We know in part, and we prophesy in part.' For when something from God (divinitus) has momentarily and, as it were, with the swiftness of a flash of light, shed its ray upon the mind in ecstasy of spirit, whether for the tempering of this too great radiance, or for the sake of imparting it to others, forthwith there present themselves, whence I know not, certain imaginary likenesses of lower things, suited to the meanings which have been infused from above, by means of which that most pure and brilliant ray of truth is in a manner shaded, and becomes both more bearable to the soul itself, and more capable of being communicated to whomsoever the latter wishes. I think that these images are formed in us by the suggestions of the holy angels, as, on the contrary, evil ones without any doubt are 'inoculations (immissiones) by bad angels' (Psalm lxxvii. 49). (*Cant.* xli. 3).

This theory as to the manner of translation or transliteration of the perception of spiritual realities in contemplation into phantasmata capable of being expressed in language intelligible to others, is of much interest in its bearing on the attempts of the mystics, preeminently Ruysbroeck, to give utterance to their experiences.

Bernard goes on in a difficult piece of much interest on the speculative side of the theory of mystical knowledge of God. I translate it quite literally:

And very likely in this way is fabricated, as by the hands of Angels, that mirror and enigma through which the Apostle saw, out of such pure and beauteous imaginations: in such wise that we both feel the Being of God, which is perceived as pure and without any phantasy of corporeal images; and we attribute to angelic ministration whatever kind of elegant similitude wherewith It appeared worthily clothed withal (*Cant.* xli. 4).

Here we seem to have expressed the common mystic claim of an experimental perception of God's Being, while the ideas under which It is apprehended are said to be supplied by the angels. This last is a piece of purely personal speculation, which did not find a place in the tradition of mystical teaching.

St Bernard likens contemplation to the sleep of the soul in the arms of God; but it is a deep sleep, alive and watchful, which enlightens the inward senses—'magis istiusmodi vitalis vigilque sopor sensum interiorem illuminat'—a sleep which dulls not the senses but ravishes them (ibid. lii. 2, 3). Here we are taught that St Bernard's contemplation is no 'quietism': although images and sense perceptions are eliminated and the faculties of the mind reduced to silence, the soul itself is full of light and operating with an intense activity.

Transiency

The transiency of contemplation, its short duration, the recoil of the soul after an act of contemplation, and the alternations of the presence and absence of the experience—all well-known phenomena illustrated copiously in the writings of SS Augustine and Gregory—are illustrated equally in those of St Bernard. Various such passages have already been cited; others occur in the later sections of this study. Here only two or three special pieces portraying Bernard's own experience will be given:

But there is a place where God is beheld as truly tranquil and in repose; it is, in fact, the place not of a judge, not of a teacher, but of a Bridegroom. I do not know how it may be with regard to others, but as far as concerns myself, that is for me a chamber into which entrance has sometimes been granted unto me. But alas! how rarely that has happened, and for how short a time it has lasted. It is there that is clearly recognized the mercy of the Lord from everlasting and to everlasting upon them that fear Him. ... Then have I felt on a sudden so great a joy and confidence arising in me, that

… it seemed to me that I was one of those blessed ones. O that it had lasted longer. Again and again do Thou visit me, O Lord, with Thy salvation (*Cant.* xxiii. 15).

If any of us finds it good for him to draw near to God, and is so filled with an earnest longing that he desires to be dissolved and to be with Christ; but desires it vehemently, thirsts for it ardently, and without ceasing dwells upon the thought of it: he shall, without doubt, receive the Word, and in no other form than that of the Bridegroom in the time of visitation; that is to say, in the hour when he shall feel himself inwardly embraced, as it were, by the arms of Wisdom, and shall receive an inpouring of the sweetness of divine Love. For the desire of his heart shall be granted him, though he is still in the body in a place of pilgrimage, and though only in part for a time, and that a short time. For when the Lord has been sought in watching and prayers, with strenuous effort, with showers of tears, He will at length present Himself to the soul; but suddenly, when He is thought to be held, He will glide away. Again He comes to the soul that follows after Him with tears; He allows Himself to be regained, but not to be retained, and anon He passes away, as out of its very hands. Yet if the devout soul shall persist in prayers and tears, He will at length return to it; He will not deprive it of the desire of its lips; but He will speedily disappear again, and will not be seen unless He be sought again with the whole desire of the heart. Thus, then, even in this body, the joy of the presence of the Bridegroom may frequently be felt; but not the fullness of His presence, because though His visitation renders the heart glad, the alternation of His absence affects it with sadness. And this the Beloved must of necessity endure [until the next life] (*Cant.* xxxii. 2).

In the book on 'the Love of God' there is a passage reminding us of words of Gregory and Augustine:

Happy is he who hath deserved to reach unto the fourth degree of love, where man may love not even himself except for the sake of God. This love is a mountain, and the high mountain of God. When shall the mind experience affection like this, so that, inebriated with divine love, forgetful of self, and become to its own self like a broken vessel, it may utterly pass over into God, and, adhering to God, become one spirit with Him? Blessed and holy should I call one to whom it has been granted to experience such a thing in this mortal life at rare intervals, or even once, and this suddenly, and for the space of hardly a moment.[1] For in a certain manner to lose thyself, as though thou wert not, and to be utterly unconscious of thyself, and to be emptied of thyself, and, as it were, brought to nothing, pertains to celestial conversation, not to human condition. And if, indeed, any mortal is suddenly, now and then (as

[1] 'Raro interdum, aut vel semel, et hoc ipsum raptim, atque unius vix momenti spatio.'

has been said), and for a moment, admitted to this, straightway the wicked world envies, the evil of the day disturbs, the body of death becomes a burden, the necessity of flesh provokes, the defect of corruption does not endure, and, what is more insistent than these, fraternal charity recalls. Alas! he is compelled to return unto himself, to fall back into his own, and miserably to exclaim: 'Unhappy man that I am, who shall deliver me from the body of this death?' (de diligendo Deo, 27; trans. Edm. Gardner).

Similarly in another treatise:

In this life the happiness of contemplation is enjoyed only 'rarely and momentarily' (raro raptimque); contemplatives alone can experience the freedom of enjoyment, 'but only in part and in small part, and on most rare occasions' (de Grat. et lib. Arbit. 15).

The language used in describing the highest intellectual contemplation is worth recalling:

When something from God has momentarily and with the swiftness of a flash of light shed its ray upon the mind—'cum divinitus aliquid raptim et veluti in velocitate corusci luminis interluxerit menti' (Cant. xli. 3).

Effects on the Soul

The lasting effects on the soul of the higher mystical experiences—love, fervour, active zeal—are sufficiently brought out in the various passages just cited, and need not be dwelt upon. It will suffice to adduce a single piece in illustration:

If any one obtains by prayer to be transported in mind to that secret place of God, he will anon return from it fired with most vehement love of God, inflamed with zeal for righteousness, and filled with extreme fervour in all spiritual desires and duties (Cant. xlix. 4).

But in St Bernard are adumbrated those difficult mystical conceptions of 'transformation' and 'deification' that obtained a well-recognized place in the later mystical theology of the West.

The idea of deification was familiar, indeed, to the Greek Fathers; it was a favourite one with Clement of Alexandria,[1] and with pseudo-Dionysius, as a result of mystical contemplation. I am not able to speak of its history in Latin Christianity. St Augustine uses the language, but apparently of the final consummation of redemption in heaven.[2] Certainly we met no trace of it in his descriptions

---

[1] The passages are collected by Mr Butterworth in Journal of Theological Studies, Jan. 1916.

[2] 'Ut totus homo deificatus inhaereat perpetuae et incommutabili veritati' (Serm. clxvi. 4).

even of the highest mystical states; nor did we meet it in those of St Gregory.[1]

In more than one passage St Bernard gives expression to the idea of transformation (*Cant.* xxv. 5, lvii. 11, lxii. 5, lxix. 7); but all these passages are based on St Paul, 2 Cor. iii. 18: 'We all, beholding the glory of the Lord with face unveiled, are transformed into the same image from glory to glory, as by the Spirit of the Lord.' In each case, however, the passage is applied to the result of mystical contemplation in this life, and gives a lead to the idea of mystical transformation as found in later mystics.

Of 'deification' I find in St Bernard only one instance, and that refers to the consummation in heaven:

It will sometime come about that, as God willed all things for Himself, so we too may will neither ourselves nor aught else to have been, or to be, save equally for His sake, for His will alone, not our pleasure. ... O holy and chaste love! O sweet and tender affection! O pure and perfect intention of the will! surely so much more perfect and pure as there is in it now nothing mixed of its own; the more sweet and tender as all is divine that is felt. To be thus affected is to be deified (sic affici, deificari est). As a drop of water mingled in wine is seen to pass away utterly from itself, while it takes on the taste and colour of the wine; as a kindled and glowing iron becomes most like the fire, having put off its former and natural form; and as the air, when flooded with the light of the sun, is transformed into the same clarity of light, so that it seems to be not merely illumined, but the light itself: so it will needs be that all human affection in the Saints will then, in some ineffable way, melt from itself and be entirely poured over into the will of God. Otherwise how will God be all in all, if in man somewhat remains over of man? (*de diligendo Deo*, 20: the following sections, 29-33, contain one of the finest and most convincing of the attempts to depict the joys of the life eternal).

It was, no doubt, owing to the popularization of the Latin translation of pseudo-Dionysius that 'deification' came into vogue just after St Bernard in the West, as it always has been in the East, as a manner of describing the experiences of mystical contemplation and union in this life. St Bernard's similes in the above piece, of the drop of water, the iron, and the air, were also freely used to describe the union of the soul with God in this life, as in the next (Ruysbroeck, St John of the Cross, and Blosius in the piece cited above, p. 9), but on the part of the Catholic mystics always with a proviso against any kind of pantheistic absorption of the soul in the Deity.

[1] On deification see App. C of Dean Inge's *Christian Mysticism*, and the Index, under 'Deification' and 'Transmutation,' to Evelyn Underhill's *Mysticism*.

Those familiar with the literature of mysticism know the considerable place held in it by the imagery of 'spiritual marriage' as an allegory of the relationship between God and the soul in the highest kinds of mystical contemplation. This imagery is not found in St Augustine or St Gregory; but it is found fully developed in St Bernard. It calls for treatment in a separate section, and to it will be devoted § D, there being no possibility in St Bernard's case of the discussion instituted under that heading on St Augustine—viz. whether his contemplation was religious or only intellectual.

D. Spiritual Marriage: Union

The idea that Jesus Christ or the Divine Word is the Bridegroom, and the devout soul the Bride of the Canticle goes back to Origen, and became acclimatized in the West by the translations of his Commentary on the Canticle made by Jerome and Rufinus. It is found not infrequently in Augustine,[1] and at least once in Gregory;[2] but the idea is not emphasized or elaborated, as by Bernard. That consecrated virgins are the 'spouses of Christ' is a very early Christian conception, found, equivalently, in Cyprian (*Ep.* 4). Though a natural step, it is a step forward in allegory to look on the union of the soul with God in contemplation as a spiritual marriage, and to develop the imagery implied therein. The first, I believe, to give utterance to the realities of the mystical experience in terms of a sublimated human love was the austerely intellectual Plotinus, so little is such imagery in itself liable to suspicion of erotic sensuousness.[3]

Mystical writers in the West from the time of St Bernard onwards use the imagery of the 'spiritual marriage' freely, and as a matter of course. I do not know that it was so definitely used by any writer before him. It is found, however, and in an accentuated form, in his younger contemporary, Richard of St Victor (died c. 1173), *de quatuor Gradibus violentae Caritatis* (Migne, Patr. Lat. cxcvi.). It passed into the common stock of mystical writers in later times, notably B. John Ruysbroeck, St John of the Cross, St Teresa.[4]

The idea of the marriage is announced by Bernard from the first

[1] See Index to his works, under 'Sponsa,' 'Sponsus'.
[2] *Hom. in Ezech.* II. iii. 8; it is frequent in the spurious or doubtful *Comm. in Cant. Solom.*
[3] *Ennead*, vi. ix. 9; translated in Taylor's *Select Works of Plotinus*, ed. 1914, pp. 316–19, and Inge's *Philosophy of Plotinus*, ii. 139.
[4] See App. D of Inge's *Christian Mysticism*, Eales's Introduction to the *Sermons on the Canticle*, and especially Evelyn Underhill, *Mysticism*, pp. 162 ff., 509 ff. (and see Index).

sermon: The Canticle is a nuptial song, the chaste and joyous embraces of minds (11). Elsewhere he says:

I cannot contain myself for joy that the Divine Majesty disdains not to stoop to a familiar and sweet companionship with our lowliness, nor the supernal Godhead to enter into a marriage (inire connubia) with a soul still in exile, and despises not to show it the affection of a bridegroom possessed of a most ardent love (*Cant.* lii. 2).

Again: When the beloved soul shall have been perfected, the Bridegroom will make with her a spiritual marriage (spirituale coniugium) and they shall be two, not in one flesh, but in one spirit, according to the saying of the Apostle: 'He that is joined unto God is one spirit' (*Cant.* lxi. i.).

In the last five or six sermons on the Canticle, preached shortly before his death, St Bernard surpasses himself in the sublimity of his thought, in the fervour of his devotion, and in the eloquence of his language. The following is the passage in which he depicts the glory of the spiritual marriage:[1]

The return of the soul is its conversion, that is, its turning to the Word; to be reformed by Him and to be rendered conformable to Him. In what respect? In charity. It is that conformity which makes, as it were, a marriage between the soul and the Word, when, being already like unto Him by its nature, it endeavours to show itself like unto Him by its will, and loves Him as it is loved by Him. And if this love is perfected, the soul is wedded to the Word. What can be more full of happiness and joy than this conformity? What more to be desired than this love, which makes thee, O soul, no longer content with human guidance, to draw near with confidence thyself to the Word, to attach thyself with constancy to Him, to address Him familiarly and consult Him upon all subjects, to become as receptive in thy intelligence as fearless in thy desires? This is the contract of a marriage truly spiritual and sacred. And to say this is to say little; it is more than a contract, it is embracement (complexus). Embracement surely, in which perfect correspondence of wills makes of two one spirit. Nor is it to be feared that the inequality of the two who are parties to it should render imperfect or halting in any respect this concurrence of wills; for love knows not reverence. Love receives its name from loving, not from honouring. Let one who is struck with dread, with astonishment, with fear, with admiration, rest satisfied with honouring; but all these feelings are absent in him who loves. Love is filled with itself, and where love has come it overcomes and transforms all other feelings. Wherefore the soul that loves, loves, and knows nought else. He who justly deserves to be honoured, justly deserves to be admired and wondered

[1] Eales's translation inclines to tone down the language; of set purpose St Bernard is here allowed to say what he says.

at; yet He loves rather to be loved. They are Bridegroom and Bride. What other bond or constraining force do you seek for between spouses than to be loved and to love? ... God says: If I be Father, where is My honour? He says that as a Father. But if He declares Himself to be a Bridegroom, will He not change the word and say: If I be Bridegroom, where is My love? For He had previously said: If I be Lord, where is My fear? God, then, requires that He should be feared as Lord, honoured as Father, but as Bridegroom loved. Which of these three is highest and most to be preferred? Surely it is love. Without it fear is painful and honour without attraction. ... Neither of these will He receive if it be not seasoned with the honey of love. Love is sufficient by itself, it pleases by itself, and for its own sake. It is itself a merit, and itself its own recompense. Love seeks neither cause nor fruit beyond itself. Its fruit is its use. I love because I love; I love that I may love. Love, then, is a great reality. It is the only one of all the movements, feelings, and affections of the soul in which the creature is able to respond to its Creator, though not upon equal terms, and to repay like with like. For example, if God is wroth with me, may I similarly be wroth with Him? Certainly not, but I shall fear and tremble and implore pardon. ... But how different is it with love! For when God loves, He desires nought else than to be loved, because He loves us for no other purpose than that He may be loved, knowing that those who love Him become blessed by their love itself. ... Love that is pure is not mercenary; it does not draw strength from hope, nor is it weakened by distrust. This is the love of the Bride, because all that she is is only love. The very being of the Bride and her only hope is love. In this the Bride abounds; with this the Bridegroom is content. He seeks for nothing else; she has nothing else. Thence it is that He is Bridegroom and she is Bride. This belongs exclusively to a wedded pair, and to it none other attains, not even a son. The Bridegroom's love, or rather the Bridegroom who is Love, requires only love in return and faithfulness. Let it then be permitted to the Bride beloved to love in return. How could the Bride not love, she who is the Bride of Love? How could Love not be loved?

Rightly then does she renounce all other affections, and devote her whole self to Him alone Who is Love, because she can make a return to Him by a love which is reciprocal. For even when she has poured her whole self forth in love, what would that be in comparison to the ever-flowing flood of that Fountain? Not with equal fullness flows the stream of love from the soul and the Word, the Bride and the Bridegroom, the creature and the Creator. What then? Shall the desire of her who is espoused perish and become of none effect, because she is unable to contend with a Giant who runs His course, to dispute the palm of sweetness with honey, of gentleness with the lamb, of brilliance with the sun, of love with Him Who is Love? No. For although, being a creature, she love less, because she is less; nevertheless if she loves with her whole self, nothing is wanting where all is given. Wherefore, as I have said, to love thus is to be wedded (nupsisse); because it is not possible to love thus and yet not to be greatly loved, and in the consent of the two parties consists a full and perfect marriage (connubium). Can any one doubt that the soul is first loved, by the Word, and more dearly? Assuredly it is both anticipated in loving and surpassed. Happy the soul whose favoured lot it is to be prevented with the benediction of a delight so great. Happy the soul to which is granted to experience the embracement (complexus) of such sweetness, which is nought else than a love holy and chaste; a love sweet and delightful; a love as serene as it is sincere; a love mutual, intimate, powerful, which not in one flesh, but in one spirit joins together two, and makes them no more two, but one, according to St Paul: 'He that is joined to God is one spirit' (*Cant.* lxxxiii., the whole sermon compressed).

Let whoso will, see in this fine piece any note of sensuousness or of selfish enjoyment of spiritual delights. No less fine is the following passage, wherein the idea of the spiritual marriage is carried on to that of spiritual fecundity:

When you shall see a soul which, having left all, cleaves unto the Word with every thought and desire, lives only for the Word, rules itself according to the Word, nay, becomes, as it were, fruitful by the Word; which is able to say, 'To me to live is Christ and to die is gain;' then you may have much assurance that this soul is a Bride, wedded to the Word. ... Assuredly the soul of the Apostle Paul was, as it were, a faithful spouse and a tender mother, as was shown by his words: 'My little children, of whom I travail in birth again until Christ be formed in you.'

But notice that in this spiritual matrimony there are two ways of travailing in birth, with different offspring, though not contrary; since saintly souls, as holy mothers, either bring forth souls by preaching, or by meditation develop spiritual intellections (intelligentias).[1] In the latter kind of travail it sometimes happens that the soul is so transported out of itself and detached from the senses, that, though conscious of the Word, it has no consciousness of itself. This is the case when the mind is drawn on by the ineffable sweetness of the Word, and, as it were, is stolen from itself; or, rather, it is rapt and abides out of itself to enjoy the Word. The mind is affected in one way when it is rendered fruitful by the Word, and in another when it enjoys the presence of the Word. In the one, necessity of its neighbour importunes it, in the other the sweetness of the Word entices it. And, indeed, a mother has joy in her offspring; but a bride has greater joy in the embraces of her spouse. Dear are children, the pledges of affection; but kisses give greater joy. It is a good work to save many souls; but to be transported and to be with the Word, that is far more delightful. But when does that happen to us, or how long does it endure? Sweet is that intercourse; but how seldom does it occur, and for how brief a time does it last. And this

---

[1] The Latin of the following passage is given below (p. 117).

is the final reason for which the soul seeks the Word; namely, that it may find delight through enjoying Him.

What is it to enjoy the Word? I reply: Let that be asked rather from him who has had the experience. Even though it were given to me to have that experience, how can you think it possible that I should explain that which is incapable of being put into words? ... It has been permitted to me to have had that experience; it is not at all permitted to me to express it in speech. And in the reference which I have just now made to it, I adapt my words, so as to speak as you are able to receive what I say. O thou who art full of curiosity to know what it is to enjoy the Word, prepare thy mind for that, not thy ear. The tongue cannot teach it, it is taught only by grace. It is hidden from the wise and prudent, and it is revealed to babes. Humility, my brethren, is a great and lofty virtue, by which that which is not taught is merited; which is worthy to attain what is beyond the province of teaching; worthy of the Word, and by the Word to conceive that which it is not itself capable of expressing in words. Why is this? Not because of any merit of its own, but because such is the good pleasure of Him Who is the Father of the Word, the Bridegroom of the soul, Jesus Christ our Lord, Who is above all, God blessed for ever (*Cant.* lxxxv. 12-14).

These were almost the dying words of Bernard, for the next sermon, the last, remains half finished, cut short by death. It seems as though, at the end, he was inspired to lift the veil and disclose the most secret intimacies of his soul with God.

As such efforts of the mystics to describe their experiences are often attended by some danger of seemingly pantheistic language, it will be well to conclude this section with selections from a passage wherein St Bernard guards himself against any misconception as to a pantheistic absorption or identification of the soul in God. The whole second half of Sermon lxxi. (5-10) deals with this subject; only a few sentences are extracted:

'He who is joined to God is one spirit.' The union between God and man is not a unity, at least if compared with the unique and sovereign unity of Father and Son. For how can there be unity where there is plurality of natures and difference of substances? The union of God and man is brought about not by confusion of natures, but by agreement of wills. Man and God, because they are not of one substance or nature, cannot be called 'one thing' ('unum', like Father and Son); but they are with strict truth called 'one spirit', if they adhere to one another by the glue of love. But this unity is effected not by coherence of essences, but by concurrence of wills. God and man, because they exist and are separate with their own wills and substances, abide in one another not blended in substance but consentaneous in will.

E. Psycho-Physical Concomitants

In pursuance of the method followed in regard to SS Augustine and Gregory, we have now to examine the evidence afforded by St Bernard's writings as to psycho-physical concomitants of prayer and contemplation. The evidence of his writings will in the first place be collected and co-ordinated.

Evidence in regard to ecstasy, rapture, and bodily phenomena

Of the words that may suggest such conditions, the most usual with St Bernard is 'excessus', departure or transport, or the verb 'mente excedere'. This is taken from St Paul: 'Sive mente excedimus, Deo; sive sobrii sumus, vobis' (2 Cor. v. 13). The Doway Bible translates: 'Whether we are transported in mind'; the Revised Version: 'are beside ourselves'. It would be beyond our scope to examine the Scriptural use of 'excessus'; but in the text the meaning is not anything of the nature of full religious ecstasy. Bernard uses also the word 'ecstasy', but not so frequently; also 'flight' (volatus, avolare); and occasionally 'stupor', 'sleep', and even 'death'. Naturally 'rapere', 'rapi', to be caught up, or ravished, are of frequent occurrence, but I have not found the noun 'raptus'.

The meaning to be attached to these various terms must now be determined by the citation of passages illustrating their use.

It will be the most satisfactory course to take, in the first place, a series of pieces from a continuous passage of some length wherein the language may seem suggestive of the physical phenomena of rapture. The translation is quite literal:

I may then, without any absurdity, call the ecstasy (ecstasis) of the Bride a death, but one which delivers her not from life, but from the snares of life. For in this life we proceed in the midst of snares; which, however, are not feared as often as the soul, by some holy and vehement thought, is carried away out of itself (a semetipsa abripitur), provided that it so far departs in mind and flies away (mente secedat et avolet), that it transcends its usual way of thought. For how should impurity be feared, where there is no consciousness of life? For when the soul is transported (excedente anima), though not from life, yet from consciousness of life, the temptations of life cannot be felt. It is a good death which does not take away life, but changes it into something better, by which the body does not fall, but the soul is elevated.

This is a death which is the lot of men. But may my soul die the death also, if I may so speak, of the angels; that, departing from the memory of things present, it may divest itself not only of the desires but of the images of things below and corporeal, and may have pure commerce with those with whom is the image of purity. Such transport (excessus) alone, or in the highest degree, is named contemplation. For while alive not to be held by the desires of things is the part of human virtue; but in the processes of thought (speculando), not to be enveloped by the images of bodies is the part of angelic purity. But both are by divine gift, both are 'to be transported', both are to transcend yourself; but one a long way, the other not long. You have not yet gone a long way unless you are able by purity of mind to fly over (transvolare) the phantasmata of corporeal images that rush in from all sides. Unless you have attained to this,[1] do not promise yourself rest. You are mistaken if you think that short of this[1] you find a place of quiet, secret solitude, serene light, a dwelling of peace. But show me him who has arrived thither, and I will straightway confess that he is enjoying rest (quiescentem). This place is truly in solitude, this dwelling is in the light. Suppose, therefore that the Bride has withdrawn into this solitude, and there through the delightfulness of the place has sweetly gone to sleep in the embrace of the Bridegroom, that is to say, has been transported in spirit [as in an ecstasy]. ... As often as the Bride is transported (excedit) in contemplation, so often is she associated with the august company of the blessed spirits (*Cant.* lii. 4-6).

The foregoing passage is typical for our purpose, employing freely the words under consideration: ecstasis, excessus, mente excedere, abripere, avolare, transvolare, transcendere. It is patent, too, that the elevations in question are of the highest order, even ecstasy. Yet the phenomena depicted appear to be purely mental; there seems no reason for supposing any physical conditions to be contemplated.

A few short pieces will be added in further illustration, those being chosen which seem most suggestive of a physical side. It will appear that 'rapere' and 'rapi' do not carry the meaning of physical rapture.

If ever it befall one to be rapt by transport to the contemplation of God's majesty, that is the Finger of God, not the temerity of man (*Cant.* lxii. 4).

Purity carries us off (rapit) to contemplation, whereby we are lifted up to things invisible (*de Grad. Hum.* 19).

The perfect soul desires to be rapt by contemplation to the chaste embraces of her Spouse (*Serm. de div.* lxxxvii. 2).

If it have ever befallen one of you at any time to be so rapt and so

---

[1] Hucusque ... citra. Eales translates 'citra', 'on this side of your earthly existence,' as meaning that the 'place of quiet' cannot be attained to in this life. But what follows shows that St Bernard considered it is attained in contemplation, albeit momentarily, not permanently.

hidden in the secret sanctuary of God, as not to be called away or disturbed by the needs of the senses, or by the sting of some care, or the pang of some sin, or, what is with greater difficulty kept off, the inrushing phantasmata of bodily images; such an one, when he comes back to us, will be able to glory and to say: 'The King hath brought me into his bed-chamber' (*Cant.* xxiii. 16).

In the following, the word 'stupor' is used:

The delight of contemplation is likened to the feeling of rest 'in the sleep of a most sweet stupor and tranquil admiration' (ibid. xxiii. 11).
Contemplation 'sometimes for brief intervals holds the admiring soul aloft in stupor and ecstasy' (*de Consid.* v. 32).

Finally, [1]there is the piece already cited from *Canticle* lxxxv. 13; the English will be found on p. 113; the Latin is given here:

(In contemplatione) interdum exceditur et seceditur etiam a corporeis sensibus, ut sese non sentiat quae Verbum sentit. Hoc fit cum mens ineffabili Verbi illecta dulcedine, quodam modo se sibi furatur, imo rapitur atque elabitur a seipsa, ut Verbo fruatur.

This passage by itself would suggest phenomena akin to trance; but there is nothing in it that need mean more than a profound absorption of mind such as may take place without any fainting away of the body; and it is sound critical method to interpret this ambiguous passage by the general tenor of St Bernard's utterances, which, as we have seen, point to the conclusion that the experiences he speaks of were not accompanied by any such psycho-physical concomitants. This stands out with conspicuous clearness in the long autobiographical relation of his own experiences, cited in § B (p. 101), in which there is no suggestion of, or room for, any bodily phenomena.

Evidence in regard to visions, locutions, revelations, &c.

In the autobiographical piece just referred to, spoken near the close of his life, St Bernard says, as plainly as man could say it, that never in his contemplations or mystical elevations of soul had he perceived any vision, audition, locution, revelation, or anything in any way perceptible to the senses or imagination. Compare the piece cited at p. 104 from *Canticle* xxxi.

It is true that the Lives do speak of certain visions and communications; but they are different in character from the visions and revelations that play so great a part in the lives of many more recent mystics. Some of the visions appear to have occurred in sleep, and the communications for the most part were psychic rather than properly mystic; nor did they enter into Bernard's mystic experiences. Thus the Lives are not counter to his own testimony, that visions and locutions were not a feature of his personal spiritual life.

St Bernard is conspicuous for his loving devotion to the Humanity of our Lord and to His Passion. The following beautiful passage is well known:

> To meditate on (the life and sufferings of Jesus Christ) I have called wisdom; in these I have placed the perfection of righteousness for me, the fullness of knowledge, the abundance of merits, the riches of salvation. There is among them for me sometimes a draught of salutary bitterness, sometimes, again, a sweet unction of consolation. In adversities they raise me up, and in prosperity repress my exuberant delight. ... It is for these reasons that I have them frequently in my mouth, as you know, and always in my heart, as God knoweth. ... In a word, my philosophy is this, and it is the loftiest in the world, to know Jesus and Him crucified (*Cant.* xliii. 4).

On the matter of pictorial meditation on the Sacred Humanity St Bernard discourses in Sermon xx. on the Canticle. Many of the *Sermons de Tempore* are devoted to stirring up a tender love of Our Lord's Humanity, by pictures of Him in His Infancy, Life, and Passion, directly appealing to the imagination and emotions of the hearers, and drawn with all the depth of feeling and picturesqueness of language that Bernard could command so well. And yet of this love of the Sacred Humanity he writes as follows:

> The love of the heart is in a certain sense carnal, in that it chiefly moves the heart of man towards the flesh of Christ and what Christ in the flesh did and said. The sacred image of the God-Man, either being born or suckled or teaching or dying or rising again, is present to one in prayer, and must needs stir up the soul to the love of virtue. But although such devotion to the flesh of Christ is a gift, and a great gift, of the Holy Ghost, nevertheless I call it carnal in comparison with that love which does not so much regard the Word which is Flesh, as the Word which is Wisdom, which is Justice, which is Truth, which is Holiness (*Cant.* xx. 6, 8).

He goes on to show how love of Christ, at first carnal or sensible, progresses when it becomes rational love, and is perfected when it becomes spiritual love, in which the images of the Sacred Humanity no longer form part. And so when he comes to speak of the vision of Christ in contemplation, he expresses himself as follows:

> In this knowing of Jesus and Him crucified, while abiding in His

wounds, and contemplating gladly the things which relate to Him, Incarnate and in His Passion ... I do not suppose that in this vision there is presented to the senses any images of His Flesh or of His Cross, or any other kinds of likenesses of our weak flesh; for in these respects 'He hath no form nor comeliness.' But that the soul beholding Him now pronounces Him fair and comely, shows He appeared to her by means of a nobler vision ... a vision certainly sublime and sweet (*Cant*. xlv. 4, 6).

This shows that in his contemplations there was no framing of pictures of the scenes of the Passion, nor any portrait presented to the mind of Our Lord's human form. It is the same in regard to the intercourse between Him and the soul:

As often as you hear or read that the Word and the soul converse together or behold each other, do not imagine that so to say bodily words pass between them, or that bodily images of those conversing are seen. Think rather that the Word is a spirit and the soul is a spirit, and they have tongues of their own by which they speak to one another and indicate their presence. The tongue of the Word is the favour of His condescension, and the tongue of the soul is her fervour (ibid. 7).

And elsewhere:

When with eager mind we ponder His testimonies and the judgements of His Mouth, and meditate on His law day and night, we should know for certain that the Bridegroom is present and is speaking to us, that we may not be wearied by our labours, being rejoiced by His words (*Cant*. xxxii. 4).

[In the union of the soul with God] the Word utters no sound, but penetrates; It is not full of words, but full of power; It strikes not on the ears, but caresses the heart; the form of its Face is not defined, and it does not touch the eyes of the body, but it makes glad the heart, not with charm of colour, but with the love it bestows (ibid. xxxi. 6).

F. THE VISION OF GOD

This subject need not detain us long. St Bernard betrays no knowledge of St Augustine's speculations concerning the vision of God accorded to Moses and St Paul. The subject is alluded to principally in *Canticle* xxxi. all, xxxii. 9, xxxiii. 6, xxxiv. 1. His doctrine is quite categorical that God's Being cannot be seen as It is by man in this life:

God now appears as He wishes, not as He is. No wise man, no saint, no prophet, is able to see Him as He is, nor has been able in this mortal body (*Cant*. xxxi. 2).

Again:

I would not say that He appears as He is, although He does not manifest Himself as something altogether other than that which He is (ibid. xxxi. 7).

The knowledge of God in contemplation is thus characterized:

The soul slumbering in contemplation dreams God; for through a mirror and in an enigma, and not face to face, does it behold Him; and it warms with the love of something conjectured rather than seen, momentarily, as if in the flash of a passing spark, and touched scantily and barely—'non tam spectati quam conjectati, idque raptim, et quasi sub quodam coruscamine scintillulae transeuntis, tenuiter vix attacti' (*Cant.* xviii. 6).

Concerning Moses's vision, this is what St Bernard says:

In olden time holy Moses, presuming greatly on the favour and familiarity that he had found with God, aspired to a certain great vision, so as to say to God: If I have found favour in Thine Eyes, show me Thyself. But he received instead of this a vision of much lower order, from which, however, he might be able at some time to come to that one which he desired (ibid. xxxiv. 1).

In contrast with this the terms used in speaking of St Benedict's vision come as a surprise:

[In the next life] the earthly creature, like the heavenly creature, no longer through a mirror and in an enigma, but face to face will see God, and His Wisdom will be contemplated with clearness in itself. Meantime the human mind has need of some kind of vehicle of a creature that it may mount up to the knowledge of the Creator; whereas the angelic nature has far more blessedly and perfectly its knowledge of the creature in the Creator. To this excellence, though only for a moment (*or* partially, 'ad modicum'), seems to have been rapt that blessed soul, which saw the whole world collected under one ray of the sun. Of this miracle St Gregory says: To him who sees the Creator, all creation is small (*Serm. de div.* ix. 1).

CONTEMPLATION

4. SUMMARY

SUMMARY : CHARACTERISTICS OF
WESTERN MYSTICISM

WE are now in a position to understand the title of this book, *Western Mysticism*, which is taken as being something different from, as being a particular phase of mysticism in the West. This latter would be a much wider and more difficult subject. The characteristic features of what is here taken as Western Mysticism, and which seem to differentiate it from other types of mysticism, will now be unfolded.

(1) Those familiar with the writings of later mystics will know how they delight to describe the highest mystic states in the terms of darkness and obscurity; of knowing God by ignorance and unknowing; of being plunged in the solitude of the Godhead or in the viewless abyss of the divine Nature. Such expressions occur in the extracts given in the Prologue and they might be multiplied indefinitely. The writer in the *Nation*, referred to in the Preface, puts the case thus:

The mystics heap up terms of negation—darkness, void, nothingness—in endeavouring to describe that Absolute which they have apprehended. It may be, of course, that their apprehension had such a fullness and richness of content that in human language it could only be described negatively. But one may, at least, point out that their method is the very opposite of the characteristically Christian one of affirmation; that where they say, 'darkness' St John says 'light', and that St John says 'fulness' where they say 'void': and St Paul stresses, not ignorance, but enhanced knowledge, as the result of religious experience.

Now it will be felt that our three Western Doctors whose teaching on contemplation has just been exposed, do not lie open to this objection: for them contemplation is a revelation of light and knowledge and fullness; what religious experience could be fuller and richer than the 'spiritual marriage' as depicted by St Bernard? We did, indeed, meet in St Gregory (above, p. 88) the idea that the knowledge of God by contemplation in this life is as seeing the sun through a cloud or mist—'clouds of darkness are round about Him' (Ps. xcvi. 2); but this idea is quite different from the divine Dark of the later mysticism: though the light be seen as through a chink or through a mist, for St Gregory it is light that is perceived in contemplation, not darkness.

The reason for the change which in this matter came over the spirit of mysticism in Western Europe is not far to seek: it may be found in the pieces from the writings of pseudo-Dionysius cited at the head of the extracts in the Prologue (p. 6). The writings of this mysterious personage now recognized as a Christian neo-Platonist, probably Syrian, of the early sixth century, especially indebted to the neo-Platonist Proclus,[1] were translated into Latin in the ninth century by John Scotus Erigena. They seem, however, not to have come into general vogue until the twelfth century. Certain of the treaties were commented on by Hugh of St Victor and the great schoolmen, including St Thomas, who knew them thoroughly and used them freely as among his principal authorities, as did the other scholastic doctors. Thus the doctrine of pseudo-Dionysius entered fully into the intellectual tradition of the West from the twelfth century onwards. His emphasis is laid strongly on the idea of the transcendence of God, and he pushes to its extreme limit the 'negative way' in attaining to knowledge of God.

The all-pervading influence of his theological conceptions is very apparent in the German Dominican mystics of the fourteenth century, Eckhart, Tauler, Suso, and in the Flemish Canon Regular, Ruysbroeck; it is very apparent also in the Carmelite St John of the Cross and the Benedictines Abbot Blosius and Fr Augustine Baker. In fact in the West, from the twelfth century onwards until modern times, the thoughts of the mystics about their own experiences in contemplation have been coloured by the philosophical and theological theories of Dionysius, and their language has been moulded in his categories.

St Augustine was prior to pseudo-Dionysius. St Gregory in one place refers to the *Celestial Hierarchy* as authority on a point concerning the angels;[2] but there is no trace in his utterances on contemplation and mystical theology of any influence of the theories or language of pseudo-Dionysius; indeed his fundamental conception of the process of contemplation is diametrically opposite. For 'Dionysius' the soul in contemplation is borne up to the ray of the divine Darkness; for Gregory it endeavours to fix its gaze on the ray of the unencompassed Light. Nor do I discern any trace of the influence of pseudo-Dionysius in St Bernard.

---

[1] See the tractate of Fr J. Stiglmair, S.J., *Die Pseudo-Dionysische Schriften*, 1895.

[2] *Hom. in Evang.* xxxiv. 12. It is obscure how St Gregory came by his knowledge of this passage, because, in spite of his sojourn in Constantinople, he could not read Greek. But the manner of citation seems to indicate that his knowledge was by hearsay rather than first-hand: 'Fertur Dionysius Areopagita, antiquus videlicet et venerabilis pater, dicere.'

The first characteristic, therefore, marking off the mystical theology of SS Augustine, Gregory, and Bernard from that which came in just after St Bernard's time, and has held sway ever since in the West, is that it is 'pre-Dionysian', untouched by the ideas and nomenclature of the religious philosophy made current by the diffusion of the Dionysiac writings in Latin in the twelfth century.

(2) Another characteristic of the mystical theology of our three Doctors is that it is 'pre-scholastic'. They discourse of contemplation as occasion arises, but make no attempt at any systematic presentation of their teaching in the form of a scientific treatise of mystical theology. But this was being done by St Bernard's contemporaries, Hugh and Richard of St Victor. The latter especially produced treatises wherein it is sought to reduce the theory and practice of contemplation to a science in the approved scholastic manner then coming into fashion.

Moreover, a speculative and philosophical treatment of the subject, according to the principles of the Platonic or Aristotelian philosophies, was introduced, and this process was carried forward by the great scholastics, so that mystical theology tended more and more to become a science of contemplation rather than contemplation itself, an intellectual system rather than a religious experience. The difference between this manner of treatment, and that which we have found in St Bernard and St Gregory, and St Augustine too, is very apparent. In them there is no philosophizing about contemplation, no thought of systematizing or schematization. All they aim at doing is to describe as best they can the personal experiences of their soul.

The features so far mentioned are recognized by Abbé Pourrat in regard to St Bernard, and what he says of him is equally applicable to St Gregory:

The mysticism of St Bernard does not present itself as a synthesis; it is exposed in an oratorical manner. It has no scientific character; it is essentially practical. Contrary to that of St Augustine and of pseudo-Dionysius, the neo-Platonic theories are wholly strangers to it, and equally so is scholastic philosophy. He speaks of mystic facts according to his own personal experience and that of the monks whose confidences he had received (*La Spiritualité Chrétienne*, ii. 98).

Here is noted a difference between St Bernard (and St Gregory) on the one hand, and St Augustine on the other, in that the mysticism of the latter is expressed in the terms of his neo-Platonism.

(3) A third characteristic. In 1910 was published by Père Poulain, S.J., a book entitled *Journal spirituel de Lucie Christine* (English,

1915). It is a selection from the diary of a devout French lady, kept by request of her confessor, wherein she recorded her religious experiences and the principal facts of her spiritual life from 1870, shortly after her marriage, until her death in 1908. It is a record of divine favours of all kinds, often almost from day to day: of words spoken in her soul by God, or by Jesus Christ, often at Communion; of visions, pictorial or intellectual; of communications and impressions of religious truths, and perceptions of things divine. This book is brought in here not in order that any kind of critique may be made of the value of its contents, but that it may serve as a standard of comparison. Because, whether a spiritual life made up of such experiences be an advance on that of SS Augustine, Gregory, and Bernard, or not, there can be no question that it is something quite different.

Now this type of mysticism, abounding in revelations and visions, so usual in later times, set in with St Gertrude and the two Mechtilds in the century after St Bernard. They were the recipients of communications and messages, seers of pictorial panoramic visions. And from that time forth these elements have tended to enter more and more into the experiences of Catholic mystics, and have almost come to be identified with mysticism itself.

And here it may be of interest to note the fact that the line of great seers of visions and hearers of revelations is made up almost wholly of women:—the names of Gertrude and the Mechtilds have just been mentioned; other well-known instances are Hildegard, Elizabeth of Schonau, Bridget of Sweden, Angela of Foligno, Catherine of Siena, Maria Magdalena de Pazzi, and in modern times, Margaret Mary Alacoque and Catherine Emerich. Of course from SS Peter and Paul and John downwards men too have seen visions and heard words. But it seems to be the case that nearly always it has been women who have had elaborate pictorial visions, often succeeding each other in a sort of panoramic series.[1] It is not suggested that the visions are any the worse for that; but it does seem that there is something in the mental or psychic make-up of women that renders them susceptible to this kind of quasi-mystical experience.

The entire absence of any such element of vision, locution, revelation, from the mysticism of SS Bernard, Gregory, and Augustine, is again a characteristic distinguishing it from more modern types.

---

[1] Fr Herbert Thurston, S.J., in a paper contributed to the Society for Psychical Research (*Proceedings*, vol. xxxii.), has pointed out that similarly, though there are a great number of apparently well-authenticated cases of 'stigmatization' in women, St Francis has been the only case among men, at least until one in our day.

(4) In various places in her writings St Teresa describes the phenomena of the state of rapture or trance as experienced by herself. Its effects on the body are such that there is for the time being complete bodily collapse (*Interior Castle*, 'Sixth Mansion', iv.; *Life*, xx.).

Neither in St Gregory nor St Bernard did we find trace of any such violent rapture as St Teresa speaks of. Nor did we in St Augustine's accounts of his own experiences; but it may be questioned whether, in the supreme ecstasy in which he believed that the Being of God may be seen, he did not intend some such physical condition, in that he held the soul to be, for the time being, gone forth from the body.

(5) Besides the phenomena of rapture and trance, there have at all times in the history of mysticism been a variety of lesser psycho-physical concomitants of mystic states. The inpouring of the Holy Spirit at Pentecost caused in the Apostles a physical state that bore the outward semblance of intoxication. The enthusiasm and excitement of highly-wrought religious emotion, as at 'revivals', always tends to manifest itself in physical expression of many kinds. Again, mystical states and psycho-physical experiences are often produced by a set process of self-hypnotization, as was the case of the Hesychast monks of Mount Athos, who by auto-hypnotism and suggestion induced at will their vision of 'the uncreated light'. Concentration of mind on a religious idea, or on other ideas, often causes physical effects on the body. The history of religious experience and of mysticism, both true and false, is full of such psycho-physical phenomena.[1] But they find no place in the descriptions given of their experiences by our three Doctors; there is no suggestion of anything more than a deep absorption of mind in prayer, such that consciousness is lost of external things and of the operations of the mind itself.

(6) Yet another point wherein SS Augustine, Gregory, and Bernard differ from later mystical writers. Those familiar with modern treatises on mystical theology, as those of Schram and Gorres, will know the great part played by the Evil One. Such subjects as diabolical obsession and possession have won a recognized place in these books. There is a constant fear of, a constant guarding against the intrusions of the Devil in prayer and in every turn of the spiritual life. We recall the case of St Teresa: she relates how once her spiritual state was investigated by a number of learned theologians who examined her personally, and after much con-

[1] Fr Thurston discusses the psycho-physical concomitants of mystical states in a long series of articles in the *Month*, 1919-21.

ferring together came to the unanimous conclusion that she was being deceived by Satan and that her prayer was his work (*Life*, xxv. 18-21).

In *Benedictine Monachism* I wrote:

> It is strange how the Devil has invaded the realm of mystical theology and shares the ground about equally with Almighty God. In Görres's *Mystik* there are two volumes of 'Divine Mysticism' and two volumes of 'Diabolical Mysticism', in great measure a systematized demonology, filthy and disgusting. Though the Devil figures largely in the stories of St Gregory's *Dialogues*, and is the object of much theological disquisition in his other works, and also in St Bernard's, neither saint manifests any fear of his intrusion in the intimate personal relations of the soul with God (p. 65).[1]

It is for the reasons just set forth that I seemed to see in the teaching on contemplation of the three great Doctors, Augustine, Gregory, and Bernard, a type of mysticism with clearly marked characteristics that differentiate it from other types of mysticism, earlier and later. It may be described as pre-Dionysian, pre-scholastic, non-philosophical; unaccompanied by psycho-physical concomitants, whether rapture or trance, or any quasi-hypnotic symptoms; without imaginative visions, auditions, or revelations; and without thought of the Devil. It is a mysticism purely and solely religious, objective and empirical; being merely, on the practical side, the endeavour of the soul to mount to God in prayer and seek union with Him and surrender itself wholly to His love; and on the theoretical side, just the endeavour to describe the first-hand experiences of the personal relations between the soul and God in contemplation and union. And it is a mysticism far removed from any kind of quietism: though images and phantasmata and sense perceptions are shut out from the imagination and memory, and the processes of reasoning silenced, and the faculties of the mind quieted, and words cease and language fails; all this produces not a blank, but makes room for the soul itself to actuate and energize with a highly wrought activity and intense concentration on God.

---

[1] A critic called in question this statement in regard to St Bernard, referring to *Serm. in Cant.* xxxiii. This is not counter to what is said in the text. Of course St Bernard accepted the New Testament doctrine that the Devil is the great Tempter, 'going about as a roaring lion seeking whom he may devour.' Of course he believed that Satan 'transforms himself into an angel of light,' so as to deceive and mislead even those that stand spiritually highest: such stories are one of the commonplaces of early monasticism, witness Cassian and Palladius. But when St Bernard speaks of contemplation and prayer and personal devotion, the Devil does not come in, and there is not that abiding sense of the danger of his intervention, such as is in some measure manifested by even the most spiritual of more modern writers, as St John of the Cross and Fr Baker. The numerous pieces given in these pages show abundantly that St Bernard was not haunted by this fear of diabolical illusion in prayer.

The foregoing description applies substantively to St Augustine's mysticism, as well as to St Gregory's and St Bernard's; but it applies more fully and more completely to theirs. Though in reality experimental, and not philosophical, St Augustine's mysticism is coloured by his neo-Platonism, and is conceived according to the ideas, and in some measure expressed in the language, of that philosophy which was such a living reality to him. But however expressed, real religious mysticism is not a philosophy; it is an experience.

It is important to insist on the fact that neither the philosophizings of the mystics nor their theological speculations, even when claiming to be based on their experiences in mystical contemplation, have anything to say to essential mysticism. Some mystics are of a metaphysical turn of mind, and have endeavoured to give utterance to the thoughts their experiences have inspired on such profound subjects as the Being and Attributes of God, the Persons of the Holy Trinity, the nature of the soul, its union with God, the problem of evil, the cosmic laws of God's working in the universe. But such speculations are no more guaranteed by the mystic state in which they were conceived, are no more to be identified with mysticism, than are the revelations received, or thought to be received, under the same conditions, but against which the great spiritual masters give such emphatic warnings. Mysticism as such has nothing to say to philosophy: some mystics, like some other people, have held philosophies, and of all kinds—Platonism, pantheism, scholasticism, idealism;—but most mystics, like most other people, have been devoid of anything that deserves the name of philosophy. For, like religion, mysticism is not the privilege of the intellectual, but is within the reach of the poor and unlearned and the little ones of Christ; and without any doubt it is most commonly and most successfully cultivated by those who know not its name. Even masters in mysticism, as St Gregory, St Bernard, St Francis, St Teresa, cannot properly be said to have belonged to any philosophical school. Mysticism finds its working expression not in intellectual speculation, but in prayer.

Of course there may be a philosophy of mysticism, as there is a philosophy of history or of politics, although neither history nor politics are themselves philosophy. It is not too much to say that St Gregory and St Bernard might have written every word they wrote on contemplation and mysticism, had neither Plato, nor Aristotle, not Plotinus, nor 'Dionysius', nor even Augustine himself, ever lived; because the personal religious experiences which they describe were in no way dependent on what they learned from any man.

If, owing to its neo-Platonic affinities, St Augustine's mysticism stands somewhat apart from that of SS Gregory and Bernard, the mysticism found in Cassian is quite identical with theirs. Cassian's teaching on the spiritual life and prayer, on contemplation and mysticism, has been worked out sufficiently in *Benedictine Monachism* (pp. 47-49, 63-67, 78-82), and need not be incorporated here; in its essential elements it falls under the definition or description given above. It is set forth by Cassian as being what he learned from the hermits of the Egyptian deserts, and no doubt it was such. Its resemblances to the teaching of SS Gregory and Bernard are doubtless due to similarity of origin: both are the result of the effort on the part of spiritually highly gifted, devout souls to express what they experienced in prayer, contemplation, and union with God, just objectively as they experienced it, and without regard to any theories or philosophies; and the identity of teaching is due to the fact that their experiences were much the same.

And so, while fully recognizing the surpassing elevation and the supreme value and interest of St Augustine's presentation of his mystical experience, it is pre-eminently to the mysticism of Cassian, Gregory, and Bernard that I venture to give the name 'Western Mysticism'. Cassian forbids us to claim it as a purely Western product, originating in the West. But it became domiciled in the West, and, owing chiefly to the overmastering influence of St Gregory, it held sway there universally during the early Middle Ages, the 'Benedictine Centuries', for the six hundred years from 550 to 1150. That it underwent no great change in all this period is shown by St Bernard's entire agreement with St Gregory. During this same period in the East, as after it also in the West, the mystical theology and theories of pseudo-Dionysius were the dominant influence; so that the simple practical mysticism of these centuries in Western Europe is a thing apart, and deserves a name to itself and separate treatment.

Abbé Pourrat (op. cit.) calls the affective practical mysticism of St Bernard, 'the Benedictine School'; but though without doubt it was the kind of spirituality and mysticism in use generally in the Benedictine monasteries of the Middle Ages, it cannot be claimed as being in any particular sense Benedictine. It was the mysticism of the Church in the West in those days, and Benedictines quite naturally adopted it. It seems to me that 'Western Mysticism' is the proper name, both because it was the mysticism of the West until foreign elements, notably pseudo-Dionysius, came in, and because its principal exponent, St Gregory, was typically Western, Roman, in mind and temperament, so that his formulation of mystical doctrine was characterized by an element of Roman soberness and practical sense, which made this type of mysticism immune from the elements of extravagance, fanaticism, and delusion, both of thought and act, which have so frequently disfigured mysticism in its concrete embodiments.

For it has to be recognized that there are few religious tendencies more dangerous, more mischievous, than a false, uncontrolled, unbalanced mysticism. It has led in all ages to deplorable excesses of fanaticism, self-deception, madness, rebellion. The like may, of course, be said of other things in themselves good—of metaphysics, politics, economics. One feels that the rulers of the Church must often have been sorely tempted, in view of the practical troubles and embarrassments occasioned by the aberrations of mystics, to rule the whole thing out. And yet they have not done so. On the contrary, the Church has blessed mysticism in her saints; for those of them who have not been martyrs or apostles, have for the most part been mystics. In spite of all errors and counterfeits, the Church has set the seal of her approval on mysticism itself, and in its highest manifestations as made in the saints.

These saints themselves, the mystics, are unanimous as to the great religious value of contemplation and the mystical experience. It is the conviction that the type of mysticism here called 'Western Mysticism', especially as presented by St Gregory and St Bernard, offers to all devout souls a kind of mysticism free from danger, intellectual or spiritual; free from bodily and psycho-physical phenomena, usually so dubious, so liable to illusion, and at best in most cases so little desirable; a mysticism that is simple and practical and downright in character, being no more than the exercise of piety and prayer and love in a very earnest and whole-hearted manner—it is this conviction that led to the writing of this book.

It is a fact to be deplored that devout souls are apt to be frightened off mysticism by the presentations commonly made of it nowadays, whereby it is almost identified with a quasi-miraculous state of visions, revelations, and extraordinary favours frequently affecting the body; so that it is placed on a sort of pedestal, as a thing to be wondered at and admired respectfully from beneath, out of reach of all but the small number of select ones called by God to a privilege so exceptional, the very thought of which as a thing to be practically desired would be presumption. Yet it was the standard teaching in the Catholic ages down to modern times that contemplation is the natural term of a spiritual life seriously lived, and is a thing to be desired, aspired to, aimed at, and not infrequently attained to by devout souls. We shall see that it is explicitly taught by SS Augustine and Gregory (under § K) that contemplation is open to all. And that this was the great Catholic tradition is shown by Abbé Saudreau in the book *La Vie d'Union à Dieu* (1901). This older view is being reasserted increasingly by Catholic writers on the subject in these our days. It is the hope that the teaching of the three great Western Doctors may promote the return to the old Catholic tradition that has prompted the undertaking of this presentation of 'Western Mysticism'.

CONTEMPLATION

EPILOGUE

EPILOGUE

THE VALIDITY OF THE MYSTICS' CLAIM

BEING now in possession of a body of first-hand material, we may come to face the question posed in the 'Prologue' as the outstanding problem of mysticism: The validity of the claim consistently made by the great mystics. The extracts there given from the utterances of a number of the best-accredited Catholic mystics show that their claim amounts to this: that in the highest mystic state the soul, already in this life, enters into conscious immediate relationship with God. It would be too much to say that on the admission of this claim depends the value of the writings of the mystics: even if it be disallowed, many of their writings would retain indeed their value and utility as spiritual instruction for those embracing an interior life of self-discipline, mortification, and prayer; but the most characteristically mystical treatises would have to find their level as the utterance of a splendid illusion, of value only to the psychologist studying religious phenomena or the historian of religious thought. Thus, St Teresa's *Way of Perfection* and the first four Mansions of the *Interior Castle* would always be of practical use to those endeavouring to lead a spiritual life; but the last three Mansions, along with the two latest and most mystical of the treatises of St John of the Cross, and a host of other such writings, would have to be classed in our libraries as outworn ideas of a bygone age, or at best as religious poetry.

At the outset it has to be premised that at all times and in many ways the idea of communion with divinity, and the effort to achieve it, and the conviction of the individual that he has achieved it, are common features in religions of all kinds, and are amongst the most universal expressions of the religious consciousness; and especially is ecstasy looked on as the means of effecting union with divinity.

The vast majority of such claims have to be set aside as unreal. Often the means taken to bring about the state of ecstasy and union are altogether repulsive—magical, orgiac, immoral; often they are hypnotic. Often a state of religious excitement and exaltation is deliberately produced by physical or psychological methods, or by playing on the religious emotions of a crowd, as in revivals. Of such methods the result is often religious frenzy and abnormal physical phenomena, akin to hysteria. Within Christianity religious excitement and expectancy frequently produce the feeling of being specially visited by God, by the Holy Ghost, by Jesus Christ. Well-authenticated and evidently sincere cases of such convictions fill volumes.¹ In most cases the experience must be set down as purely subjective, the result of highly-wrought religious emotions, nothing more than an excess of sensible devotion. Similarly, visions, revelations, locutions, auditions, impulses, movements, experiences, are a field wherein is endless scope for illusion, self-deception, auto-suggestion, as is very well recognized by the most accredited authorities on the spiritual life; concerning a nun who claimed to hear locutions from God, St John of the Cross said: 'All this that she says: God spoke to me; I spoke to God; seems nonsense.—Such an one has only been speaking to herself' (after the Letters, and *Ascent*, ii. 29). Bodily conditions, indistinguishable on the physical side from ecstasy and rapture, but without any religious content, can be produced by hypnotism, or may be the results of hysteria or neurasthenia or other morbid pathological conditions. And there is a series of well-authenticated cases of what may be called 'nature ecstasies', non-religious in the manner of production, and non-religious or vaguely religious in content, but akin on the phenomenal side to religious ecstasy.

In short it is not to be denied that the mystics find themselves in bad company. The question is: From all this welter of unpromising stuff do the experiences of the great mystics stand out with such distinction and such compelling force as to impose themselves by their quality, so that they constitute a class apart, able to carry the weight of their tremendous claim, and to assert its validity?

For myself, I believe that it is so. To prevent misconception, I say quite simply that I have never had any such experience myself, never anything that could be called an experimental perception of God or His Presence. But I do accept the witness of the great mystics of the Catholic Church: it is one of the best equipped of modern writers on mysticism, not a Catholic, who has declared that 'the greatest mystics have been Catholic saints.'² The reports of the greatest among them come home to me with convincing signs not only of truthfulness, but of objective truth. I cannot think they were under such grievous delusion in what they believed they had been through.

It will be helpful to know the position in regard to mystical experiences of a modern psychologist like William James. He sums up

¹ See Starbuck, *Psychology of Religion*, and William James, *Varieties of Religious Experience*.
² Evelyn Underhill, *Mysticism*, p. 126.

the subject at the end of the lectures on Mysticism (*Varieties of Religious Experience*, pp. 422-4):

> Mystical experiences are, and have the right to be, authoritative for those that have had them, and those who have had them not are not in a position to criticize or deny the validity of the experience; the mystic is invulnerable and must be left in undisturbed possession of his creed.

But, on the other hand, he says, those that have not had the experience are not called upon to accept the validity of the claim on the authority of the mystics; though James himself evidently is prepared to admit that there may be validity in it:

> It must always remain an open question whether mystical states may not possibly be superior points of view, windows through which the mind looks out upon a more extensive and inclusive world (p. 428).

So it comes back to the question of evidence, and it would seem that the only way of bringing the claim to the test is to listen to what the greatest of the mystics report of their experience, and to judge in accordance with the impressions of truthfulness, reality, sanity, religious elevation, made by their reports. Copious collections of extracts from the writings of very many of them are to be found in the standard works on mysticism; but it seems preferable to allow a small number of master-mystics to speak at some length as representatives of the race, and give a short, connected account of what they declare their individual personal experiences to have been. We have already heard three such master-mystics thus speaking in the persons of SS Augustine, Gregory, and Bernard; and I propose adducing as a fourth witness St John of the Cross. But before doing so it will be well to clear the ground by making certain general considerations.

(1) Let us then consider the claim of the mystics in the light of Christian theology, beginning with the New Testament.

Such texts as the following at once meet us: 'If a man love me, he will keep my words, and my Father will love him, and we will come unto him and make our abode with him' (John xiv. 23). The indwelling of the Holy Ghost in the souls of the just is affirmed by St Paul in a number of places: 'Know ye not that ye are the temple of God, and that the Spirit of God dwelleth in you?' (1 Cor. iii 16). 'Know ye not that your body is the temple of the Holy Ghost who is in you, whom ye have from God?' (1 Cor. vi. 19).

In Catholic theology, and I believe in old-fashioned Protestant theology, these texts are taken as being literally true—in the regenerate soul in a state of grace God dwells, and in an especial manner the Holy Ghost. Thus St Thomas says: 'The Holy Ghost inhabits the mind by His substance.'[1] The effect of this indwelling is further described by St Paul: 'The love of God hath been shed abroad in our hearts through the Holy Ghost who hath been given unto us' (Rom. v. 5); and along with love the other virtues too, and the Seven Gifts of the Holy Ghost, which make the Twelve Fruits of the Spirit grow in the soul. All this results in a wondrous beautifying of the soul. On this subject Fathers, theologians, preachers wax eloquent; they find it difficult to depict the spiritual beauty of the soul in the state of God's grace and friendship, inhabited by the Holy Ghost, and adorned with His Gifts. They adopt the words of 2 Peter, 'partakers of the divine nature' (i. 4), and rise to the idea of 'deification': 'All those in whom the Holy Ghost abides become deified by this reason alone.'[2]

And not only in the order of grace, but in that of nature is God present in every soul: 'He is not far from each one of us, for in Him we live and move and have our being' (Acts xvii. 27). As the theologians say, God is present in all creatures in a threefold way: by essence, by power, by presence or inhabitation; and He is in a special way present in spiritual beings. According to the Catholic sense of divine immanence, God working in man is more intimately present in him than man is even in himself.[3] This reminds us of Augustine: 'Thou art more inward to me than my most inward part.'[4]

When these elements of Christian doctrine are kept in view, it appears that the claim of the mystics is hardly more than this: that what is accepted by Christian belief as realities of faith in the case of all souls in the state of grace, becomes consciously realized in the mystic vision. It involves hardly more than momentary liftings of the veil that keeps hidden from the mind's eye the soul's super- natural estate. It is an experimental perception of the presence of God in the soul, Who at all times is there.

If it be said that on this showing what would be surprising is not that the mystical experience should sometimes take place, but rather that it should so seldom take place; should it not be expected to be a more ordinary experience of the spiritual life devotedly lived? To

---

[1] 'Spiritus Sanctus per suam substantiam mentem inhabitat' (c. Gent. iv. 18).
[2] Athanasius, Ep. ad Serap. i. 24.
[3] 'Sunt qui in eo collocant (divinam immanentiam), quod Deus agens intime adsit in homine, magis quam ipse sibi homo; quod plane, si recte intelligitur, reprehensionem non habet' (Encyclical 'Pascendi').
[4] Tu, autem eras interior intimo meo' (Conf. iii. 11).

such questions the answer must be the same as that to all questions
and difficulties concerning God's distribution of graces and favours,
whether in the supernatural order or the natural—We do not know.
Our only answer can be that confession of ignorance with which
St Paul concludes the discussion of these mysterious subjects: 'O the
depth of the riches both of the wisdom and of the knowledge of
God!'

There is an answer given in the *Imitation of Christ*: 'This is the
reason why there are found so few contemplative persons, because
few know how to separate themselves wholly from created and
perishing things' (iii. 31). And this would be the answer of St John
of the Cross, that few are willing to pay the full price in renunciation
at which alone the mystic experience can be purchased; few are
prepared to make the Ascent of Mount Carmel with him.

(2) Let us now consider the claim from the side of psychology.

The modern psychologists, who, while not accepting the objective
truth of the mystics' claim, still very well recognize that there is
something there that is not to be explained as hallucination or
hysteria or degeneracy, such as William James and H. Delacroix,[1]
have recourse to recent theories of the 'subliminal self' or 'sub-
conscious self.' Great attention is being paid in modern psychology
to the sub-conscious regions of the mind; yet no one has explored
them better than did St Augustine in Book x. of the *Confessions*,
where he speaks of the Memory as the mysterious storehouse of vast
quantities of forgotten knowledge and impressions. And not only
forgotten knowledge is there, but powers, instincts, intuitions, good
and bad, highest and lowest, they are all working in this unconscious
region, and only now and then, and imperfectly, come to the surface
of consciousness. It is the idea of William James and others that
mystical states are part of the stuff of the sub-conscious region, and
are an emergence of latent powers from sub-consciousness into
consciousness—'inroads from the sub-conscious life, of the cerebral
activity correlative to which we as yet know nothing' (*Varieties*,
p. 427). To offer as an explanation of the mystic experience such
bursting into consciousness of powers from this unknown region
seems a case of 'ignotum per ignotius'.

But should it be said that it is the sub-conscious or subliminal self
that emerges into consciousness, we seem to be near the idea of the
mystics. Behind the faculties of the soul, behind intellection and
understanding and reason and will and emotion and imagination,
is the soul itself, the spiritual principle that is the root of all the
faculties: as St Thomas says: 'all the powers of the soul are rooted

[1] *Études d'histoire et de psychologie du Mysticisme; les grands mystiques Chrétiens.*

in the one essence of the soul.'[1] This at least will be held by all who regard the mind as something other than a bundle of sensations, phantasmata, emotions, cognitions, volitions.

This essence of the soul, the soul itself, is what the mystics mean when they speak of the centre of the soul, or its apex, or ground, or the fund of the spirit, or the synteresis.[2] It has been called also in modern terminology the core of personality, and the transcendental self.

For the Catholic mystics it is this essence of the soul that enters into union with God. This we learned from St Gregory: he says that the mind must first clear itself of all sense perceptions and of all images of things bodily and spiritual, so that it may be able to find and consider itself as it is in itself, i.e., its essence; and then, by means of this realization of itself thus stript of all, it rises to the contemplation of God (*Hom. in Ezech.* ii. v. 8, 9; see p. 98).

The following is Fr Baker's account, certainly based on personal experience:

According to the doctrine of mystics, this union passes above both the understanding and will, namely, in that supreme portion of the spirit which is visible to God alone, and in which He alone can inhabit; a portion so pure, noble, and divine, that it neither hath nor can have any name proper to it, though mystics endeavour to express it by divers, calling it the summit of the mind, the fund and centre of the spirit, the essence of the soul, its virginal portion (*Sancta Sophia*, p. 533).

At the end of the *Book of Spiritual Instruction* Blosius sets forth at some length the doctrine of the Catholic mystics on this hidden essence of the soul.

Few rise above their natural powers; few ever come to know the apex of the spirit and the hidden fund or depth of the soul. It is far more inward and sublime than are the three higher faculties, for it is their origin. It is wholly simple, essential, and uniform, and so there is not multiplicity in it, but unity, and in it the three higher faculties are one thing. Here is perfect tranquillity, deepest silence, because never can any image enter here. By this depth, in which the divine image lies hidden, we are deiform. This same depth is called the heaven of the spirit, for the Kingdom of God is in it, as the Lord said: 'The Kingdom of God is within you'; and the Kingdom of God is God Himself with all His riches. Therefore this naked and unfigured depth is above all created things, and is raised above

---

[1] 'Omnes potentiae animae in una essentia animae radicantur' (*Summa*, 1 2ae, qu. xxxvii, art. 1).

[2] They speak also of 'the spark of the soul'; and some, as Eckhart, regard this essence of the soul as a spark or emanation of divinity, and so uncreated. Such idea was not commonly held.

all senses and faculties; it transcends place and time, abiding by a certain perpetual adhesion in God its beginning; yet it is essentially within us, because it is the abyss of the mind and its most inward essence. This depth, which the uncreated light ever irradiates, when it is laid open to a man and begins to shine on him, powerfully affects and attracts him. ... May God, the uncreated Abyss, vouchsafe to call unto Himself our spirit, the created abyss, and make it one with Him, that our spirit, plunged in the deep sea of the Godhead, may happily lose itself in the Spirit of God.

When this inmost sanctuary of the soul, wherein God abides, has been entered and the soul itself is consciously realized, then like to like, spirit with Spirit, real with Real, the soul of man, being one of the spiritual realities, is capable of union with the Supreme Ultimate Reality, God, and thus may the union of the two Realities be experienced that is spoken of by the mystics.

The modern psychologist does not commonly accept the doctrine of the presence of God in the soul or the indwelling of the Holy Ghost; but if he did, it would seem possible to conciliate with the experience of the mystics his idea of the subliminal self taken as the soul itself. William James, at any rate, is a representative modern psychologist, and he is able to say: 'The overcoming of all the usual barriers between the individual and the Absolute is the great mystic achievement' (*Varieties*, p. 419). The language is different, and the underlying thought is different; but the psychologist and the mystics are speaking of the same thing.

(3) In many minds, no doubt, the objection will arise that the conception of the mystical experience just put forward implies a supernatural character. This is the case. The mystical experience as here represented is in the order of grace, and the order of grace is supernatural. In proclaiming the supernatural character of the mystical experience as the definite operation of God, the Christian mystics are surely right. For if God working in man is more intimately present in him than man is even in himself; if the indwelling of the Holy Ghost in the souls of the just is a reality; then we are already in the presence of the supernatural. And if the veil be momentarily lifted, so that man is made experimentally aware of God's presence, if (to use St Gregory's favourite symbol) he 'catches a glimpse of the uncircumscribed light as coming through a chink,'— then this too, still more, must be supernatural, must be brought about by God's own working in the soul.

Is it then miraculous? It is difficult in the extreme to draw a line of demarcation between the ordinary and the miraculous in the supernatural order.

Yet all who believe in the reality of the life of grace in the soul, believe that there are supernatural workings of God and effects in the soul that would not be called miraculous. It is Catholic doctrine, fixed at the Pelagian controversies, that prayer which shall be meritorious unto life everlasting, or which shall be even the beginning of sanctification, is supernatural, being completely beyond the power of unassisted nature;[1] but it is not therefore miraculous. It is hard to say whether there be any recognizable established order of supernature, as there is a recognizable established order of nature. And so it seems that the mystical experience should be said to be supernatural, but not, at any rate in most cases, miraculous. But to modern 'naturalists' the whole Catholic conception of the supernatural order of grace will be intolerable.

(4) In appraising the value of the evidence of the mystics, it is necessary to examine their character as witnesses, if they be worthy of credit. Their *bona fides* will not be questioned by any who know them: they are possessed by the most utter conviction of the truth of what they say. What will be questioned is the correctness of their judgement as to the objective nature of their experience. It would not be to the point to urge that they readily believed in the miraculous, some of them with an avidity amounting to credulity. What is in question is not external happenings, but the most intimately personal religious experience of their souls. It is character, and soundness of judgement, and general good sense, and spiritual elevation, that will carry conviction. Judged by these tests many of the mystics must be accepted as witnesses with good credentials.

The first called may be St Paul, whose being caught up to the third heaven into Paradise, whatever this symbolizes, was surely a mystical experience, almost unique.

Next St Augustine: he is on all hands recognized as having a place in the inmost circle of greatest minds of the whole human race, and as a spiritual genius of the highest order. Equal to his power of intellectual vision were his good judgement and practical sense, as is shown by the whole tenor of his life. He is a witness of the highest quality, little likely to have been mistaken as to the true nature of the experiences he claims to have had.

Our two other doctors, SS Gregory and Bernard, though on a much lower intellectual level than St Augustine, are witnesses that must command respect. They were both men of high intelligence and character and good sense, and each of them was in his day probably the predominant personality of the Western Church. They were not dreamers, but public men, born rulers, who left their mark

[1] Bishop Hedley, *Prayer and Contemplation*, p. 13.

on the history of the Church and of the world. Their lives were lived on high spiritual levels, and we have learned to admire their earnest personal religion and their spiritual insight. It is not likely that they should have misinterpreted their religious experiences.

In his book *Degeneracy* (p. 64) Max Nordau brings in St Teresa in illustration. But St Teresa was not a degenerate. On the contrary, she is universally recognized as one of the great women, a fine, strong character, virile yet womanly, who achieved great things through her courage and perseverance. And, what is especially to the point, her robust good sense in things spiritual, no less than secular, is the quality that stands forth most conspicuously in her writings. She also is a witness who must inspire confidence.

I am not going to prolong a litany of the great Catholic mystics, but many others might be adduced whose lives and personalities proclaim them witnesses worthy of credit: such are the two Catherines, of Siena and Genoa, St Francis, St Ignatius, St John of the Cross. It will be admitted that their own account of what happened in their personal experience, when given by such witnesses, is entitled to carry great weight.

'There is about mystical utterances an eternal unanimity which ought to make a critic stop and think'[1]

(5) The surpassing richness and fruitfulness of the content of the mystics' experiences as described by themselves is another element to be taken into account when we estimate the credibility of what they say. If the great and first commandment be to love God with all our heart and all our soul and all our mind and all our strength; and if, therefore, acts of love of God be the highest and richest acts of the human mind and soul; how rich are the experiences described by St Augustine, and by St Bernard in the fine passage on the Spiritual Marriage! Such descriptions of the spiritual espousal and marriage as are given by St John of the Cross in his treatises *The Spiritual Canticle of the Soul* and *The Living Flame of Love*, and by St Teresa in the last three Mansions of the *Interior Castle*, should be read in order that the fullness and richness of their mystical experience may be understood. Psychologists and others recognize and emphasize the bliss that, according to all mystics, accompanies the highest experiences. But not ecstatic joy so much as ecstatic love, is the characteristic feature of the experience.

The Spiritual Marriage is not a passing experience, but a lasting state, and the love conceived in the mystic experience is an abiding possession which colours the whole life of the mystics, as is seen in well-nigh every page of St Augustine's *Confessions*, or in the prayers

[1] W. James, *Varieties*, p. 419.

and affections into which St Teresa so continually breaks forth in the pages of her *Autobiography*, or in the *Confessions of a Lover* by Dame Gertrude More, Fr Baker's disciple. The following words are taken from her Twenty-eighth Confession, but the same refrain runs through them all:

O my God, let me walk in the way of love which knoweth not how to seek self in anything whatsoever. Let this love wholly possess my soul and heart, which, I beseech Thee, may live and move only in, and out of, a pure and sincere love to Thee. Oh! that Thy pure love were so grounded and established in my heart, that I might sigh and pant without ceasing after Thee, and be able in the strength of this Thy love to live without all comfort and consolation, human or divine. Oh, sight to be wished, desired, and longed for, because once to have seen Thee is to have learned all things! Nothing can bring us to this sight but love. But what love must it be? Not a sensible love only, a childish love, a love which seeketh itself more than the Beloved. No, it must be an ardent love, a pure love, a courageous love, a love of charity, a humble love, and a constant love, not worn out with labours, nor daunted with any difficulties. O Lord, give this love into my soul, that I may never more live nor breathe but out of a most pure love of Thee, my All and only Good. Let me love Thee for Thyself, and nothing else but in and for Thee. Let me love nothing instead of Thee, for to give all for love is a most sweet bargain. ... Let Thy love work in me and by me, and let me love Thee as Thou wouldst be loved by me. I cannot tell how much love I would have of Thee, because I would love Thee beyond all that can be imagined or desired by me. Be Thou in this, as in all other things, my chooser for me, for Thou art my only choice, most dear to me. The more I shall love Thee, the more will my soul desire Thee, and desire to suffer for Thee.[1]

A writer well read in the literature of mysticism has said:

The language of human passion is tepid and insignificant beside the language in which the mystics try to tell the splendours of their love. 'This monk can give lessons to lovers!' exclaimed Arthur Symonds in astonishment of St John of the Cross.[2]

I refrain from entering on the matter of intellectual illumination that is so frequent an element of the mystics' claim;[3] I only cite the judgement passed by Dean Inge:

The fact of intuition into Divine truth, during states of spiritual exaltation (ecstasy), seems incontrovertible, and the admission can cause no difficulty to a theist.[4]

---

[1] *Life and Writings of Dame Gertrude More*, ed. 1911, ii. 83.
[2] Evelyn Underhill, *Mysticism*, p. 106. A. Symonds translated St John's poems.
[3] Augustine (above, p. 49), Ruysbroeck, St John of the Cross (below, pp. 222-3), St Teresa, St Ignatius, are conspicuous examples.
[4] Hastings, *Encyclopaedia of Religion*, art. 'Ecstasy'.

It is necessary, however, to emphasize how alien from any kind of 'quietism' are even the highest states of the great mystics. What I said in *Benedictine Monachism* concerning Cassian's account of the 'richest' and 'glowing' prayer of the Egyptian monks, is applicable to the experiences of the classical mystics:

It is true that in this prayer words cease, and language fails, and sense impressions are transcended; but the powers of mind and soul are operating and energizing with a highly-wrought activity, utterly removed from quietism (p. 57).

Though the mind is emptied of sense perceptions and images, and though reasoning ceases, and the faculties seem at rest, the soul itself is all the time actuating with a concentration and energy unsurpassed in this life, 'acting', says Fr Baker, 'by a portion of the spirit above all the faculties' (*Sancta Sophia*, p. 545).[1]

Some psychologists are prone to speak of the ecstasy of the mystics as a state of mental blank without content, akin to hypnotic sleep. This may have an element of truth in certain oriental cases. But in the case of the great Christian mystics of the West, if their own evidence, which is the only evidence we possess, be accepted, it has to be said that nothing could be further from the truth. Intellectually, emotionally, religiously, the experience, according to all that they tell us, is of a fullness and a richness beyond all power of expression.

Whoever will read the accounts given of their experiences by the great classical mystics will find a coherence and quiet sanity in the midst of a mysterious elevation; and in the midst of exuberance of religious feeling, a dignity and sobriety, and a conviction of reality, which is all deeply impressive; it creates a sense of spiritual life and experience on high levels, and seems even to command assent to its claims.

[1] No one is more emphatic in his condemnation of 'quietism' than that highest of contemplatives, Ruysbroeck: 'When a man is bare and imageless in his senses, and empty and idle in his higher powers, he enters into rest through mere nature. Now mark the way in which this natural rest is practised. It is a sitting still without either outward or inward acts, in vacancy, in order that rest may be found and may remain untroubled. But a rest which is practised in this way is unlawful. Such a rest is nought else than idleness, and is wholly contrary to the supernatural rest, which one possesses in God; for that is a loving self-mergence joined to a simple gazing into the incomprehensible Brightness. This rest in God is actively sought with inward longing, and is found in fruitive inclination, and is eternally possessed in the self-mergence of love, and when possessed is sought none the less. When a man wishes to possess inward rest in idleness, without inward and desirous cleaving to God, then he is ready for all errors. ... These men maintain themselves in pure passivity, without any activity towards above or towards below. For they deem that if they worked themselves, God would be hindered in His work. They have no knowledge and no love, no will, no prayer, no desire' (*Adornment of the Spiritual Marriage*, ii. c. 66, to be read in its entirety, also c. 67).

(6) Lastly we must consider the effects upon life of the mystical experience.

Ecstasy is often accompanied by a physical condition of rapture or trance, and such conditions are well known medically as pathological symptoms in hysterical and neurotic subjects. These latter trances are bad in their effects, physical, mental, and moral alike, and are rightly set down as signs and effects of degeneracy. But the day has passed when doctors and psychologists classed St Teresa's raptures as hysteria. It is recognized that not all ecstasies are degeneracy, and that the only valid criterion in judging them is their content: What takes place in them; and their effect on life. 'By their fruits shall you know them'. William James recognized this very clearly:

To pass a spiritual judgement upon these states, we must not content ourselves with superficial medical talk, but inquire into their fruits for life. [The result of his inquiry is that in natively strong minds and characters mysticism exercises a strengthening effect]: the great Spanish mystics, who carried the habit of ecstasy as far as it has often been carried, appear for the most part to have shown indomitable spirit and energy, and all the more so for the trances in which they indulged.

He introduces one of St Teresa's descriptions of the effects of her ecstasies by the words:

Where in literature is there a more evidently veracious account of the formation of a new centre of spiritual energy?

And of St Ignatius he says:

He was a mystic, but his mysticism made him assuredly one of the most powerfully practical human engines that ever lived.[1]

This puts the thing in its true light: the mystics were what they were, not in spite of their mysticism, but because of it. This is particularly evident in the case of St Teresa. The first twenty years of her life as a nun were quite ordinary, lived on an average level, and had she so lived on and died, her name would have been indistinguishable among the crowd of Spanish nuns of her day. But the 'conversion' of 1555, described in the ninth chapter of her *Autobiography*, heralded in the great and ever-growing series of mystical experiences that went on until her death. And that it was precisely these experiences that enlarged and strengthened her character, and spiritualized and elevated her nature, and made her into the great saint, and great woman, and great personality in religious history that she

[1] *Varieties of Religious Experience*, pp. 413, 414.

is, this must be evident to every one who reads her *Life*, written by herself. For it is the case that her power and influence, and her mystical experiences, began together and went on developing together.

Their own accounts of their experiences given by St Augustine, St Gregory, St Bernard, which we have seen, show the effects of them on life, both the inner life of the soul and the life lived among men. One other account, that of Fr Augustine Baker, of the effects on soul and character of a 'passive union purely intellectual' is reproduced here, as being a certainly first-hand record of personal experience:

The change that is made by this supernatural union with regard to the will and affections is admirable, insomuch as many years spent in mortification and other internal exercises will not so purify the soul as a few minutes passed in such a divine inaction. Here it is, indeed, that a soul perfectly feels her own nothing and God's totality, and thereby is strangely advanced in humility and the divine love; for being so immediately united to God, so illustrated with His heavenly light, and inflamed with His love, all creatures (and herself above all) are become as nothing, yea, perfectly odious to her. Besides, there are many secret defects in a soul, so subtle and intime, that they can neither be cured nor so much as discovered but by a passive union, insomuch as hereby the soul is advanced to perfection in a manner and degree not to be imagined, far more efficaciously than by all the former actions of herself put together, so that the following aspirations and elevations of the spirit become far more pure and efficacious than before. And, indeed, were it not for such good fruits and effects upon the will, such passive unions would be little profitable to the soul; for our merit consists in our own free acts produced in virtue of divine grace assisting us, and not by the operations simply wherein God is only agent, and we patients (*Sancta Sophia*, p. 534).

These considerations will prepare the way for a judgement on the mystic claim. Reasons have been brought forward showing that from the standpoints of theology and of psychology the claim is not incredible; and that it is recommended by the high calibre of the principal witnesses, and by the qualities of richness of content and fruitfulness for character and life of the experience they describe. St John of the Cross may now be allowed to speak, as representative of the mystics, in behalf of the mystic claim. After hesitating between him and Blessed John Ruysbroeck, the two who probably combine in the greatest measure the achievement of heights of contemplation with systematic and powerful description, I have chosen St John as the one on whom to stake the issue. This choice I have made because he is more coherent and in his expositions more easily intelligible than Ruysbroeck. In his two treatises, *The Spiritual Canticle of the Soul* and *The Living Flame of Love*, he attains to a sustained elevation of thought and language probably not equalled—certainly not surpassed—by any other who has essayed to describe the highest mystical experiences. Besides being saint and mystic, St John is at once poet, orator, psychologist, and theologian; and to no one has it been given to depict with more daring and actuality the relations that may be possible, even in this life, between the soul of man and God.

The following catena from these works has been formed principally on the basis of psychology, as recording the mental states he had experienced, and which he entirely believed to correspond to realities. But no mere selection of passages can do justice to the case for the mystics as presented by St John. No one can be in possession of the evidence that would give him a cognizance of the case sufficient to justify him in passing an adverse verdict on the claim of the mystics, who has not read in their entirety St John's two mystical treatises, *The Spiritual Canticle* and *Living Flame*: nor can any one understar.d St John who has not read also the two ascetical treatises, *The Ascent of Mount Carmel* and *The Dark Night*, for only so can be appreciated the price paid for the attainment to the Spiritual Marriage; verily it was the pearl of great price, to purchase which he went and sold, quite literally, all that he had. His writings produce the conviction that they are autobiography from beginning to end: whether he inculcates appalling—inhuman, it will be said,—renunciation and detachment in the ascetical treatises, or depicts the intimacies of the divine union in the mystical, we feel in both cases alike that he speaks of nothing but what he had himself been through. The peculiar fascination of his writings is probably due to this. The effect on us of reading him is as though we had been climbing the first slopes of a mountain range, and having reached an eminence, should look out over the plain below, and think how high we had got—till we look round and see behind us the great peaks and crags, tier after tier, towering up to heaven; and as we gaze aloft we descry on the sky-line, among the hard, ice-bound rocks, but bathed in the warmth and light of the sunshine, a solitary climber wending his way with steady head and sure foot at heights that make us dizzy even to look at.

Let us now hear him:[1]

---

[1] The following extracts have been revised by Fr Benedict Zimmerman, Prior of the Carmelites in Kensington, on the text of the critical edition produced by the Spanish Carmelites in 1912.

St John starts from the theological position that God permanently resides in the inmost depth of each one's soul.

We must remember that the Word, the Son of God, together with the Father and the Holy Ghost, is hidden in essence and in presence in the inmost being of the soul. That soul, therefore, that will find Him, must go out from all things in will and affection, and enter into the profoundest self-recollection, and all things must be to it as if they existed not. ... Go not to seek Him out of thyself, for that will be but distraction and weariness, and thou shalt not find Him; because there is no fruition of Him more certain, more ready, more intimate than that which is within (*Cant.* stanza i. 7-9).

We must keep in mind that God dwells in a secret and hidden way in all souls, in their very substance, for if He did not, they could not exist at all. This dwelling of God is very different in different souls: in some He dwells contented, in others displeased; in some as in His own house, giving His orders and ruling it; in others, as a stranger in a house not His own, where He is not permitted to command or to do anything at all (*Living Flame*, stanza iv. 14).

In stanza iv. of the *Living Flame*, St John tells of the 'awakening of God in the soul', and the soul's consequent awakening to a realization of God's presence within it:

This awakening is a movement of the Word in the depth of the soul, of such grandeur, authority, and glory, and of such profound sweetness, that all the balsams, all the aromatic herbs and flowers of the world, seem to be mingled and shaken together for the production of that sweetness (*Living Flame*, iv. 3).

Then is felt the Touch of God:

There occurs that most delicate touch of the Beloved, which the soul feels at times, even when least expecting it, and which sets the heart on fire with love, as if a spark had fallen upon it and made it burn. Then the will in an instant, like one roused from sleep, burns with the fire of love, longs for God, praises Him and gives Him thanks, worships and honours Him, and prays to Him in the sweetness of love (*Cant.* xxv. 5).

He apostrophizes the Touch of God:

O gentle subtile touch, the Word, the Son of God, Who because of the pureness of Thy divine nature dost penetrate subtilely the very substance of my soul, and touching it gently, absorbest it wholly in divine ways of sweetness. O touch of the Word, so gentle, so wonderfully gentle to me. O blessed soul, most blessed, which Thou, Who art so terrible and so strong, touchest so gently. Proclaim it to the world, O my soul—no, proclaim it not, for the world knoweth not the gentle air, neither will it listen to it. O gentle touch! as in Thee there is nothing material, so Thy touch is the more penetrating, changing what in me is human into divine, for Thy divine Essence, wherewith Thou touchest me, is foreign to all modes and manners. O gentle touch and most gentle, for Thou touchest me with Thy most simple Substance and innermost Essence; therefore is this touch so subtile, so loving, so deep, and so delicious (*Living Flame*, ii. 18-21).

What the soul tastes now in this touch of God is in truth, though not perfectly, a certain foretaste of everlasting life. It is not incredible it should be so, when we believe, as we do believe, that this touch is most substantial, and that the Substance of God touches the substance of the soul. The sweetness of delight which this touch occasions baffles all description (ibid. 22).

In the *Living Flame of Love* these Touches are considered to be the Holy Ghost playing on the soul as a Fire:

As the fire of love is infinite, so when God touches the soul somewhat sharply the burning heat within it becomes so extreme as to surpass all the fires of the world. This is why this touch of God is said to be a 'burn'; for the fire there is more intense and more concentrated, and the effect of it surpasses all other fires. When the divine fire shall have transformed the soul into itself, the soul not only feels the burn, but itself is become wholly and entirely burnt up in this vehement fire (*Living Flame*, ii. 3, 4).

O delicious wound, and the more delicious the more the burn of love penetrates the inmost substance of the soul, burning all it can burn, that it may supply all the delight it can give. This burning and wound, in my opinion, are the highest condition attainable in this life; for this is the touch of the Divinity without form or figure, either intellectual or imaginary (ibid. ii. 9).

In that burn the flame rushes forth and surges vehemently, as in a glowing furnace or forge. The soul feels that the wound it has thus received is sovereignly delicious. It feels its love to grow, strengthen, and refine itself to such a degree as to seem to itself as if seas of fire were in it, filling it with love. ... The soul beholds itself as one immense sea of fire (*Living Flame*, 10, 11).

The second half of the *Spiritual Canticle of the Soul* (stanzas xxii.-xl.) treats of the Spiritual Marriage, on which we have heard St Bernard:

The gifts of love which the Bridegroom bestows on the soul in the spiritual marriage are inestimable; the praises and endearing expressions of divine love which pass so frequently between them are beyond all utterance. The soul is occupied in praising Him and in giving Him thanks; and He in exalting, praising, and thanking the soul (*Cant.* xxxiv. pref. note).

We have seen in St Bernard that ecstatic love, unto inebriation, is the characteristic of the state of Spiritual Marriage. So is it for St John:

God sometimes bestows an exceeding great grace upon advanced souls, when the Holy Spirit inebriates them with the sweet, luscious, and strong wine of love. This love communicates to the soul such a strong abundant inebriation when God visits it, that it pours forth with great effect and force acts of rapturous praise, love, and worship, with a marvellous longing to labour and suffer for Him (*Cant.* xxv. 8).

God is sometimes so merciful to the Bride-soul as to manifest to it its interior treasures and to reveal to it all its beauty. So abundant are these favours at times that the soul seems enveloped in delight and bathed in inestimable bliss (ibid. xvii. 6, 7).

If we speak of that light of glory which, in the soul's embrace, God sometimes produces within it, and which is a certain spiritual communion wherein He causes it to behold and enjoy the abyss of delight and riches He has laid up within it, there is no language to express any degree of it (*Cant.* xx. 16).

It cannot be doubted that St John believed he had experienced 'transformation' of the soul in God and 'deification':

God, to make the soul perfect and to raise it above the flesh more and more, assails it divinely and gloriously, and these assaults are really encounters wherein God penetrates the soul, deifies the very substance of it, and renders it godlike, divine. The Substance of God absorbs the soul, because He assails and pierces it to the quick by the Holy Ghost, Whose communications are vehement where they are of fire (*Living Flame*, i. 34).

He guards himself, however, against suspicion of any pantheistic absorption of the soul in God:

The thread of love binds so closely God and the soul, and so unites them, that it transforms them and makes them one by love; so that, though in essence different, yet in glory and appearance the soul seems God and God the soul. Such is this marvellous union. God Himself is here the suitor[1] Who, in the omnipotence of His unfathomable love, absorbs the soul with greater violence and efficacy than a torrent of fire a single drop of the morning dew (*Cant.* xxxi. pref. note).

[1] This reminds us of Francis Thompson's 'Hound of Heaven'.

Elsewhere:

The soul seems God by participation, though in reality pre-
serving its own natural substance as distinct from God, as it did
before, although transformed in Him (*Ascent of Mt. Carmel*, ii. 5).

In the state of transformation and perfect union of love the soul
thus expresses the unification:

Let me be so transformed in Thy beauty, that, being alike in
beauty, we may see ourselves both in Thy beauty; so that one beholding the other, each may see his own beauty in the other, the
beauty of both being Thine only, and mine absorbed in it. And
thus I shall see Thee in Thy beauty, and myself in Thy beauty,
and Thou shalt see me in Thy beauty; and I shall see myself in
Thee in Thy beauty, and Thou Thyself in me in Thy beauty; so
shall I seem to be Thyself in Thy beauty, and Thou myself in Thy
beauty; my beauty shall be Thine, Thine shall be mine, and I shall
be Thou in it, and Thou myself in Thine own beauty; for Thy
beauty will be my beauty, and so we shall see, each the other, in
Thy beauty (*Cant.* xxxvi. 3).

Intellectual illumination and intuition of the mysteries and
secrets of God are for St John, as for the other great mystics, an
integral part of the mystical experience:

[In the 'awakening of the soul' it beholds what God is in Himself,
and what He is in creatures.] This awakening and vision of the soul
is as if God drew back some of the many veils and coverings that
are before it, so that it might see what He is; then indeed—but still
dimly, because all the veils are not drawn back—the divine Face,
full of grace, bursts through and shines, which as it moves all things
by its power, appears together with the effect it produces (*Living
Flame*, iv. 7).

St John does not follow the idea of SS Augustine and Thomas,
that the divine Essence can be seen in this life:

The communication and sense of God's presence, however great
they may be, and the most sublime and profound knowledge of
God which the soul may have in this life, are not God essentially,
neither have they any affinity with Him, for in very truth He is
still hidden from the soul (*Cant.* i. 2).
We are not to imagine that the soul sees God essentially and
clearly because it has so deep a sense of Him; for this is only a strong
and abundant communication from Him, a glimmering light of
what He is in Himself (ibid. xiv. 6).

It is utterly impossible to describe what the soul in its awakening knows and feels of the majesty of God in the inmost depths of its being (*Living Flame*, iv. 9).

A most sublime and sweet knowledge of God and of His attributes overflows into the understanding from the contact of the attributes of God with the substance of the soul. This is the most supreme delight of which the soul is capable in this life (*Cant.* xiv. 16). The soul is admitted to a knowledge of the wisdom, secrets and graces, and gifts and powers of God, whereby it is made so beautiful and rich (ibid. xxiv. 2). The knowledge of God communicated to the understanding is not only substantial knowledge, but a manifestation also of the truths of the Divinity, and a revelation of the secret mysteries thereof (ibid. xiv. 20).

St John does not claim, like Ruysbroeck, to have been admitted to the vision of the Three Divine Persons and to have penetrated into the Unity of the Godhead that lies behind Them; but he does claim to have been granted an intimate understanding of the Mystery of the Incarnation:

When the soul has been raised to the high state of spiritual marriage the Bridegroom reveals to it His own marvellous secrets most readily and most frequently. The chief matter of His communications are the sweet mysteries of His Incarnation, and the ways and means of Redemption, which is one of the highest works of God (*Cant.* xxiii. pref. note).

He claims, too, to have been accorded a cosmic revelation, imparting a deeper insight into the relations of creatures with God:

The divine life and being and the harmony of creation are revealed with marvellous newness (*Living Flame*, iv. 6).

Though it is true that the soul here sees that all creatures are distinct from God, in that they have a created existence; it understands them in Him in their power, root, and energy; it knows also that God in His own Essence is, in an infinitely pre-eminent way, all these things, so that it understands them better in Him, their First Cause, than in themselves. This is the great joy of this awakening, namely to know creatures in God, and not God in His creatures: this is to know effects in their cause, and not cause by its effects (ibid. iv. 5).

[The soul is able to hear the great Concert of Creation praising its Maker]:

In this silence and tranquillity, and in this knowledge of the divine light, the soul discerns a marvellous arrangement and disposition of God's wisdom in the diversities of His creatures and operations. All these, and each one of them, have a certain correspondence with God, whereby each, by a voice peculiar to itself, proclaims what there is in itself of God, so as to form a concert of sublimest melody, transcending all the harmonies of the world (*Cant.* xv. 5).

Again:

In this tranquil contemplation the soul beholds all creatures, not only the highest but the lowest also, each one according to the gift of God to it, sending forth the voice of its witness to what God is. It beholds each one magnifying Him in its own way, and possessing Him according to its particular capacity. And thus all these voices together unite in one strain in praise of God's greatness, wisdom, and marvellous knowledge (*Cant.* xv. 7).

It only remains to put the question: Is this the language of illusion? For my part I do not believe that it is.

PART II: PRACTICAL

THE CONTEMPLATIVE AND ACTIVE LIVES

I. ST AUGUSTINE

ANALYSIS

ST AUGUSTINE

As in so many other departments of Christian thought in the West; as in formulating the theory and fixing the terminology of the Christian spiritual life;[1] so in the matter of the contemplative life and the active life, the relations between them, and the claims of each upon the individual, St Augustine laid down the great lines along which all subsequent thought in the Catholic Church has run. I do not know that any co-ordinated presentation of his teaching as a whole has hitherto been made. Yet I think it will appear that hardly any writer, if any, has discoursed on these topics with such fullness and insight as has Augustine.

G. The Two Lives

The simplest and most distinct definition given by St Augustine of the 'Two Lives' is, I believe, the following: The study and pursuit of wisdom lies in action and in contemplation, so that one part of it may be called 'active', the other 'contemplative'. The active has to say to living one's life and to moral conduct; the contemplative to beholding the causes of nature and most pure truth (*de Civ. Dei*, viii. 4). The words employed are 'contemplativa' and 'activa'.

Here the familiar piece in the Breviary for the Feast of St John the Apostle comes to mind, wherein the two lives are contrasted in a series of sharp antitheses:

The Church knows two lives divinely preached and commended unto her: whereof the one is in faith, the other in 'specie'; the one is in the time of pilgrimage, the other in eternity of abiding; the one is in labour, the other in rest; the one is on the way, the other in the [true] country; the one is in the work of action, the other in the reward of contemplation; the one turns away from evil and does good, the other has no evil from which to turn away, and has great good to enjoy; the one wars with the foe, the other reigns without a foe; the one is strong in things adverse, the other has no sense of aught adverse; the one bridles the lusts of the flesh, the other is given up to the joys of the spirit; the one is anxious with the care of getting the victory, the other in the peace of victory is without care; the one is helped in temptations, the other, without any temptation, rejoices in its Helper Himself; the one assists the needy, the other is where it finds none needy; the one pardons the sins of others that its own sins may be pardoned, the other suffers nothing

[1] See Abbé P. Pourrat's *Spiritualité Chrétienne*, i. 270–330.

that it can pardon, nor does anything that calls for pardon; the one is scourged with evil that it be not lifted up with good things, the other through so great fullness of grace is without any evil, so that without temptation of pride it cleaves to the Supreme Good; the one discerns between good and evil, the other sees things which are only good: therefore the one is good, but still in miseries; the other is better and in beatitude (*Tract. in Ioan.* cxxiv. 5).

A contemplative life such as is described in this passage up to this point is for the next world, not for this. But what follows shows that Augustine's meaning is that there may be some beginnings of the contemplative life in this world, but its perfection only in the next; whereas the active life may be fully carried out in this world, and ceases with it.

The active life is signified by the Apostle Peter, the contemplative by John. The first is wholly carried out here until the end of this world, and there finds an end; the last is deferred, to be completed after the end of this world, but in the world to come it hath no end. … Let perfected action *follow Me*, informed by the ensample of My Passion: but let contemplation that has been begun, *tarry till I come*, to be perfected when I come (ibid.).

In the following similar piece the treatment is less absolute; the contemplative life is less definitely allocated to the other world, and at the end the nature of a contemplative life in this world is indicated:

Two virtues are set before the soul of man, the one active, the other contemplative; the one whereby we journey, the other whereby we reach our journey's end; the one whereby we toil that our heart may be cleansed for the vision of God, the other whereby we repose and see God; the one lies in the precepts for carrying on this temporal life, the other in the doctrine of that life which is eternal. Hence it is that the one toils, and the other reposes; for the former is in the purgation of sins, the latter in the light [*or* illumination] of the purgation effected. Hence it is that, in this mortal life, the former consists in the work of leading a good life, the latter more in faith, and with some few, through a mirror in enigma and in part, in some vision of unchangeable Truth. These two virtues are seen figured in the two wives of Jacob, concerning whom I discoursed in my work 'Against Faustus'. The three first Evangelists, who principally record the words and deeds of our Lord for the right conduct of the present life, are chiefly concerned with active virtue; but John is chiefly concerned in commending contemplative virtue (*de Cons. Evang.* i. 8).

The following is the passage on Jacob's wives referred to:

Two lives are held out to us in the Body of Christ—the one temporal, in which we labour; the other eternal, in which we shall contemplate the delights of God. The names of Jacob's wives teach us to understand this. For it is said that Lia is interpreted 'Labouring', and Rachel 'the Beginning seen', or 'the Word by which is seen the Beginning'. Therefore the action of human and mortal life, in which we live by faith, doing many laborious works, is Lia. But the hope of the eternal contemplation of God, which has a sure and delightful understanding of the truth, is Rachel (c. Faust. xxii. 52).

The remainder of this chapter, and all the six that follow, are of great interest for the matter in hand, and are (so far as is known to me) the source of one phase of teaching on the contemplative life that runs through the medieval mystical writers of the West. The whole is an elaborate allegorical interpretation, worked out in minutest detail, of the story of Jacob's wives (Gen. xxix. xxx.). It would be much too long (six columns in Migne) to be reproduced in its entirety; so an attempt will be made to summarize the heads of its teaching, detached from the allegory:

It is for the hope of the eternal contemplation of God that everyone is converted and undergoes the process of repentance and purification from sin. No one in the works of justice loves the actual toil of the things done and suffered; no one seeks the active life for its own sake: it is undertaken and endured as the means of attaining to contemplation. For everyone would wish, were it possible, without undergoing the labour that has to be embraced in the active life, to arrive straightway at the delights of contemplation. But this is not possible in this world, where the labour of working the works of righteousness precedes the pleasure of contemplating truth. To see the Beginning is what every rational mind that desires the truth chiefly longs for. But this longing should make it not refuse but endure the active life, without which there is no coming to that which is so ardently loved. But when this latter is attained to, then will be united in this world the beauty of contemplation and the labours of righteousness. However keenly and clearly unchangeable truth is seen by mortal man, the corruptible body weighs down the soul. Therefore must we tend to the One, but for its sake bear the Many. So the one life is loved, the other endured. But the one which is endured is more abundantly fertile, so that it becomes beloved, if not for its own sake, at any rate for its offspring. For the labour of the just bears great fruit in those they beget for the Kingdom of God by preaching the Gospel. But the life given up to the pursuit of contemplation desires to be free from all business, and therefore is sterile. For by striving after leisure, whereby the pursuit of contemplation is enkindled, it is not brought into touch with men's infirmities, who desire to be helped in their needs. But the contemplative life also is aflame with the love of generating, for it desires to teach what it knows. Mankind have more appreciation for the active life, whereby their infirmities and necessities are cared for, than for the contemplative, from which what is divine and unchangeable is learned. But those who spend their life in active good works, and are good pastors, will bear witness to that other life, which is at leisure for sake of the endeavour to attain to and to contemplate truth. It would not be right that the contemplative life should keep in leisure one fit and apt for the administration of ecclesiastical charges, or that those who are worthy of being entrusted with the government of the Church, should, through being inflamed with the desire of pursuing and contemplating wisdom, withdraw themselves wholly from the troubles attendant on action, and bury themselves in the leisure of contemplation. So those who are enamoured with the contemplative life are often called upon, by the needs of the Church, to undertake the works of the active life; and thereby the contemplative life is held in greater esteem by the generality of men (*c. Faust.* xxii. 52, 58).

The contemplative life spoken of in the foregoing passage is such a contemplative life as may be lived in this world. It is perhaps the most important single exposition of St Augustine's theories on the relations between the Two Lives, and supplies a valuable summary of the chief points of doctrine that will be further illustrated from other of his writings. As Augustine here sets the interpretation that became traditional in the west, whereby Lia represents the active life and Rachel the contemplative, so did he also initiate the chief features of the Western treatment of the case of Martha and Mary as representing the Two Lives.

H. THE CONTEMPLATIVE LIFE THE BETTER

St Augustine has no hesitation in affirming the superiority of the contemplative life over the active. This judgement he, in common with the rest of theologians, bases on the story of Martha and Mary, which forms the theme of his discourses in various of the *Sermons* (ciii., civ., clxix., clxxix., cclv.). His exegesis became the tradition with the Western mystical writers. Its most salient points of teaching may be summarized as follows:

Martha chose a good part, but Mary the better. What Martha chose passes away. She ministered to the hungry, the thirsty, the homeless: but all these pass away,—there will be when none will hunger nor thirst. Therefore will her care be taken from her. 'Mary hath chosen the better part (meliorem), which shall not be taken away from her'. She hath chosen to contemplate, to live by the Word (clxix. 17).

Martha's part is holy and great: yet Mary hath chosen the better, in that while her sister was solicitous and working and caring for many things, she was at leisure and sat still and listened. Mary's part will not be taken from her, Martha's will—for the ministering to the saints will pass away; to whom will food be given, where none hungers? Mary's part does not pass away, for her delight was in justice and truth, and in this same will be her delight in eternity. What Mary chose waxes greater; for the delight of the human heart,—of a faithful and holy human heart,—in the light of truth and the affluence of wisdom, if it be sweet now, will then be sweeter far (clxxix.).

The sweetness of truth is eternal: it will not be taken away but increased—increased in this life, and perfected in the next (ciii. 5).

In these two women, both pleasing the Lord, two lives were figured:
    the present and the future,
    the laborious and the quiet,
    the troublous and the happy,
    the temporal and the eternal.
Both are praiseworthy: but the one is laborious, the other leisured. What Martha was doing, there we are; what Mary, that we hope for. While in this life how much can we have of Mary's part? For even now we do somewhat of her work, when removed from businesses and laying aide our ordinary cares. Inasmuch as we do thus, we are like to Mary (civ. 4).

Even Mary only signified the life of contemplation; she did not yet lay hold of it (cclv.).

In the following passage also he treats of Martha and Mary:

Jesus Christ will bring those who believe to the contemplation of God, where is the end of all good actions, and everlasting rest, and joy that never will be taken from us. A similitude of this joy Mary prefigured, sitting at the feet of the Lord, and intent on His words; resting, that is, from all action, and intent on the truth in such wise as this life is capable of, whereby she prefigured what is to be in eternity. For while her sister Martha was occupied about things that had to be done, good indeed and useful, but destined to pass away when rest succeeds them, she was resting on the word of the Lord. And when Martha complained, He said, not that what she was doing was a bad part, but that Mary's was the best, which should not be taken away. For that which lies in ministering to want, when want is no more, is taken away. And abiding rest is the reward of a transient good work. In that contemplation God will be all in all; because nought else will be sought from Him, but it will suffice to be illumined by Him and to enjoy Him (de Trin. i. 20).

The relations between contemplation and action, and the superiority of contemplation, are treated of in a series of passages based on 1 Cor. xii. 8-10, wherein are contrasted 'wisdom' and 'knowledge'—'sapientia' and 'scientia' (*de Trin.* xii. 22, 25, xiii. 1; *Enar. in Psalm.* cxxxv. 8; *Conf.* xiii. 21, 23). The same idea, the same exegesis, runs through these passages, and their import may be thus summarized:

Action, whereby we use aright things temporal, is different from the contemplation of things eternal; and contemplation is assigned to 'wisdom', action to 'knowledge'.[1] Here action is taken as being the right ordering of the present life, in so far as it is concerned with transitory things. And so he goes on to explain that 'knowledge' has to do with the abstaining from evil and the striving after good, wherein our action is exercised.[2] Thus it includes the practice of the moral virtues: also the exercising of works of mercy, both spiritual and corporal.

Contemplation, or 'wisdom', is the intellectual cognition of things eternal.[3] In its wide sense it has to do with Platonic Ideas—abstract ideas and universals; but pre-eminently it lies in the cognition and love of That which always is and unchangeably abides, viz. God;[4] for what among eternal things is so excellent as God, Whose nature alone is unchangeable?[5]

The pre-eminence of contemplation over action is unequivocally asserted in the following passages:

We have distinguished the function of the rational mind in things temporal, wherein not only cognition but also our action is concerned, from that more excellent function of the same mind which is exercised in contemplating things eternal, and is completed in cognition alone.[6]

And he says that no one can doubt that the intellectual cognition of things eternal (i.e. wisdom, contemplation) is to be placed above the rational cognition of things temporal (i.e. knowledge, action).[7]

The same teaching is enforced in a passage near the end of the *Confessions*. It occurs in a highly elaborated allegorical interpretation of the first chapter of Genesis.

The souls that thirst after Thee and that appear before Thee, Thou waterest by a sweet spring, that the earth may bring forth her fruit, and Thou Lord God so commanding, our soul may bud forth works of mercy according to their kind [divers spiritual and corporal works of mercy are enumerated]: which fruits, having sprung out of

---

[1] *de Trin.* xii. 22.   [2] Ibid. 21, 22.
[3] Ibid. 25.   [4] *Enar. in Psalm.* cxxxv. 8.
[5] *de Trin.* xii. 22.   [6] Ibid. xiii. 1.
[7] Ibid. xii. 25.

the earth, see it is good; and let ourselves, from this lower fruitfulness of action arriving at the delights of contemplation, appear like lights in the world.

He goes on to explain that day and night signify respectively those who give themselves to the things of the mind (intelligibilia) and those who are preoccupied with the things of sense (sensibilia); and that of the gifts of the Spirit enumerated in 1 Cor. xii. 7-10, 'word of wisdom', i.e. contemplation, is 'the greater light, for their sakes who are delighted with the light of perspicuous truth, as it were for the rule of the day'; whereas the 'word of knowledge' is the lesser light, and the other gifts the stars, 'for the rule of the night', the regulation of the things of this life—'inasmuch as they come short of that brightness of wisdom which gladdens the fore-mentioned day' (*Conf.* xiii. 21-23).

The following passage declares that contemplation is the supreme act of the human soul:

The going to God, that is to the very contemplation of Truth, ... the striving to grasp intellectually those things which truly and supremely are, is the highest act of seeing (aspectus) of the soul, than which it has none more perfect or better (*de Quant. Anim.* 74, 75).

J. CLAIMS OF THE TWO LIVES

The practical conciliation of the claims of the Two Lives on the individual is treated of by Augustine, as it had been by philosophers before him. At the end of the passage on Rachel and Lia, already cited, he lays down quite definitely that it is not proper for one who is capable of the administration of ecclesiastical charges, or of the government of the Church, to withdraw himself wholly from the active life in order to give himself up to the contemplative.[1] The same principle is set forth in the following piece:

In the persons of them who know how to hear gladly and humbly, and to pass a quiet life in sweet and wholesome studies, let holy Church take her delight and say, 'I sleep, and my heart waketh',—I so rest that I may hear; my leisure is not bestowed on the nourishing of sloth, but on the getting of wisdom: I am unoccupied, and see that Thou art the Lord: I rest from the hurry of business, and my mind bends itself up for godly affections.

But in them who in this manner sweetly and humbly rest, while in their persons the Church doth leisurely take her delight, behold He knocketh Who saith, 'That which ye hear in the ear, preach ye upon the house-tops.' ... He knocketh to break the repose of the

---

[1] *c. Faust.* xxii. 57 (*supra*, p. 232).

saints who live in leisure, and crieth, 'Open to me.' ... Hence it comes to pass that also these who love the leisure of virtuous studies, and are loth to have to bear the troubles of laborious active duties, because they feel themselves ill-suited to minister in these things, and to do them without blame—the Church, turning her regard to them who have, in whatever sort, the ability to preach, to win new flocks and to rule them, and so open unto Christ, but in the diffi-culties of these active duties fear to sin, saith, 'I have washed my feet; how shall I defile them?' When we preach Thee, we tread upon earth that we may open unto Thee. Wash our feet, once cleansed, but while we walk through earth to open unto Thee, again defiled (*Tract in Ioan.* lvii. compressed).

In similar terms he writes to the Abbot of a community of monks on the island of Capraria. He exhorts them to hold fast to their manner of life and to persevere in it to the end; and if Mother Church desires any work from them, neither to take it on with keen elation, nor to refuse it through indolence: 'and do not prefer your own leisure to the needs of the Church; for if no good men were willing to help her in childbirth, how would her children come to the birth?' (*Ep.* xlviii.)

In the nineteenth Book of the 'City of God' he defines more accurately his ideas on the relations between the Two Lives and the manner in which their claims are to be conciliated in practice. Here he does not employ the terms 'contemplative' and 'active', but speaks of 'otium' (leisure) and 'negotium' (business), and so of a 'vita otiosa' and a 'vita negotiosa', a life leisured for contemplation, and a life busied in action.

First of all he defines that there are three kinds of life, 'one which, not lazily, but in the contemplation and examination of the truth, is leisured; another which is busied in carrying on human affairs; and a third which combines both of these' (*de Civ. Dei*, xix. 2).

Just before he had thus expressed himself:

Men may love a leisured life, as those who have desired, and have been able, to give themselves up only to the pursuit of doctrine; or a busied life, as those who, though they cultivated intellectual things, were greatly occupied in administering and directing affairs; or one combined of both, as those who gave up the alternating times of their life partly to learned leisure and partly to necessary business (ibid. xix. 1).

In a later passage he reverts to this division, and gives practical advice as to the principles that should govern the choice to be made.

Concerning the three kinds of life—the leisurely [contemplative], the busy [active], and the life which combines the two [mixed]—

though any one may without prejudice to his faith spend his life
in any one of them and attain to an everlasting reward, for all that
it does matter what a man holds to through love of truth, and what
he expends himself on through the service of charity. For no one
should be so at leisure as in his leisure not to think of his neighbour's
welfare; nor so busied as not to seek after the contemplation of God.
In his leisure he should not find delight in an idle vacancy, but it
should be a seeking and finding of the truth: so that each one may
advance in this, and not grudge to others what he finds. In the life
of action honour in this life is not to be loved, nor power; but the
work itself which is done in virtue of the said honour and power, if
it be rightly and usefully done, that is, if it work the salvation of
those under us. ... No one is precluded from the pursuit of knowing
the truth, which is the work of a leisure that is praiseworthy. ...
Wherefore the love of truth seeks for a holy leisure; and the obligations of charity make us undertake righteous business.

If no one lays this burden on us, we should give ourselves up in
leisure to the perception and contemplation of truth; but if it be
laid upon us, it must be undertaken because of the obligation of
charity: but even so, we must not wholly abandon the delight in
truth, lest that sweetness be withdrawn from us, and the obligations
we have undertaken overwhelm us.[1]

Elsewhere St Augustine emphasizes the warning here given, that
idleness is the danger in the leisured or contemplative life: 'Mary's
life was leisured (otiosa) but not idle (desidiosa), from which the
leisured life must be on its guard.'[2] Also, commenting on the words
of Psalm xlv. 11, 'Vacate et videte quia Ego sum Deus,' which he
cites in the Old Latin form, 'Agite otium', he says: 'Be at leisure—
not the leisure of idleness, but the leisure of thought.'[3] St Benedict
uses 'otiositas' in the bad sense of idleness: 'Otiositas inimica est
animae' (c. 48).

In an autobiographical note in the *Confessions* Augustine tells how
he himself combined the two lives, giving up to contemplation the
time he was able to save from the duties imposed by the calls of the
active life. Speaking of his inner communion with God, he says:

This I often do, this delights me, and as far as I may be freed from
necessary duties, unto this pleasure have I recourse. And sometimes
Thou dost admit me to an interior experience most unwonted, to
a wondrous sweetness (*Conf.* x. 65).

[1] 'Quamobrem otium sanctum quaerit caritas veritatis: negotium iustum
suscipit necessitas caritatis. Quam sarcinam si nullus imponit, percipiendae et
intuendae vacandum est veritati: si autem imponitur, suscipienda est propter
caritatis necessitatem: sed nec sic omni modo veritatis delectatio descrenda est,
ne subtrahatur illa suavitas, et opprimat ista necessitas' (*de Civ. Dei*, xix. 19).
[2] *Serm.* civ. 4.   [3] *de Vera Relig.* 65.

K. CONTEMPLATION OPEN TO ALL

St Augustine in more than one place describes a contemplative life in practice, as it may be lived in this world. One of these passages St Thomas adopts as a practical definition of a contemplative life:

Let them choose for themselves the better part: let them devote themselves to the word of God; let them yearn for the sweetness of doctrine; let them occupy themselves with the knowledge that leads to salvation (*Serm.* civ. 2).[1]

Elsewhere he describes as follows those given up to the contemplative life:

Inflamed with the desire of doctrine and of searching out and contemplating wisdom, they desire to remove themselves from all the troubles of action, and to bury themselves in a leisure of learning and teaching (*c. Faust.* xxii. 57).

After saying that the act of contemplation is the highest act—(literally 'look', 'summus aspectus')—of the soul, he goes on to say that certain choice souls who have been admitted to it, have in some measure described its joys. He continues:

I now dare to aver that we, if we steadfastly hold to the course that God commands us, and that we have undertaken to hold to, we shall come by the Power and Wisdom of God to that First Cause, or First Principle of all things; which when we have intellectually seen, we shall truly see the vanity of all things under the sun (*de Quant. Anim.* 76).

Contemplation, and, be it noted, in this life, is here promised to those who faithfully pursue the way laid down by God for attaining to it. This teaching is illustrated by other passages, as the following, which is of value also as a set-off against the apparent pervading intellectualism of St Augustine's accounts of contemplation; it shows that, to his mind, those who arrive there are not the 'intellectuals', but the 'little ones' who follow the path of Christ crucified:

If we be faithful, we have already arrived at the way of faith; and if we do not abandon it, we shall without doubt arrive at not merely so great an understanding of things incorporeal and unchangeable as cannot in this life be grasped by all, but even to the height of contemplation, which the Apostle calls 'face to face'. For some of the least ones, who yet perseveringly walk in the path of faith, come to that most blessed contemplation: while others who have knowledge of what invisible, unchangeable, incorporeal nature is, but

[1] Cf. St Thomas, 'Summa', Secunda Secundae, quaest. clxxxi. art. 3.

refuse to follow the path leading to the abode of such happiness, which seems folly to them, viz. Christ crucified, are not able to come to the shrine of that quiet, although their mind is already, as at a distance, touched by the ray of its light.[1]

But he recognizes that the hermits, such as those of Egypt, have unique advantages for the pursuit of contemplation:

They enjoy converse with God, to Whom with pure minds they inhere, and are most blessed in the contemplation of His beauty, which cannot be perceived save by the intellect of the holy.[2]

[1] *Ep.* cxx. 4. [2] *de Mor. Eccl. Cath.* 66.

THE CONTEMPLATIVE AND ACTIVE LIVES

2. ST GREGORY THE GREAT

ANALYSIS

ST GREGORY THE GREAT

St Gregory treats of this branch of the subject with great copiousness and in many places. His indebtedness to St Augustine is much more apparent here than in Part I., where he treats of contemplation; but his teaching, if it falls short of the intellectual inspiration of Augustine's, is characterized by a practicality and good sense, essentially Roman, that make it a truly valuable guide for the shaping of life. Much of it was written for his own monks in the *Morals*, and so has a value and interest all its own, as being the ideas on one of the most fundamental aspects of the theory of the monastic life held by its first and greatest Western exponent, next to St Benedict himself. As such it has profoundly influenced Benedictine life in subsequent ages. But no less profoundly has St Gregory's teaching on the contemplative and active lives influenced all clerical life, of secular priests and religious alike, in the West. His great book on the Pastoral Office, the *Regula Pastoralis*, was the first to lay down the master principles that should regulate the lives of the pastoral clergy. For though intended primarily for bishops, it is equally applicable to all pastors of souls, to all who hold posts of spiritual superiority, or exercise the cure of souls in any form. Thus what he has to teach should be of surpassing interest and value not only to monks but to all priests.

The section from the *Homilies on Ezechiel*, II ii., which characterizes the act of contemplation, was taken in Part I. as the basis of the investigation of St Gregory's teaching on contemplation. In that same Homily he gives the first formal definition of the Two Lives, the active and the contemplative, which has ever since been taken as the classical and standard definition:

There are two lives in which Almighty God by His holy word instructs us—the active and the contemplative.

The active life is: to give bread to the hungry, to teach the ignorant the word of wisdom, to correct the erring, to recall to the path of humility our neighbour when he waxes proud, to tend the sick, to dispense to all what they need, and to provide those entrusted to us with the means of subsistence.

But the contemplative life is: to retain indeed with all one's mind the love of God and neighbour, but to rest from exterior action, and cleave only to the desire of the Maker, that the mind may now take no pleasure in doing anything, but having spurned all cares, may be aglow to see the face of its Creator; so that it already knows how to bear with sorrow the burden of the corruptible flesh, and with all its desires to seek to join the hymn-singing choirs of angels, to mingle with the heavenly citizens, and to rejoice at its everlasting incorruption in the sight of God (§§ 7, 8).

The subsequent paragraphs unfold St Gregory's theory on the relations between the Two Lives. As a bird's-eye view of his theory this section will now be cited in full:

8. While placed in this life we taste only the beginnings of intimate contemplation; whereas the active life can be fully laid hold of.

9. The two women, Martha and Mary, well symbolized these two lives; whereof one was busied about much service, but the other sat at the Lord's feet and listened to the words of His mouth. And on Martha complaining of her sister, that she neglected to help her, the Lord answered saying: 'Martha, thou art occupied and busied about many things; only one is necessary. But Mary hath chosen the best part, which shall not be taken away from her.' See Martha's part is not blamed but Mary's is praised. Nor does He say that Mary hath chosen 'the good' part but 'the best', that Martha's also may be shown to be good. And the reason why Mary's part is the best is indicated: because it shall not be taken away from her. For the active life ceases with the body. For who in our everlasting country will give bread to the hungry, where none hungers? Who will bury the dead, where none dies? Wherefore the active life ceases with this present world; but the contemplative life begins here, that it may be perfected in the heavenly country, because the fire of love which begins to burn here, when it sees Him whom it loves, will in His love blaze up the more. Therefore the contemplative life is by no means taken away, for when the light of the present world is withdrawn it is perfected.

10. The two wives of Jacob, Lia and Rachel, also symbolized these two lives. For Lia is interpreted 'laborious', and Rachel 'the sight of the Beginning' [lit. 'the beginning seen'—'visum principium']. The active life is laborious, because it exerts itself in work; but the contemplative, being single-minded, pants only for the sight of the Beginning,—Him, namely, Who said: 'I am the Beginning'. But holy Jacob desired Rachel, but in the night received Lia; because every one who is converted to the Lord, desires the contemplative life, longs for the rest of the everlasting Country; but first it is necessary that in the night of the present life he work what good he can, and exert himself in labour: that is to say, receive Lia, that afterwards in the embraces of Rachel he may rest in the sight of the Beginning. Rachel was beautiful but sterile, because the contemplative life is lovely in the mind, but while it longs to rest in silence, it does not generate sons by preaching; it sees but brings not forth, because while it loves the pursuit of its quiet, it is less inflamed in gathering in others; and what it sees within it is unable to open

out to others by preaching. Lia, on the other hand, was dim-eyed but fruitful; because the active life, while it is occupied in work, sees less; but while now by word, now by example, it incites others to imitate itself, it generates many children in its good work. And if it is not able to stretch the mind in contemplation, yet from the fact that it acts exteriorly, it is able to beget followers. The active life is lived first, that afterwards the contemplative may be attained to.

11. But we must know that just as it is the right order of living to pass from the active life to the contemplative, so usually it is useful for the mind to turn back from the contemplative to the active, that by the very fact that the contemplative has inflamed the mind, the active may be more perfectly held. Therefore the active life ought to pass us on to the contemplative, and yet sometimes the contemplative, by that which we have inwardly seen with the mind, ought better to call us back to the active. Thus Jacob after the embrace of Rachel returned to that of Lia, because after the sight of the Beginning the laborious life of good works is not to be wholly given up (*Hom. in Ezech.* II. ii. 8-11).

Similar continuous expositions of St Gregory's theory of the Two Lives will be found in *Morals*, vi. 56-61, and *Homilies on Ezechiel*, I. iii. 9-12.

His theory will now be developed in detail along the same lines as were followed in developing the theory of St Augustine.

G. THE TWO LIVES

In the passages cited from St Augustine under this heading, where he contrasts the Two Lives, we saw his first principle to be that the active life is for this world, wherein it can be fully and perfectly carried out, and with which it ceases; whereas the contemplative life, fully and perfectly carried out, is for the next world, only some slight and imperfect beginning of it being possible in this. St Gregory teaches the same, as we have just seen in the passage from the *Homilies on Ezechiel*, II. ii. 9.

And elsewhere:

The silence of contemplation cannot be perfect in this life. ... Contemplation is by no means perfected here, even though it be ardently begun. ... The elect fully perform all the works that are to be done, but as yet look on only the beginnings of contemplation (*Mor.* xxx. 53).

In the long passage from *c. Faust.* xxii. (summarized in AUGUSTINE, § G, above) wherein St Augustine takes Jacob's wives as typifying the Two Lives, he lays down as axiomatic that no one can come to contemplation without having exercised the works of the active life, so that the active life is necessary for all, whereas the contemplative is not necessary. Here again St Gregory reproduces his teaching: and first, that the active life is necessary, the contemplative optional:

Though each life is by the gift of grace, yet as long as we live among our neighbours one is by necessity, the other by choice. For who that knows God enters into His Kingdom, unless he first works well? Without the contemplative life, therefore, those can enter into the heavenly Kingdom who neglect not to do the good that they can; but without the active life they cannot enter, if they neglect to do the good they can. Therefore the active life is by necessity, the contemplative by choice (*Hom. in Ezech.* i. iii. 10).

Then, that the active life must be first exercised, and only so can any one come to the contemplative:

The active life is lived first, that afterwards the contemplative may be attained to (*Hom. in Ezech.* ii. ii. 10).
Perfectness of practice having been received, we come to contemplation (*Mor.* xxii. 50).
Every one that is perfect is first joined to an active life for productiveness, and afterwards united to a contemplative life for rest (ibid. vi. 61).
The season for action comes first, for contemplation last. ... The mind should first spend itself in labour, and afterwards it may be refreshed by contemplation (ibid. vi. 60).
We ascend to the heights of contemplation by the steps of the active life (ibid. xxxi. 102).
The active life is before the contemplative in time, because by good works we tend to contemplation (*Hom. in Ezech.* i. iii. 9).

H. The Contemplative Life the Better

St Gregory follows closely St Augustine in the teaching that though the active life is more productive than the contemplative, the contemplative is better and greater than the active. The passages of Augustine which Gregory adopts are, in respect of the greater productiveness of the active life, the allegory on Lia and Rachel in *c. Faust.* xxii. 54 (see AUGUSTINE, § G, p. 231;) and in respect of the superiority of the contemplative, the pieces on Martha and Mary brought together in AUGUSTINE, § H, p. 232. In the following places the cases of Lia and Rachel and of Martha and Mary are coupled together: *Hom. in Ezech.* ii. ii. 9, 10; *Mor.* vi. 61; *Ep.* i. 5; but in *Hom. in Ezech.* i. iii. 9, Martha and Mary are dealt with alone. The principal passage on Lia and Rachel and the greater productiveness of the active life is introduced by the words: 'sicut et ante nos dictum est', referring clearly to Augustine as the source. It is § 10 in the

continuous passage just cited from *Hom. in Ezech.* II. ii., and it should
be read again, along with § 9 (on Martha and Mary). A similar
passage is the following:

Rachel is beautiful but barren, Lia dim-eyed but fruitful, truly in
that when the mind seeks the ease of contemplation, it sees more
but it is less productive in children to God. But when it betakes itself
to the labour of preaching, it sees less but it bears more largely
(*Mor.* vi. 61).

For all that, it is the quite firm teaching of St Gregory, as of all
theologians, that the contemplative life is greater and better than
the active.

See *Hom. in Ezech.* II. ii. 9. Also:

The contemplative life is greater in merit than the active, which
labours in the exercise of present work, whilst the other already
tastes with inward savour the rest that is to come. Although the
active life is good, the contemplative is better (*Hom. in Ezech.* I. iii. 9).

The contemplative life is second indeed in time, but in merit
greater than the active. Martha's concern is not reproved, but that
of Mary is even commended; for the merits of the active life are
great, but those of the contemplative far better (*Mor.* vi. 61).

Here it is worth noticing the manner in which St Gregory uses
St Augustine. A comparison of *Homilies on Ezechiel*, II. ii. 9, 10, the
principal piece wherein he reproduces Augustine's ideas on the
relative advantages of the Two Lives, with the originals, shows that
the borrowing has been done with much judgement and skill, the
very marrow of Augustine's thought having been extracted, shorn
of its rhetoric and eloquence, and expressed in simple terms of dignity
and weight—indeed a model of condensation. This is especially
striking in the piece on Martha and Mary, which is based not on
any one of Augustine's passages, but certainly on two of them, if not
three. In these places it may safely be said that Augustine's thought
loses nothing in Gregory's presentment.

When treating of the productiveness of the active life, Augustine
says that the contemplative life too has a productiveness of its own:
'it is aflame with the love of generating, for it desires to teach what
it knows' (*c. Faust.* xxii. 54).

Similarly Gregory:

Holy men when they soar aloft to the contemplation of things on
high, when they bind the first-fruits of their spirit in the love of the
heavenly Country, but weighed down by the load of human life,
return to themselves, they declare unto their brethren the heavenly

goods they were able to contemplate at any rate in a mirror, and inflame their minds with the love of that inward brightness, which they are able neither to see as it is, nor to utter as they saw it; but while they speak their words pierce and set on fire the hearts of those that hear (*Hom. in Ezech.* I. v. 13).

Again:

Whoever reaps benefit by seeing spiritual things, is bound by speaking to lay them before others. For he sees in order that he may announce, who, by the fact that he reaps benefit for himself, by preaching has a care also for the advance of his neighbour (*Hom. in Ezech.* II. ii. 4).

J. CLAIMS OF THE TWO LIVES

St Gregory's foregoing exposition of the theory of the Two Lives and their relations, though quite clear and sensible, is jejune in comparison with St Augustine's treatment of the subject. On the other hand, on the conciliation of their claims on the individual, and on the way in which they may both play their part in a well-ordered spiritual life, his teaching is fuller, more detailed, more practical, richer, than Augustine's. It is indeed his great contribution to the theory and practice of the spiritual life for all succeeding generations in Western Christianity; and as such it merits to be set forth here with much care and fullness. His doctrine is to be found chiefly in the *Morals* and in the *Book on the Pastoral Care*: the former originally addressed to his monks; the latter an instruction for all who exercise the cure of souls.

(1) *The union of the two lives, after the example of Christ, should be aimed at, especially by preachers.*

Christ set forth in Himself patterns of both lives, that is the active and the contemplative, united together. For the contemplative life differs very much from the active. But our Redeemer by coming incarnate, while He gave a pattern of both, united both in Himself. For when He wrought miracles in the city, and yet continued all night in prayer on the mountain, He gave His faithful ones an example not to neglect, through love of contemplation, the care of their neighbours; nor again to abandon contemplative pursuits through being too immoderately engaged in the care of their neighbours: but so to keep together their mind, in applying it to the two cases, that the love of their neighbour may not interfere with the love of God; nor again the love of God cast out, because it transcends, the love of their neighbours (*Mor.* xxviii. 33).

Whosoever opens his mind in holy works, has over and above to extend it to the secret pursuits of inward contemplation. For he is no perfect preacher who either, from devotion to contemplation, neglects works that ought to be done, or, from urgency in business, puts aside the duties of contemplation. ... It is hence that the Redeemer of mankind in the daytime exhibits His miracle in cities, and spends the night in devotion to prayer upon the mountain, namely, that He may teach all perfect preachers, that they should neither entirely leave the active life from love of the speculative, nor wholly slight the joys of contemplation from excess in working; but in quiet imbibe by contemplation what in employment they may pour back to their neighbours by word of mouth. For by contemplation they rise into the love of God, but by preaching they return back to the service of their neighbour ... In the sight of the internal judge our charity should be coloured with the love both of God and of our neighbour, that the converted soul may neither so delight in repose for the sake of the love of God, as to put aside the care and service of our neighbour; nor, busying itself for the love of our neighbour, be so wedded thereto that, entirely forsaking quiet, it extinguish in itself the fire of love of the Most High. Whosoever then has already offered himself as a sacrifice to God, if he desires perfection, must needs take care that he not only stretch himself out to breadth of practice, but likewise up to the heights of contemplation (ibid. vi. 56).

(2) *In particular, all pastors of souls and superiors must exercise both lives.*

The ruler [he who has the cure of souls] should be close to all by compassion, but hung aloft above all by contemplation; so that by the bowels of kindness he may take unto himself the weakness of others, and by the loftiness of speculation he may transcend himself in seeking after things invisible; lest either by seeking the heights, he despise the weaknesses of his neighbours, or by adapting himself to their infirmities, he give over to climb the heights (*Reg. Past.* ii. 5; the whole passage occurs also in *Ep.* i. 25).

Because that preacher is raised to the height of perfection, who is made firm not only by the active, but also by the contemplative life; this very perfection of preachers is rightly expressed by 'locusts', which, as often as they endeavour to raise themselves into the air, first impel and raise themselves with their legs, and afterwards fly with their wings. Thus doubtless are holy men, who, when they aim at heavenly things, rely in the first place on good works of the active life, and afterwards raise themselves in flight to sublime truths by the spring of contemplation. They plant their legs firmly, and spread their wings, because they strengthen themselves by good doings, and are exalted to lofty things by their way of life. But, while dwelling in this life, they cannot remain long in divine contemplation, but, as if like locusts, they catch themselves on their feet from the leap they have given, when, after the sublimities of contemplation, they return to the necessary doings of the active life; but yet they are not content to remain in the same active life. But when they eagerly spring forth to contemplation, they again as it were seek the air in flight; and they pass their life, like locusts, soaring up and sinking down, while they ever unceasingly endeavour to behold the highest objects, and are thrown back on themselves by the weight of their corruptible nature (*Mor.* xxxi. 49).

Holy men are sent and go forth as lightnings, when they come forth from the retirement of contemplation to the public life of employment. They are sent and they go, when from the secrecy of inward meditation, they spread forth into the wide space of active life. But after the outward works which they perform, they always return to the bosom of contemplation, there to revive the flame of their zeal, and to glow as it were from the touch of heavenly brightness. For they would freeze too speedily amid their outward works, good though they be, did they not constantly return with anxious earnestness to the fire of contemplation. ... Holy men, though they come forth, for our sakes, from the sight of their Creator, whose brightness they endeavour to behold with their mind, to the ministry of active life, yet they unceasingly recur to the holy study of contemplation; and if in their preaching they pour themselves out into our ears by bodily words from without, yet do they ever return in their silent thoughts to consider the Fount of life Itself. Did they not constantly return with anxious mind to the contemplation of God, their inward drought would doubtless dry up even their outward words of preaching (*Mor.* xxx. 8).

(3) *The reasons why pastors must not neglect either the contemplative life or external good works.*

Let not the pastor diminish his care of things within through his occupation about things without; nor forsake the oversight of things without through his anxiety about things within: lest either being given up to things external, he fall away within; or being occupied wholly with internal matters, he fail to pay that which is due to his neighbours abroad.

For oftentimes there are those who, having, as it were, forgotten that they are set over their brethren for the sake of their souls, make themselves servants with all the strength of their heart to the cares of this world; they delight to follow them, when they have them; they pant after them night and day, even when they have them not, with the fever of a troubled mind. And when, perchance, by the absence of opportunity, they are quiet from them, they are still more wearied by their very quiet: for they think it pleasure if they are drowned in business; they count it toil if they are not toiling in earthly affairs. And so it cometh to pass, while they rejoice in the pressure of worldly commotions, that they are ignorant of those inward things which they ought to have taught others: whence also the life of those who are under them is, without doubt, benumbed. ...

On the other hand, there are some who undertake the charge of a flock, but are so desirous of leisure for themselves for spiritual exercises, that they are not engaged in outward things at all. And since they utterly neglect to take care for bodily things, they are far from meeting the wants of those who are under them. And no wonder their preaching is generally looked down upon; for while they reprove the deeds of transgressors, but yet do not furnish them with things needful for this present life, they are not heard with any willingness; for the word of doctrine maketh no way into the soul of a man in want, if the hand of mercy commend it not to his mind. ... Let pastors, therefore, be in such wise zealous about the inner pursuits of those that are under them, as not to abandon provision for their outward life; for the mind of the flock is broken off, and naturally, from listening to preaching, if the care of outward aid be neglected by the shepherd (*Reg. Past.* ii. 7).

(4) *External works should be undertaken by contemplatives with a certain reluctance.*

There are two commands of charity, the love of God and of our neighbour. Isaias, desiring by the life of action to do good to his neighbours, seeketh the office of preaching. Jeremias, wishing by the life of contemplation to cleave diligently to the love of his Maker, speaketh against his being bound in duty to be sent to preach. What, therefore, the one laudably sought, that the other laudably dreaded; the latter, lest he should squander the gain of silent contemplation by speaking; the former, lest by keeping silence he should have experience of the loss of diligent labour. But this is nicely to be observed in both; that he who refused resisted not to the end, and he who would be sent had first seen himself purged by the coal from off the altar: that no one who is not purged should dare to approach the sacred ministry, nor he whom heavenly grace had chosen, prove a proud gainsayer under colour of humility. Seeing, then, that it is very difficult for any man to know that he is purged, the office of preaching is more safely declined; and yet it ought not stubbornly to be declined, when the divine Will is discerned that it should be undertaken (*Reg. Past.* i. 7).

Secular business is sometimes to be borne with, out of compassion, but never to be sought for love (ibid. ii. 7).

Pastors must always fear and take watchful heed, lest whiles they are concerned with external cares they sink from their inward purpose. For generally speaking, while the minds of rulers incautiously serve the ends of temporal solicitude, they grow cold in inward love; and being spent on things abroad, they are not afraid to forget that they have undertaken the government of souls. The solicitude, therefore, which is bestowed on their subjects exteriorly, must needs be kept within certain bounds (ibid. ii. 7).

One who is submissive to the divine disposals, when a high position of authority is enjoined upon him, if he be already endowed with qualities by which he may do good to others, ought from his heart to flee from it, and to obey unwillingly (ibid. i. 6).

(5) *Yet contemplatives should accept offices of superiority when called on to do so.*

There is a chapter (*Reg. Past.* i. 5) on the duty of contemplatives accepting high positions of authority or superiority (culmen regiminis): Concerning those who might be useful by their example of virtues in a high position of authority, but refuse in pursuit of their own quiet.

If they refuse when called upon to take upon themselves high positions of authority, they take away for the most part from themselves the very gifts which they received, not for themselves only, but also for others. And while they think of their own gain, and not of that of others, they deprive themselves of those very good things which they desire to keep for themselves. ... There are some who, being enriched with great gifts, while they are eager for the pursuit only of contemplation, fly from complying with the advantage of their neighbour by preaching, loving the privacy of quiet and seeking the retirement of contemplation. And if they be judged strictly concerning this, they are doubtless answerable for all the good they might have done had they come into public. For with what conscience can he who would be distinguished for his usefulness to his neighbours put his own privacy before the benefit of others, when the Only-begotten of the Father Most High Himself came forth from the bosom of His Father into public amongst us, that He might do good to many? (*Reg. Past.* i. 5).

(6) *In a dearth of workers, contemplatives should undertake the works of the active life.*

We ought to bear in mind that when those are wanting who might fitly minister to the exterior needs of their neighbours, those too who are full of spiritual gifts ought to condescend to their weakness, and as far as they may with propriety be able, lend themselves with the condescension of charity to the earthly necessities of others. Nor should it weary the mind, if its perception, being ever intent on the contemplation of spiritual things, is sometimes as it were bent down, diminished in managing the least concerns (*Mor.* xix. 45).

(7) *Periods of retirement for contemplation are necessary for those in superiority or engaged in active works.*

Those that bear themselves well in authority rest, in that they lay aside at intervals the din of earthly business for the love of God, lest while the lower concerns incessantly occupy the heart, it fall away wholly from the highest. For they know that the mind can never be lifted up to things above, if it be continually busied in those below with tumultuous care. ... They who are busied in temporal affairs, then manage external things aright, when they betake themselves with solicitude to those of the interior, and repose within themselves in the bosom of tranquil rest (ibid. v. 19).

Holy men who are obliged by the necessity of their employments to engage in outward ministrations, are ever studiously betaking themselves to the secrets of their hearts; and there do they ascend the height of most inward thought, while they put aside the tumults of temporal activities and at the summit of their contemplation search out the sentence of the divine Will. Hence it is that Moses frequently retires to the Tabernacle on doubtful points, and there secretly consults God, and learns what certain decision to come to. For to leave the crowd and retire to the Tabernacle, is to put aside the tumults of outward objects, and enter into the secret recess of the mind. For the Lord is there consulted, and we hear inwardly and in silence what we must do openly and without. This course good Rulers (rectores) daily pursue; when they are aware they cannot settle doubtful points, they betake themselves to the secret recesses of their mind, and what they first hear in silence, they afterwards make known to the world in their conduct. For in order that they may engage in outward employments without injury to themselves, they constantly take care to withdraw to the secrets of their heart. And thus they hear the voice of God while they withdraw themselves in the thoughts of their mind from the influence of carnal things (*Mor.* xxiii. 38).

(8) *The contemplative life will be aided by an admixture of the active.*

Each soul the broader it is in the love of its neighbour, the higher also will it be in the knowledge of God. For while by love it enlarges itself alongside itself, by knowledge it bears itself aloft; and it becomes the higher above itself in proportion as it stretches itself out alongside itself to the love of neighbour.

But let us love God and our neighbour from the bottom of our heart. Let us enlarge ourselves in the affection of love, that we may be exalted in the glory of loftiness. Let us compassionate our neighbour by love, that we may be joined to God by knowledge. Let us condescend to our least brethren on earth, that we may be the equals of the angels in heaven (*Hom. in Ezech.* II. ii. 15).

Hence the very Truth, manifested to us by taking our human nature, cleaved unto prayer on the mountain, and worked miracles in the cities, laying down a way for imitation by good Rulers of souls; so that even though they already scale the heights by contemplation, by compassion, for all that, they share in the needs of the weak; for love then wonderfully mounts to the heights, when it mercifully draws itself to the lowliness of its neighbours; and in proportion as it kindly descends to what is weak, does it mightily return to the heights (*Reg. Past.* ii. 5; also in *Ep.* i. 25).

(9) *For contemplation tranquillity of mind is necessary.*

St Gregory when Pope found that even when he had despatched

his businesses, he was unable to secure sufficient tranquillity of mind for exercising contemplation:

When my business is done I try to return to my inner self, but cannot, for I am driven away by vain tumultuous thoughts (*Ep.* i. 5, ad Theoctistam).

It ought to be known that we do not at all reach the height of contemplation, if we cease not from the oppression of outward care (*Mor.* xxx. 54).

Anger that comes of evil blinds the eye, but anger that come of zeal disturbs it. Since necessarily, in whatever degree one is moved by a zeal for virtue, the world of contemplation, which cannot be known save by a heart in tranquillity, is broken up. For zeal for the cause of virtue in itself, in that it fills the mind with disquietude and agitation, presently bedims the eye thereof, so that in its troubled state it can no longer see those objects far up above which it afore-time clearly beheld in a state of tranquillity. To perturbation con-templation is never joined, nor is the mind when disturbed enabled to see that which, even when in a tranquil state, it scarcely has power to gaze on (ibid. v. 82).

Often we wax angry in correcting faults and perturb our tran-quillity of mind. Only a tranquil mind is able to hold itself aloft in the light of contemplation. While we pursue faults in anger we are necessarily thrown into confusion and disturbed from the con-templation of things on high (Gregory's Letter answering the ques-tions put him by Augustine, Question viii. towards end; preserved in Ven. Bede's *Eccl. Hist.* i. 27. The thought and latinity of this passage afford strong confirmation of the authenticity of the Letter, which has been questioned).[1]

These are the things the soul is employed withal: she both wholly withdraws herself from the restless appetite of this world, and gives over the turmoil of earthly actions, and in pursuit of tranquillity, bent on virtuous attainments, she sleeps waking. For she is never led on to contemplate internal things, unless she be heedfully with-drawn from those which entwine themselves about her without ... Inward knowledge is not cognizable unless there is a cessation from outward embarrassments, and our mind is never caught up to the force of inward contemplation, unless it be first carefully lulled to rest from all agitation of earthly desires (*Mor.* v. 55).

If we wish to contemplate things within, let us rest from outward

[1] The authenticity of St Gregory's 'Responsions', though questioned from an early date, may now be said to be accepted, Mommsen and the editors in the *Mon. Germ. Hist.* having declared for it; Mgr Duchesne, too, after having rejected it, accepted it in the later editions of his *Origines du Culte Chrétien.* The only general treatment of the question seems to be a memoire by Cardinal Gasquet and Mr Edmund Bishop, read in Rome in 1890. The text, without the illustrative notes, was first printed in the *Downside Review*, 1904, and then, with the notes, which add greatly to its value, in a volume of *Miscellanea*, celebrating Abbot Amelli's jubilee of priesthood (Monte Cassino, 1920). The case for authenticity seems quite conclusive, though the argument from style has not been brought to bear. The piece in the text is redolent of St Gregory.

engagements. The voice of God is heard when, with minds at ease, we rest from the bustle of this world, and the divine precepts are pondered by us in the deep silence of the mind (ibid. xxiii. 37).

(10) *Conciliation of contemplative life with external works.*

It is by an active life perfectly carried out that one passes to the freedom of the contemplative life. And very often such an one is able to pass to the contemplative life, and yet not give up the active life, so that he who has arrived at contemplation does not abandon the activity of good works whereby he is able to be of use to others (*Hom. in Ezech.* I. iii. 11, 12).

God will often send one who has passed from the active life to the contemplative back to the active, and will keep him in alternations of the two lives. St Gregory makes Him say:

I adapt My preachers, when I will, after the grace of contemplation to the ministry of active life. And yet I ever call them back from outward good deeds to the inward height of contemplation, in order that they may one while go forth, when commanded, to perform their tasks, and that at another they may dwell with Me more familiarly when recalled to the pursuit of speculation (*Mor.* xxx. 8).

It sometimes happens that they who love the heavenly country alone, seem to be subjected to the charges of the earthly country. Being full of wisdom from above, they distinguish how they may at once be free to one thing inwardly, and busied with another thing outwardly, ... and when the affairs of business make a din without, within the most peaceful repose is maintained in love. For as force of mind is at the head for bridling the motions of the flesh, so very often the love of tranquillity regulates aright the imposed turmoils of business, because external charges, if they be not desired with a wrong affection, may be executed with a mind not disordered but regulated. For holy men never court them, but lament them when put upon them by secret appointment; and though in respect of a better aim they shun them, yet in respect of a submissive mind they bear them, which same they are above everything eager to avoid if it might be; but fearing the secret dispensations of God, they lay hold of that they eschew, and execute what they avoid. For they go into their conscience, and they there take counsel what the secret will of God would have, and being conscious that they ought to be subject to the appointments on high, they humble the neck of the heart to the yoke of divine Providence. But he that is such as this, whatever turmoils are at work without, they never reach to his interior parts. And so it comes to pass that there is one thing maintained within in wish and another thing maintained without in office, and that with this wisdom their hearts are filled, being no longer troubled and disordered, but in a state of tranquillity (*Mor.* xviii. 70).

(11) *A true 'mixed life' the most excellent.*

St Gregory places in the highest grade the excellence of preachers; then that of pure contemplatives who practice continence and silence; and lowest that of the married who lead good lives in the world: yet, though not equal in merit and dignity, they all are rewarded equally according to their desires and efforts.

The excellence of preachers is far above that of the continent and silent, and the eminence of the continent outdistances greatly that of married people. The married, though they do well and desire to see God, yet are occupied by domestic cares and are divided in mind. The continent are remote from the affairs of this world and restrain carnal pleasure even from lawful wedlock; they are implicated in no care of wife and children and no troublesome and difficult thoughts of providing for a family. But preachers not only withhold themselves from vices, but restrain others from sinning, lead them to the faith, and instruct them in the pursuit of holy living. Yet there is for all three the same faith, the same reward of everlasting life, the same joy in the vision of God (*Hom. in Ezech.* II. iv. 6).

Taken in conjunction with what has gone before, on the necessity of preachers practising both lives, we have here quite clearly adumbrated the later doctrine, formulated by St Thomas, that the contemplative life is higher than the active, and the mixed life, such as this, the highest of all.

(12) *St Gregory's conception of 'the contemplative life' as actually lived.*

We can remain fixed in the active life, but in the contemplative we are by no means able to keep our mind on the stretch. ...

When we mount from the active life to the contemplative, as the mind is not able to stand long in contemplation, but whatever it gazes on of eternity in a mirror and an enigma, it beholds, so to say, by stealth and in passing, the mind, repelled by the immensity of so great a height, sinks back into itself. And it has to return to the active life and to exercise itself for long in the practice of good works: so that when the mind is not able to rise to the contemplation of heavenly things, it may not refuse to do the good that it can. And so it comes about that, helped by its good deeds, it again mounts aloft unto contemplation, and receives nourishment of love from the pasture of contemplated truth. And as the very weakness of corruption cannot for long maintain itself in contemplation, coming back again to good works, it feeds on the memory of the sweetness of God, and is nourished externally by good actions, and internally by holy desires (*Hom. in Ezech.* I. v. 12).

There are some good deeds wherein we persevere unwearied, and again there are some from which we are continually giving over and falling away. and we are restored to these not without great en-

deavours at intervals of time: for in the active life the mind is
stablished without failing; but from the contemplative, being overcome by the load of its infirmity, it faints away. For the first endures
the more steadfastly in proportion as it opens itself to things about
it for our neighbour's weal; the latter falls away the more swiftly in
proportion as, passing beyond the barriers of the flesh, it endeavours
to soar up above itself. The first directs its way through level places,
and therefore plants the foot of practice more strongly; but the other,
as it aims at heights above itself, the sooner descends wearied to
itself. When the minds of the elect, through the grace of an active
life being vouchsafed them, abandon the paths of error, they never
return to the evil courses of the world, which they have forsaken;
but when through the gaze of contemplation they are led to stay
themselves from this same active life, they 'go and return', in that
because they are never able to continue for long in contemplation,
they again let themselves out in action, that by busying themselves
in such things as are immediately near them, they may recruit their
strength, and may be enabled by contemplation again to soar above
themselves. But while this practice of contemplation is in due method
resumed at intervals of time, we hold on assuredly without failing
to all its entireness (soliditas); for though the mind, being overcome
by the weight of its infirmity, falls short, yet, being restored again
by continual efforts, it lays hold thereof. Nor should it be said to
have lost its stability in that which, though it be ever failing in, it is
ever pursuing, even when it has lost the same[1] (*Mor.* x. 31).

In *Benedictine Monachism* (p. 99) this passage is commented on, and
its importance for the theory of Benedictine life brought out. It will
be dwelt on again later (p. 207).

(13) *A reminder to contemplatives of their indebtedness to active livers.*

In the following piece St Gregory, both in respect to spiritual
common sense with a gentle irony, and to felicity in allegory, is at
his best:

There are some, who if they have made ever so small a beginning
in spiritual conversation, on observing that their rulers fix their
thoughts only on worldly and temporal objects, begin to blame the
disposition of supreme Providence as if they were improperly
appointed to rule, since they set an example of worldly conversation.
But because the power of office cannot be exercised without our
engaging in worldly cares, therefore Almighty God frequently im-
poses the burden of rule on hard and laborious hearts, in order that

[1] The Latin of the closing portion is as follows: 'Sed dum haec eadem contemplatio more debito per temporum intervalla repetitur, indeficienter procul
dubio et in eius soliditate persistitur: quia etsi infirmitatis suae pondere superata
mens deficit, haec tamen iterum continuis conatibus reparata comprehendit. Nec
stabilitatem suam in ea perdidisse dicenda est, a qua etsi semper deficit, hanc et
cum perdiderit semper inquirit.'

the tender minds of spiritual men may be released from worldly cares: in order that the one may be more safely concealed from the bustle of the world, the more willingly the others employ themselves in worldly anxieties.

And how properly this is ordered in the Church by divine appointment is signified by the very construction of the tabernacle. For Moses is commanded by the voice of God to weave curtains of fine linen and scarlet and blue, for the covering of the Holy of Holies within. And he was ordered to spread, for the covering of the tabernacle, curtains of goats' hair and skins, to sustain the rain and wind and dust. What then do we understand by the skins and goats' hair, with which the tabernacle is covered, but the gross minds of men, which are sometimes hard though they be placed on high in the Church by the secret judgements of God? And because they are not afraid of being employed in worldly concerns, they must needs bear the winds and storms of temptation which arise from the opposition of this world. But what is signified by the blue, scarlet, and fine linen, but the life of holy men, delicate, but brilliant? And while it is carefully concealed in the tabernacle under goats' hair and skins, its beauty is preserved entire. For in order that the fine linen may shine, the scarlet glitter, and the blue be resplendent with azure brilliance, the skins and the goats' hair endure the rains, the winds, the dust from above. They then who advance in great excellence within the bosom of holy Church, ought not to despise the doings of their rulers, when they see that they are engaged in the business of the world. For that they penetrate in safety into secret mysteries, is owing to the help of those who buffet with the storms of this world from without. For how would the fine linen retain the grace of its brightness, if the rain were to touch it? Or what splendour or brightness would the scarlet or blue display, should the dust light on and defile them? Let the strong texture of the goats' hair, then, be placed above, to resist dust; and the brightness of the blue, fitted for ornament, be placed beneath. Let those who are engaged in spiritual pursuits alone, adorn the Church. Let those guard her, who are not wearied with the labours of the world. But let not him who now gleams with spiritual brightness within holy Church, murmur against his superior, who is employed in worldly business. For if thou glitterest securely within, like scarlet, why dost thou blame the goats' hair with which thou art protected? (*Mor.* xxv. 38, 39).

K. Contemplation Open to All

That St Gregory believed contemplation not to be the perquisite of any small select spiritual circles, but open to all sincere livers of a good Christian life, appears from the circumstance that his principal expositions of contemplation and the contemplative life were given, not in conferences to his monks, but in public sermons preached in the Lateran Basilica to mixed congregations of all comers, viz. the two Homilies on Ezechiel, II. ii. and II. v., already many times cited. At the close of the former he says: 'See, beloved brethren, while wishing to explain to you the theory of each life, we have spoken at undue length. But good minds, who love to carry out both of these two lives (quibus utraque eadem vita est ad agendum amabilis) should not find it burdensome to hear about them' (§ 14). This shows he thought a considerable number of his hearers were likely to be concerned with the contemplative life.

Similarly at the close of the other Homily he quite definitely declares that contemplation may be the lot of all, no state or condition of life being debarred:

It is not the case that the grace of contemplation is given to the highest and not given to the lowest; but often the highest, and often the most lowly, and very often those who have renounced,[1] and sometimes also those who are married, receive it. If therefore there is no state of life (officium) of the faithful, from which the grace of contemplation can be excluded, any one who keeps his heart within him (cor intus habet) may also be illumined by the light of contemplation; so that no one can glory in this grace as if it were singular. It is not the high and pre-eminent members of holy Church only that have the grace of contemplation; but very often those members receive this gift, who, although by desire they already mount to the heights, are still occupying low positions. Almighty God inpours the light of contemplation into those also who appear to be lowly in the eyes of men, but secretly give themselves up to the pursuit of divine wisdom, pant after heavenly things, and think on the everlasting joys (*Hom. in Ezech.* II. v. 19, 20).

Elsewhere are found such utterances as the following:

We see daily in holy Church that very many, while they manage well external things that come to them, are by the grace given them led moreover to mystic intelligence;[2] so that they faithfully administer outward things and are gifted greatly with inward understanding (*Hom. in Evang.* ix. 5).

The book on the Pastoral Care is addressed to bishops, but it applies also to all who exercise the pastoral office or the cure of souls in any capacity. The passages already cited from this work show that St Gregory considered an admixture of the contemplative life to be a condition of the fruitful performance of the pastoral office, and that he took for granted that all pastors of souls may,

---

[1] 'Remoti': cf. 'continentes et tacentes ... ab huius mundi actione remoti sunt' (*Hom. in Ezech.* II. iv. 6; the whole piece is cited p. 184 above). Also: 'Qui a praesentis vitae actione remoti sunt' (*Mor.* v. 55). Thus it appears to be equivalent to Cassian's word for monks, 'renunciantes'.

[2] 'Intellectus mysticus'; the use of the word 'mystic' in its later sense is to be noted.

and should, exercise contemplation: among the disqualifications for the pastoral office he names 'ignorance of the light of heavenly contemplation' (i. 11). Thus by contemplation he means something that he believes to be ordinarily open to all priests.

For some characters an active life is best, for some a contemplative; for restless minds, and those lacking spiritual discernment, there are dangers in a contemplative life, which are pointed out in the following passage:

It is above all things necessary to know that the compositions of souls are infinitely varied one with another; for there are some so restless that if they have cessation from labour, they have only the worse labour, in that they are subject to worse tumults of mind in proportion as they have more time and liberty for their thoughts. Whence it behoves that neither the tranquil mind should open itself wide in immoderate exercising of works, nor the restless mind stint itself by the pursuit of contemplation. For often they who might have contemplated God in quiet, have fallen, being overcharged with business; and often they who might live advantageously occupied with the service of their fellow-creatures, are killed by the sword of their quiescence. It is hence that some restless spirits, whilst by contemplation they hunt out more than their wits compass, launch out even to the length of wrong doctrines, and whilst they have no mind to be the disciples of truth in a spirit of humility, they become the masters of falsities. There are some who are quite unable to behold the world above and spiritual things with the eye of discernment, yet enter upon the heights of contemplation, and therefore, by the mistake of a perverted understanding, they fall away into the pit of misbelief. These then the contemplative life, adopted to an extent beyond their powers, causes to fall from the truth, which same persons the active life by itself might have kept safe in lowliness of mind in the firm seat of their uprightness. ... When thou art not qualified for the contemplative life by a fitting degree of discretion, keep more safely the active life alone. ... On the other hand, if it were not that the contemplative life suited some minds more than the active life, the Lord would never say by the voice of the Psalmist: 'Be still, and know that I am God' (Mor. vi. 57).

Thus the active life is the more ordinary call: 'The active life is the lot of many, the contemplative of few' (Mor. xxxii. 4). But for the spiritually minded the active life alone is unsatisfying:

Whosoever already looks down upon all earthly objects of desire, whosoever spreads himself out in the labours of an active life, finds that it by no means suffices him to do great things without, unless by contemplation he also have power to penetrate into interior mysteries (ibid. vi. 55).

THE CONTEMPLATIVE AND ACTIVE LIVES

3. ST BERNARD

ANALYSIS

ST BERNARD

WE have from St Bernard no such reasoned exposition of the nature and theory of the Two Lives as we have from Augustine and Gregory. He makes various allusions, indeed, to Lia and Rachel, Martha and Mary, but, except in *Serm. de Assumpt. B.V.M.* iii., they are mere passing references. They follow the lines of exposition or allegory made current in the West by the two earlier doctors, without bringing anything new to the treatment. I believe that Bernard is here based on Gregory; I see no ground for supposing he had direct acquaintance with Augustine's treatment of the two cases. And in general, I am not aware of any reason for supposing he was beholden to Augustine, otherwise than through Gregory, for his mystical doctrine.[1]

In these circumstances there is nothing to be said under the headings G and H of this part of the subject, and we pass at once to J, where Bernard has much to say that is of interest.

J. CLAIMS OF THE TWO LIVES

St Bernard's solution of the problem of the claims of the Two Lives on the individual, and their conciliation in practice, is substantially the same as St Gregory's, and is no doubt derived from it. But St Bernard's strong personality bestows on his treatment an originality and a freshness that make it something new. It is not possible to follow quite the same lines of exposition as were adopted in the case of St Gregory, but the general method of treatment will be similar.

The Gospel story of Martha and Mary shows that the contemplative life is in itself to be preferred: Mary chose the best part, even though the humble life of Martha be perchance of no less merit with God. But Mary is praised for her choice, because her part is altogether, so far as it rests with us, to be chosen; but Martha's part, if it be laid upon us, is to be patiently borne (*Serm. de aiv.* ix. 4).

Addressing his monks, pledged to the contemplative state, he exhorts them to cling to it:

By no means should one who is at leisure to attend to God (qui

[1] In other words, I doubt the correctness of Dean Inge's note, that 'in the speculative side of his teaching (on mysticism) he depends almost entirely upon Augustine' (*Christian Mysticism*, p. 140).

vacat Deo) aspire to the tumultuous life of the officials of the monastery (*Serm. de assumpt. B.V.M.* iii. 2).

The solitude of the contemplative life is described as follows:

O holy soul, remain alone, so as to preserve thyself for Him alone of all things Whom thou hast chosen to thyself from among all. Avoid appearing in public, shun even those who dwell in the house with thee, withdraw thyself from friends and intimates. ... Withdraw thyself; I do not mean in body, but withdraw in mind, in intention, in devotion, in spirit. ...

The only solitude prescribed to you is solitude of mind and spirit. You are alone if you are not thinking of common things, if you are not interested in things present, if you think little of that which many esteem highly, if you despise what all desire, if you avoid disputes, do not take to heart losses, nor bear injuries in mind. You may be alone in a crowd, or in a crowd when alone. However large the throng of men in which you find yourself, you are alone if only you take care not to pry curiously into the lives and doings of others, nor to judge them rashly (*Cant.* xl. 4, 5).

But in this life it is not possible for any one to be given up wholly to contemplation:

There is no doubt that in a right-thinking soul the love of God is preferred to the love of man, heaven to earth, eternity to time, the soul to the body. And yet in well-regulated action the opposite order is found frequently, or almost always, to prevail. For we are both more frequently occupied, and more busily, with cares for our neighbour; we apply ourselves, by the right of humanity and the necessity of the case, more to promote the peace of the earth than the glory of heaven; in our anxiety about temporal interests we scarcely permit ourselves to think anything about those which are eternal. ... Who doubts that a man when he is in prayer is speaking to God? and yet how often are we withdrawn from prayer, and that at the very dictate of charity, because of those who are in need of our assistance or our advice! How often does holy quiet give place, and that from a pious motive, to the tumult of business affairs! (ibid. l. 5).

St Gregory's teaching of the union of the two lives, of contemplation and action, is endorsed by St Bernard:

A soul accustomed to quiet draws consolation from good works rooted in a faith unfeigned, whenever the light of holy contemplation is withdrawn from it, as is often the case. For who is able to enjoy the light of holy contemplation—I do not say continually, but even for a considerable time—while he remains in this body? But, as

I have said, as often as he falls from the state of contemplation he resorts to that of action, as to a convenient refuge from whence he may be able more easily to return into contemplation. For these two things are intimately related; they are chamber companions and dwell together. Martha is sister to Mary, and although she comes forth from the light of contemplation, she never suffers herself to fall into the darkness of sin, or subside into slothful leisure, but remains still in the light of good works (*Cant.* li. 2).

Similarly:

Recognize what I have said to you more than once about the two alternations of sacred repose and of necessary action, and that there is not in this life space for lengthened contemplation or prolonged repose, because the duties of office and the usefulness of work press upon us more urgently, and are more immediately necessary. The Bridegroom, therefore, as is His wont, when His beloved has been for a while reposing in sacred communion with Him, does not delay to summon her to duties which seem to be more needful. ... But for the Bride to know a wish of her Bridegroom is for her at once to feel the desire to be enabled to fulfil it, the desire for good works, the desire to bear fruit for the Bridegroom (ibid. lviii. 1).

Like St Gregory, St Bernard insists that those who work for the spiritual good of others, must themselves be spiritual men, exercising prayer and contemplation. This is the burden of Sermon xviii. on the Canticle.

The gifts of the Holy Ghost are of two kinds, those given us for our own sake, and those given us for the sake of others. He gives the warning:

We must take heed of two dangers: that of giving to others what is meant for ourselves, and of keeping for ourselves what is given to us for others. You are certainly retaining for yourself that which belongs to your neighbour, if, for example, being not only full of virtues, but also outwardly adorned with the gifts of knowledge and of eloquence, fear, perhaps, or sloth, or an ill-judged humility, restrains your good gift of speech, which might be of service to many people, in a useless, or, rather, blamable silence; and thus you are evil spoken of because you withhold corn from the people. On the other hand, you dissipate and lose that which is your own if, before you have received a complete inpouring, and while you are, so to speak, but half filled, you hasten to pour yourself forth. ...

If, then, you are wise, you will show yourself rather as a reservoir than as a canal. For a canal spreads abroad water as it receives it, but a reservoir waits until it is filled before overflowing, and thus communicates, without loss to itself, its superabundant water. ... In the Church at the present day we have many canals, few reservoirs (*Cant.* xviii. 2, 3).

The course of the spiritual life is traced in § 5, from conversion through penitence, good works, prayer, up to contemplation (the passage has been cited in Part I., p. 99). The effect of contemplation is to generate a love that makes such an one a good and worthy pastor of souls; thus the last three stages are: prayer, contemplation, spiritual fecundity.

That momentary and passing contemplation does not fail to arouse in him an ardent and burning love. Such a love is full of zeal; and with that love a faithful and prudent servant, whom the Lord hath set over His household, ought to feel himself aglow. It fills and warms the soul, it boils over and spreads itself fearlessly, it bursts forth, and it says: Who is weak and I am not weak? Who is scandalized and I am not on fire? Let him who is possessed by that love preach and bear fruit; let him do marvels, let him even work miracles; vanity will find no place in him who is wholly occupied by charity. ... It is very full of peril to promote [to ecclesiastical functions] one who has not yet attained this perfect charity, however great be the talents which, in other respects, he may appear to possess. ...
Behold with how many and great graces it behoves us to be previously filled, that we may venture to impart to others, so that we may bestow out of fullness, not out of poverty. In the first place we ought to have compunction; secondly, devotion; thirdly, a laborious penitence; fourthly, works of piety; fifthly, earnestness in prayer; sixthly, the repose of contemplation; and in the seventh place, the fullness of charity (*Cant.* xviii. 6).

Warnings are uttered against a false mysticism, a contemplation not properly prepared for by penitence, self-discipline, the exercise of the virtues, and the performance of good works, and indulged in to the disregard of works of obedience:

Perhaps you desire the repose of contemplation; and in this you do well, provided that you do not forget the flowers with which the Couch of the Bride is strewed. Therefore do thou take great care similarly to wreathe around thine the blossoms of good works, and to make the exercise of virtues precede that holy leisure. Otherwise it would be self-indulgence that you should so earnestly desire to rest before you have earned that rest by labour, and you would be neglecting the fruitfulness of Lia in desiring to enjoy only the embraces of Rachel. But it would be a reversing of the proper order to ask for the reward without having earned it, and to take food before having done the labour. The taste of contemplation is emphatically not due, except to obedience to God's commandments. Do not imagine, then, that the love of your own repose is to be in any wise made a hindrance to works of holy obedience, or to the traditions of the elders. Do not suppose that you will have the company of the

Bridegroom for that bed[1] which you have strewed, not with the flowers of obedience, but with the weeds and nettles of disobedience. How should He approve the empty leisure of that contemplation of yours?[2] (*Cant.* xlvi. 5).

The good actions of a holy life are well compared to flowers in a bridal-chamber, because they produce the testimony of a quiet and safe conscience. After a good work one more securely reposes (slumbers) in contemplation; and the more fully a man is conscious of not having been wanting through inertness or love of self in the performance of good works, the more confidence will he have in endeavouring to see and to investigate things on high. (ibid. xlvii. 4).

We have already seen in Part I. § D (p. 113) when speaking of the Spiritual Marriage, that the imagery of marriage is carried on to the idea of spiritual fecundity.

This conception entered into the traditional mystical doctrine of later times; therefore it is worth while signalizing other places where St Bernard dwells upon it.

Commenting on the opening words of the Canticle, 'Thy breasts are better than wine', he explains them as meaning that the effect of union with the Bridegroom in contemplation is that the Bride's breasts become filled with spiritual milk for the nourishment of the children she brings forth:

Suddenly the Bridegroom is present and gives assent to her petition; He gives her the kiss asked, of which the fullness of breasts is witness. For so great is the efficacy of this holy kiss that the Bride on receiving it conceives, the swelling breasts rich with milk being the evidence. Those whose endeavour it is to pray frequently have made proof of what I say. Often we approach the altar and give ourselves to prayer with a heart lukewarm and dry. But if we persist, grace comes suddenly in a flood upon us, our breast grows full of increase, a wave of piety fills our inward heart; and if we press on, the milk of sweetness conceived in us will soon spread over us in fruitful flood. And the Bridegroom will say: Thou hast, O my Spouse, that which thou prayedst for; and this is the sign: Thy breasts have become better than wine. By this may you know that you have received the kiss, in that you have conceived, and that your breasts are filled with milk. Her companions say to the Bride, Why do you still ask for the wine of contemplation? For that which He has already given is of far greater value. That which you ask for delights you indeed; but the breasts by which you nourish the children whom you bring forth are better, that is, more necessary, than the wine of contemplation. The one is that which makes glad the heart of one man alone; but the other that which edifies many. For though Rachel is fairer, Lia is more fruitful. Do not therefore too

---

[1] 'Non dormiet tecum sponsus in lecto uno.'
[2] 'Contemplationis tuae inane otium.'

much linger over the kisses of contemplation, because the breasts of preaching are better (*Cant*. ix. 7, 8).

The above may appear unduly realistic in treatment; the following is not liable to such criticism:

Notice how, while desiring one thing, the Bride receives another. She strives for the repose of contemplation, and the labour of preaching is laid upon her; and while she is thirsting for the presence of the Bridegroom, the care of bringing forth children for Him and of nourishing them is entrusted to her. She must recognize herself to be a mother, and to be bound to give milk to her little ones, and to nourish her children.
[Again the illustration of Rachel, beautiful but barren, and Lia, dim-eyed but fertile.]
From this we are taught that it is often needful to leave the sweets of contemplation for the sake of labours which give nourishment (lactantia ubera), and that no one must live for himself alone, but for the good of all (*Cant*. xli. 5, 6).

We have seen (p. 184) St Gregory's idea of a contemplative life as actually lived; the following piece makes it clear that St Bernard's idea is the same:

After this divine look, so full of condescension and goodness, comes a Voice, gently and sweetly presenting to the mind the Will of God; and this is no other than Love itself, which cannot remain in leisure, soliciting and persuading to the fulfilment of the things that are of God. Thus the Bride hears that she is to arise and hasten, no doubt to work for the good of souls. This is indeed a property of true and pure contemplation, that it sometimes fills the mind, which it has vehemently inflamed with divine fire, with a fervent zeal and desire to gain for God others to love Him in like manner, and to that end it very willingly lays aside the leisure of contemplation for the labour of preaching. And again, when it has attained the object desired, to a certain extent, it returns with the more eagerness to that contemplation, in that it remembers that it laid it aside for the sake of gaining more fruit. Then, when it has tasted again the delights of contemplation, it recurs with increased power, and with its accustomed keenness, to its labours for the good of souls.
But the mind frequently hesitates between these continual changes, being profoundly anxious and fearful, lest when drawn to one or other of these alternatives by the attractions and advantages it discerns in each, it should give itself up too much to one or other of them, and should deviate by ever so little from the divine will. ... Even a holy man feels grave uncertainty between the claims of fruitful labour and of restful contemplation; and although he is always occupied about good things, yet he always feels a sense of regret as if he had been doing that which is wrong, and from one

moment to another entreats with groans to be shown the will of God. In these uncertainties, the one and only remedy is prayer and frequent upliftings of the soul to God, that He would deign to make continually known to us what we ought to do, and when, how, and in what manner we should do it. You have, as I think, these three things pointed out and commended in the words of the Bridegroom, 'My love, my dove, my beautiful one,'—namely, preaching, prayer, and contemplation.

For rightly is the Bride called 'love', in that by preaching, advising, ministering, she zealously and faithfully seeks to make gain for the Bridegroom. Rightly is she called 'dove', in that she ceases not in prayer to win the divine mercy for her sins. Rightly too is she called 'beautiful' in that, radiant with heavenly desire, she takes on herself the beauty of divine contemplation, but only at the hours when it may be done conveniently and opportunely (*Cant.* lvii. 9).

K. CONTEMPLATION OPEN TO ALL

On this point St Bernard's testimony is less clear than St Augustine's and St Gregory's, because in what he says of contemplation he is addressing his monks. He certainly encourages them all to aspire to contemplation and declares it to be open to any of them who strives in the right way to attain to it. But in some passages he may be understood as speaking more generally of all devout Christians. For instance:

'My beloved is mine, and I am His.' It is the Church that speaks thus. But what shall we say of each of us individually? Are we to think that there is any one among us to whom what is said by the Bride is capable of being applied? Anyone, do I say, among us? I should think that there is no one at all among the faithful members of the Church with respect to whom it may not justly be inquired whether the Bride's mystical saying is not realized in some degree in him (*Cant.* lxviii. 3, 4).

At the beginning of the exposition after describing the Kiss of the Hands and Feet of Christ, he goes on:

And after you have made in those two kisses a double proof of the Divine condescension, perhaps you may be so bold as to enter upon the endeavour to reach still higher and more sacred things. For in proportion as you grow in grace, your confidence also will augment, you will love more fervently, and knock at the door with more assurance of success, to seek that in which you feel you are wanting: for to him who knocks it shall be opened. And to you, when in such a disposition of mind and soul, I believe there will not be refused that kiss, the loftiest and most sacred of all, which contains in itself at once a supreme condescension and a sweetness ineffable (ibid. iii. 5).

Again:

If there be among us one who feels it is good to draw near to
God; one in such way a man of desires that he longs to be dissolved
and to be with Christ; but longs for it vehemently, thirsts for it
ardently, and meditates on it assiduously; such an one assuredly will
receive the Word, and in none other form than Bridegroom, in the
time of visitation, in the hour when he feels himself inwardly embraced, as it were, in the arms of Wisdom, and feels himself bathed
in the sweetness of holy love (ibid. xxxii. 2).

THE CONTEMPLATIVE AND ACTIVE LIVES

4. SUMMARY

SUMMARY: THE CONTEMPLATIVE LIFE

THE nature of the contemplative (theoretic, speculative) life and the problems to which it gives rise had occupied the attention of the Greek philosophers, and the subject has been dealt with from many standpoints by many writers on ethics and religion ever since. Yet I do not know that the history of thought on the contemplative life and the active, and the relations between them, has ever been made the object of a special study, or that any treatise has been composed on the subject. So comprehensive a work as Hastings's *Encyclopaedia of Religion and Ethics* has no article on 'contemplative life'; yet would the subject be fraught with interest. If this history ever comes to be worked out, it will, I think, appear that no previous writer had discoursed with such fullness and insight as Augustine on the nature of the Two Lives and the claims of each of them on the individual; and no later writer with such discerning judgement and practicality as Gregory.

In any such investigation one thing would soon become manifest: that, not unlike many other philosophical terms, 'contemplative life' has borne many connotations, hardly any of the authorities meaning exactly the same thing by the term.

In order to make some beginning of the investigation here proposed, and at the same time to serve the practical purpose that has inspired this book, a few notes will be given indicating some of the principal conceptions that have been entertained of the contemplative life.

There is a tradition that Pythagoras formulated a theory of the contemplative life and established in South Italy communities living it; little, however, is known of the actual teaching of Pythagoras, and in later times a myth grew up concerning him, so that we are in great uncertainty about him. Thus in the matter of contemplative life we do not touch *terra firma* until we come to Plato.

Plato and Aristotle

Plato speaks of contemplation in various places, but it is at the end of Book vii. of the *Republic* that he speaks of the contemplative life, without, however, using the term:

Those who are to be the guardians of the state and the upbringers of the coming generation, after having been in early manhood exercised in all the civic functions of peace and war, 'when they have reached fifty years, let those who have distinguished themselves in every action of their lives and in every branch of knowledge, come at last to their consummation: the time has now arrived at which they must raise the eye of the soul to the universal light which lightens all things, and behold the Absolute Good (τὸ ἀγαθὸν αὐτό); for that is the pattern according to which they are to order the State and the lives of individuals, and the remainder of their own lives also; making philosophy their chief pursuit, but, when their turn comes, each one devoting himself to the hard duties of public life and holding office, not as a desirable but as an unavoidable occupation' (540: Jowett).

This conception of a contemplative life as liable to alternations of return to the active at the call of duty, is not fundamentally different from what we have found in Augustine or Gregory. Plato's idea of contemplation may be gathered from the following:

The soul when using the body as an instrument of perception, that is to say, when using the sense of sight or hearing or some other sense, is dragged by the body into the region of the changeable, and wanders and is confused. But when returning to herself she reflects, then she passes into the other world, the region of purity and eternity and immortality and unchangeableness, which are her kindred, and with them she ever lives when she is by herself and is not let or hindered; then she ceases from her erring ways, and being in communion with the unchanging, is unchanging. And this state of the soul is called wisdom (*Phaedo*, 79; cf. Augustine, above, p. 161). Of contemplation itself he speaks thus: In the heaven above the heavens there abides Being Itself with which true knowledge is concerned; the colourless, formless, intangible essence, visible only to mind. The mind which is capable of it rejoices in beholding reality and in gazing upon truth. It beholds knowledge absolute in existence absolute, and the other true existences in like manner, and feasts upon them (*Phaedrus*, 247). This is the contemplation of the celestials, or, as we should say, of the next life; in this life, according to Plato, the soul can have only desires and glimpses of such contemplation.

Aristotle distinguishes three lives, the sensual (that of the senses), the political or civic (of which virtue is the object), and the speculative, i.e. theoretic or contemplative (*Ethics*, i. 3). He treats of the speculative in *Ethics*, Book x.:

Happiness is the activity of the highest part of our nature; but the speculative is the highest activity, as the intuitive reason (νοῦς) is the highest of our faculties, and the objects with which the intuitive reason is concerned are the highest of things that can be known. There is no virtuous activity so pleasant as the activity of wisdom or philosophic reflexion. Speculative activity will be the perfect happiness of man, if perfect length of life is given it. But such a life will be too good for man. He will enjoy such a life not in virtue of his humanity, but in virtue of some divine element within him. If the reason is divine in comparison with the rest of man's nature, the life which accords with reason will be divine in comparison with human life in general. A man should do all that is in his power to live in accordance with the highest part of his nature. The activity of God, being pre-eminently blissful, will be speculative; and if so, then the human activity most nearly related to it will be most capable of happiness. The life of men is blessed in so far as it possesses a certain resemblance to God's speculative activity. Happiness is co-extensive with speculation, and the greater a person's power of speculation, the greater will be his happiness. Happiness must be a kind of speculation (cc. 7, 8, Welldon).

It is to be noted that the conception of contemplation held by Aristotle and Plato alike is purely intellectual, a philosophical concentration of thought on absolute Good or ultimate Truth.

Philo

With Philo a fully religious conception of the contemplative life enters the field. The description of the Therapeutae in the treatise *de Vita Contemplativa* portrays a community living apart in seclusion and silence, practising ascetical and religious exercises, given up to prayer, the reading of the Scriptures, and the contemplation of divine truth. In his other writings Philo speaks incidentally in like manner of contemplation and the contemplative life: the passages have been brought together by Mr F. C. Conybeare in the 'Excursus' to his edition of *de Vita Contemplativa*, 1895. Philo insists that no one should enter on the contemplative life before the age of fifty, after having exercised faithfully the duties and functions of family and civic life; this idea, no doubt, is derived from Plato.

Clement and Origen

Any treatise on the Two Lives would have to take count of Clement of Alexandria, the first Christian writer on the subject, even though the idea underlying his 'lower' and 'higher', or 'gnostic', life is somewhat different from that of the active and contemplative lives (see Bigg, *Christian Platonists of Alexandria*, pp. 82-99). Origen is more in the line of tradition; in a fragment on John ix. 18, he takes Martha as typifying the practical or active life, and Mary as typifying the theoretic or contemplative (*Comm. in Ioan.* 'Berlin Corpus', p. 547); for him the contemplative life is one given up

mainly to searching the Scriptures and wearying itself in invest-
igating the meaning of the Sacred Writings (see Dissertation of
W. Borneman, *In investiganda Monachatus Origine quibus de causis ratio
habenda sit Origenis*, 1884).

Cassian

What Cassian says of the contemplative life has been summarized
in *Benedictine Monachism*; the summary may be reproduced here:

In the beginnings of Christian monachism, among the monks of
Egypt as represented by various hermits in Cassian (especially
Collations, xix. xxiv.), we find the conception of the contemplative
life pushed to the extreme limit. It could not be lived in a cenobium
(community), but only in a hermitage: 'the cenobite cannot attain
to the fullness of contemplative purity' (xix. 9); 'the heavenly
transports' frequently experienced in solitude, and the 'sublimity of
contemplation' are lost by return to the cenobium (5). Anything
that withdraws the hermit from the precincts of his cell and court-
yard, and compels him to go out for any work in the open air,
'dissipates his concentration of mind and all the keenness of the
vision of his aim' (xxiv. 3). 'Agricultural work is incompatible with
the contemplative life, because the multitude of thoughts generated
by such work makes unbearable the prolonged silence and quiet of
the hermit's cell' (4), and the excitement of cultivating a fertile
garden is too great a distraction, and incapacitates the mind for
spiritual exercises (12): of course it was recognised that contemplation cannot be continual in this life (xxiii. 5) (p. 67).

On this I commented: 'It is at once evident that the three great
cenobitic founders, Pachomius, Basil, and Benedict, all turned away
from the idea of a contemplative life such as this, and all made agricultural work an integral part of the monastic life they instituted.
Judged by the Egyptian standard, Trappist life is not contemplative,
nor any form of Western monastic life for men, except, perhaps, the
Camaldolese and Carthusian, who are half-hermits.' But this ideal
of the contemplative life has prevailed in the East from that day
to this.

It may be well just to refer to Cassian's teaching on the 'actual'
or 'practical' life, set forth in *Collation* xiv., and summarized in
Benedictine Monachism, p. 47. Cassian's actual life is not the same as
the active life defined by St Gregory, though to some extent the
two are coincident. The actual life is ethical training and self-
discipline, and may, but does not necessarily, include the good
works of the active life.

St Augustine

We have seen very fully St Augustine's idea of the contemplative
life, and we have seen his conciliation of the claims of the two lives.

He speaks of the contemplative life and the active; also of a leisured life and a busied (otiosa, negotiosa); and though he does not employ the term 'mixed life', he does speak of a life made up of both the others (ex utroque genere composita). His practical solution of the problem, given in a passage that set the standard in the West (de Civ. Dei, xix. 19, cited p. 165 in Latin and English), is that, whatever be the superior attractions or the greater intrinsic worth of contemplation, it has to be interrupted at the calls of duty or charity.

We have already been at some pains to show that Augustine's contemplations, whatever the language in which they are expressed, are really and fully religious in character, and not merely the joy felt in intellectual speculation (Part I. § D). Still, in most of the places where he speaks of the contemplative life the dominant idea appears to be the intellectual perception or intuition of truth. Thus in the passage just referred to, the contemplative life is characterized as a life in which one is given up to perceiving and intuing truth. It is not open to question that when, on his conversion, he betook himself with his intimate friends to the country retreat at Cassiciacum, it was to give himself up to a course of philosophical speculation on the great truths of religion; or that at that time he tended to identify true knowledge and virtue: in the Retractions he rectifies in various points the over-emphasized intellectualism of these early dialogues. For all that, many indications in these same dialogues show that he was giving himself up at the same time frequently and with great earnestness to the practice of prayer and devotion (e.g. de Ord. i. 22, 25, 29; Ep. iii. 4).[1]

[1] Reference has already been made (p. 41) to the questions mooted recently as to St Augustine's intellectual and religious position at the time of the Conversion and during the subsequent months. The problem is the conciliation of the account in the Confessions with the mentality manifested in the series of Dialogues. It is contended that the Confessions cannot be taken as an historical account of his mental processes, but are rather an idealized projection backwards of the fully religious Catholic attitude into which he finally grew. The new theory has been pushed to its extreme limit in the book of M. Prosper Alfaric, L'Évolution Intellectuelle de S. Augustin (1918), which contains a careful and useful analysis of the Dialogues. For M. Alfaric the Conversion was not one of the intellect to Catholic Christianity, but only a moral change of life, the intellect remaining neo-Platonist, so that some years passed during which Augustine was but a neo-Platonist, not a Christian, in intellect.

Such a position appears to me altogether unbalanced and extravagant, and not borne out by a reasonable interpretation of the documents. There is in Book iii. of the Dialogue contra Academicos, one of the Cassiciacum series, a passage that quite unmistakably portrays his attitude of mind: 'No one can doubt that we are impelled to learn by a twofold weight, of authority and of reason. In regard to authority, it is for me certain never to depart from that of Christ, for I can find none more powerful. But in regard to what is to be sought out by subtlest reason— for I am so made that I impatiently desire to apprehend truth not only by believing but also by intellectually understanding—I am confident of finding with

We are accustomed to distinguish sharply between philosophical contemplation and religious. Thus Fr Baker says:

To this rank of philosophical contemplations may be referred those scholastic wits which spend much time in the study and subtle examination of the mysteries of faith (*Sancta Sophia*, p. 503).

And, on the other hand:

Experience demonstrates that all the most sublime exercises of contemplation may as purely and perfectly be performed by persons the most ignorant and unlearned (so they be sufficiently instructed in the fundamental articles of Catholic faith) as by the learnedst doctors, inasmuch as not any abilities in the brain are requisite thereto, but only a courageous affection of the heart (ibid. 39; cf. 136).

But for Augustine there could be no such distinction—his intellectual perception of truth was religious, and his religious experience was intellectual. God as absolute Being, Good, Truth, Beauty, was the object not only of his intellectual vision, but at the same time of his religious emotion. Probably in a higher degree than any other saint or seer has he synthesized in his religious consciousness the two faculties of knowing and loving. So that his contemplative life was intellectual, and simultaneously religious, in a measure perhaps not achieved by any other.

Julianus Pomerius

This writer, an African who lived at Arles about 500, is introduced as being the author of the first Christian treatise entitled *de Vita Contemplativa* (Migne, Patr. Lat. lix. 415). It used to be attributed to Prosper of Aquitaine, and as such St Thomas cites it. It is a work of pastoral instruction for the clergy, and it treats of the contemplative life (Book i.) and the active life (Book ii.). The contemplative life properly belongs to the next world, but an earnest living of the spiritual life may be some beginning of a contemplative life even in this world. Such beginning is open to holy bishops and priests, who, for all their ministrations and occupations, may enjoy

---

the Platonists what is not repugnant to our sacred books' (or doctrines—sacris nostris) (op. cit. 43).

This shows, on the one hand, his full acceptance of Christian faith and belief on the authority of Christ; and, on the other, that he was one of those who feel the need of a philosophical basis for his Christian belief, and that he looked to Platonism, i.e. neo-Platonism, to supply it. To label the man who wrote these words as a mere neo-Platonist, and not yet a Catholic Christian, is preposterous. St Augustine was not a neo-Platonist in any other way than that in which St Thomas was an Aristotelian.

some taste of contemplation. The contemplative life consists of four elements: the knowledge of hidden things, the vision of God, vacancy from mundane pursuits, reading of Scripture. Nothing stands in the way of holy bishops and priests attaining to this—to some taste of the first two, as far as may be possible in this life, and to the last two adequately. Thus those who faithfully exercise their pastoral duties may be partakers in the contemplative life.

St Gregory the Great

We have seen St Gregory's definition of the contemplative life (p. 171), that it lies in resting from exterior action and cleaving to the desire of God, so that the mind takes no pleasure in doing anything, but is aglow with the longing for the eternal life. We have seen also that he recognizes this cannot be the permanent state of the mind, for no mind in this life can be kept thus on the stretch for spiritual things; consequently his idea is that the exercise of the contemplative life can be carried on only by way of alternation with the works of the active life. The intervals between bouts of contemplation are not to be vacant periods of resting or waiting, but should be filled up by the exercise of the good works of the active life. Furthermore, in the striking passage cited on pp. 184-185, St Gregory lays it down that he who ordinarily carries on the good works of the active life, but ever and anon strives to recollect himself and raise himself to contemplation, is not failing in leading a contemplative life, but assuredly holds on to the fullness of that which, though ever falling short of, he is at frequent intervals striving to attain to.

This is what is now understood by the 'mixed life', though the term is not used by St Gregory. What is now called a purely contemplative life, in which the works of the active life are sought to be reduced almost to a vanishing point, lay quite outside St Gregory's mental horizon: he seems to take for granted that such a life is not livable in this world.

A great part of St Gregory's utterances on the subject were made to his monks, to whom the *Morals* were addressed; and therefore in *Benedictine Monachism* (p. 99) the thesis is maintained that St Gregory's teaching is the most authentic historical formulation of the theory of Benedictine contemplative life.

Cluny

But another conception of the contemplative life introduced itself among Benedictines under the tendencies set going by St Benedict of

Aniane in the ninth century, and carried to their utmust limit by the Cluniacs in the eleventh and twelfth, whereby there was so great an increase in the celebration of masses and offices that they took up the greater part of the waking hours, to the exclusion of all other work (see *Benedictine Monachism*, p. 295). And this manner of life, spent mostly in church, came to be looked on as realizing the idea of the contemplative life. In the curious twelfth-century Dialogue between a Cluniac and a Cistercian, the Cluniac twits the Cistercian, saying that the Cistercians, spending most of their time in manual labour in the fields, live the active life, whereas the Cluniacs live the contemplative life.[1] Owing to the enormous influence of Cluny, this became the currently accepted idea of the contemplative life in Benedictine circles, and beyond them, during several centuries.

St Bernard and Richard of St Victor

The Cistercian movement was in great measure a reaction against the Cluniac interpretation of Benedictine life, and included a restoration of the element of manual and field work as provided by St Benedict. In regard to the theory of the contemplative life, St Bernard reasserted St Gregory's idea that a contemplative life can only be one made up of alternations of contemplation and the exercise of the works of the active life for the good of others (see pp. 192-193, and especially p. 196).

But St Bernard takes the theory a step forward. As we have seen (p. 113), he carries on the imagery of the spiritual marriage to the idea of spiritual fecundity, so that the ensuing zeal for souls and work for souls is not merely a process of needful repose and recuperation of the spiritual forces of the soul after contemplation, but is positively the direct effect of the highest kind of contemplation, that of the spiritual marriage, which propels the soul to leave its quiet and go forth to bear spiritual offspring to its Lord.

St Bernard's contemporary, Richard of St Victor, 'in contemplation more than man' (Dante), works out this imagery with a literalness that is almost startling. He dwells upon the four phases of the spiritual marriage, espousals, marriage, wedlock, child-bearing (desponsatio, nuptiae, copula, puerperium): after having been in the third admitted to the closest union with God, in the fourth the contemplative comes down with Christ from the Mount of Transfiguration and works in imitation of Him among men, preferring their good to his own. Thus does the spiritual marriage issue in spiritual fecundity.[2]

---

[1] Martène, *Thesaurus Anecdotorum*, v. 1574.
[2] *De iv Gradibus violentae Caritatis* (Migne, Patr. Lat. cxcvi. 1216, 1222-4).

St Thomas Aquinas

St Thomas's teaching on contemplation and the contemplative life may be found conveniently in the volume entitled *On Prayer and the Contemplative Life, by St Thomas Aquinas*, being the relevant Questions of the 'Summa', translated by Fr Hugh Pope, O.P. The doctrine is thus summarized by Fr Pope: 'For St Thomas the contemplative life is but the natural life of a man who is serving God and who devotes a certain portion of his time to the study and contemplation of divine things' (p. 4).

In a careful analysis of St Thomas's idea of contemplation, Dom John Chapman thus sums up his teaching on the point:

> In his disquisitions on the active and contemplative lives (*in 3 Sent.* dist. xxxv., qu. 1, and *Summa*, 2 2ae, qu. clxxx.), he describes contemplation humano modo', as the brief rest of the mind upon the great verities at which it has arrived by argument and investigation, avoiding any mention of mystical prayer. He means by the contemplative life the life of study and passion for truth, as opposed to the life which uses the body to do external works. In the Order of Preachers, to which he belonged, he thinks the perfect admixture of the two is to be found in the combination of study with preaching. He did not simply distinguish the two lives as that of prayer and that of works of charity.[1]

In thus stressing the intellectual side of contemplation, St Thomas is in line with Aristotle and St Augustine. The Index to the Opera shows that only the marrow of his teaching is in the *Summa*; he treats with extreme care in many other places the whole range of questions concerning this subject. I do not find that he ever employs the very term 'mixed life'; he recognizes the thing, however, and says it is the highest form of life—but on certain conditions: if to a contemplative life be united works of the active, it must be by way of addition, not by way of subtraction; and the works of the active life must flow from the fullness of contemplation.[2]

Blessed John Ruysbroeck

John Ruysbroeck, 'the Admirable', is in some ways the most wonderful of the mystics. As a descriptive mystic he stands alongside of St John of the Cross in the daring and eloquence with which he ventures to utter in human language the experiences of union and knowledge to which he was admitted. If he lacks St John's Latin clarity of thought and expression, he more than makes up for it by

---

[1] Hastings's *Encyclopaedia of Religion and Ethics*, ix. 96.
[2] *Summa*, 2 2ae, qu. clxxxii. 1, clxxxviii. 6.

a certain massive mysteriousness that may be called Teutonic—he
was a Fleming of Brabant—through which we seem ever and anon
to catch glimpses of realities deeply impressive though at times bewildering. But there is a consistency and a sanity through it all, and
a restraint due to his sound theological formation, which make an
overwhelming impression of truth and reality. It may with all
probability be said, that than him there has been no greater contemplative; and certainly there has been no greater mystical writer.
His contemplation is highly intellectual, and at the same time fully
mystical. Whether in the sublimity of his elevations or in the power
of recording his experiences, Ruysbroeck stands as one of the very
greatest of the mystics.[1]

Ruysbroeck's principal work, *The Adornment of the Spiritual
Marriage*, is divided into three books. The first is concerned with
the active life; it is a treatise on the acquirement of the virtues, and
is rather Cassian's actual than St Gregory's active life. The second
book deals with contemplation and the contemplative life, which
Ruysbroeck calls the 'inward life'. And still above the heights of
contemplation and union to which the inward life rises, are further
and higher heights unfolded in Book iii. on the 'superessential life'.
Though he does not use the imagery of 'fecundity', for him also, as
for St Bernard, the final state, the result of the highest contemplation, is that the contemplative is inspired with zeal to labour actively
for God's glory.

In contemplation God comes to us without ceasing and demands
of us both action and fruition, in such a way that the one never im-
pedes but always strenghtens the other. And therefore the most inward man lives his life in these two ways, namely, in work and in
rest. And in each he is whole and undivided, and he is perpetually
called by God to renew both the rest and the work (*Adornment*, ii. 65).

In the prologue to the *Sparkling Stone* he lays down that 'the man
who would live in the most perfect state of Holy Church must be
a good and zealous man, an inward and ghostly man, an uplifted
and God-seeing man, and an outflowing man to all in common.'
What is meant by an 'outflowing man' is explained in the final
chapter, as following the highest contemplation, that of the superessential life:

The man who is sent down by God from these heights into the

[1] Ruysbroeck's works were written in old Flemish. The best edition is the
French translation, made from the critical edition of the Flemish by the French
Benedictines of Wisques; it is to be in four volumes, whereof three have appeared
(Brussels: Vromont). Three of the principal treatises have been well translated
into English from the Flemish in a volume published in 1916 (London: Dent).
There are also other translations in English.

world is full of truth and rich in all virtues. He possesses a rich and generous ground, which is set in the richness of God: and therefore he must always spend himself on those who are in need of him. He is a living and willing instrument of God, with which God works whatsoever He will, and howsoever He will. And he remains ready and willing to do in the virtues all that God commands, and strong and courageous in suffering all that God allows to befall him. And by this he possesses an universal life, for he is ready alike for contemplation and for action, and is perfect in both of them. And none can have this universal life save the God-seeing man [i.e. the one who has been raised to the superessential or highest mystical life].

Here we have the same idea as is contained in St Bernard's 'fecundity', that the highest mystical experience has as one of its effects the sending back him who attains it to the active life with an enhanced zeal to work for the good of others.

St Teresa is the same: the Seventh Mansion of the *Interior Castle* is devoted to the spiritual marriage, and though she does not speak of fecundity, she does say that the effect of the marriage is to cause in the soul an intense longing to serve God by striving to gain souls for Him (c. 3).

St John of the Cross

He strikes another note, out of harmony with the trend of the Western tradition, but akin to that of Cassian and the East.

[In the state of the spiritual marriage] of a truth the soul is now lost to all things, and gained only to love, and the mind is no longer occupied with anything else. It is, therefore, deficient in what concerns the active life and other external duties, that it may apply itself in earnest to the one thing which the Bridegroom has pronounced necessary. ... When the soul has reached the state of unitive love, it is not requisite it should occupy itself in other and exterior duties—unless they be matters of obligation—which might hinder, were it but for a moment, the life of love in God, though they may minister greatly to His service; because an instant of pure love is more precious in the eyes of God and the soul, and more profitable to the Church, than all other good works together, though it may seem as if nothing were done. ...

When the soul, then, in any degree possesses the spirit of solitary love, we must not interfere with it. We should inflict a grievous wrong upon it, and upon the Church also, if we were to occupy it, were it only for a moment, in exterior or active duties, however important they might be. Let those men of zeal, who think by their preaching and exterior works to convert the world, consider that they would be much more edifying to the Church, and more pleasing unto God—to say nothing of the good example they would give—if they would spend at least one-half their time in prayer, even though they may not have attained to unitive love. Certainly they would do more, and with less trouble, by one single good work than by a thousand, because of the merit of their prayer and the spiritual strength it supplies (*Spiritual Canticle*, note prefatory to Stanza xxix.).

There is no need to pursue the subject through later writers: what has been adduced suffices to delineate the great Western tradition on the contemplative life and the necessary admixture with it of the active life. In modern times this life has come to be called the 'mixed life', and the ideal expressed by St John of the Cross, the old Oriental conception, has tended to come into general acceptance as the ideal of the contemplative life. The current modern conception of the contemplative life is well summed up by Bishop Hedley in the sentence: 'For a contemplative life both social recreation and apostolic work must be reduced to their lowest degree.'[1]

It will be recognized that such a conception of a contemplative life is fundamentally different from that of St Gregory. But in another place Bishop Hedley reverts to the older idea. The final chapter of the posthumous *Spiritual Retreat for Priests* is addressed to the Benedictine priests of the English Congregation; and with the pastoral and educational activities to which they are devoted clearly in view, and with full cognizance of the facts, the Bishop says to them: 'It is a life of contemplation to which our vows bind us. The religious state is always one of contemplation, more or less'. It is not to be doubted that Cardinal Manning[2] and Cardinal Mercier[3] would say the like to all secular priests; and we have seen that St Gregory does say it to them quite emphatically; also that he teaches that contemplation is open to all—to the devout laity as well as to clergy. This is Bishop Hedley's sense, too.

It is the very aim of the teaching of Fr Baker and his school that 'extraordinary' prayer (contemplation) should be an ordinary state for Christian souls; for priests, for religious, for devout layfolk, and for the poor and unlearned, who love God with all their heart.[4]

Here is a problem none the less interesting because it is of practical import for wide circles, for all priests, be they secular or regular, for devout souls of all conditions whose endeavour is to live a life of union with God. The old tradition of the Christian Church was

[1] *Dublin Review*, 1876, art. on Fr Baker's *Sancta Sophia*; re-edited by the present writer as a Catholic Truth Society tract, under the title 'Prayer and Contemplation' (1916).
[2] *The Eternal Priesthood.*
[3] Retreats to his Seminarists and to his Clergy.
[4] *Prayer and Contemplation*, p. 12.

that contemplation is open to all such, as a thing that may be aspired to and grasped, being the objective of a spiritual life earnestly lived. The modern idea is rather that contemplation is a thing practically out of reach of all save a very restricted number of specially called and favoured souls, a thing to be wondered at from afar, but hardly to be aspired to without presumption. The process of this change of attitude is traced by Dom John Chapman in the article on 'Mysticism' already referred to.[1] The solution of the problem must depend on a right understanding of what 'contemplation' is. This ascertained, it will be possible to form just judgements on the derivative terms 'contemplative prayer', 'a contemplative', 'contemplative state', 'contemplative life'. This book has been written in the conviction that the teaching on contemplation and the contemplative life of the three Doctors would prove not only intellectually illuminating, but also practically helpful; and therefore, with this practical purpose in view, an attempt is here made to determine the meanings to be attached to these terms.

Contemplation

Contemplation at its highest limit is identical with the mystical experience, and involves the claim of the mystics, made in such passages as those cited in the Prologue, to an experimental perception of God's Being and Presence. These are the elevations named the spiritual marriage, or passive union, or the intellectual ecstasy spoken of by St Augustine. The validity of such claims has been vindicated in the Epilogue. But there must be true contemplation that falls short of such heights.

We have seen that St Gregory, among the qualifications of the pastor of souls, requires him to soar aloft in contemplation, and that he reckons it a bar to the pastoral office if one 'knows not the light of heavenly contemplation.'[2] Now it is not to be supposed that St Gregory, shrewd knower of men that he was, imagined that all pastors of souls, all bishops even, do, or ought to, or could, enjoy contemplation of the kind we have heard him describe, evidently his own experiences. Not in his time, nor in any time, have bishops and priests commonly been so spiritually favoured as to be raised to these heights of prayer.

It is impossible to suppose that he regarded such contemplation as the condition of a fruitful ministry, still less as the condition of exercising the pastoral office. Consequently, unless we are to think

---

[1] Hastings's *Encyclopaedia of Religion and Ethics*, ix. 100.
[2] *Regula Pastoralis*, i. 11, ii. 5.

he was spinning theories out of all touch with reality and merely setting up a quite unrealizable ideal, which in a book intended as an eminently practical instruction for pastors is unthinkable, we must take it that he recognized lower grades of contemplation within the reach of ordinary fervent and devout priests, which all may be expected to attain to.

The easiest and most satisfactory manner of answering the question thus posed, will be to have recourse to the digression on the first steps in contemplation, that so unexpectedly meets us at the middle of the last and highest of the mystical treatises of St John of the Cross.[1] We read:

In order to have a better knowledge of the state of beginners, we must keep in mind that it is one of meditation and of acts of reflection. It is necessary to furnish the soul in this state with matter for meditation, that it may make reflections and interior acts, and avail itself of the sensible spiritual heat and fervour, for this is necessary in order to accustom the senses and desires to good things, that, being satisfied by the sweetness thereof, they may be detached from the world.

When this is in some degree effected, God begins at once to introduce the soul into the state of contemplation, and that very quickly, especially religious, because these, having renounced the world, quickly fashion their senses and desires according to God; they have therefore to pass at once from meditation to contemplation. This passage, then, takes place when the discursive acts and meditation fail, when sensible sweetness and first fervours cease, when the soul cannot make reflections as before, nor find any sensible comfort, but is fallen into aridity. ... Souls in this state are not to be forced to meditate or to apply themselves to discursive reflections laboriously effected, neither are they to strive after sweetness and fervour, for if they did so, they would be thereby hindering the principal agent, Who is God Himself. ... The soul must be lovingly intent upon God, without distinctly eliciting other acts beyond those to which He inclines it; making no efforts of its own, purely, simply, and lovingly intent upon God, as a man who opens his eyes with loving attention (§§ 33-36).

This fading away of images in the mind at prayer, and failure in ability for discursive meditation, and drying up of sensible sweetness with consequent aridity, St John calls 'the Dark Night of Sense'. It marks the transition from the state of beginners to that of proficients, as the 'Dark Night of the Spirit' marks the transition

---

[1] *The Living Flame*, stanza iii. §§ 29–77, ed. 1912; stanza iii. line 3, §§ 4–16, ed. 1864.

from the state of proficients to that of the perfect. The 'Dark Night of Sense' forms the first book of the treatise called *The Dark Night of the Soul*.

The night of sense is common and the lot of many: these are the beginners. The night of the spirit is the portion of very few. [It is what Fr Baker calls 'the Great Desolation': Père Grou also speaks of it in many places, *Manuel des Ames intérieures*.] The night of sense is of ordinary occurrence. Recollected persons enter the dark night sooner than others after they have begun their spiritual course. In general there elapses no great length of time after they have begun, before they enter the night of sense, and most of them do enter it, for they generally suffer aridities (i. 8).

During the aridities of the night of sense God is drawing the soul out of the way of sense into that of spirit, from meditation to contemplation. ... God is leading them by the road of contemplation, which knows no imagination or reasoning. Persons in this state will do enough if they keep patience and persevere in prayer; all they have to do is to keep their soul unembarrassed and at rest from all thoughts and all knowledge, contenting themselves simply with directing their attention lovingly and calmly towards God; and all this without anxiety or effort, or desire to feel and taste His presence. For all such efforts disquiet the soul, and distract it from the calm repose and sweet tranquillity of contemplation, to which they are now admitted (i. 10).

The foregoing words of St John, who, if any one, had tasted what contemplation is, and certainly cannot be suspect of any low ideas about it, suffice to make it clear that besides the supreme heights of the spiritual marriage, there was for him a lowlier kind of prayer, which he recognized as being in truth contemplation: the beginnings of it, but still essentially the thing itself. Many pass into the dark night of sense, though usually without realizing what it is; they do not imagine they are passing through a spiritual state that bears so formidable a name! We are apt to think, when ability to make a set discursive meditation, with the workings of imagination and reasoning, fails us, and sensible devotion and spiritual sweetness dry up, and aridity invades the soul, that it is a sign of failure; but St John assures us that it is a sign of progress, if only we behave ourselves duly, for the prayer we can now exercise is contemplation —'arid contemplation' he calls the prayer of aridity, and 'dim and secret contemplation', and says that such souls are in 'the dark and arid night of contemplation'. This is strangely at variance with the popular idea, which associates contemplation with inundations of spiritual joy and light.

In order to make St John's meaning clear, the following words from the *Ascent of Mount Carmel* should be kept in view:

This attention, or general loving knowledge of God, is necessary when the spiritual man passes from the state of meditation to that of contemplation. If the soul were without this knowledge or sense of God's presence at that time, the result would be that it would have nothing and do nothing—every act of the worship of God would be wanting. If the soul be idle, not occupied either with its intellectual faculties in meditation and reflection, or with its spiritual faculties in contemplation and pure knowledge, it is impossible to say it is occupied at all (ii. 14).

This shows that he will have no quietism in prayer.

Modern writers on mystical theology commonly distinguish two kinds of contemplation, the one acquired, active, ordinary; the other infused, passive, extraordinary. Of course, according to Catholic teaching, all contemplation, all prayer, is made by the help of God's grace, and without this help we cannot pray at all. But the more elementary kind of contemplation is exercised by the help of ordinary grace that we may count on receiving if we dispose ourselves properly for it; so that by a course of self-discipline and training in prayer, and perseverant practice in concentration of mind, in recollection, introversion and devotion, we can prepare ourselves for acquired or ordinary contemplation, and put ourselves into a state in which God usually will bestow on us the prayer of ordinary contemplation. But the higher kinds of contemplation, passive union, spiritual marriage, are entirely beyond the power of the soul to prepare for or to bring about, being, according to the theologians, wholly the operation of God, working on the soul by an extraordinary grace.

There is a tendency among quite recent authors to react against this distinction of the two kinds of contemplation, as unused by and unknown to the older writers on mystical theology. The distinction, in fact, seems to have been first drawn in the fifteenth century by Denis the Carthusian.[1] But this surely does not matter; what matters is, whether the distinction corresponds to realities and conduces to clearness of thought. Now it cannot be doubted that anyone who, after reading the passages just given, wherein St John describes the elementary contemplation of beginners, should then read the later portion of the *Spiritual Canticle* (stanzas xxii.-xl.), or the *Living Flame*, would recognize that the contemplation spoken of in the latter, and that spoken of in the former, are divided by a difference not merely of degree, but of kind. The one is simple and of quite ordinary

[1] So Pourrat, *Spiritualité Chrétienne*, ii. 476.

occurrence, being easily within the reach of very many souls who cultivate seriously the spiritual life and the practice of prayer; the other is most rare, being in heights scaled by few, and (if real) must surely be due to a very special enablement and grace from God. Thus it cannot be doubted that the distinction is founded on fact and is useful, even if the passage from lower to higher is so graded that it be not possible to draw a line of demarcation at any precise point. [But see 'Afterthoughts'.]

Thus it is of acquired, active, ordinary contemplation that we must understand the early writers to be speaking, when they say that contemplation is the natural and normal issue of the spiritual life; and Bishop Hedley when he says that 'the end and object of the man of prayer is to attain to contemplation';[1] and above all, St Gregory when he says that all bishops, all pastors, all rulers of souls, should be hung aloft in contemplation.

Contemplative Prayer

By contemplative prayer is meant the kind of prayer in which or by which contemplation is exercised. It has to be clearly asserted, in the first place, that vocal prayer may be contemplative, and this whether it be private vocal prayer or the public prayer of the Divine Office. Such is quite definitely the teaching of Cassian (see *Benedictine Monachism*, p. 70): 'A verse of a psalm may be the occasion of glowing prayer (contemplation) while we are singing'. What the chanting of the Office was for the monks of the Middle Ages may be understood from the 'Instituta Patrum', a ninth-century manual on the manner of chanting.[2] After a number of practical instructions the old monk concludes thus:

It is in the presence of the Holy Trinity and all the angels that we both chant and sing. So with compunction of heart, with lowly fear, with devout mind, with fervour of spirit, inflamed with inmost longing for the things above, raised by the words which we employ to the contemplation of heavenly mysteries, with sweetness of feeling, with purity of soul, with pleasing gravity, with befitting cheerfulness, in suave melodies, in delicious passages, with musical voices and gladness ineffable, let us sing joyfully to God our Maker.

Such singing of the Office assuredly is contemplative prayer.

At the page referred to of *Benedictine Monachism* it is shown that in modern times such apostles of mental prayer as St Teresa and Fr Baker assert strongly that contemplation may be arrived at by

[1] *Prayer and Contemplation*, p. 42.
[2] Printed in Gerbert's *Scriptores*, i.; translation by D. Alphege Shebbeare in *Downside Review*, 1919.

vocal prayer; the former declaring that while saying the 'Our Father' we may be raised to perfect contemplation.[1]

Those familiar with *Sancta Sophia* will know the place held in Fr Baker's scheme for the life of prayer by 'forced acts' of the will. It is his theory of mental or interior prayer, that if a soul has the propension for contemplative prayer, at no long time after its entrance on a spiritual course of prayer will it feel drawn to quit discursive meditation and cease from the operations of the imagination and reasoning in its prayer, so that the prayer becomes almost wholly the working of affections and acts of the will. When this becomes its habitual prayer, the soul, according to him, has entered on the ways of contemplation, and exercises contemplative prayer.

A soul that by a divine call, as being in a state of maturity for it, relinquisheth meditation to the end to betake herself to a more sublime exercise, which is that of immediate acts or affections of the will, only then begins to enter into the ways of contemplation; for the exercises of the will are the sublimest that any soul can practise, and all the difference that hereafter follows is only in regard of the greater or lesser promptitude, or in regard of the degrees of purity wherewith a soul produces such acts. The whole latitude of internal prayer of the will, which is contemplative prayer, may be comprehended under these two distinct exercises: (1) forced acts or affections of the will, (2) aspirations.[2]

Under the name 'Prayer of Simplicity', or 'Prayer of Simple Regard', borrowed from Bossuet,[3] Père Poulain in the second chapter of his book, *The Graces of Interior Prayer*, treats of acquired or ordinary contemplation, for which, as he says, 'Prayer of Simplicity' is only another name. He gives clear and excellent explanation and instruction, and recommends all who feel the enablement to respond to it by passing from meditation to the prayer of contemplation. Prayer of this kind he regards as a quite usual state of prayer.[4]

[1] *Way of Perfection*, xxv. 1.
[2] *Sancta Sophia*, p. 431. As an assistance to souls practising the prayer of acts, various collections of such acts have been provided. Those most easily accessible in English are by Blosius (*The Oratory of the Faithful Soul*, Art and Book Co., London), and by Dame Gertrude More, grand-daughter of B. Thomas, and disciple of Fr Baker. Her collection appeared as an appendix to *Sancta Sophia*, and also separately in various forms (see *Benedictine Monachism*, p. 118). Quite recently, a small pocket volume, containing a new collection of several hundred such acts, has been compiled by Dom Anselm Rutherford, *Acts for Mental Prayer* (Downside Abbey, 1921).
[3] See the excellent opuscule of Bossuet printed at end of Père Grou's *Manuel des Ames Intérieures* (also in the English translation).
[4] This chapter has been separately printed by the present writer as a Catholic Truth Society tract, *The Prayer of Simplicity*. Exception has been taken to it as departing from the traditional teaching found in St John of the Cross. But the

From what has been said it is seen that affective prayer, whether vocal or mental, forced acts of the will, aspirations, the prayer of simplicity, all are forms of contemplative prayer. Much sound instruction on such contemplation will be found scattered through the pages of Père Grou's *Manuel* and *Maximes*, both translated into English.

It has to be observed, however, that mere passing moments of such prayer could not merit the name of contemplation. Moments or minutes of 'loving attention to God' are a common experience of good souls in their ordinary religious exercises. In order to merit the name contemplative prayer or contemplation, the prayer has to be sustained; Père Poulain lays down that for it to be the prayer of simplicity or contemplation, the loving attention and regard has to be maintained for a notable time, not less than a quarter of an hour;[1] Fr Baker asks for half an hour. On this point, and on the others treated of here, much excellent instruction is to be found in the two little Catholic Truth Society tracts already many times referred to: Bishop Hedley's *Prayer and Contemplation* and Père Poulain's *Prayer of Simplicity*.

A Contemplative

The obvious definition of a 'contemplative' is, 'one who practises contemplation'. Such exercise of contemplation would have to be understood as no mere isolated experience, but as an object systematically pursued. But if there be two kinds of contemplation, ordinary (acquired, active) and extraordinary (infused, passive), it follows that there will be two kinds of contemplatives. In one of his minor treatises, still in manuscript, on the 'Variety of Spirits in Religion', Fr Baker distinguishes and defines the two kinds of contemplatives, calling them 'perfect' and 'imperfect' contemplatives respectively. The perfect contemplatives are those with a strong interior spirit and propensity for contemplative exercises, and who in the midst of business can keep the mind in singleness and fixed on God; they are those who experience the higher mystic states and

---

departure from St John lies not in the conception of the prayer of simplicity itself, which agrees fully with St John's elementary contemplation, but in the misunderstanding and misplacing of the 'night of sense', which Père Poulain will not take as the simple and elementary thing St John means by it. Moreover he uses the word 'mystical' in a restricted sense, not applying it to ordinary contemplation, but making mystical prayer equivalent to infused, passive, or extraordinary contemplation. In this his usage differs from that commonly accepted.

[1] There is a mistake in the English translation at p. 18 of the Catholic Truth Society tract; it reads: 'they should continue for an hour or more.' The French is: 'un quart d'heure ou davantage.'

extraordinary contemplation. Fr Baker's description of imperfect contemplatives is so much to the point that it is reproduced here:

The imperfect contemplative spirit commonly in his business is full of multiplicity; yet for all that, when the businesses are laid aside, and he betakes himself to his recollection [or set exercise of mental prayer] at the season for it, he, having as it were a natural and habitual propension towards God and His immediate presence, with a loathing, or at least a neglect or disesteem of all creatures, doth easily surmount all multiplicity of images that could be occasioned by his precedent employments, whereon the soul had never fixed her love, as who was not, nor could be, satisfied or much delighted with them; and therefore he now easily getteth an unity and simplicity in soul, which is an emptying or casting out of all images of creatures. Whereupon in such unity and simplicity of soul, overcoming multiplicity which is distraction, he easily findeth and treateth with the unity and simplicity of God, which immediately appeareth unto him.

All contemplatives, perfect and imperfect, agree in this, which is it that distinguisheth their way from the other ways, that they immediately, without the means of images or creatures, apply themselves to God, or to seek union with Him by the powers of their soul, but especially by the most noble power of it, called the will.

In *Sancta Sophia* there is a chapter similarly laying down the principle that in the character of the prayer habitually exercised lies the distinction between contemplative and active spirits:

Though all internal dispositions of souls may conveniently enough be ranged under these two states, yet we are not to conceive that each soul is by its temper entirely and absolutely either contemplative or active; for, on the contrary, the most part are of a disposition mixed between both, and partaking somewhat, more or less, of each. But they receive the denomination from that whereto the propension is more strong. ... Now that wherein diversity of spirits is principally discerned is their prayer. ... The prayer of the contemplative life is a quiet affective prayer of the heart alone; that of the active life, the busy methods of discoursive meditation.[1]

It cannot be questioned that in thus distinguishing between contemplation and meditation or consideration, and in making the exclusion of images the determining note of contemplation, Fr Baker and St John of the Cross are in the full current of Catholic tradition from the beginning. In regard to SS Augustine, Gregory, Bernard, this has appeared in the foregoing pages with an abundance of proof that leaves no room for doubt. And in the article on

[1] *Sancta Sophia*, p. 37.

'Catholic Mysticism' already referred to, Dom John Chapman shows that the same was the universally accepted idea in West and East alike from Clement of Alexandria onwards until the sixteenth century.[1] Meditation, the thinking out of a point by dint of imagination and reasoning, is the very antithesis of the traditional idea of contemplation.

Contemplative State

As the 'state of perfection' is one wherein those who embrace it are bound to 'aim at perfection', and to take reasonable measures to make progress in the endeavour to attain to it, so the 'contemplative state' may be defined as one wherein is the obligation of aiming at contemplation and of taking reasonable measures calculated to bring the soul to it, first in the lower grade, and then, if the call and enablement come, in the higher. Of these measures, the principal and indispensable one is the serious cultivation of contemplative prayer.

In this sense, the monastic state is a contemplative state : St Thomas says so (*Summa* 2 2ae, clxxxviii. 2) ; and Benedictine tradition says so, the latest witness being, as we have just seen, the English Benedictine spiritual writer, Bishop Hedley. (See *Benedictine Monachism* p. 110.)

Contemplative Life

And finally we come again to that from which this investigation started, and ask if it be possible to attach a definite historical meaning to the term 'contemplative life', concerning which the great authorities have been found to differ among themselves so materially.

In the first place, it has to be observed that their differences are due in large measure to an ambiguity in the use of the term. 'Contemplative life' has two meanings. It has an objective meaning: a manner of corporate life ordinated with the primary object of facilitating and promoting the exercise of contemplation, by removal or reduction of the usual obstacles. And it has a subjective or personal meaning, according to which, whatever be the external conditions, that man is leading a contemplative life who effectively practises contemplation. In this sense, whatever be his calling or manner of life, a contemplative is leading a contemplative life: it is a matter of personal experience, not of external conditions.

The first is the modern technical sense of 'contemplative life', whereby many Orders of women, pre-eminently the Carmelites and Poor Clares, and among men the Carthusians and Trappists, are said to lead a contemplative life. But the second is the old Western

[1] Hastings's *Encyclopaedia of Religion and Ethics*, ix.

meaning, as defined by St Gregory and endorsed by St Bernard. According to this conception, the test of a contemplative life does not lie in the absence of activity, but in the presence of contemplation; it is a life in which the good works of the active life have their place, provided the contemplation be there as a reality. Fr Baker's imperfect contemplatives lead St Gregory's contemplative life. According to this, the historical Western sense, it may be said that a contemplative life is one in which contemplative prayer is practised in an adequate measure. To Fr Baker's mind, what suffices for this is, in addition to the obligatory vocal prayer of the Office, two half-hours a day, or at least one, of contemplative mental prayer: and this is all he asks for. For the rest, the time may be spent in the ordinary avocations and duties of our state of life.[1]

If what has been set forth in these pages, based as it is on the utterances of well-accredited teachers, be a correct appreciation, there is contemplation that is a simple thing. This it is that the old writers mean, when they take for granted that contemplation is the natural aim and the normal issue of a spiritual life; it is the elementary grades of contemplation and contemplative prayer that they have in mind. Such contemplation is practised by countless souls who know nothing of the divisions and definitions of interior prayer, and who would be as much surprised on learning that they were exercising contemplation, as was Molière's 'bourgeois gentilhomme' on learning that he had been speaking prose all his life. There is a strong current running in these days along the way of return to the old tradition, and a principal motive of the writing of this book has been the hope that it may help on this return.

The Eastern tradition on contemplative life, contemplation, mysticism, has differed from the old authentic Western tradition, and has during these past few centuries obscured it even in the West. As differing from the Eastern tradition, the Western may be stated somehow thus: There are four elements in religion: the institutional or external element of Church, sacraments, and public worship; the intellectual element of doctrine and dogma and theology; the mystical element of will and emotion and personal religious experience; and the element of service of others. A fully developed, properly balanced, personal religious life must be the result of an harmonious blending of these four elements, not one of which may be neglected except at the cost of a one-sided, distorted, enfeebled type of religion. In regard to the mystical element itself, it is not to be cultivated as a thing apart from the every-day duties of life:

[1] See citations from 'The Alphabet' (manuscript) in *Benedictine Monachism*, p. 108.

our life may not be divided into water-tight compartments; it is only by means of self-discipline in the spiritual formation of our own characters, and of the discipline of life in our relations with our fellow men; it is only by bearing ourselves bravely and overcoming in our appointed station in the great battle of life—it is only thus that those most intimate personal relations of our souls with God, which are the mystical element of religion, will attain to their highest and noblest and most fruitful consummation. Nor are these things the preserve of the intellectual and the educated, or of any spiritually leisured class; they are open to all—to the poor and the unlettered and the lowly workers, who spend their lives in alternation between the conscientious performance of their daily round of humble duties and the regular recourse to God in affective prayer and rudimentary contemplation—a union so commonly met with among the peasantry in Catholic districts. And so again we learn that mysticism, like religion itself, is within the reach of all: 'It is not too hard for thee, neither is it far off. It is not in heaven, that thou shouldst say, Who shall go up for us to heaven, and bring it unto us? ... But it is very nigh unto thee, in thy mouth, and in thy heart, that thou mayest do it.'

APPENDIX

to re gior ave religious intuitions. William James himself supplies the answer. We have listened (p. 12) to the 'babblings' of Pascal in the effort to seize and fix the impressions of his mystical experience; and William James supplies a page of the babblings whereby he tried to do the same while coming to from the gas-intoxication. Here are some of them:

What's a mistake but a kind of take?
Sober, drunk, -unk, astonishment.
Reconciliation of opposites; sober, drunk, all the same.
Good and evil reconciled in a laugh!
That sounds like nonsense, but is pure onsense.

Only one of them has a religious refrain:

Medical school; divinity school, school! SCHOOL!
Oh my God, oh God, oh God!

William James himself pronounces these utterances the veriest nonsense—at best, they look like Hegelianism gone mad—'a pessimistic fatalism, depth within depth of impotence and indifference, reason and silliness united, not in a higher synthesis, but in the fact that whatever you choose it is all one—this is the upshot of a revelation that began so rosy bright'. But not such is the upshot of the revelation of the mystics.

Above this is the higher grade of nature ecstasies not produced by artificial means. There are certain regularly cited cases, as Wordsworth and Tennyson.

Wordsworth's occurs in the 'Lines composed above Tintern Abbey'; Tennyson's is as follows:

I have never had any revelations through anaesthetics but a kind of waking trance—this for lack of a better word—I have frequently had, quite up from boyhood, when I have been alone. This has come upon me through repeating my own name two or three times to myself silently, till all at once, as it were out of the intensity of consciousness of individuality, individuality itself seemed to dissolve and fade away into boundless being, and this not a confused state, but the clearest of the clearest, and the surest of the surest, the weirdest of the weirdest, utterly beyond words, where death was an almost laughable impossibility, the loss of personality (if so it were) seeming no extinction, but the only true life. I am ashamed of my feeble description. Have I not said the state is utterly beyond words?

And elsewhere:

By God Almighty! there is no delusion in the matter! It is no nebulous ecstasy, but a state of transcendant wonder, associated

APPENDIX

ONE criticism likely to be passed upon this book will be that its scope is too exclusively limited to Christian and even Catholic mysticism. The answer is that the book was not intended to be a treatment of mysticism in general, but a study of a particular phase of mysticism, that represented by SS Augustine, Gregory, and Bernard, supplemented by St John of the Cross. What has been brought together as the outcome of this study may, however, be illuminated and enforced by a comparison with other kinds of mystical or quasi-mystical experiences, not in the same way religious in character, yet bearing some superficial resemblance to the fully mystical experiences of the great Catholic mystics. It will evidently be of interest and of value to present some first-hand materials for forming a judgement on such experiences.

Consequently in this Appendix are given: (1) Authentic Cases of Nature Ecstasy; (2) Intellectual Ecstasies of Plotinus as described by himself.

1. *Nature Ecstasy*

By 'nature ecstasy' is meant an exaltation of mind, without abnormal physical concomitants, akin to ecstasy, non-religious in the manner of its production, and non-religious, or vaguely religious, in its content. That such nature ecstasies frequently occur is a well-established fact. In a lower grade they may be produced by drugs (we think of de Quincey's opium reveries) or by ether or nitrous oxide. William James relates how he experimented on himself with nitrous oxide and the effect it had upon him:

The keynote of the experience is the tremendously exciting sense of an intense metaphysical illumination. Truth lies open to the view in depth beneath depth of almost blinding evidence. The mind sees all the logical relations of being with an apparent subtlety and instantaneity to which its normal consciousness offers no parallel.[1]

This is interesting: we seem to have vision and insight in the metaphysical order analogous to those of mysticism in the religious order—and produced by artificial physical means. And is not the experience just coloured by temperament?—as a mind attuned to metaphysics has metaphysical intuitions, so will a mind attuned

[1] *The Will to Believe, and other Essays*, p. 294; cf. *Varieties*, p. 387.

with absolute clearness of mind (*Memoirs of Alfred Tennyson*, cited by James and Inge, op. cit.).

Here is another example:

I had spent the evening in a great city, with two friends, reading and discussing poetry and philosophy. We parted at midnight. I had a long drive in my hansom to my lodging. My mind, deeply under the influence of the ideas, images, and emotions called up by the reading and talk, was calm and peaceful. I was in a state of quiet, almost passive enjoyment, not actually thinking, but letting ideas, images, and emotions flow of themselves, as it were, through my mind. All at once, without warning of any kind, I found myself wrapped in a flame-coloured cloud. For an instant I thought of fire, an immense conflagration somewhere close by in that great city; the next, I knew that the fire was within myself. Directly afterward there came upon me a sense of exultation, of immense joyousness accompanied or immediately followed by an intellectual illumination impossible to describe. Among other things, I did not merely come to believe, but I saw that the universe is not composed of dead matter, but is, on the contrary, a living Presence; and I became conscious in myself of eternal life. I saw that all men are immortal; that the cosmic order is such that without any peradventure all things work together for the good of each and all. The vision lasted a few seconds and was gone; but the memory of it and the sense of the reality of what it taught has remained during the quarter of a century which has since elapsed.

This is an account of his own experience by Dr R. M. Bucke in the book *Cosmic Consciousness* (1901), wherein he collects a number of similar experiences, one of Balzac. A description by J. A. Symonds of trances he used to experience in youth is often cited; but William James declares them suggestive of pathology,[1] and indeed they seem like complete mental collapse.

Instead of adducing a number of cases, I propose concentration on that of Richard Jefferies, who is not mentioned in this connexion by James, nor by any writer known to me, except Mr E. I. Watkin, who devotes a chapter to him, but from a somewhat different point of view.[2] I cannot but think that in Richard Jefferies we have the nature ecstasy at its highest and best, and the most nearly resembling the religious mystical experience; and so, for our purpose, it will be most instructive. The material is all to be found in the little book *The Story of my Heart*.[3]

Jefferies's mental attitude was extraordinary, probably unique.

[1] *Varieties*, p. 386.
[2] *Philosophy of Mysticism*.
[3] The references are to the Pocket Edition.

He rejected as vain things all creeds, religions, philosophies, science, accumulations of civilization. He rejected impatiently all idea of design, intelligence, providence in the world, being overwhelmed by the problem of evil. Passages shock by their even blatant atheism. But for all that, it is hard to resist the feeling that his atheism was on the surface, and that deep down there existed a fund of beliefs that save him from the stigma of irreligion or even non-religion. He had a profound belief in the soul, in immortality, in deity—super-deity he calls it—and he was full of the sense of the supernatural enveloping him. The consuming craving and endeavour of his life was to get into touch with this super-nature, super-deity, he so ardently believed in. This was the cause of his nature ecstasies, descriptions of which will now be cited to afford matter of comparison and contrast with those the Christian mystics have given of their experiences.

Sometimes I have concentrated myself, and driven away by continued will all sense of outward appearances, looking straight with the full power of my mind inwards on myself. I find 'I' am there; an 'I' I do not wholly understand or know—something is there distinct from earth and timber, from flesh and bones. Recognizing it, I feel on the margin of a life unknown, very near, almost touching it: on the verge of powers which if I could grasp would give me an immense breadth of existence, an ability to execute what I now only conceive; most probably of far more than that. To see that 'I' is to know that I am surrounded with immortal things (p. 36).

This passage strikingly recalls the prescriptions of St Gregory for the first step in contemplation, namely, recollection and introversion, whereby the soul strives to see itself as it is in itself, stript of all phantasms of things bodily or spiritual (p. 70). This shows that the process is no Asiatic or neo-Platonic infusion, but the natural process whereby the soul tries to enter into itself and get into touch with higher realities.

Jefferies relates how in the earliest morning he would go to some elms where he could see across the fields to the distant hills over which the sun rose:

I looked at the hills, at the dewy grass, and then up through the elm branches to the sky. In a moment all that was behind me—the house, the people, the sounds—seemed to disappear, and to leave me alone. Involuntarily I drew a long breath, then I breathed slowly. My thought, or inner consciousness, went up through the illumined sky, and I was lost in a moment of exaltation. This only lasted a very short time, perhaps only part of a second, and while it lasted there was no formulated wish. I was absorbed; I drank the beauty of the morning; I was exalted. When it ceased I did wish for some increase or enlargement of my existence to correspond with the largeness of feeling I had momentarily enjoyed(p. 54).

These feelings would come upon him whenever he put himself in favourable conditions—under an oak or an elm, by some fir trees, in a grassy hollow, on the seashore—anywhere in nature—and he used to seek and find the experience daily:

It was a necessity to have a few minutes of this separate life daily (p. 55); these pilgrimages [to the fir trees] gave me a few sacred minutes daily; the moment seemed holy when the thought or desire came in its full force (p. 58).

[On London Bridge in the bright morning summer sun] I felt the presence of the immense powers of the universe; I felt out into the depths of the ether. So intensely conscious of the sun, the sky, the limitless space, I felt too in the midst of eternity then, in the midst of the supernatural, among the immortal, and the greatness of the material realized the spirit. By these I saw my soul; by these I knew the supernatural to be more intensely real than the sun. I touched the supernatural, the immortal, there that moment (p. 61).

One midsummer I went out of the road into the fields, and sat down on the grass between the yellowing wheat and the green hawthorn bushes. The sun burned in the sky, the wheat was full of a luxuriant sense of growth, the grass high, the earth giving its vigour to tree and leaf, the heaven blue. The vigour and growth, the warmth and light, the beauty and richness of it entered into me; an ecstasy of soul accompanied the delicate excitement of the senses: the soul rose with the body. Rapt in the fullness of the moment, I prayed there with all that expansion of mind and frame; no words, no definition, inexpressible desire of physical life, of soul-life, equal to and beyond the highest imagining of my heart (p. 77).

Elsewhere he gives expression to his prayer. After a passage asserting that the existance of evil shows there is no deity, no god, in nature, he says:

I conclude that there is an existence, a something higher than soul—higher, better, and more perfect than deity. Earnestly I pray to find this something better than a god. There is something superior, higher, more good. For this I search, labour, think, and pray. With the whole force of my existence, with the whole force of my thought, mind, and soul, I pray to find this Highest Soul, this greater than deity, this better than god. Give me to live the deepest soul-life now and always with this Soul. For want of words I write soul, but I think that it is something beyond soul (p. 51).

The expression 'super-deity' will shock: yet it is the very expression also of 'Dionysius': 'the all-transcending super-essentially super-existing super-deity.' Jefferies was but feeling after, if haply he might find, the transcendental God of the mystics and of the theologians, only he knew it not. For all the somewhat thin atheism, who will say that that soul was irreligious? Mr Watkin's chapter on Richard Jefferies is of much interest; he claims him as being, in spite of himself, a religious mystic. Especially interesting is the statement on the last page, given as being a certain fact, that on his death-bed the knowledge of God and of Jesus Christ came to him, and when 'he came to die that divine name uttered in fervent prayer was among the last words to pass his lips.'[1]

2. *Intellectual Ecstasy of Plotinus*

Mention has been made more than once of Plotinus in the foregoing pages, in connection with St Augustine, over whom he exercised a great influence, and for whom he was as pre-eminently 'the Philosopher' as Aristotle was for St Thomas. St Augustine's language in describing his ecstasies is reminiscent of Plotinus, and Plotinus's own ecstasies hold a prominent and even unique position in the history of mysticism. Therefore the material for forming an estimate of these ecstasies will be laid before the reader. I have to confess that I can lay no claim to any first-hand acquaintance with Plotinus; such knowledge as I possess is derived almost wholly from Dean Inge's Gifford Lectures, *The Philosophy of Plotinus* (1918).

Plotinus was born in Egypt in the first years of the third century; he studied at Alexandria under Ammonius Saccas, the founder of the neo-Platonic school of philosophy, and about the year 250 he migrated to Rome, where he lectured until his death. He is the most authentic and copious exponent of neo-Platonism. We are not concerned with his philosophy, but only with his ecstasies. The principal passages wherein he speaks of the ecstsasies, which were certainly genuine personal experiences of Plotinus's own, are brought together and discussed by Dean Inge (ii. 125-62), and also by Rev. W. Montgomery, the joint editor with Dr Gibbs of St Augustine's *Confessions* in the Cambridge 'Patristic Texts', in an unpublished paper, 'St Augustine and Plotinus', reprinted from *Transactions of the London Society for the Study of Religion* (1914). The following critique of the ecstasies is from this paper:

It is an axiom of neo-Platonism that the highest being must be absolutely simple, excluding all differentiation. It is another axiom

[1] *Philosophy of Mysticism*, p. 388.

that like can be known only by like. Now, the highest form of ordinary thought involves differentiation, at the very least the differentiation of subject and object in consciousness. Therefore the highest being, the primal One, can only be known by transcending the ordinary process of thought and leaving behind the duality of consciousness. But it is strictly by transcending, not by negating thought that we arrive at it. It lies beyond thought, but, so to speak, on the same line produced; though the production involves its passing through a critical point at which its character is changed. The character of the neo-Platonic ecstasy is, in short, determined by the fact that it comes as the culminating point of a process of the most intense thought. Ethics also enters into the matter, inasmuch as it is the ethical will which keeps thought to its task in these high efforts. The special effort of strenuous thought, working upwards and inwards from phenomena to the ultimate principle of things, constitucs the *Ascent*. And the point on which I wish to insist is that the ecstasy, coming as the culminating point of this ascent, has its character determined by what goes before, and is widely different from a trance produced by mechanical hypnotism or any other negation of thought (op. cit. 177).

The following is, says Mr Montgomery, 'the most determined attempt of Plotinus to describe the indescribable':

[During the vision] the beholder was in himself one, having in himself no difference either in relation to himself or in regard to other things. There was no movement in him such as wrath or desire, or any intellection; nor was he, so to say, wholly himself, but as though in a rapture or enthusiasm, he was wholly quiescent and alone, in a condition of unmoved calm, with no inclination outward from his own essence, nor even any movement of revolution about himself, but wholly in repose, and, as it were, identified with repose; and perhaps this is hardly to be called vision; it is rather another kind of seeing, an ecstasy, a becoming absolutely simple, an abandonment of self, a desire for contact, a state of calm and of knowledge leading to harmonization (*Ennead*, vi. ix. 11) (ibid. 179.)

The following pieces are selected from Dean Inge's versions of the principal passages wherein Plotinus describes his ecstasies (loc. cit. 132-42); he has somewhat modernized them and stript them of technicalities.

The preliminary step is recollection and introversion:

It is impossible for any one who has in his soul any extraneous image to conceive of the One while that image distracts his attention. The soul must forsake all that is external, and turn itself wholly to

that which is within; it will not allow itself to be distracted by anything external, but will ignore them all, as at first by not attending
to them, so now at last by not seeing them; it will not even know
itself; and so it will come to the vision of the One and will be united
with it; and then, after a sufficient converse with it, it will return
and bring word, if it be possible, to others of its heavenly intercourse.

For last clause compare St Augustine and St Gregory, p. 175.
The union itself is thus characterized:

Because the soul is different from God, and yet springs from him,
she loves him of necessity. It is natural for the soul to love God and
to desire union with him. Yonder is the true object of our love, which
it is possible to grasp, and to live with and truly to possess, since
no envelope of flesh separates us from it. He who has seen it knows
what I say, that the soul then has another life, when it comes to
God, and having come possesses him, and knows, when in that
state, that it is in the presence of the Dispenser of true life, and
that it needs nothing further. On the contrary, it must put off all
else, and stand in God alone, which can only be when we have
pruned away all else that surrounds us. We must then hasten to
depart hence, to detach ourselves as much as we can from the body
to which we are unhappily bound, to endeavour to embrace God
with all our being, and to leave no part of ourselves which is not
in contact with him. Then we can see God and ourselves, as far as
is permitted: we see ourselves glorified, full of spiritual light, or
rather we see ourselves as pure, subtle, ethereal light; we become
divine, or rather we know ourselves to be divine. In the vision of
God that which sees is not reason, but something greater than and
prior to reason. We ought not to say that the seer will *see*, but he
will *be* that which he sees, if indeed it be possible any longer to distinguish seer and seen, and not boldly to affirm that the two are
one. In this state the seer does not see or distinguish or imagine two
things; he becomes another, he ceases to be himself and to belong
to himself. He belongs to God and is one with him. If a man could
preserve the memory of what he was when he was mingled with the
divine, he would have in himself an image of God, for he was then
one with God.[1]

The soul is above Being while in communion with the One. If
then a man sees himself to have become one with the One, he has
in himself a likeness of the One, and if he passes out of himself, as
an image to its archetype, he has reached the end of his journey.
And when he comes down from his vision, he can again awaken the
virtue that is in him, and seeing himself fitly adorned in every
part, he can again mount upward through virtue to spirit, and
through wisdom to God. Such is the life of the gods and of godlike

[1] These ideas might be strangely paralleled from Ruysbroeck and St John of
the Cross.

and blessed men; a liberation from all earthly bonds, a life that takes no pleasure in earthly things, a flight of the alone to the Alone.

The foregoing pieces are taken from *Ennead*, VI. ix. 7 onwards; in them the intellectual element of the ecstasy or contemplation is paramount, but elsewhere other elements are emphasized—as ecstatic love:

[It is in view of the very highest] that the soul takes fire and is carried away by love. The fullest life is the fullest love; and the love comes from the celestial light which streams forth from the absolute One, the absolute Good, the supreme Principle which made life and made spirit (VI. vii. 23). In this vision of the One 'the spirit is in love' (νοῦς ἐρῶν), and is inebriated with the intoxication of love (VI. vii. 35).

The idea of the 'spiritual marriage' is foreshadowed in the following:

The soul sees the One suddenly appearing in itself, for there is nothing between, nor are they any longer two, but one; for you cannot distinguish between them while the vision lasts: it is that union of which the union of earthly lovers, who wish to blend their being with each other, is a copy (VI. vii. 34).
The soul loves God, wishing to be united to him, being as it were the desire of a noble virgin to be united to a noble Love (VI. ix. 9)

Plotinus speaks also of the ecstatic bliss of the union:

When, after having sought the One, the soul finds itself in its presence, it goes to meet it and contemplates it instead of itself. What itself is when it gazes, it has no leisure to see. When in this state the soul would exchange its present condition for nothing, no, not for the very heaven of heavens; for there is nothing better, nothing more blessed than this. It judges rightly and knows that it has what it desired, and that there is nothing higher. It is not deceived in its happiness; it fears no evil while it is with the One, or even while it sees him; though all else perish around it, it is content, if it can only be with him: so happy is it (VI. vii. 34).

Again:

In order to attain to the Good we must mount up to the supernal regions, leaving behind in the ascent all that is foreign to the deity, so that by ourself alone we behold It alone in all its simplicity and purity, that upon which all things depend, to which all things look, from which they derive their being and life and thought. This then, if any one beholds, what transports of joy does he feel, with what ardour does he desire to be united with it, how is he ravished with delight (i. vi. 7) (Montgomery, op. cit. 184).

As Dean Inge rightly says:

An examination of pathological symptoms, such as fill the now popular books on 'religious experience', would not be of any help towards understanding the passages just quoted.

He says further:

The influence of the psychological school on the philosophy of religion seems to me to be on the whole mischievous. Psychology treats mental states as the data of a science. But intuition changes its character completely when treated in this way. This is why a chilling and depressing atmosphere seems to surround the psychology of religion. The whole method is external; it is a science not of validity but of origins; in limiting itself to the investigation of mystical vision as a state of consciousness, it excludes all consideration of the relation which the vision may bear to objective truth. There are some, no doubt, who regard this last question as either meaningless or unanswerable; but such are not likely to trouble themselves about the philosophy of Plotinus (*Plotinus*, ii. 142).

To judge from the foregoing extracts, Plotinus's ecstasies have all the characteristics of authentic personal experiences. He had such ecstasies but rarely, four times during the six years that his biographer Porphyry lived with him. No attempt will here be made to arrive at any judgement on their character. Only it will be pointed out that St Augustine accepted them as fully religious mystical experiences. His words, already cited in Latin (p. 43), are:

What joys, what fruition of the highest and true Good, what breath of serenity and eternity are in the vision and contemplation of Truth, why should I tell? Certain great and incomparable souls have told it, as far as they thought it should be told, whom we believe to have seen and to see these things (*de Quantitate Animae*, 76).

There is little room for doubt that here he has in mind the descriptions of ecstasy given by Plotinus. The expression 'great and incomparable souls' finds its counterpart in other expressions he uses of Plotinus and the neo-Platonists: as 'great and almost inspired men' (magni homines et pene divini, *de Ordine*, ii. 28).[1] If this appear extravagant, it is to be remembered that at this time, just after his conversion, he confidently looked to neo-Platonism to supply the philosophy of Christian belief (*c. Academicos*, iii. 43, see p. 205).

[1] Compare the language he uses of Pythagoras: 'Venerabilis ac prope divina Pythagorae disciplina' (*de Ordine*, ii. 53).

ADDITION

A criticism passed on the Appendix by more than one reviewer is to the effect that the cases of natural and intellectual ecstasy should not have been merely stated and left alone, but should have been discussed and dealt with. This I refrained from attempting, partly from a sense of insufficient equipment in theology and psychology, and partly in the hope that others more competent might come forward to deal with the problems involved. This hope has been in some measure realized.

But as a preliminary to any such discussion, it is well to emphasize the fact that more and more clearly and fully is it coming to be recognized that there need be nothing miraculous or supernatural in ecstasy, rapture, or trance in themselves; on the physical and psychological side they are often induced in purely natural ways; if there be any supernatural element in them, it arises from that which takes place during them. Religious ideas more easily and more powerfully than others cause such concentration and absorption of mind as passes into ecstasy; but often it is quite non-religious in its origin. It is not questioned that ecstasy often is caused supernaturally, in order, as St Augustine says, that 'to the spirit may be shown what is to be shown' (p. 51). But even then the physical and psychological side of the ecstasy is natural. It is recognized, too, that some people are so made physically and psychologically as to be temperamentally apt for ecstsasics. This whole matter of ecstasy is treated with knowledge and discernment by Fr Henry Browne in various places of his excellent book on mysticism, *Darkness or Light*, a book characterized by a well-balanced sound judgement, that I have read with almost entire agreement (see its Index).

These considerations may call for a modification of P. Garrigou-Lagrange's position in ranging ecstasy among the extraordinary elements, like the charismata of the Corinthians, as prophecies, miracles, revelations, visions, and so forth. It is not a thing to be desired or prayed for; but it is not in itself miraculous. It is a question if ecstasy be not the usual accompaniment of certain phases of contemplation. For St Augustine ecstasy is the condition of the highest mystical experiences (p. 53). Fr Baker's words on ecstasy were remarkable at that date:

In ecstasies there is an alienation and suspension of the use of the outward senses, which I have styled supernatural graces of God; not as if the like might not be produced by a natural way, for history informs us of some that, by a wonderful intention of mind upon philosophical verities, have drawn the operations of the spirit so much inward that the exercise of the outward senses has been suspended, and an ecstasy ensued; and, therefore, no doubt the like may even naturally happen in the contemplating of divine verities; in which case, the imagination being full of divine and spiritual images only, no wonder if during such a suspension there be represented internal discoursings with God and angels, &c., which to the persons may seem to have been real. However, even in these circumstances, an ecstasy so following according to the exigence and disposition of natural causes may properly be termed supernatural, since the preceding contemplation, which caused it, did proceed from a more than ordinary supernatural grace, and the imaginations occurring during such an ecstasy are no doubt ordered by an especial and supernatural providence of God (*Sancta Sophia*, p. 530).

The old treatment of natural ecstasy and contemplation of a religious character outside of Christianity, as made by theologians before the great advances of recent times in the study of comparative religion and of experimental psychology and mental physiology, is no longer adequate, and the subject has not yet received from theologians the consideration it calls for. Consequently the remarks of those who have ventured on this not yet properly explored ground are naturally tentative in character. I know of three Catholic theologians who since the publication of this book have faced the problem—all of them Jesuits. The first was Fr Thomas Slater, a very competent theologian, who in reviewing the book took up the case of Plotinus.[1] After citing some of the pieces given above he says:

There is a tone of sincerity and of personal experience in these descriptions written by a pagan philosopher. ... But what is the relation between these and the mystical experiences of St Augustine and other Christian saints? Are the claims of Plotinus or of some Indian mystic equally valid with those of St Teresa, St Augustine, St Gregory, and St Bernard? All Christians must admit that God loves all men and illumines every man that cometh into the world. The Spirit breatheth where He will, and He can choose his friends wherever He will, as He chose holy Job of old. ... Our faith does not require that we should at once reject the claims made by non-Catholic or non-Christian mystics. ... But really it is not necessary to have recourse to preternatural influences in order to explain the ecstasies of Plotinus. The natural powers of the human soul are quite sufficient to explain them. They were merely the natural effect of philosophical contemplation. After careful preparation, the follower of Plato made the ascent of the ladder of being, concentrated his attention on the contemplation of the One, the True, and the Good, and if circumstances were favourable he was occasionally

---

[1] The review was three articles in the *Catholic Times*, Jan. 1923; it has been reprinted, 'The Mystics' Quest', in a volume, *Points of Church Law, Mysticism, and Morality*.

rewarded by the vision of perfect Beauty fashioned by himself. Unless I am mistaken, that is the simple explanation of the ecstasies of Plotinus and of many another so-called mystic (op. cit. pp. 149-53).

Whether this be a fully satisfying account of Plotinus' language each one must judge for himself; it will be satisfying to those who think that there is nothing more than this in any mystical experience.

Fr Henry Browne has in *Darkness or Light* a chapter of over forty pages on 'Natural Contemplation', which carries the thing a step further than Fr Slater. He limits the enquiry to 'natural contemplation', considered as the culmination of natural religion:

What, he asks, are we to think of those souls—and surely there may be many—who though cut off from the light of Christian Faith have yet honestly sought communion with the God revealed to them by their own nature and by the world around? Is there such a thing as natural contemplation; and what assistance is offered by God's Providence to non-Christians who in good faith practise such mystic prayer? (p. 41).

He has not in mind special cases: 'Our enquiry does not relate merely to a few cases of those on whom God may have chosen to confer exceptional favours. We are thinking rather of masses—perhaps large masses—of human kind' (p. 47). He speaks of Plato and Plotinus, of the religions of India, both Brahmanism and Buddhism, and their contemplatives and mystics. He thus concludes:

When the spirit of man in its native weakness, without the saving grace of regeneration, uses its natural freedom and intelligence to draw towards the Author of its being, what kind of help does God extend to it, not as belonging to any covenant with a fallen race, but still as viewing His creatures with friendly sympathy and fatherly compassion? When the human soul in silence and solitude seems to call upon the Author of all beauty and grandeur in nature, tries to commune with Him at least as present in His works—what is the response which is vouchsafed to such a contemplative by God? There seems to us to be no difficulty in believing that the merciful God may extend to natural contemplatives, within the province of their own psychology, a strengthening and steadying influence, which will enable them to put their cognitive and appetitive faculties to the best account: and this without elevating them beyond the confines of their own nature. Thus natural contemplation may sometimes be carried to a point which has a sublimity of its own, even when without any real relation to Christian mysticism or Christian faith (p. 83).

Fr Browne adds in a note that in thus confining the case to natural religion and natural contemplation, he has no idea of *limiting*

God's operation to aids in the natural order even among Pagans—
how far God may or does grant supernatural aids is a matter which
concerns the theologians.

The theological problem lies in this: it is the firm unanimous
teaching of all the Catholic mystics and theologians alike, that contemplation, and especially the higher mystical states are supernatural in the strict sense of the word, the work of God Himself, the
result of the indwelling of the Holy Ghost in the soul, and of the
divine graces and gifts He bestows. But the experiences of all the
mystics, non-Christian as well as Christian, are couched in the same
language; all make, in one way or another, the same claim of
entering into immediate relation and contact with the Divinity or
with Ultimate Reality. The resemblance, the identity, of the
descriptions are unmistakable for any one who will read the experiences on the one side and the other; for instance, Fr Browne says
that the experience of Plotinus strongly suggests the mystical union
of St Teresa and St John of the Cross (p. 62). Non-Catholic writers
assume and assert the full identity of all such higher experiences,
Catholic, Protestant, Mohammedan, Hindu. Has Catholic theology
a place for fully supernatural religious mystical experiences outside
of Catholic Christianity? Does God in fact bestow His mystical
graces beyond the pale of His Church?

Frs Slater and Browne pass by this issue, while guardedly leaving
it open; but Père Maréchal, S.J., does explicitly face it. It should
be said that he is more than psychologist; he is a scholastic meta-
physician of standing, the author of a comprehensive work in six
volumes, *Le Point de Départ de la Métaphysique*; he is also a good
theologian.

The three essays contained in the volume of *Études sur la Psychologie
des Mystiques*, 1924, had all appeared in periodicals before the War.
In the second and third essays he deals with the question in hand;
and he announces that the greater part of the second volume will
be devoted to this very question of 'comparative mysticism', with
special regard to India and to Islam. The treatment in Vol. I is
therefore but a sketch. In two places (pp. 144 ff., 222 ff.) are given,
for purpose of comparison, texts on mystical experience selected
from sources of all origins. Finally, on the last page are formulated
the definite questions:

Are there outside of Catholicism, among dissident Christians, true
supernatural ecstasies?

Since every one admits that, if they are in good faith, the baptized participate in the grace of Christ, nothing stands in the way,

as matter of principle, of their enjoying, as a personal privilege, the very highest mystical favours.

But contemplatives outside the pale of Christianity—Mussulmans, Brahmans, Buddhists—or mere philosophers without positive religion?

We recognize gladly that there are some such whose lives or writings carry such a stamp of sincerity and of elevation of soul, that it would be repugnant to deny to their ecstasies all religious value. We must remember, too, that natural contemplation can have a high religious efficacity, as it improves the moral life and so prepares the way for supernatural grace.

Granted (*sans doute*): but does not Catholic theology teach that supernatural grace, whatever be the way of its bestowal, is not denied to any soul of good will? Then why deny that God can manifest Himself sometimes more directly still, outside the pale of Christianity, to some devout ascetic, who seeks Him with groping, with humble and perseverant energy, even though by methods of strange and touching 'bizarrerie'?

Friendly reader, let us hope it may be so! (p. 257).

We may remark in passing that Fr A. B. Sharpe in *Mysticism, its True Nature and Value* (1910) in his chapter on Plotinus hovers between the two alternatives, whether his ecstasies are to be looked on as natural, in Fr Slater's sense; or are to be taken as fully supernatural religious ecstasies: and he shows himself quite prepared to accept the second alternative.

To return to P. Maréchal; one of the promised essays, 'Le problème de la grâce mystique en Islam', has appeared in an article, fifty pages long, in the *Recherches de Science Religieuse*, 1923.[1] It is an account of the life, writings, prayers, mystical experiences, of Mansour al-Hallâj, put to death A.D. 922 as a heretic by the Mohammedan religious authorities. It is in all a wonderful and most arresting story, but any attempt to summarize it would be impossible here.[2] Hallâj's accounts of his mystical experiences, and his teaching and prayers, are in language hardly distinguishable from that of the Christian mystics. A special feature is his devotion to Jesus Christ, not of course as the Word made Flesh, but as the greatest and most perfect creation of God's grace. Maréchal thus sums up the articles of his creed:

The One transcendent God, the great Rewarder; a supernatural destiny, attaining to an immediate possession of the divine Essence, a destiny made possible only by a special grace, the grace of benevolent love; a knowledge and veneration of Jesus as the model of

[1] An English translation is being prepared of P. Maréchal's essays, including this one.

[2] See art. 'Hallâj' in Hastings's *Encyclopaedia of Religion and Ethics*.

holiness, the perfect type of union with God, and the Prince of the spiritual kingdom of grace.

This belief Hallâj got from the Koran, but the Koran got it from the Scriptures. And there are in it the essential elements of an act of faith. P. Maréchal comments in the four concluding pages of the article:

Let us now place ourselves definitely in the point of view of Catholic theology.

To the Christian, who knows by Scripture and by personal experience, something of the Saviour's divine love, it will hardly be conceivable that an appeal to Jesus, even distant, will be rejected by Him, or that a homage imperfect but sincere, will remain without answer. So far as it is possible to conjecture the invisible realities from exterior indications, it seems that 'the mystic martyr of Islam', by his heroic fidelity in embracing the partial truth that had filtered down to him, must have drawn to himself the merciful predilection of that Jesus, who is not only the supreme human creation of divine grace, as Hallâj believed Him, but the Author and Finisher of that grace.

That God can give particular revelations and mystical gifts, even very eminent ones, to 'negative misbelievers', kept outside the visible body of the Church by invincible ignorance, is not in doubt, according to received doctrine—and we speak of graces strictly supernatural. What, then, did Hallâj need in order to make an act of supernatural faith? Only the enlightening motion, wholly interior, which should put his mind in perfect consonance with the supernatural revealed truth: the 'grace of faith', which God refuses to no sincere mind to which is proposed the object of faith.

He adds: Perhaps other cases, more difficult than that of Hallâj, more difficult than that of Islamism in general, may be resolved by the same principles.[1]

[1] On Mohammedan Mysticism may be read C. Field, *Mystics and Saints of Islam* (London, 1910); R. A. Nicholson, *Studies in Islamic Mysticism* (Cambridge, 1921); R. P. Masani *The Conference of the Birds*, a Sufi allegory of Farid-ud-din Attar (Oxford, 1924).

Revised February 1966

hARPER TORCHBOOKS

HUMANITIES AND SOCIAL SCIENCES

American Studies: General

THOMAS C. COCHRAN: The Inner Revolution: *Essays on the Social Sciences in History* TB/1140

EDWARD S. CORWIN: American Constitutional History. *Essays edited by Alpheus T. Mason and Gerald Garvey* TB/1136

CARL N. DEGLER, Ed.: Pivotal Interpretations of American History TB/1240, TB/1241

A. HUNTER DUPREE: Science in the Federal Government: *A History of Policies and Activities to 1940* TB/573

OSCAR HANDLIN, Ed.: This Was America: *As Recorded by European Travelers in the Eighteenth, Nineteenth and Twentieth Centuries. Illus.* TB/1119

MARCUS LEE HANSEN: The Atlantic Migration: 1607-1860. *Edited by Arthur M. Schlesinger. Introduction by Oscar Handlin* TB/1052

MARCUS LEE HANSEN: The Immigrant in American History. *Edited with a Foreword by Arthur M. Schlesinger* TB/1120

JOHN HIGHAM, Ed.: The Reconstruction of American History TB/1068

ROBERT H. JACKSON: The Supreme Court in the American System of Government TB/1106

JOHN F. KENNEDY: A Nation of Immigrants. *Illus. Revised and Enlarged. Introduction by Robert F. Kennedy* TB/1118

RALPH BARTON PERRY: Puritanism and Democracy TB/1138

ARNOLD ROSE: The Negro in America: *The Condensed Version of Gunnar Myrdal's An American Dilemma* TB/3048

MAURICE R. STEIN: The Eclipse of Community: *An Interpretation of American Studies* TB/1128

W. LLOYD WARNER and Associates: Democracy in Jonesville: *A Study in Quality and Inequality* ‖ TB/1129

W. LLOYD WARNER: Social Class in America: *The Evaluation of Status* TB/1013

American Studies: Colonial

BERNARD BAILYN, Ed.: The Apologia of Robert Keayne: *Self-Portrait of a Puritan Merchant* TB/1201

BERNARD BAILYN: The New England Merchants in the Seventeenth Century TB/1149

JOSEPH CHARLES: The Origins of the American Party System TB/1049

LAWRENCE HENRY GIPSON: The Coming of the Revolution: 1763-1775. † *Illus.* TB/3007

LEONARD W. LEVY: Freedom of Speech and Press in Early American History: *Legacy of Suppression* TB/1109

PERRY MILLER: Errand Into the Wilderness TB/1139

PERRY MILLER & T. H. JOHNSON, Eds.: The Puritans: *A Sourcebook of Their Writings* Vol. I TB/1093; Vol. II TB/1094

EDMUND S. MORGAN, Ed.: The Diary of Michael Wigglesworth, 1653-1657: *The Conscience of a Puritan*

EDMUND S. MORGAN: The Puritan Family: *Religion and Domestic Relations in Seventeenth-Century New England* TB/1227

RICHARD B. MORRIS: Government and Labor in Early America TB/1244

KENNETH B. MURDOCK: Literature and Theology in Colonial New England TB/99

WALLACE NOTESTEIN: The English People on the Eve of Colonization: 1603-1630. † *Illus.* TB/3006

LOUIS B. WRIGHT: The Cultural Life of the American Colonies. 1607-1763. † *Illus.* TB/3005

American Studies: From the Revolution to 1860

JOHN R. ALDEN: The American Revolution: 1775-1783. † *Illus.* TB/3011

MAX BELOFF, Ed.: The Debate on the American Revolution, 1761-1783: *A Sourcebook* TB/1225

RAY A. BILLINGTON: The Far Western Frontier: 1830-1860. † *Illus.* TB/3012

EDMUND BURKE: On the American Revolution: *Selected Speeches and Letters.* ‡ *Edited by Elliott Robert Barkan* TB/3068

WHITNEY R. CROSS: The Burned-Over District: *The Social and Intellectual History of Enthusiastic Religion in Western New York, 1800-1850* TB/1242

GEORGE DANGERFIELD: The Awakening of American Nationalism: 1815-1828. † *Illus.* TB/3061

CLEMENT EATON: The Freedom-of-Thought Struggle in the Old South. *Revised and Enlarged. Illus.* TB/1150

CLEMENT EATON: The Growth of Southern Civilization: 1790-1860. † *Illus.* TB/3040

LOUIS FILLER: The Crusade Against Slavery: 1830-1860. † *Illus.* TB/3029

DIXON RYAN FOX: The Decline of Aristocracy in the Politics of New York: 1801-1840. ‡ *Edited by Robert V. Remini* TB/3064

FELIX GILBERT: The Beginnings of American Foreign Policy: *To the Farewell Address* TB/1200

FRANCIS J. GRUND: Aristocracy in America: *Social Class in the Formative Years of the New Nation* TB/1001

ALEXANDER HAMILTON: The Reports of Alexander Hamilton. ‡ *Edited by Jacob E. Cooke* TB/3060

THOMAS JEFFERSON: Notes on the State of Virginia. ‡ *Edited by Thomas P. Abernethy* TB/3052

JAMES MADISON: The Forging of American Federalism: *Selected Writings of James Madison. Edited by Saul K. Padover* TB/1226

---

† The New American Nation Series, edited by Henry Steele Commager and Richard B. Morris.

‡ American Perspectives series, edited by Bernard Wishy and William E. Leuchtenburg.

* The Rise of Modern Europe series, edited by William L. Langer.

‖ Researches in the Social, Cultural, and Behavioral Sciences, edited by Benjamin Nelson.

§ The Library of Religion and Culture, edited by Benjamin Nelson.

∑ Harper Modern Science Series, edited by James R. Newman.

○ Not for sale in Canada.

BERNARD MAYO: Myths and Men: *Patrick Henry, George Washington, Thomas Jefferson* TB/1108

JOHN C. MILLER: Alexander Hamilton and the Growth of the New Nation TB/3057

RICHARD B. MORRIS, Ed.: The Era of the American Revolution TB/1180

R. B. NYE: The Cultural Life of the New Nation: 1776-1801. † *Illus.* TB/3026

FRANCIS S. PHILBRICK: The Rise of the West, 1754-1830. † *Illus.* TB/3067

TIMOTHY L. SMITH: Revivalism and Social Reform: *Protestantism on the Eve of the Civil War* TB/1229

FRANK THISTLETHWAITE: America and the Atlantic Community: *Anglo-American Aspects, 1790-1850* TB/1107

A. F. TYLER: Freedom's Ferment: *Phases of American Social History from the Revolution to the Outbreak of the Civil War. 31 illus.* TB/1074

GLYNDON G. VAN DEUSEN: The Jacksonian Era: 1828-1848. † *Illus.* TB/3028

LOUIS B. WRIGHT: Culture on the Moving Frontier TB/1053

American Studies: The Civil War to 1900

THOMAS C. COCHRAN & WILLIAM MILLER: The Age of Enterprise: *A Social History of Industrial America* TB/1054

W. A. DUNNING: Essays on the Civil War and Reconstruction. *Introduction by David Donald* TB/1181

W. A. DUNNING: Reconstruction, Political and Economic: 1865-1877 TB/1073

HAROLD U. FAULKNER: Politics, Reform and Expansion: 1890-1900. † *Illus.* TB/3020

HELEN HUNT JACKSON: A Century of Dishonor: *The Early Crusade for Indian Reform. ‡ Edited by Andrew F. Rolle* TB/3063

ALBERT D. KIRWAN: Revolt of the Rednecks: *Mississippi Politics, 1876-1925* TB/1199

ROBERT GREEN MCCLOSKEY: American Conservatism in the Age of Enterprise: 1865-1910 TB/1137

WHITELAW REID: After the War: *A Tour of the Southern States, 1865-1866. ‡ Edited by C. Vann Woodward* TB/3066

CHARLES H. SHINN: Mining Camps: *A Study in American Frontier Government. ‡ Edited by Rodman W. Paul* TB/3062

VERNON LANE WHARTON: The Negro in Mississippi: 1865-1890 TB/1178

American Studies: 1900 to the Present

RAY STANNARD BAKER: Following the Color Line: *American Negro Citizenship in Progressive Era. ‡ Illus. Edited by Dewey W. Grantham, Jr.* TB/3053

RANDOLPH S. BOURNE: War and the Intellectuals: *Collected Essays, 1915-1919. ‡ Ed. by Carl Resek* TB/3043

A. RUSSELL BUCHANAN: The United States and World War II. † *Illus.* Vol. I TB/3044; Vol. II TB/3045

ABRAHAM CAHAN: The Rise of David Levinsky: *a documentary novel of social mobility in early twentieth century America. Intro. by John Higham* TB/1028

THOMAS C. COCHRAN: The American Business System: *A Historical Perspective, 1900-1955* TB/1080

FOSTER RHEA DULLES: America's Rise to World Power: 1898-1954. † *Illus.* TB/3021

JOHN D. HICKS: Republican Ascendancy: 1921-1933. † *Illus.* TB/3041

SIDNEY HOOK: Reason, Social Myths, and Democracy TB/1237

ROBERT HUNTER: Poverty: *Social Conscience in the Progressive Era. ‡ Edited by Peter d'A. Jones* TB/3065

WILLIAM L. LANGER & S. EVERETT GLEASON: The Challenge to Isolation: *The World Crisis of 1937-1940 and American Foreign Policy* Vol. I TB/3054; Vol. II TB/3055

WILLIAM E. LEUCHTENBURG: Franklin D. Roosevelt and the New Deal: 1932-1940. † *Illus.* TB/3025

ARTHUR S. LINK: Woodrow Wilson and the Progressive Era: 1910-1917. † *Illus.* TB/3023

GEORGE E. MOWRY: The Era of Theodore Roosevelt and the Birth of Modern America: 1900-1912. † *Illus.* TB/3022

RUSSEL B. NYE: Midwestern Progressive Politics: *A Historical Study of its Origins and Development, 1870-1958* TB/1202

WALTER RAUSCHENBUSCH: Christianity and the Social Crisis. ‡ *Edited by Robert D. Cross* TB/3059

PHILIP SELZNICK: TVA and the Grass Roots: *A Study in the Sociology of Formal Organization* TB/1230

GEORGE B. TINDALL, Ed.: A Populist Reader ‡ TB/3069

TWELVE SOUTHERNERS: I'll Take My Stand: *The South and the Agrarian Tradition. Intro. by Louis D. Rubin, Jr. Biographical Essays by Virginia Rock* TB/1072

WALTER E. WEYL: The New Democracy: *An Essay on Certain Political Tendencies in the United States. ‡ Edited by Charles B. Forcey* TB/3042

Anthropology

JACQUES BARZUN: Race: *A Study in Superstition. Revised Edition* TB/1172

JOSEPH B. CASAGRANDE, Ed.: In the Company of Man: *Twenty Portraits of Anthropological Informants. Illus.* TB/3047

W. E. LE GROS CLARK: The Antecedents of Man: *Intro. to Evolution of the Primates.* ○ *Illus.* TB/559

CORA DU BOIS: The People of Alor. *New Preface by the author. Illus.* Vol. I TB/1042; Vol. II TB/1043

RAYMOND FIRTH, Ed.: Man and Culture: *An Evaluation of the Work of Bronislaw Malinowski* ‖ ○ TB/1133

DAVID LANDY: Tropical Childhood: *Cultural Transmission and Learning in a Rural Puerto Rican Village* |, TB/1235

L. S. B. LEAKEY: Adam's Ancestors: *The Evolution of Man and His Culture. Illus.* TB/1019

ROBERT H. LOWIE: Primitive Society. *Introduction by Fred Eggan* TB/1056

EDWARD BURNETT TYLOR: The Origins of Culture. *Part I of "Primitive Culture."* § *Intro. by Paul Radin* TB/33

EDWARD BURNETT TYLOR: Religion in Primitive Culture. *Part II of "Primitive Culture."* § *Intro. by Paul Radin* TB/34

W. LLOYD WARNER: A Black Civilization: *A Study of an Australian Tribe.* ‖ *Illus.* TB/3056

Art and Art History

WALTER LOWRIE: Art in the Early Church. *Revised Edition. 452 illus.* TB/124

EMILE MÂLE: The Gothic Image: *Religious Art in France of the Thirteenth Century.* § *190 illus.* TB/44

MILLARD MEISS: Painting in Florence and Siena after the Black Death: *The Arts, Religion and Society in the Mid-Fourteenth Century. 169 illus.* TB/1148

ERICH NEUMANN: The Archetypal World of Henry Moore. *107 illus.* TB/2020

DORA & ERWIN PANOFSKY: Pandora's Box: *The Changing Aspects of a Mythical Symbol. Revised Edition. Illus.* TB/2021

ERWIN PANOFSKY: Studies in Iconology: *Humanistic Themes in the Art of the Renaissance. 180 illustrations* TB/1077

ALEXANDRE PIANKOFF: The Shrines of Tut-Ankh-Amon. *Edited by N. Rambova. 117 illus.* TB/2011

JEAN SEZNEC: The Survival of the Pagan Gods: *The Mythological Tradition and Its Place in Renaissance Humanism and Art. 108 illustrations* TB/2004

OTTO VON SIMSON: The Gothic Cathedral: *Origins of Gothic Architecture and the Medieval Concept of Order. 58 illus.* TB/2018

HEINRICH ZIMMER: Myths and Symbols in Indian Art and Civilization. *70 illustrations* TB/2005

Business, Economics & Economic History

REINHARD BENDIX: Work and Authority in Industry: *Ideologies of Management in the Course of Industrialization*   TB/3035

GILBERT BURCK & EDITORS OF FORTUNE: The Computer Age: *And Its Potential for Management*   TB/1179

THOMAS C. COCHRAN: The American Business System: *A Historical Perspective, 1900-1955*   TB/1080

THOMAS C. COCHRAN: The Inner Revolution: *Essays on the Social Sciences in History*   TB/1140

THOMAS C. COCHRAN & WILLIAM MILLER: The Age of Enterprise: *A Social History of Industrial America* TB/1054

ROBERT DAHL & CHARLES E. LINDBLOM: Politics, Economics, and Welfare: *Planning & Politico-Economic Systems Resolved into Basic Social Processes* TB/3037

PETER F. DRUCKER: The New Society: *The Anatomy of Industrial Order*   TB/1082

EDITORS OF FORTUNE: America in the Sixties: *The Economy and the Society*   TB/1015

ROBERT L. HEILBRONER: The Great Ascent: *The Struggle for Economic Development in Our Time*   TB/3030

FRANK H. KNIGHT: The Economic Organization   TB/1214

FRANK H. KNIGHT: Risk, Uncertainty and Profit   TB/1215

ABBA P. LERNER: Everybody's Business: *Current Assumptions in Economics and Public Policy*   TB/3051

ROBERT GREEN MCCLOSKEY: American Conservatism in the Age of Enterprise, 1865-1910   TB/1137

PAUL MANTOUX: The Industrial Revolution in the Eighteenth Century: *The Beginnings of the Modern Factory System in England* °   TB/1079

WILLIAM MILLER, Ed.: Men in Business: *Essays on the Historical Role of the Entrepreneur*   TB/1081

RICHARD B. MORRIS: Government and Labor in Early America   TB/1244

HERBERT SIMON: The Shape of Automation: *For Men and Management*   TB/1245

PERRIN STRYKER: The Character of the Executive: *Eleven Studies in Managerial Qualities*   TB/1041

PIERRE URI: Partnership for Progress: *A Program for Transatlantic Action*   TB/3036

Contemporary Culture

JACQUES BARZUN: The House of Intellect   TB/1051

JOHN U. NEF: Cultural Foundations of Industrial Civilization   TB/1024

NATHAN M. PUSEY: The Age of the Scholar: *Observations on Education in a Troubled Decade*   TB/1157

PAUL VALÉRY: The Outlook for Intelligence   TB/2016

Historiography & Philosophy of History

JACOB BURCKHARDT: On History and Historians. *Intro. by H. R. Trevor-Roper*   TB/1216

WILHELM DILTHEY: Pattern and Meaning in History: *Thoughts on History and Society. ° Edited with an Introduction by H. P. Rickman*   TB/1075

J. H. HEXTER: Reappraisals in History: *New Views on History & Society in Early Modern Europe*   TB/1100

H. STUART HUGHES: History as Art and as Science: *Twin Vistas on the Past*   TB/1207

RAYMOND KLIBANSKY & H. J. PATON, Eds.: Philosophy and History: *The Ernst Cassirer Festschrift. Illus.*   TB/1115

GEORGE H. NADEL, Ed.: Studies in the Philosophy of History: *Selected Essays from History and Theory*   TB/1208

JOSE ORTEGA Y GASSET: The Modern Theme. *Introduction by Jose Ferrater Mora*   TB/1038

KARL R. POPPER: The Open Society and Its Enemies
  Vol. I: *The Spell of Plato*   TB/1101
  Vol. II: *The High Tide of Prophecy: Hegel, Marx and the Aftermath*   TB/1102

KARL R. POPPER: The Poverty of Historicism °   TB/1126

G. J. RENIER: History: Its Purpose and Method   TB/1209

W. H. WALSH: Philosophy of History: *An Introduction*   TB/1020

History: General

L. CARRINGTON GOODRICH: A Short History of the Chinese People. *Illus.*   TB/3015

DAN N. JACOBS & HANS H. BAERWALD: Chinese Communism: *Selected Documents*   TB/3031

BERNARD LEWIS: The Arabs in History   TB/1029

History: Ancient

A. ANDREWES: The Greek Tyrants   TB/1103

ADOLF ERMAN, Ed.: The Ancient Egyptians: *A Sourcebook of Their Writings. New material and Introduction by William Kelly Simpson*   TB/1233

MICHAEL GRANT: Ancient History °   TB/1190

SAMUEL NOAH KRAMER: Sumerian Mythology   TB/1055

NAPHTALI LEWIS & MEYER REINHOLD, Eds.: Roman Civilization. *Sourcebook I: The Republic*   TB/1231

NAPHTALI LEWIS & MEYER REINHOLD, Eds.: Roman Civilization. *Sourcebook II: The Empire*   TB/1232

History: Medieval

P. BOISSONNADE: Life and Work in Medieval Europe: *The Evolution of the Medieval Economy, the 5th to the 15th Century. ° Preface by Lynn White, Jr.*   TB/1141

HELEN CAM: England before Elizabeth   TB/1026

NORMAN COHN: The Pursuit of the Millennium: *Revolutionary Messianism in Medieval and Reformation Europe*   TB/1037

G. G. COULTON: Medieval Village, Manor, and Monastery   TB/1022

HEINRICH FICHTENAU: The Carolingian Empire: *The Age of Charlemagne*   TB/1142

F. L. GANSHOF: Feudalism   TB/1058

EDWARD GIBBON: The Triumph of Christendom in the Roman Empire *(Chaps. XV-XX of "Decline and Fall," J. B. Bury edition). § Illus.*   TB/46

W. O. HASSALL, Ed.: Medieval England: *As Viewed by Contemporaries*   TB/1205

DENYS HAY: The Medieval Centuries °   TB/1192

J. M. HUSSEY: The Byzantine World   TB/1057

FERDINAND LOT: The End of the Ancient World and the Beginnings of the Middle Ages. *Introduction by Glanville Downey*   TB/1044

G. MOLLAT: The Popes at Avignon: 1305-1378   TB/308

CHARLES PETIT-DUTAILLIS: The Feudal Monarchy in France and England: *From the Tenth to the Thirteenth Century* °   TB/1165

HENRI PIRENNE: Early Democracies in the Low Countries: *Urban Society and Political Conflict in the Middle Ages and the Renaissance. Introduction by John H. Mundy*   TB/1110

STEVEN RUNCIMAN: A History of the Crusades.
  Volume I: *The First Crusade and the Foundation of the Kingdom of Jerusalem. Illus.*   TB/1143
  Volume II: *The Kingdom of Jerusalem and the Frankish East, 1100-1187. Illus.*   TB/1243

FERDINAND SCHEVILL: Siena: *The History of a Medieval Commune. Intro. by William M. Bowsky*   TB/1164

SULPICIUS SEVERUS et al.: The Western Fathers: *Being the Lives of Martin of Tours, Ambrose, Augustine of Hippo, Honoratus of Arles and Germanus of Auxerre. Edited and translated by F. R. Hoare*   TB/309

HENRY OSBORN TAYLOR: The Classical Heritage of the Middle Ages. *Foreword and Biblio. by Kenneth M. Setton*   TB/1117

F. VAN DER MEER: Augustine the Bishop: *Church and Society at the Dawn of the Middle Ages*   TB/304

J. M. WALLACE-HADRILL: The Barbarian West: *The Early Middle Ages, A.D. 400-1000*   TB/1061

L. B. NAMIER: Vanished Supremacies: *Essays on European History, 1812-1918* ° TB/1088

JOHN U. NEF: Western Civilization Since the Renaissance: *Peace, War, Industry, and the Arts* TB/1113

FREDERICK L. NUSSBAUM: The Triumph of Science and Reason, 1660-1685. * *Illus.* TB/3009

JOHN PLAMENATZ: German Marxism and Russian Communism. ° *New Preface by the Author* TB/1189

RAYMOND W. POSTGATE, Ed.: Revolution from 1789 to 1906: *Selected Documents* TB/1063

PENFIELD ROBERTS: The Quest for Security, 1715-1740. * *Illus.* TB/3016

PRISCILLA ROBERTSON: Revolutions of 1848: *A Social History* TB/1025

ALBERT SOREL: Europe Under the Old Regime. *Translated by Francis H. Herrick* TB/1121

N. N. SUKHANOV: The Russian Revolution, 1917: *Eyewitness Account. Edited by Joel Carmichael* Vol. I TB/1066; Vol. II TB/1067

A. J. P. TAYLOR: The Habsburg Monarch, 1809-1918: *A History of the Austrian Empire and Austria-Hungary* ° TB/1187

JOHN B. WOLF: The Emergence of the Great Powers, 1685-1715. * *Illus.* TB/3010

JOHN B. WOLF: France: 1814-1919: *The Rise of a Liberal-Democratic Society* TB/3019

Intellectual History & History of Ideas

HERSCHEL BAKER: The Image of Man: *A Study of the Idea of Human Dignity in Classical Antiquity, the Middle Ages, and the Renaissance* TB/1047

R. R. BOLGAR: The Classical Heritage and Its Beneficiaries: *From the Carolingian Age to the End of the Renaissance* TB/1125

RANDOLPH S. BOURNE: War and the Intellectuals: *Collected Essays, 1915-1919. ‡ Edited by Carl Resek* TB/3043

J. BRONOWSKI & BRUCE MAZLISH: The Western Intellectual Tradition: *From Leonardo to Hegel* TB/3001

ERNST CASSIRER: The Individual and the Cosmos in Renaissance Philosophy. *Translated with an Introduction by Mario Domandi* TB/1097

NORMAN COHN: The Pursuit of the Millennium: *Revolutionary Messianism in Medieval and Reformation Europe* TB/1037

C. C. GILLISPIE: Genesis and Geology: *The Decades before Darwin* § TB/51

G. RACHEL LEVY: Religious Conceptions of the Stone Age and Their Influence upon European Thought. *Illus. Introduction by Henri Frankfort* TB/106

ARTHUR O. LOVEJOY: The Great Chain of Being: *A Study of the History of an Idea* TB/1009

FRANK E. MANUEL: The Prophets of Paris: *Turgot, Condorcet, Saint-Simon, Fourier, and Comte* TB/1218

PERRY MILLER & T. H. JOHNSON, Editors: The Puritans: *A Sourcebook of Their Writings* Vol. I TB/1093; Vol. II TB/1094

MILTON C. NAHM: Genius and Creativity: *An Essay in the History of Ideas* TB/1196

ROBERT PAYNE: Hubris: *A Study of Pride. Foreword by Sir Herbert Read* TB/1031

RALPH BARTON PERRY: The Thought and Character of William James: *Briefer Version* TB/1156

GEORG SIMMEL et al.: Essays on Sociology, Philosophy, and Aesthetics. ‖ *Edited by Kurt H. Wolff* TB/1234

BRUNO SNELL: The Discovery of the Mind: *The Greek Origins of European Thought* TB/1018

PAGET TOYNBEE: Dante Alighieri: *His Life and Works. Edited with Intro. by Charles S. Singleton* TB/1206

ERNEST LEE TUVESON: Millennium and Utopia: *A Study in the Background of the Idea of Progress. ‖ New Preface by the Author* TB/1134

PAUL VALÉRY: The Outlook for Intelligence TB/2016

PHILIP P. WIENER: Evolution and the Founders of Pragmatism. *Foreword by John Dewey* TB/1212

Literature, Poetry, The Novel & Criticism

JAMES BAIRD: Ishmael: *The Art of Melville in the Contexts of International Primitivism* TB/1023

JACQUES BARZUN: The House of Intellect TB/1051

W. J. BATE: From Classic to Romantic: *Premises of Taste in Eighteenth Century England* TB/1036

RACHEL BESPALOFF: On the Iliad TB/2006

R. P. BLACKMUR et al.: Lectures in Criticism. *Introduction by Huntington Cairns* TB/2003

ABRAHAM CAHAN: The Rise of David Levinsky: *a documentary novel of social mobility in early twentieth century America. Intro. by John Higham* TB/1028

ERNST R. CURTIUS: European Literature and the Latin Middle Ages TB/2015

GEORGE ELIOT: Daniel Deronda: *a novel. Introduction by F. R. Leavis* TB/1039

ADOLF ERMAN, Ed.: The Ancient Egyptians: *A Sourcebook of Their Writings. New Material and Introduction by William Kelly Simpson* TB/1233

ÉTIENNE GILSON: Dante and Philosophy TB/1089

ALFRED HARBAGE: As They Liked It: *A Study of Shakespeare's Moral Artistry* TB/1035

STANLEY R. HOPPER, Ed.: Spiritual Problems in Contemporary Literature § TB/21

A. R. HUMPHREYS: The Augustan World: *Society, Thought and Letters in 18th Century England* ° TB/1105

ALDOUS HUXLEY: Antic Hay & The Giaconda Smile. ° *Introduction by Martin Green* TB/3503

ALDOUS HUXLEY: Brave New World & Brave New World Revisited. ° *Introduction by Martin Green* TB/3501

HENRY JAMES: Roderick Hudson: *a novel. Introduction by Leon Edel* TB/1016

HENRY JAMES: The Tragic Muse: *a novel. Introduction by Leon Edel* TB/1017

ARNOLD KETTLE: An Introduction to the English Novel. Volume I: *Defoe to George Eliot* TB/1011 Volume II: *Henry James to the Present* TB/1012

ROGER SHERMAN LOOMIS: The Development of Arthurian Romance TB/1167

JOHN STUART MILL: On Bentham and Coleridge. *Introduction by F. R. Leavis* TB/1070

KENNETH B. MURDOCK: Literature and Theology in Colonial New England TB/99

SAMUEL PEPYS: The Diary of Samuel Pepys. ° *Edited by O. F. Morshead. Illus. by Ernest Shepard* TB/1007

ST.-JOHN PERSE: Seamarks TB/2002

GEORGE SANTAYANA: Interpretations of Poetry and Religion § TB/9

HEINRICH STRAUMANN: American Literature in the Twentieth Century. *Third Edition, Revised* TB/1168

PAGET TOYNBEE: Dante Alighieri: *His Life and Works. Edited with Intro. by Charles S. Singleton* TB/1206

DOROTHY VAN GHENT: The English Novel: *Form and Function* TB/1050

E. B. WHITE: One Man's Meat. *Introduction by Walter Blair* TB/3505

MORTON DAUWEN ZABEL, Editor: Literary Opinion in America Vol. I TB/3013; Vol. II TB/3014

Myth, Symbol & Folklore

JOSEPH CAMPBELL, Editor: Pagan and Christian Mysteries. *Illus.* TB/2013

MIRCEA ELIADE: Cosmos and History: *The Myth of the Eternal Return* § TB/2050

MERCEA ELIADE: Rites and Symbols of Initiation: *The Mysteries of Birth and Rebirth* § TB/1236

C. G. JUNG & C. KERÉNYI: Essays on a Science of Mythology: *The Myths of the Divine Child and the Divine Maiden* TB/2014

DORA & ERWIN PANOFSKY: Pandora's Box: *The Changing Aspects of a Mythical Symbol. Revised Edition. Illus.* TB/2021

CHARLES H. SHINN: Mining Camps: *A Study in American Frontier Government.* ‡ *Edited by Rodman W. Paul*
TB/3062

Psychology

ALFRED ADLER: The Individual Psychology of Alfred Adler. *Edited by Heinz L. and Rowena R. Ansbacher*
TB/1154

ALFRED ADLER: Problems of Neurosis. *Introduction by Heinz L. Ansbacher*
TB/1145

ANTON T. BOISEN: The Exploration of the Inner World: *A Study of Mental Disorder and Religious Experience*
TB/87

HERBERT FINGARETTE: The Self in Transformation: *Psychoanalysis, Philosophy and the Life of the Spirit* ||
TB/1177

SIGMUND FREUD: On Creativity and the Unconscious: *Papers on the Psychology of Art, Literature, Love, Religion.* § *Intro. by Benjamin Nelson*
TB/45

C. JUDSON HERRICK: The Evolution of Human Nature
TB/545

WILLIAM JAMES: Psychology: *The Briefer Course. Edited with an Intro. by Gordon Allport*
TB/1034

C. G. JUNG: Psychological Reflections
TB/2001

C. G. JUNG: Symbols of Transformation: *An Analysis of the Prelude to a Case of Schizophrenia. Illus*
Vol. I: TB/2009; Vol. II TB/2010

C. G. JUNG & C. KERÉNYI: Essays on a Science of Mythology: *The Myths of the Divine Child and the Divine Maiden*
TB/2014

JOHN T. MC NEILL: A History of the Cure of Souls
TB/126

KARL MENNINGER: Theory of Psychoanalytic Technique
TB/1144

ERICH NEUMANN: Amor and Psyche: *The Psychic Development of the Feminine*
TB/2012

ERICH NEUMANN: The Archetypal World of Henry Moore. *107 illus.*
TB/2020

ERICH NEUMANN: The Origins and History of Consciousness
Vol. I *Illus.* TB/2007; Vol. II TB/2008

C. P. OBERNDORF: A History of Psychoanalysis in America
TB/1147

RALPH BARTON PERRY: The Thought and Character of William James: *Briefer Version*
TB/1156

JEAN PIAGET, BÄRBEL INHELDER, & ALINA SZEMINSKA: The Child's Conception of Geometry °
TB/1146

JOHN H. SCHAAR: Escape from Authority: *The Perspectives of Erich Fromm*
TB/1155

Sociology

JACQUES BARZUN: Race: *A Study in Superstition. Revised Edition*
TB/1172

BERNARD BERELSON, Ed.: The Behavioral Sciences Today
TB/1127

ABRAHAM CAHAN: The Rise of David Levinsky: *A documentary novel of social mobility in early twentieth century America. Intro. by John Higham* TB/1028

THOMAS C. COCHRAN: The Inner Revolution: *Essays on the Social Sciences in History* TB/1140

ALLISON DAVIS & JOHN DOLLARD: Children of Bondage: *The Personality Development of Negro Youth in the Urban South* ||
TB/3049

ST. CLAIR DRAKE & HORACE R. CAYTON: Black Metropolis: *A Study of Negro Life in a Northern City. Revised and Enlarged. Intro. by Everett C. Hughes*
Vol. I TB/1086; Vol. II TB/1087

EMILE DURKHEIM et al.: Essays on Sociology and Philosophy: *With Analyses of Durkheim's Life and Work.* || *Edited by Kurt H. Wolff* TB/1151

LEON FESTINGER, HENRY W. RIECKEN & STANLEY SCHACHTER: When Prophecy Fails: *A Social and Psychological Account of a Modern Group that Predicted the Destruction of the World* ||
TB/1132

ALVIN W. GOULDNER: Wildcat Strike: *A Study in Worker-Management Relationships* ||
TB/1176

FRANCIS J. GRUND: Aristocracy in America: *Social Class in the Formative Years of the New Nation* TB/1001

KURT LEWIN: Field Theory in Social Science: *Selected Theoretical Papers.* || *Edited with a Foreword by Dorwin Cartwright*
TB/1135

R. M. MAC IVER: Social Causation
TB/1153

ROBERT K. MERTON, LEONARD BROOM, LEONARD S. COTTRELL, JR., Editors: Sociology Today: *Problems and Prospects* ||
Vol. I TB/1173; Vol. II TB/1174

ROBERTO MICHELS: First Lectures in Political Sociology. *Edited by Alfred De Grazia* || °
TB/1224

BARRINGTON MOORE, JR.: Political Power and Social Theory: *Seven Studies* ||
TB/1221

BARRINGTON MOORE, JR.: Soviet Politics—The Dilemma of Power: *The Role of Ideas in Social Change* ||
TB/1222

TALCOTT PARSONS & EDWARD A. SHILS, Editors: Toward a General Theory of Action: *Theoretical Foundations for the Social Sciences*
TB/1083

JOHN H. ROHRER & MUNRO S. EDMONSON, Eds.: The Eighth Generation Grows Up: *Cultures and Personalities of New Orleans Negroes* ||
TB/3050

ARNOLD ROSE: The Negro in America: *The Condensed Version of Gunnar Myrdal's An American Dilemma*
TB/3048

KURT SAMUELSSON: Religion and Economic Action: *A Critique of Max Weber's The Protestant Ethic and the Spirit of Capitalism.* || ° *Trans. by E. G. French. Ed. with Intro. by D. C. Coleman* TB/1131

PHILIP SELZNICK: TVA and the Grass Roots: *A Study in the Sociology of Formal Organization* TB/1230

GEORG SIMMEL et al.: Essays on Sociology, Philosophy, and Aesthetics. | *Edited by Kurt H. Wolff* TB/1234

HERBERT SIMON: The Shape of Automation: *For Men and Management* TB/1245

PITIRIM A. SOROKIN: Contemporary Sociological Theories. *Through the First Quarter of the 20th Century* TB/3046

MAURICE R. STEIN: The Eclipse of Community: *An Interpretation of American Studies* TB/1128

FERDINAND TÖNNIES: Community and Society: *Gemeinschaft und Gesellschaft. Translated and edited by Charles P. Loomis* TB/1116

W. LLOYD WARNER & Associates: Democracy in Jonesville: *A Study in Quality and Inequality* || TB/1129

W. LLOYD WARNER: Social Class in America: *The Evaluation of Status* TB/1013

RELIGION

Ancient & Classical

J. H. BREASTED: Development of Religion and Thought in Ancient Egypt. *Introduction by John A. Wilson*
TB/57

HENRI FRANKFORT: Ancient Egyptian Religion: *An Interpretation* TB/77

G. RACHEL LEVY: Religious Conceptions of the Stone Age *and their Influence upon European Thought. Illus. Introduction by Henri Frankfort* TB/106

MARTIN P. NILSSON: Greek Folk Religion. *Foreword by Arthur Darby Nock* TB/78

ALEXANDRE PIANKOFF: The Shrines of Tut-Ankh-Amon. *Edited by N. Rambova. 117 illus.* TB/2011

H. J. ROSE: Religion in Greece and Rome TB/55

Biblical Thought & Literature

W. F. ALBRIGHT: The Biblical Period from Abraham to Ezra TB/102

C. K. BARRETT, Ed.: The New Testament Background: *Selected Documents* TB/86

C. H. DODD: The Authority of the Bible TB/43

M. S. ENSLIN: Christian Beginnings TB/5

M. S. ENSLIN: The Literature of the Christian Movement
TB/6

7

Christianity: The Roman and Eastern Traditions

Oriental Religions: Far Eastern, Near Eastern

Philosophy of Religion

Religion, Culture & Society

NATURAL SCIENCES
AND MATHEMATICS

Biological Sciences

LUDWIG VON BERTALANFFY: Modern Theories of Development: *An Introduction to Theoretical Biology* TB/554
LUDWIG VON BERTALANFFY: Problems of Life: *An Evaluation of Modern Biological and Scientific Thought* TB/521
HAROLD F. BLUM: Time's Arrow and Evolution TB/555
JOHN TYLER BONNER: The Ideas of Biology. Σ *Illus.* TB/570
A. J. CAIN: Animal Species and their Evolution. *Illus.* TB/519
WALTER B. CANNON: Bodily Changes in Pain, Hunger, Fear and Rage. *Illus.* TB/562
W. E. LE GROS CLARK: The Antecedents of Man: *Intro. to Evolution of the Primates. ⁰ Illus.* TB/559
W. H. DOWDESWELL: Animal Ecology. *Illus.* TB/543
W. H. DOWDESWELL: The Mechanism of Evolution. *Illus.* TB/527
R. W. GERARD: Unresting Cells. *Illus.* TB/541
DAVID LACK: Darwin's Finches. *Illus.* TB/544
J. E. MORTON: Molluscs: *An Introduction to their Form and Functions. Illus.* TB/529
ADOLF PORTMANN: Animals as Social Beings. ⁰ *Illus.* TB/572
O. W. RICHARDS: The Social Insects. *Illus.* TB/542
P. M. SHEPPARD: Natural Selection and Heredity. *Illus.* TB/528
EDMUND W. SINNOTT: Cell and Psyche: *The Biology of Purpose* TB/546
C. H. WADDINGTON: How Animals Develop. *Illus.* TB/553
C. H. WADDINGTON: The Nature of Life: *The Main Problems and Trends in Modern Biology* TB/580

Chemistry

J. R. PARTINGTON: A Short History of Chemistry. *Illus.* TB/522
J. READ: A Direct Entry to Organic Chemistry. *Illus.* TB/523
J. READ: Through Alchemy to Chemistry. *Illus.* TB/561

Communication Theory

J. R. PIERCE: Symbols, Signals and Noise: *The Nature and Process of Communication* TB/574

Geography

R. E. COKER: This Great and Wide Sea: *An Introduction to Oceanography and Marine Biology. Illus.* TB/551
F. K. HARE: The Restless Atmosphere TB/560

History of Science

W. DAMPIER, Ed.: Readings in the Literature of Science. *Illus.* TB/512
A. HUNTER DUPREE: Science in the Federal Government: *A History of Policies and Activities to 1940* TB/573
ALEXANDRE KOYRÉ: From the Closed World to the Infinite Universe: *Copernicus, Kepler, Galileo, Newton, etc.* TB/31
A. G. VAN MELSEN: From Atomos to Atom: *A History of the Concept Atom* TB/517
O. NEUGEBAUER: The Exact Sciences in Antiquity TB/552
H. T. PLEDGE: Science Since 1500: *A Short History of Mathematics, Physics, Chemistry and Biology. Illus.* TB/506
HANS THIRRING: Energy for Man: *From Windmills to Nuclear Power* TB/556
LANCELOT LAW WHYTE: Essay on Atomism: *From Democritus to 1960* TB/565
A. WOLF: A History of Science, Technology and Philosophy in the 16th and 17th Centuries. ⁰ *Illus.* Vol. I TB/508; Vol. II TB/509

A. WOLF: A History of Science, Technology, and Philosophy in the Eighteenth Century. ⁰ *Illus.* Vol. I TB/539; Vol. II TB/540

Mathematics

E. W. BETH: The Foundations of Mathematics: *A Study in the Philosophy of Science* TB/581
H. DAVENPORT: The Higher Arithmetic: *An Introduction to the Theory of Numbers* TB/526
H. G. FORDER: Geometry: *An Introduction* TB/548
GOTTLOB FREGE: The Foundations of Arithmetic: *A Logico-Mathematical Enquiry* TB/534
S. KÖRNER: The Philosophy of Mathematics: *An Introduction* TB/547
D. E. LITTLEWOOD: Skeleton Key of Mathematics: *A Simple Account of Complex Algebraic Problems* TB/525
GEORGE E. OWEN: Fundamentals of Scientific Mathematics TB/569
WILLARD VAN ORMAN QUINE: Mathematical Logic TB/558
O. G. SUTTON: Mathematics in Action. ⁰ *Foreword by James R. Newman. Illus.* TB/518
FREDERICK WAISMANN: Introduction to Mathematical Thinking. *Foreword by Karl Menger* TB/511

Philosophy of Science

R. B. BRAITHWAITE: Scientific Explanation TB/515
J. BRONOWSKI: Science and Human Values. *Revised and Enlarged Edition* TB/505
ALBERT EINSTEIN et al.: Albert Einstein: Philosopher-Scientist. *Edited by Paul A. Schilpp* Vol. I TB/502 Vol. II TB/503
WERNER HEISENBERG: Physics and Philosophy: *The Revolution in Modern Science* TB/549
JOHN MAYNARD KEYNES: A Treatise on Probability. ⁰ *Introduction by N. R. Hanson* TB/557
KARL R. POPPER: The Logic of Scientific Discovery TB/576
STEPHEN TOULMIN: Foresight and Understanding: *An Enquiry into the Aims of Science. Foreword by Jacques Barzun* TB/564
STEPHEN TOULMIN: The Philosophy of Science: *An Introduction* TB/513
G. J. WHITROW: The Natural Philosophy of Time ⁰ TB/563

Physics and Cosmology

STEPHEN TOULMIN & JUNE GOODFIELD: The Fabric of the Heavens: *The Development of Astronomy and Dynamics. Illus.* TB/579
DAVID BOHM: Causality and Chance in Modern Physics. *Foreword by Louis de Broglie* TB/536
P. W. BRIDGMAN: The Nature of Thermodynamics TB/537
P. W. BRIDGMAN: A Sophisticate's Primer of Relativity TB/575
A. C. CROMBIE, Ed.: Turning Point in Physics TB/535
C. V. DURELL: Readable Relativity. *Foreword by Freeman J. Dyson* TB/530
ARTHUR EDDINGTON: Space, Time and Gravitation: *An Outline of the General Relativity Theory* TB/510
GEORGE GAMOW: Biography of Physics Σ TB/567
MAX JAMMER: Concepts of Force: *A Study in the Foundation of Dynamics* TB/550
MAX JAMMER: Concepts of Mass in Classical and Modern Physics TB/571
MAX JAMMER: Concepts of Space: *The History of Theories of Space in Physics. Foreword by Albert Einstein* TB/533
EDMUND WHITTAKER: History of the Theories of Aether and Electricity
Volume I: *The Classical Theories* TB/531
Volume II: *The Modern Theories* TB/532
G. J. WHITROW: The Structure and Evolution of the Universe: *An Introduction to Cosmology. Illus.* TB/504